GW01339468

Financial Risk Forecasting

For other titles in the Wiley Finance Series please see
www.wiley.com/finance

Financial Risk Forecasting

The Theory and Practice of Forecasting Market Risk, with Implementation in R and Matlab

Jón Daníelsson

WILEY

A John Wiley and Sons, Ltd, Publication

This edition first published 2011
Copyright © 2011 Jón Daníelsson

Registered office
John Wiley & Sons Ltd, The Atrium, Southern Gate, Chichester, West Sussex, PO19 8SQ, United Kingdom

For details of our global editorial offices, for customer services and for information about how to apply for permission to reuse the copyright material in this book please see our website at www.wiley.com

The right of the author to be identified as the author of this work has been asserted in accordance with the Copyright, Designs and Patents Act 1988.

Reprinted January 2012

All rights reserved. No part of this publication may be reproduced, stored in a retrieval system, or transmitted, in any form or by any means, electronic, mechanical, photocopying, recording or otherwise, except as permitted by the UK Copyright, Designs and Patents Act 1988, without the prior permission of the publisher.

Wiley also publishes its books in a variety of electronic formats. Some content that appears in print may not be available in electronic books.

Designations used by companies to distinguish their products are often claimed as trademarks. All brand names and product names used in this book are trade names, service marks, trademarks or registered trademarks of their respective owners. The publisher is not associated with any product or vendor mentioned in this book. This publication is designed to provide accurate and authoritative information in regard to the subject matter covered. It is sold on the understanding that the publisher is not engaged in rendering professional services. If professional advice or other expert assistance is required, the services of a competent professional should be sought.

ISBN 978-0-470-66943-3 (hardback)
ISBN 978-1-119-97710-0 (ebook)
ISBN 978-1-119-97711-7 (ebook)
ISBN 978-1-119-97712-4 (ebook)

A catalogue record for this book is available from the British Library.

Project management by OPS Ltd, Gt Yarmouth, Norfolk
Typeset in 10/12pt Times
Printed in Great Britain by CPI Antony Rowe, Chippenham, Wiltshire

Contents

Preface xiii

Acknowledgments xv

Abbreviations xvii

Notation xix

1 Financial markets, prices and risk 1
   1.1 Prices, returns and stock indices 2
       1.1.1 Stock indices 2
       1.1.2 Prices and returns 2
   1.2 S&P 500 returns 5
       1.2.1 S&P 500 statistics 6
       1.2.2 S&P 500 statistics in R and Matlab 7
   1.3 The stylized facts of financial returns 9
   1.4 Volatility 9
       1.4.1 Volatility clusters 11
       1.4.2 Volatility clusters and the ACF 12
   1.5 Nonnormality and fat tails 14
   1.6 Identification of fat tails 16
       1.6.1 Statistical tests for fat tails 16
       1.6.2 Graphical methods for fat tail analysis 17
       1.6.3 Implications of fat tails in finance 20
   1.7 Nonlinear dependence 21
       1.7.1 Sample evidence of nonlinear dependence 22
       1.7.2 Exceedance correlations 23
   1.8 Copulas 25
       1.8.1 The Gaussian copula 25
       1.8.2 The theory of copulas 25
       1.8.3 An application of copulas 27
       1.8.4 Some challenges in using copulas 28
   1.9 Summary 29

2 Univariate volatility modeling — 31
- 2.1 Modeling volatility — 31
- 2.2 Simple volatility models — 32
  - 2.2.1 Moving average models — 32
  - 2.2.2 EWMA model — 33
- 2.3 GARCH and conditional volatility — 35
  - 2.3.1 ARCH — 36
  - 2.3.2 GARCH — 38
  - 2.3.3 The "memory" of a GARCH model — 39
  - 2.3.4 Normal GARCH — 40
  - 2.3.5 Student-t GARCH — 40
  - 2.3.6 (G)ARCH in mean — 41
- 2.4 Maximum likelihood estimation of volatility models — 41
  - 2.4.1 The ARCH(1) likelihood function — 42
  - 2.4.2 The GARCH(1,1) likelihood function — 42
  - 2.4.3 On the importance of σ_1 — 43
  - 2.4.4 Issues in estimation — 43
- 2.5 Diagnosing volatility models — 44
  - 2.5.1 Likelihood ratio tests and parameter significance — 44
  - 2.5.2 Analysis of model residuals — 45
  - 2.5.3 Statistical goodness-of-fit measures — 45
- 2.6 Application of ARCH and GARCH — 46
  - 2.6.1 Estimation results — 46
  - 2.6.2 Likelihood ratio tests — 47
  - 2.6.3 Residual analysis — 47
  - 2.6.4 Graphical analysis — 48
  - 2.6.5 Implementation — 48
- 2.7 Other GARCH-type models — 51
  - 2.7.1 Leverage effects and asymmetry — 51
  - 2.7.2 Power models — 52
  - 2.7.3 APARCH — 52
  - 2.7.4 Application of APARCH models — 52
  - 2.7.5 Estimation of APARCH — 53
- 2.8 Alternative volatility models — 54
  - 2.8.1 Implied volatility — 54
  - 2.8.2 Realized volatility — 55
  - 2.8.3 Stochastic volatility — 55
- 2.9 Summary — 56

3 Multivariate volatility models — 57
- 3.1 Multivariate volatility forecasting — 57
  - 3.1.1 Application — 58
- 3.2 EWMA — 59
- 3.3 Orthogonal GARCH — 62
  - 3.3.1 Orthogonalizing covariance — 62
  - 3.3.2 Implementation — 62
  - 3.3.3 Large-scale implementations — 63

			Contents	vii
	3.4	CCC and DCC models		63
		3.4.1 Constant conditional correlations (CCC)		64
		3.4.2 Dynamic conditional correlations (DCC)		64
		3.4.3 Implementation		65
	3.5	Estimation comparison		65
	3.6	Multivariate extensions of GARCH		67
		3.6.1 Numerical problems		69
		3.6.2 The BEKK model		69
	3.7	Summary		70
4	**Risk measures**			73
	4.1	Defining and measuring risk		73
	4.2	Volatility		75
	4.3	Value-at-risk		76
		4.3.1 Is VaR a negative or positive number?		77
		4.3.2 The three steps in VaR calculations		78
		4.3.3 Interpreting and analyzing VaR		78
		4.3.4 VaR and normality		79
		4.3.5 Sign of VaR		79
	4.4	Issues in applying VaR		80
		4.4.1 VaR is only a quantile		80
		4.4.2 Coherence		81
		4.4.3 Does VaR really violate subadditivity?		83
		4.4.4 Manipulating VaR		84
	4.5	Expected shortfall		85
	4.6	Holding periods, scaling and the square root of time		89
		4.6.1 Length of holding periods		89
		4.6.2 Square-root-of-time scaling		90
	4.7	Summary		90
5	**Implementing risk forecasts**			93
	5.1	Application		93
	5.2	Historical simulation		95
		5.2.1 Expected shortfall estimation		97
		5.2.2 Importance of window size		97
	5.3	Risk measures and parametric methods		98
		5.3.1 Deriving VaR		99
		5.3.2 VaR when returns are normally distributed		101
		5.3.3 VaR under the Student-t distribution		102
		5.3.4 Expected shortfall under normality		103
	5.4	What about expected returns?		104
	5.5	VaR with time-dependent volatility		106
		5.5.1 Moving average		106
		5.5.2 EWMA		107
		5.5.3 GARCH normal		108
		5.5.4 Other GARCH models		109
	5.6	Summary		109

6	**Analytical value-at-risk for options and bonds**		111
	6.1 Bonds		112
		6.1.1 Duration-normal VaR	112
		6.1.2 Accuracy of duration-normal VaR	114
		6.1.3 Convexity and VaR	114
	6.2 Options		115
		6.2.1 Implementation	117
		6.2.2 Delta-normal VaR	119
		6.2.3 Delta and gamma	120
	6.3 Summary		120
7	**Simulation methods for VaR for options and bonds**		121
	7.1 Pseudo random number generators		122
		7.1.1 Linear congruental generators	122
		7.1.2 Nonuniform RNGs and transformation methods	123
	7.2 Simulation pricing		124
		7.2.1 Bonds	125
		7.2.2 Options	129
	7.3 Simulation of VaR for one asset		132
		7.3.1 Monte Carlo VaR with one basic asset	133
		7.3.2 VaR of an option on a basic asset	134
		7.3.3 Options and a stock	136
	7.4 Simulation of portfolio VaR		137
		7.4.1 Simulation of portfolio VaR for basic assets	137
		7.4.2 Portfolio VaR for options	139
		7.4.3 Richer versions	139
	7.5 Issues in simulation estimation		140
		7.5.1 The quality of the RNG	140
		7.5.2 Number of simulations	140
	7.6 Summary		142
8	**Backtesting and stress testing**		143
	8.1 Backtesting		143
		8.1.1 Market risk regulations	146
		8.1.2 Estimation window length	146
		8.1.3 Testing window length	147
		8.1.4 Violation ratios	147
	8.2 Backtesting the S&P 500		147
		8.2.1 Analysis	150
	8.3 Significance of backtests		153
		8.3.1 Bernoulli coverage test	154
		8.3.2 Testing the independence of violations	155
		8.3.3 Testing VaR for the S&P 500	157
		8.3.4 Joint test	159
		8.3.5 Loss-function-based backtests	159
	8.4 Expected shortfall backtesting		160
	8.5 Problems with backtesting		162

	8.6	Stress testing	163
		8.6.1 Scenario analysis	163
		8.6.2 Issues in scenario analysis	165
		8.6.3 Scenario analysis and risk models	165
	8.7	Summary	166
9	**Extreme value theory**		**167**
	9.1	Extreme value theory	168
		9.1.1 Types of tails	168
		9.1.2 Generalized extreme value distribution	169
	9.2	Asset returns and fat tails	170
	9.3	Applying EVT	172
		9.3.1 Generalized Pareto distribution	172
		9.3.2 Hill method	173
		9.3.3 Finding the threshold	174
		9.3.4 Application to the S&P 500 index	175
	9.4	Aggregation and convolution	176
	9.5	Time dependence	179
		9.5.1 Extremal index	179
		9.5.2 Dependence in ARCH	180
		9.5.3 When does dependence matter?	180
	9.6	Summary	181
10	**Endogenous risk**		**183**
	10.1	The Millennium Bridge	184
	10.2	Implications for financial risk management	184
		10.2.1 The 2007–2010 crisis	185
	10.3	Endogenous market prices	188
	10.4	Dual role of prices	190
		10.4.1 Dynamic trading strategies	191
		10.4.2 Delta hedging	192
		10.4.3 Simulation of feedback	194
		10.4.4 Endogenous risk and the 1987 crash	195
	10.5	Summary	195

APPENDICES

A	**Financial time series**		**197**
	A.1	Random variables and probability density functions	197
		A.1.1 Distributions and densities	197
		A.1.2 Quantiles	198
		A.1.3 The normal distribution	198
		A.1.4 Joint distributions	200
		A.1.5 Multivariate normal distribution	200
		A.1.6 Conditional distribution	200

		A.1.7	Independence	201
	A.2	Expectations and variance		201
		A.2.1	Properties of expectation and variance	202
		A.2.2	Covariance and independence	203
	A.3	Higher order moments		203
		A.3.1	Skewness and kurtosis	204
	A.4	Examples of distributions		206
		A.4.1	Chi-squared (χ^2)	206
		A.4.2	Student-t	206
		A.4.3	Bernoulli and binomial distributions	208
	A.5	Basic time series concepts		208
		A.5.1	Autocovariances and autocorrelations	209
		A.5.2	Stationarity	209
		A.5.3	White noise	210
	A.6	Simple time series models		210
		A.6.1	The moving average model	210
		A.6.2	The autoregressive model	211
		A.6.3	ARMA model	212
		A.6.4	Random walk	212
	A.7	Statistical hypothesis testing		212
		A.7.1	Central limit theorem	213
		A.7.2	p-values	213
		A.7.3	Type 1 and type 2 errors and the power of the test	214
		A.7.4	Testing for normality	214
		A.7.5	Graphical methods: QQ plots	215
		A.7.6	Testing for autocorrelation	215
		A.7.7	Engle LM test for volatility clusters	216
B	**An introduction to R**			**217**
	B.1	Inputting data		217
	B.2	Simple operations		219
		B.2.1	Matrix computation	220
	B.3	Distributions		222
		B.3.1	Normality tests	223
	B.4	Time series		224
	B.5	Writing functions in R		225
		B.5.1	Loops and repeats	226
	B.6	Maximum likelihood estimation		228
	B.7	Graphics		229
C	**An introduction to Matlab**			**231**
	C.1	Inputting data		231
	C.2	Simple operations		233
		C.2.1	Matrix algebra	234
	C.3	Distributions		235
		C.3.1	Normality tests	237
	C.4	Time series		237

			Contents	xi
	C.5	Basic programming and M-files		238
		C.5.1 Loops		239
	C.6	Maximum likelihood		242
	C.7	Graphics		243
D	**Maximum likelihood**			245
	D.1	Likelihood functions		245
		D.1.1 Normal likelihood functions		246
	D.2	Optimizers		247
	D.3	Issues in ML estimation		248
	D.4	Information matrix		249
	D.5	Properties of maximum likelihood estimators		250
	D.6	Optimal testing procedures		250
		D.6.1 Likelihood ratio test		251
		D.6.2 Lagrange multiplier test		252
		D.6.3 Wald test		253

Bibliography 255

Index 259

Preface

The focus in this book is on the study of market risk from a quantitative point of view. The emphasis is on presenting commonly used state-of-the-art quantitative techniques used in finance for the management of market risk and demonstrate their use employing the principal two mathematical programming languages, R and Matlab. All the code in the book can be downloaded from the book's website at www.financialrisk forecasting.com

The book brings together three essential fields: finance, statistics and computer programming. It is assumed that the reader has a basic understanding of statistics and finance; however, no prior knowledge of computer programming is required. The book takes a hands-on approach to the issue of financial risk, with the reading material intermixed between finance, statistics and computer programs.

I have used the material in this book for some years, both for a final year undergraduate course in quantitative methods and for master level courses in risk forecasting. In most cases, the students taking this course have no prior knowledge of computer programming, but emerge after the course with the ability to independently implement the models and code in this book. All of the material in the book can be covered in about 10 weeks, or 20 lecture hours.

Most chapters demonstrate the way in which the various techniques discussed are implemented by both R and Matlab. We start by downloading a sample of stock prices, which are then used for model estimation and evaluation.

The outline of the book is as follows. Chapter 1 begins with an introduction to financial markets and market prices. The chapter gives a foretaste of what is to come, discussing market indices and stock prices, the forecasting of risk and prices, and concludes with the main features of market prices from the point of view of risk. The main focus of the chapter is introduction of the three stylized facts regarding returns on financial assets: volatility clusters, fat tails and nonlinear dependence.

Chapters 2 and 3 focus on volatility forecasting: the former on univariate volatility and the latter on multivariate volatility. The aim is to survey all the methods used for volatility forecasting, while discussing several models from the GARCH family in considerable detail. We discuss the models from a theoretical point of view and demonstrate their implementation and evaluation.

This is followed by two chapters on risk models and risk forecasting: Chapter 4 addresses the theoretical aspects of risk forecasting—in particular, volatility, value-at-risk (VaR) and expected shortfall; Chapter 5 addresses the implementation of risk models.

We then turn to risk analysis in options and bonds; Chapter 6 demonstrates such analytical methods as delta-normal VaR and duration-normal VaR, while Chapter 7 addresses Monte Carlo simulation methods for derivative pricing and risk forecasting.

After developing risk models their quality needs to be evaluated—this is the topic of Chapter 8. This chapter demonstrates how backtesting and a number of methodologies can be used to evaluate and compare the risk forecast methods presented earlier in the book. The chapter concludes with a comprehensive discussion of stress testing.

The risk forecast methods discussed up to this point in the book are focused on relatively common events, but in special cases it is necessary to forecast the risk of very large, yet uncommon events (e.g., the probability of events that happen, say, every 10 years or every 100 years). To do this, we need to employee extreme value theory—the topic of Chapter 9.

In Chapter 10, the last chapter in the book, we take a step back and consider the underlying assumptions behind almost every risk model in practical use and discuss what happens when these assumptions are violated. Because financial risk is fundamentally *endogenous*, financial risk models have the annoying habit of failing when needed the most. How and why this happens is the topic of this chapter.

There are four appendices: Appendix A introduces the basic concepts in statistics and the financial time series referred to throughout the book. We give an introduction to R and Matlab in Appendices B and C, respectively, providing a discussion of the basic implementation of the software packages. Finally, Appendix D is focused on maximum likelihood, concept, implementation and testing. A list of the most commonly used abbreviations in the book can be found on p. xvii. This is followed by a table of the notation used in the book on p. xix.

Jón Daníelsson

Acknowledgments

This book is based on my years of teaching risk forecasting, both at undergraduate and master level, at the London School of Economics (LSE) and other universities, and in various executive education courses. I am very grateful to all the students and practitioners who took my courses for all the feedback I have received over the years.

I was fortunate to be able to employ an exemplary student, Jacqueline Li, to work with me on developing the lecture material. Jacqueline's assistance was invaluable; she made significant contributions to the book. Her ability to master all the statistical and computational aspects of the book was impressive, as was the apparent ease with which she mastered the technicalities. She survived the process and has emerged as a very good friend.

A brilliant mathematician and another very good friend, Maite Naranjo at the Centre de Recerca Matemàtica, Bellaterra in Barcelona, agreed to read the mathematics and saved me from several embarrassing mistakes.

Two colleagues at the LSE, Stéphane Guibaud and Jean-Pierre Zigrand, read parts of the book and verified some of the mathematical derivations.

My PhD student, Ilknur Zer, who used an earlier version of this book while a masters student at LSE and who currently teaches a course based on this book, kindly agreed to review the new version of the book and came up with very good suggestions on both content and presentation.

Kyle T. Moore and Pengfei Sun, both at Erasmus University, agreed to read the book, with a special focus on extreme value theory. They corrected many mistakes and made good suggestions on better presentation of the material.

I am very grateful to all of them for their assistance; without their contribution this book would not have seen the light of day.

Jón Daníelsson

Abbreviations

ACF	Autocorrelation function
AR	Autoregressive
ARCH	Autoregressive conditional heteroskedasticity
ARMA	Autoregressive moving average
CCC	Constant conditional correlations
CDF	Cumulative distribution function
CLT	Central limit theorem
DCC	Dynamic conditional correlations
DJIA	Dow Jones Industrial Average
ES	Expected shortfall
EVT	Extreme value theory
EWMA	Exponentially weighted moving average
GARCH	Generalized autoregressive conditional heteroskedasticity
GEV	Generalized extreme value
GPD	Generalized Pareto distribution
HS	Historical simulation
IID	Identically and independently distributed
JB test	Jarque–Bera test
KS test	Kolmogorov–Smirnov test
LB test	Ljung–Box test
LCG	Linear congruental generator
LM	Lagrange multiplier
LR	Likelihood ratio
MA	Moving average
MC	Monte Carlo
ML	Maximum likelihood
MLE	Maximum likelihood estimation
MVGARCH	Multivariate GARCH
NaN	Not a number
NLD	Nonlinear dependence
OGARCH	Orthogonal GARCH
P/L	Profit and loss
PC	Principal component

PCA	Principal components analysis
PDF	Probability density function
POT	Peaks over thresholds
QML	Quasi-maximum likelihood
QQ plot	Quantile–quantile plot
RN	Random number
RNG	Random number generator
RV	Random variable
SV	Stochastic volatility
VaR	Value-at-risk
VR	Violation ratio

Notation

Chapter 1: Financial markets, prices and risk

T Sample size
$t = 1, \ldots, T$ A particular observation period (e.g., a day)
P_t Price at time t
$R_t = \dfrac{P_t - P_{t-1}}{P_{t-1}}$ Simple return
$Y_t = \log \dfrac{P_t}{P_{t-1}}$ Continuously compounded return
y_t A sample realization of Y_t
σ Unconditional volatility
σ_t Conditional volatility
K Number of assets
ν Degrees of freedom of the Student-t
ι Tail index

Chapter 2: Univariate volatility modeling

W_E Estimation window
λ Decay factor in EWMA
Z_t Residuals
α, β Main model parameters
ζ, δ Other model parameters
L_1, L_2 Lags in volatility models

Chapter 3: Multivariate volatility models

Σ_t Conditional covariance matrix
$Y_{t,k}$ Return on asset k at time t
$y_{t,k}$ Sample return on asset k at time t
$y_t = \{y_{t,k}\}$ Vector of sample returns on all assets at time t
$y = \{y_t\}$ Matrix of sample returns on all assets and dates
A and B Matrices of parameters
R Correlation matrix

Chapter 4: Risk measures

- p Probability
- Q Profit and loss
- q Observed profit and loss
- w Vector of portfolio weights
- X and Y Refers to two different assets
- $\varphi(\cdot)$ Risk measure
- ϑ Portfolio value

Chapter 5: Implementing risk forecasts

- $\gamma(p)$ Significance level as a function of probability
- μ Mean

Chapter 6: Analytical value-at-risk for options and bonds

- T Delivery time/maturity
- r Annual interest rate
- σ_r Volatility of daily interest rate increments
- σ_a Annual volatility of an underlying asset
- σ_d Daily volatility of an underlying asset
- τ Cash flow
- D^* Modified duration
- C Convexity
- Δ Option delta
- Γ Option gamma
- $g(\cdot)$ Generic function name for pricing equation

Chapter 7: Simulation methods for VaR for options and bonds

- F Futures price
- g Derivative price
- S Number of simulations
- x^b Portfolio holdings (basic assets)
- x^o Portfolio holdings (derivatives)

Chapter 8: Backtesting and stress testing

- W_T Testing window size
- $T = W_E + W_T$ Number of observations in a sample
- $\eta_t = 0, 1$ Indicates whether a VaR violation occurs (i.e., $\eta_t = 1$)
- $v_i,\ i = 0, 1$ Number of violations ($i = 1$) and no violations ($i = 0$) observed in $\{\eta_t\}$
- v_{ij} Number of instances where j follows i in $\{\eta_t\}$

Chapter 9: Extreme value theory

- ι Tail index
- $\xi = 1/\iota$ Shape parameter
- M_T Maximum of X
- C_T Number of observations in the tail
- u Threshold value
- ψ Extremal index

1
Financial markets, prices and risk

The focus of this chapter is on the statistical techniques used for analyzing prices and returns in financial markets. The concept of a stock market index is defined followed by a discussion of prices, returns and volatilities. Volatility clusters, the fat-tailed property of financial returns and observed sharp increases in correlations between assets during periods of financial turmoil (i.e., nonlinear dependence) will also be explored.

Various statistical techniques are introduced and used in this chapter for the analysis of financial returns. While readers may have seen these techniques before, Appendix A contains an introduction to basic statistics and time series methods for financial applications. The most common statistical methods presented in this chapter are implemented in the two programming languages discussed in this book: R and Matlab. These languages are discussed in more detail in Appendix B for R and Appendix C for Matlab.

We illustrate the application of statistical methods by using observed stock market data, the S&P 500 for univariate methods and a portfolio of US stocks for multivariate methods. The data can be downloaded from sources such as finance.yahoo.com directly within R and Matlab, as demonstrated by the source code in this chapter.

A key conclusion from this chapter is that we are likely to measure risk incorrectly by using volatility because of the presence of volatility clusters, fat tails and nonlinear dependence. This impacts on many financial applications, such as portfolio management, asset allocation, derivatives pricing, risk management, economic capital and financial stability.

The specific notation used in this chapter is:

T — Sample size
$t = 1, \ldots, T$ — A particular observation period (e.g., a day)
P_t — Price at time t
$R_t = \dfrac{P_t - P_{t-1}}{P_{t-1}}$ — Simple return
$Y_t = \log \dfrac{P_t}{P_{t-1}}$ — Continuously compounded return
y_t — A sample realization of Y_t
σ — Unconditional volatility
σ_t — Conditional volatility
K — Number of assets
ν — Degrees of freedom of the Student-t
ι — Tail index

1.1 PRICES, RETURNS AND STOCK INDICES

1.1.1 Stock indices

A stock market index shows how a specified portfolio of share prices changes over time, giving an indication of market trends. If an index goes up by 1%, that means the total value of the securities which make up the index has also increased by 1% in value.

Usually, the index value is described in terms of "points"—we frequently hear statements like "the Dow dropped 500 points today". The points by themselves do not tell us much that is interesting; the correct way to interpret the value of an index is to compare it with a previous value. One key reason so much attention is paid to indices today is that they are widely used as benchmarks to evaluate the performance of professionally managed portfolios such as mutual funds.

There are two main ways to calculate an index. A *price-weighted index* is an index where the constituent stocks are weighted based on their price. For example, a stock trading at $100 will make up 10 times more of the total index than a stock trading at $10. However, such an index will not accurately reflect the evolution of underlying market values because the $100 stock might be that of a small company and the $10 stock that of a large company. A change in the price quote of the small company will thus drive the price-weighted index while combined market values will remain relatively constant without changes in the price of the large company. The Dow Jones Industrial Average (DJIA) and the Nikkei 225 are examples of price-weighted stock market indices.

By contrast, the components of a *value-weighted index* are weighted according to the total market value of their outstanding shares. The impact of a component's price change is therefore proportional to the issue's overall market value, which is the product of the share price and the number of shares outstanding. The weight of each stock constantly shifts with changes in a stock's price and the number of shares outstanding, implying such indices are more informative than price-weighted indices.

Perhaps the most widely used index in the world is the Standard & Poor 500 (S&P 500) which captures the top-500 traded companies in the United States, representing about 75% of US market capitalization. No asset called S&P 500 is traded on financial markets, but it is possible to buy derivatives on the index and its volatility VIX. For the Japanese market the most widely used value-weighted index is the TOPIX, while in the UK it is the FTSE.

1.1.2 Prices and returns

We denote asset prices by P_t, where the t usually refers to a day, but can indicate any frequency (e.g., yearly, weekly, hourly). If there are many assets, each asset is indicated by $P_{t,k} = P_{\text{time,asset}}$, and when referring to portfolios we use the subscript "port". Normally however, we are more interested in the *return* we make on an investment—not the price itself.

Definition 1.1 (Returns) *The relative change in the price of a financial asset over a given time interval, often expressed as a percentage.*

Returns also have more attractive statistical properties than prices, such as stationarity and ergodicity. There are two types of returns: simple and compound. We ignore the dividend component for simplicity.

Definition 1.2 (Simple returns) *A simple return is the percentage change in prices, indicated by R:*

$$R_t = \frac{P_t - P_{t-1}}{P_{t-1}}.$$

Often, we need to convert daily returns to monthly or annual returns, or vice versa. A multiperiod (*n*-period) return is given by:

$$R_t(n) = (1 + R_t)(1 + R_{t-1})(1 + R_{t-2}) \cdots (1 + R_{t-n+1}) - 1$$

$$= \frac{P_t}{P_{t-1}} \frac{P_{t-1}}{P_{t-2}} \cdots \frac{P_{t-n+1}}{P_{t-n}} - 1 = \frac{P_t}{P_{t-n}} - 1$$

where $R_t(n)$ is the return over the most recent *n*-periods from date $t - n$ to t.

A convenient advantage of simple returns is that the return on a portfolio, $R_{t,\text{port}}$, is simply the weighted sum of the returns of individual assets:

$$R_{t,\text{port}} = \sum_{k=1}^{K} w_k R_{t,k}$$

where K is the number of assets; and w_k is the portfolio weight of asset i. An alternative return measure is continuously compounded returns.

Definition 1.3 (Continuously compounded returns) *The logarithm of gross return, indicated by Y_t:*

$$Y_t = \log(1 + R_t) = \log\left(\frac{P_t}{P_{t-1}}\right) = \log P_t - \log P_{t-1}.$$

The advantages of compound returns become clear when considering multiperiod returns:

$$Y_t(n) = \log(1 + R_t(n)) = \log((1 + R_t)(1 + R_{t-1})(1 + R_{t-2}) \cdots (1 + R_{t-n+1}))$$
$$= \log(1 + R_t) + \log(1 + R_{t-1}) + \cdots + \log(1 + R_{t-n+1})$$
$$= Y_t + Y_{t-1} + \cdots + Y_{t-n+1}.$$

Continuously compounded multiperiod returns are the sum of continuously compounded single-period returns. In contrast to simple returns, it is much easier to derive the time series properties of sums than of products.

The situation is different for portfolio returns since the log of a sum does not equal the sum of logs:

$$Y_{t,\text{port}} = \log\left(\frac{P_{t,\text{port}}}{P_{t-1,\text{port}}}\right) \neq \sum_{k=1}^{K} w_k \log\left(\frac{P_{t,k}}{P_{t-1,k}}\right).$$

where $P_{t,\text{port}}$ is the portfolio value on day t; and $Y_{t,\text{port}}$ is the corresponding return. The difference between compound and simple returns may not be very significant for small returns (e.g., daily),

$$Y_{\text{port}} \approx \sum_{k=1}^{K} w_k R_k$$

and as the time between observations goes to zero, so does the difference between the two return measures:

$$\lim_{\Delta t \to 0} Y_{\text{port}} = R_{\text{port}}.$$

It will not usually matter much which measure we choose to use. For example, suppose $P_t = 1{,}000$ and $P_{t-1} = 950$ then:

$$R_t = \frac{1{,}000}{950} - 1 = 0.0526$$

$$Y_t = \log\left(\frac{1{,}000}{950}\right) = 0.0513.$$

The discrepancy between them becomes significant only when percent changes are high—for example, if $P_t = 1{,}000$ and $P_{t-1} = 700$, then:

$$R_t = \frac{1{,}000}{700} - 1 = 0.429$$

$$Y_t = \log\left(\frac{1{,}000}{700}\right) = 0.357.$$

In some situations, such as accounting, simple returns need to be used.

Another common type of returns is excess returns (i.e., returns in excess of some reference rate, often the risk free rate).

We should think of simple returns and compound returns as two different definitions of returns. They are also known as arithmetic and logarithmic returns, respectively. Simple returns are of course *correct*; investors are primarily interested in simple returns. But there are reasons for continuously compounded returns being preferable.

A key advantage is that they are symmetric, while simple returns are not. This means an investment of $100 that yields a simple return of 50% followed by a simple return of −50% will result in $75, while an investment of $100 that yields a continuously compounded return of 50% followed by a continuously compounded return of −50% will remain at $100.

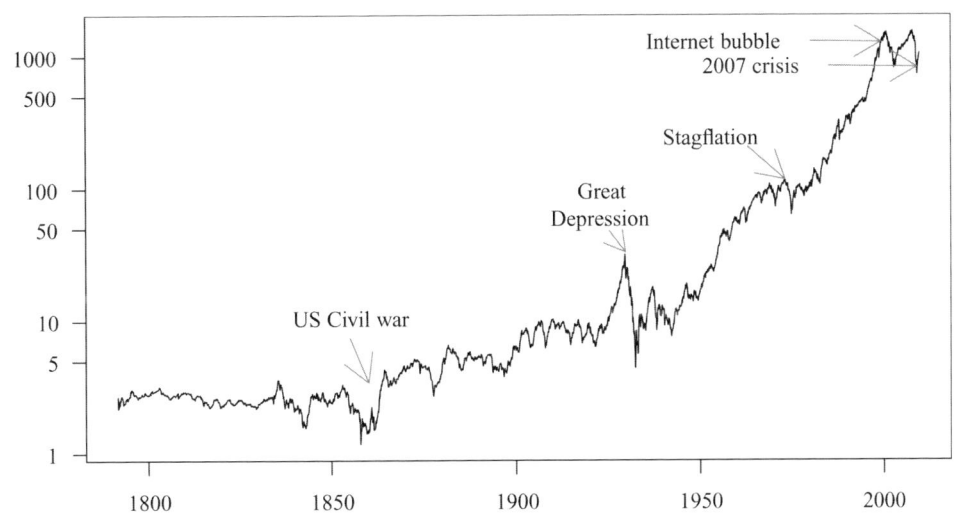

Figure 1.1. S&P 500 index August 1791 to December 2009, log scale.
Data source: Global Financial Data.

Continuously compounded returns also play an important role in the background of many financial calculations. They are a discrete form of *continuous time* Brownian motion,[1] which is the foundation for derivatives pricing and is used to model the changes in stock prices in the Black–Scholes model.

1.2 S&P 500 RETURNS

The S&P 500 index has been published since 1957 but Global Financial Data, a commercial vendor, go back as far as 1791. The log of the monthly close of the S&P 500 from 1791 until 2009 can be seen in Figure 1.1. One needs to be careful when looking at a long time series of prices as it is easy to reach misleading conclusions.

The first observation is on 1791/08/31 when the index had a value of $2.67, while the value on the last day of the sample, 2009/12/31, was $1,115.1. This implies that the index has risen in value by 41,660%, or 2% per year. This analysis, however, overlooks depreciation in the value of the dollar (i.e., inflation). We can calculate how much one dollar has increased in value from 1791 to 2009 using the five different techniques shown in Table 1.1.

Using the CPI, the real increase in the value of the index has actually been a measly 1.4% per year. This does not, however, represent the total returns of an investor as it ignores dividend yield.

We show the compound returns in Figure 1.2. There is high volatility during the American Civil War in the 1860s, the Great Depression in the 1930s, the stagflation of the 1970s and the Asian crisis in 1997, among others. Prolonged periods of high volatility are generally associated with great uncertainty in the real economy.

---

[1] Brownian motion, also called Wiener process, is a centered, zero mean Gaussian process $\{W_t; t\}$.

Table 1.1. Increase in value of one dollar from 1791 to 2009 using five different techniques.

$23.66	Consumer price index
$22.73	GDP deflator
$397.91	Unskilled wage
$942.48	Nominal GDP per capita
$70,902.74	Relative share of GDP

Calculated from http://www.measuringworth.com/uscompare

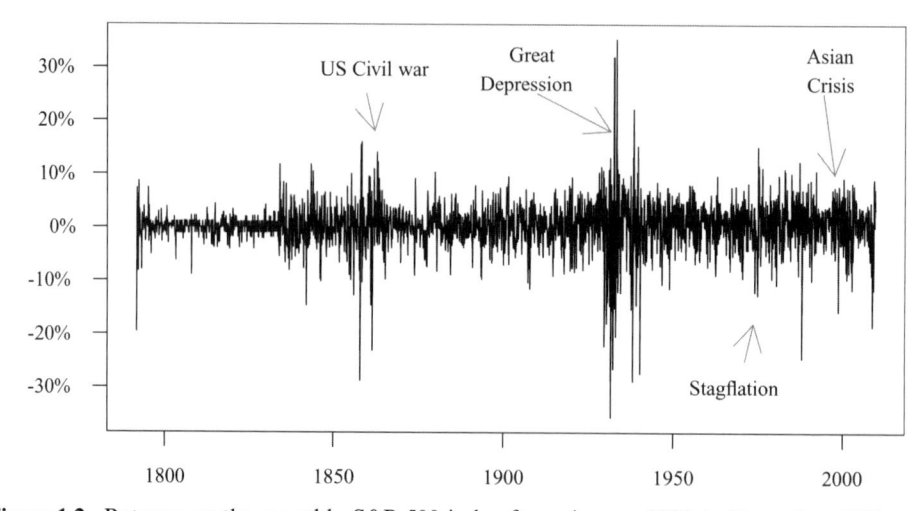

Figure 1.2. Returns on the monthly S&P 500 index from August 1791 to December 2009.

1.2.1 S&P 500 statistics

A selection of summary statistics for daily S&P 500 returns from 1928 to 2009 is presented in Table 1.2. The daily mean is very small at 0.019% while daily volatility is around 1.2%. The fact that the daily mean is only one-fiftieth of daily volatility will simplify the construction of risk measures as we can effectively assume it is zero, without

Table 1.2. S&P 500 daily return summary statistics, 1928–2009

Mean	0.019%
Standard deviation	1.16%
Min	−22.9%
Max	15.4%
Skewness	−0.4
Kurtosis	22.5
Autocorrelation (one lag) of returns	3.4%
Autocorrelation (one lag) of squared returns	21.7%
Jarque–Bera (p-value)	0.0%
Ljung–Box 20 lags (p-value)	0.0%
Ljung–Box squared returns 20 lags (p-value)	0.0%

loss of generality. Furthermore, the mean grows at a linear rate while volatility grows approximately at a square root rate, so over time the mean dominates volatility.

The lowest daily return of -23% corresponds to the stock market crash of 1987, while the best day in the index, 15%, was at the end of the Great Depression. The returns have a small negative skewness and, more importantly, quite high kurtosis.

Finally, the returns have a daily autocorrelation of about 3% while squared returns have an autocorrelation of 22%. Squared returns are a proxy for volatility. The 22% autocorrelation of squared returns provides very strong evidence of the predictability of volatility and volatility clusters.

The table also shows a test for normality, the Jarque–Bera (JB) test, first-order autocorrelations of returns and returns squared, and finally a test for the presence of an autocorrelation up to 20 lags, a Ljung–Box (LB) test.

1.2.2 S&P 500 statistics in R and Matlab

The results in Table 1.2 can be easily generated using R or Matlab. It is possible to directly download stock prices into R or Matlab from several websites, such as finance.yahoo.com. In some of the examples in this chapter we use data going back to the 1700s; data that old were obtained from Global Financial Data.

The following two R and Matlab code listings demonstrate how S&P 500 daily prices from 2000 until 2009 can be downloaded from finance.yahoo.com, where the stock market symbol for the S&P 500 is ^gspc. An active internet connection is required for this code to work, but it is straightforward to save the returns after downloading them. One issue that comes up is which data field from finance.yahoo.com to use. One might think it best to use closing prices, but that is usually not correct, because over time we observe actions that change the prices of equities such as stock splits and stock buybacks, without affecting the value of the firm. We therefore need to use the *adjusted closing prices* which automatically take this into account. For the S&P 500 this makes no difference, but for most stock prices it does. Therefore, it is good practice to use adjusted closing prices by default.

We use the R function get.hist.quote() from the tseries library. We then convert the prices into returns, and plot the returns. By default, get.hist.quote() returns a four-column matrix with open and closing prices, as well as the high and low of prices. To get adjusted closing prices in R we need to include quote="AdjClose" in the get.hist.quote() statement. Note that prices and returns in R are represented as a time series object while in Matlab they are simply vectors. The function {\tt coredata} is discussed on p. 94.

Listing 1.1. Download S&P 500 data in R

```
library("tseries")              # load the tseries library
price = get.hist.quote(instrument = "^gspc", start = "
   2000-01-01", quote="AdjClose")  # download the prices,
   from January 1, 2000 until today
y=diff(log(price))              # convert the prices into returns
plot(y)                         # plot the returns
y=coredata(y)                   # strip date information from returns
```

In Matlab it is equally straightforward to download prices. It is possible to use the GUI function, `FTSTool` from the financial and data feed toolboxes; however, it may be easier to use the Matlab function `urlread()` which can directly read web pages, such as finance.yahoo.com. Several free user-contributed functions are available to ease the process, such as `hist_stock_data()`.[2] finance.yahoo.com returns the data sorted from the newest date to the oldest date, so that the first observation is the newest. We want it sorted from the oldest to newest, and the R procedure does it automatically; unfortunately, the Matlab procedure does not, so we have to do it manually by using a sequence like `end:-1:1`. Of course, it would be most expedient to just modify the `hist_stock_data()` function.

Listing 1.2. Download S&P 500 data in Matlab

```
price = hist_stock_data('01012000','31122000','^gspc');
                                % download the prices, from
                                  January 1, 2000 until
                                  December 31, 2009
y=diff(log(price.Close(end:-1:1)))   % convert the prices into
                                       returns
plot(y)                         % plot the returns
```

After having obtained the returns, y, we can calculate some sample statistics; they are given in Listing 1.3.

Listing 1.3. Sample statistics in R

```
library(moments)
sd(y)
min(y)
max(y)
skewness(y)
kurtosis(y)
acf(y,1)
acf(y^2,1)
jarque.bera.test(y)
Box.test(y, lag = 20, type = c("Ljung-Box"))
Box.test(y^2, lag = 20, type = c("Ljung-Box"))
```

---

[2] It can be obtained directly from the webpage of the Matlab vendor http://www.mathworks.com/matlabcentral/fileexchange/18458-historical-stock-data-downloader.

Listing 1.4. Sample statistics in Matlab

```
% JPL and MFE toolboxes
mean(y)
std(y)
min(y)
max(y)
skewness(y)
kurtosis(y)
sacf(y,1,[],0)
sacf(y.^2,1,[],0)
jarquebera(y)
[q, pval]=ljungbox(y,20)
[q, pval]=ljungbox(y.^2,20)
```

1.3 THE STYLIZED FACTS OF FINANCIAL RETURNS

Extensive research on the properties of financial returns has demonstrated that returns exhibit three statistical properties that are present in most, if not all, financial returns. These are often called the three *stylized facts* of financial returns:

Volatility clusters

Fat tails

Nonlinear dependence

The first property, volatility clusters, relates to the observation that the magnitudes of the volatilities of financial returns tend to cluster together, so that we observe many days of high volatility, followed by many days of low volatility.

The second property, fat tails, points to the fact that financial returns occasionally have very large positive or negative returns, which are very unlikely to be observed, if returns were normally distributed.

Finally, nonlinear dependence (NLD) addresses how multivariate returns relate to each other. If returns are linearly dependent, the correlation coefficient describes how they move together. If they are nonlinearly dependent, the correlation between different returns depends on the magnitudes of outcomes. For example, it is often observed that correlations are lower in bull markets than in bear markets, while in a financial crisis they tend to reach 100%.

Each of those stylized facts is discussed in turn in the following sections.

1.4 VOLATILITY

The most common measure of market uncertainty is volatility.

Definition 1.4 (Volatility) *The standard deviation of returns.*

10   Financial markets, prices and risk

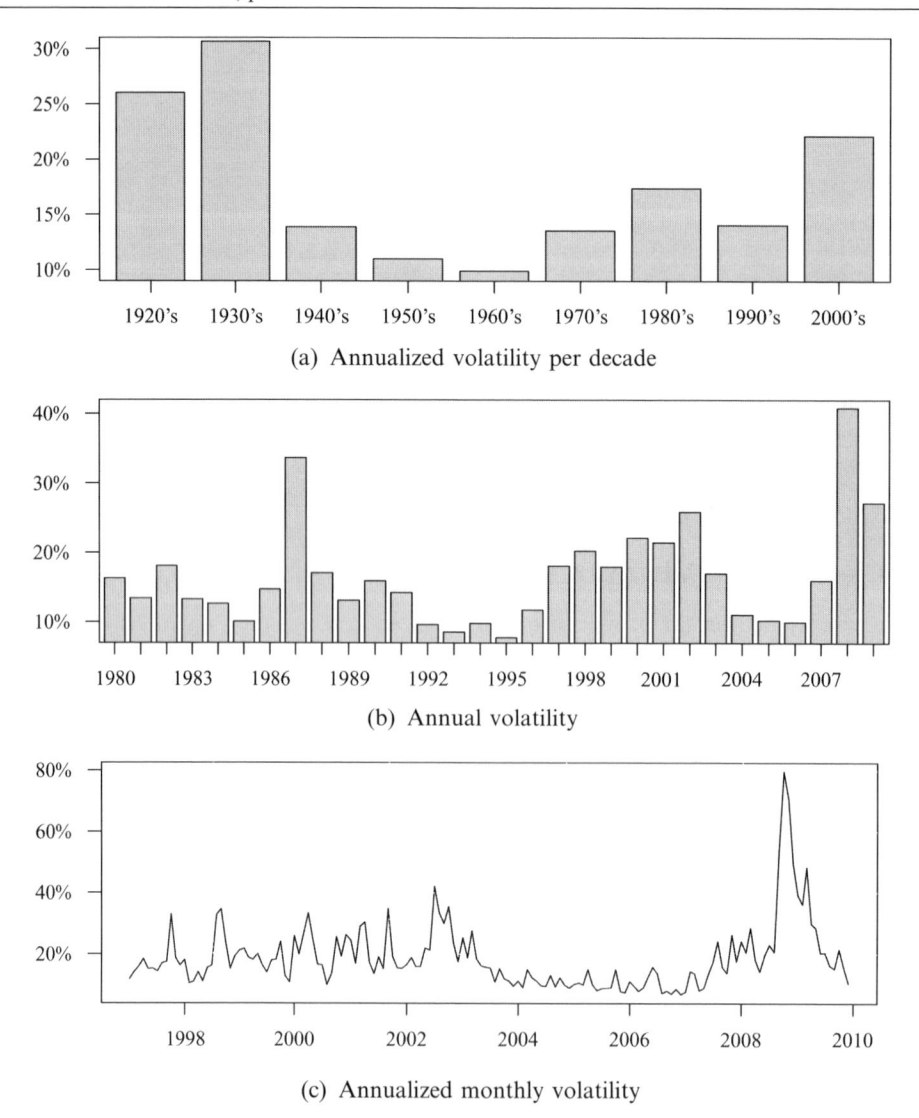

Figure 1.3. Volatility cycles.

(a) Annualized volatility per decade

(b) Annual volatility

(c) Annualized monthly volatility

We further explore the nature of volatility in the S&P 500 index by calculating volatility in subperiods of the data. This calculation is repeated for daily returns over decades, years and months (see Figure 1.3).

Panel (a) of Figure 1.1 shows volatility per decade from 1928 to 2009; we can see clear evidence of cyclical patterns in volatility from one decade to the next. Volatility is lowest in the 1960s and highest during the Great Depression in the 1930s. Note that 1920s' values only contain a part of 1929 and that the Great Depression started in 1929.

Focusing on more recent events, panel (b) shows volatility per year from 1980. The most volatile year is 2008, during the 2007–2009 crisis, followed by the stock market crash year of 1987. The calmest year is 1995, right before the Asian crisis; 2004–2006 are also quite relaxed.

However, the fact that volatility was very low in 1995 and 2005 does *not* imply that risk in financial markets was low in those years, since volatility can be low while the tails are fat. In other words, it is possible for a variable with a low volatility to have much more extreme outcomes than another variable with a higher volatility. This is why volatility is a misleading measure of risk.

Finally, panel (c) shows average daily volatility per month from 1995. Again, it is clear that volatility has been trending downwards, and has been very low from 2004. This is changing as a result of the 2007–2009 crisis.

Taken together, the figures provide substantial evidence that there are both long-run cycles in volatility spanning decades, and short cycles spanning weeks or months. In this case, we are observing cycles within cycles within cycles. However, given we have many fewer observations at lower frequencies—such as monthly—there is much more statistical uncertainty in that case, and hence the plots are much more jagged.

The crude methods employed here to calculate volatility (i.e., sampling standard errors) are generally considered unreliable, especially at the highest frequencies; more sophisticated methods will be introduced in the next chapter.

1.4.1 Volatility clusters

We use two concepts of volatility: *unconditional* and *conditional*. While these concepts are made precise later, for our immediate discussion unconditional volatility is defined as volatility over an entire time period, while conditional volatility is defined as volatility in a given time period, conditional on what happened before. Unconditional volatility is denoted by σ and conditional volatility by σ_t.

Looking at volatility in Figure 1.3, it is evident that it changes over time. Furthermore, given the apparent cycles, volatility is partially predictable. These phenomena are known as *volatility clusters*.

We illustrate volatility clusters by simulations in Figure 1.4, which shows exaggerated simulated volatility clusters. Panel (a) shows returns and panel (b) shows volatility. In the beginning, volatility increases and we are in a high-volatility cluster, then around day 180 volatility decreases only to increase again after a while and so on.

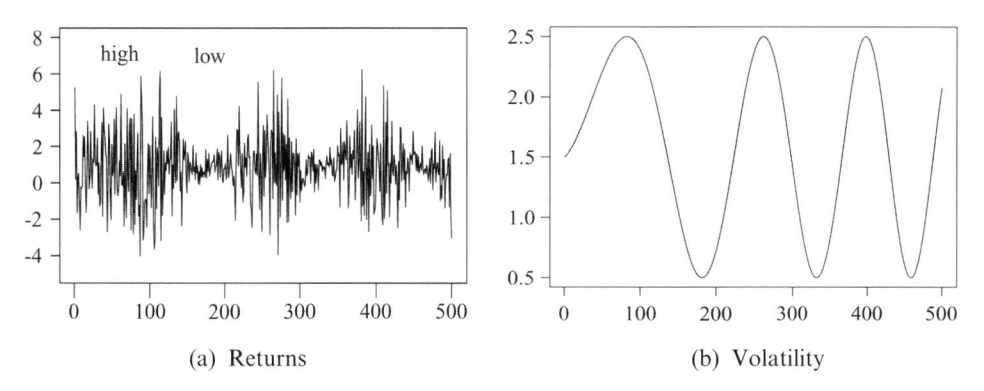

(a) Returns

(b) Volatility

Figure 1.4. Exaggerated simulated volatility clusters.

Almost all financial returns exhibit volatility clusters (i.e., the market goes through periods when volatility is high and other periods when volatility is low). For example, in the mid-1990s volatility was low, while at the beginning and end of the decade it was much higher. This feature of financial time series gained widespread recognition with the publication of Engle (1982) and is now one of the accepted stylized facts about asset returns. If we can capture predictability in volatility, it may be possible to improve portfolio decisions, risk management and option pricing, among other applications.

1.4.2 Volatility clusters and the ACF

A standard graphical method for exploring predictability in statistical data is the *autocorrelation function* (ACF). The ACF measures how returns on one day are correlated with returns on previous days. If such correlations are statistically significant, we have strong evidence for predictability.

Panel (a) of Figure 1.5 shows the ACF of S&P 500 returns along with a 95% confidence interval, where most autocorrelations lie within the interval. Contrast this with the ACF of squared returns in panel (b) where it is significant even at long lags, providing strong evidence for the predictability of volatility.

We can test for the joint significance of autocorrelation coefficients over several lags by using the Ljung–Box (LB) test. We do the LB test using 21 lags of daily S&P 500

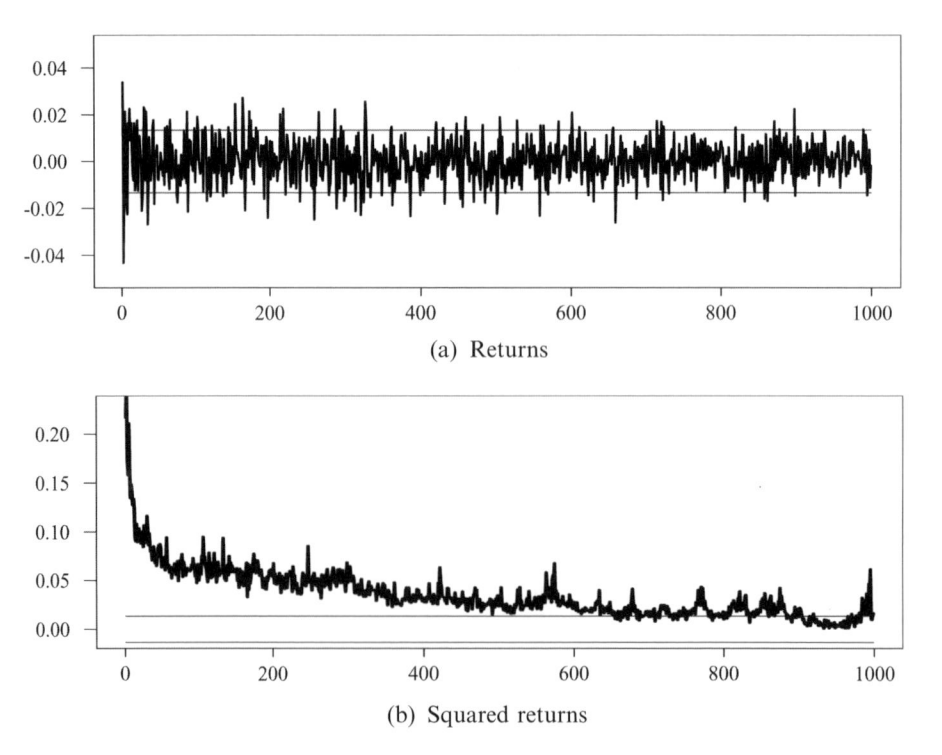

Figure 1.5. Autocorrelation plots of daily S&P 500 returns, 1929–2009, along with a ±95% confidence interval.

Table 1.3. Ljung–Box test for daily S&P 500 returns, 1929–2009

T	Ljung–Box test, 21 lags	p-value
21,334	147.7	$<2.2e^{-16}$
2,500	110.0	$4.763e^{-14}$
100	14.5	0.846

Table 1.4. Ljung–Box test for squared S&P 500 returns, 1929–2009

T	Ljung–Box test, 21 lags	p-value
21,334	9,158.1	$<2.2e^{-16}$
2,500	3,812.1	$<2.2e^{-16}$
100	33.2	0.0438

returns (i.e., approximately the number of trading days in a calendar month). The test is performed using the full sample size, as well as the most recent 2,500 and 100 observations; the results are given in Table 1.3. We can also use the Engle LM test to test for volatility clusters.

Table 1.3 shows there is significant return predictability for the full sample, but not for the most recent observations. This does not mean a violation of market efficiency, since we would need to adjust the returns for risk, the risk-free rate and transaction costs.

The same procedure is repeated for squared returns; the results are shown in Table 1.4. The reason for focusing on squared returns is that they are proxies for volatilities; most forecast procedures for volatilities, like those in the next chapter, use squared returns as their main input. The *p*-value for the smallest sample size of squared returns is much lower than the corresponding value for returns. Tables 1.3 and 1.4 demonstrate that it is easier to predict volatility than the mean.

The code necessary to carry out ACF plots and the Ljung–Box test in R and Matlab is given in the following listings.

Listing 1.5. ACF plots and the Ljung–Box test in R

```
library(MASS,stats)    # load stats and MASS package
q = acf(y,20)
plot(q[2:20])
q = acf(y^2,20)
plot(q[2:20])
b = Box.test(y,lag=21,type="Ljung-Box")
```

Listing 1.6. ACF plots and the Ljung–Box test in Matlab

```
sacf(y,20)
sacf(y.^2,20)
ljungbox(y,20)
```

1.5 NONNORMALITY AND FAT TAILS

Many applications assume that S&P 500 index returns are normally distributed. Table 1.5 shows some return outcomes and probabilities based on this assumption (e.g., where the probability of a return less than -2% is 3.5%).

Table 1.2 shows that the biggest one-day drop in the index was 23%. If S&P 500 index returns were indeed normally distributed, then the probability of that one-day crash would be 2.23×10^{-97} according to Table 1.5. In other words, the crash is supposed to happen once every 10^{95} years (accounting for weekends and holidays). To put this into context, scientists generally assume that the earth is about 10^7 years old and the universe 10^{13} years old. Assuming normality this equates to believing that the crash of 1987 only happens in one out of every 12 universes. We are doing slightly better on the best day of the index which only has a probability of occurrence once every 10^{41} years under normality.

However, it can argued that the crash of 1987 was an anomaly, so assuming normality for all the other days would be relatively innocuous. But is this really the case? Figures 1.6(a, b) show the most extreme daily returns per decade and year, respectively. It is clear that there are still many more extremes than Table 1.5 predicts.

Table 1.5. Outcomes and probabilities of daily S&P 500 returns assuming normality, 1929–2009

Returns above or below	Probability
1%	0.865
2%	0.035
3%	0.00393
5%	2.74×10^{-06}
15%	2.70×10^{-43}
23%	2.23×10^{-97}

An alternative way of analyzing the distribution of the S&P 500 index is shown in Figure 1.7. Panel (a) plots the histogram of the returns and superimposes the normal distribution with the same mean and variance. Panel (b) shows both the normal distribution and the empirical distribution of the returns, while panel (c) blows up the left tail of the distributions. We can observe from these three figures that

1. The peak of the return distribution is much higher than for the normal distribution.
2. The sides of the return distribution are lower than for the normal distribution.
3. The tails of the return distribution are much thicker (fatter) than for the normal distribution.

In other words, there are more days when very little happens in the market than predicted by the normal and more days when market prices change considerably.

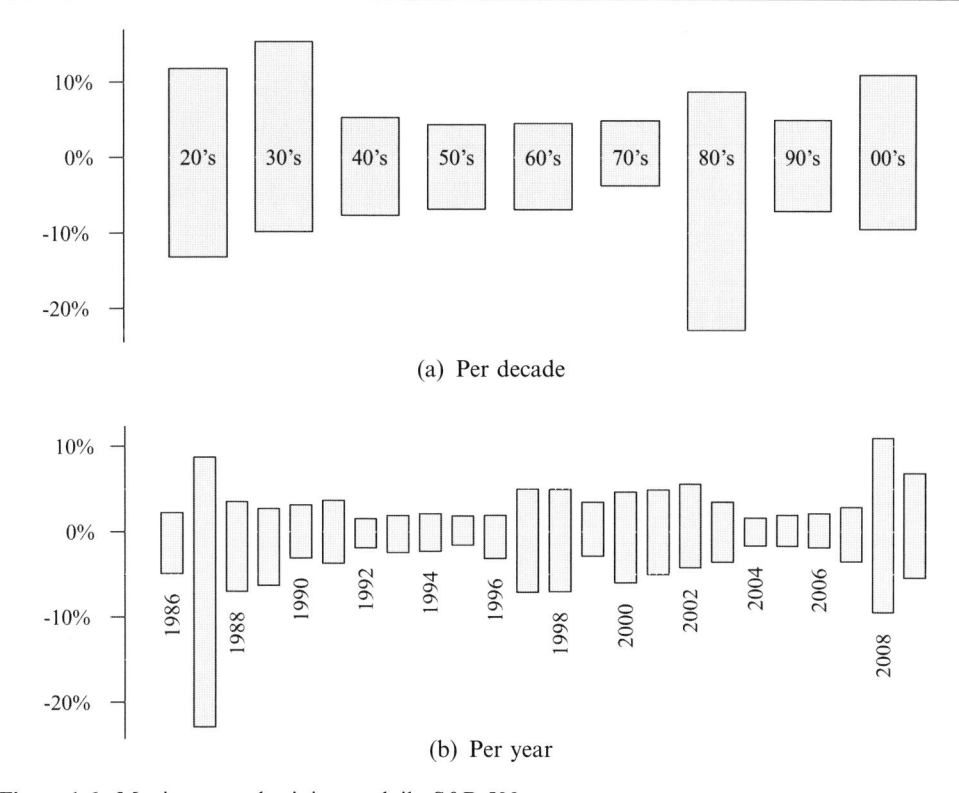

Figure 1.6. Maximum and minimum daily S&P 500 returns.

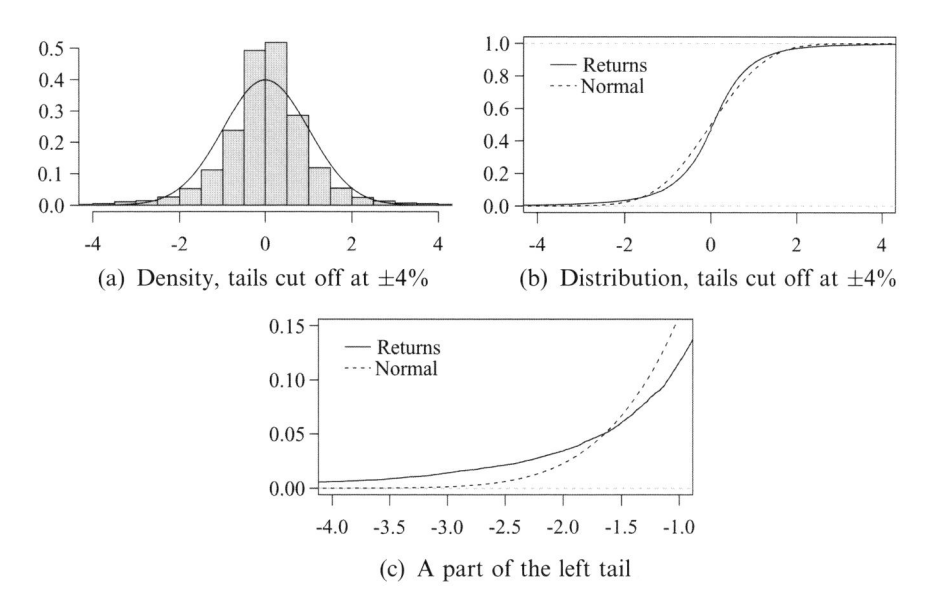

Figure 1.7. Empirical density and distribution of S&P 500 index returns for 2000–2009 compared with the normal distribution.

1.6 IDENTIFICATION OF FAT TAILS

There are two main approaches for identifying and analyzing the tails of financial returns: statistical tests and graphical methods. Statistical tests compare observed returns with some base distribution, typically but not always the normal. Graphical methods relate observed returns with values predicted from some distribution, often the normal.

1.6.1 Statistical tests for fat tails

From the above we can see that one important feature of financial returns is that they exhibit what is known as *fat tails*. We give an informal definition of fat tails below, while the formal definition can be found in Definition 9.1.

> **Definition 1.5 (Fat tails)** *A random variable is said to have fat tails if it exhibits more extreme outcomes than a normally distributed random variable with the same mean and variance.*

This implies that the market has more relatively large and small outcomes than one would expect under the normal distribution, and conversely fewer returns of an intermediate magnitude. In particular, the probability of large outcomes is much higher than the normal would predict. The fat-tailed property of returns has been known since Mandelbrot (1963) and Fama (1963, 1965).

A basic property of normally distributed observations is that they are completely described statistically by the mean and the variance (i.e., the first and second moments). This means that both skewness and kurtosis are the same for all normally distributed variables (i.e., 0 and 3, respectively). Skewness is a measure of the asymmetry of the probability distribution of a random variable and kurtosis measures the degree of peakedness of a distribution relative to the tails. High kurtosis generally means that more of the variance is due to infrequent extreme deviations than predicted by the normal, and is a strong, but not perfect, signal that a return series has fat tails. Excess kurtosis is defined as kurtosis over and above 3.

This suggests that a quick and dirty (makeshift) test for fat tails is to see if kurtosis exceeds 3. Recall that in Table 1.2 we found excess kurtosis to be 20, which is pretty strong evidence against normality.

Consequently, one can test for normality by seeing if skewness and excess kurtosis are significantly different from zero. A well-known test in this category is the Jarque–Bera (JB) test. Another common test for normality is the Kolmogorov–Smirnov test (KS) which is based on minimum distance estimation comparing a sample with a reference probability distribution (e.g., the normal distribution).

The KS test has the advantage of making no assumptions about the data distribution except the continuity of both distribution functions (i.e., technically speaking it is nonparametric and distribution free). It is sometimes claimed that the KS test is more powerful than the JB test because it considers the entire distribution. The KS test is sensitive to differences in both the location and shape of the cumulative distribution function, and a relatively large number of observations are required to reject the null in practice. However, in most cases the KS and JB tests coincide. The KS test is done in R using the function `ks.test()`, while in Matlab one can use `kstest()` from the statistics toolbox.

1.6.2 Graphical methods for fat tail analysis

A number of graphical methods exist to detect the presence of fat tails. While such graphical methods cannot provide a precise statistical description of data, they can indicate if tails are fat or thin and can reveal information about the nature of how data deviate from normality. We have seen an example of this already in Figure 1.6(a) but better techniques exist.

QQ plots

Perhaps the most commonly used graphical method for analyzing the tails of distributions is the QQ plot (quantile–quantile plot). It is similar to the comparison of distributions in Figure 1.6(a), but is more accurate. QQ plots are used to assess whether a set of observations have a particular distribution, or whether two datasets have the same distribution. The QQ plot compares the quantiles of the sample data against the quantiles of a reference distribution. The code to draw QQ plots in R and Matlab is given in the following listings.

Listing 1.7. QQ plots in R

```
library(car)
qq.plot(y, envelope=F)                          # normal
qq.plot(y,distribution="t", df=5, envelope=F)   # Student-t
```

Listing 1.8. QQ plots in Matlab

```
% Statistics toolbox
qqplot(y)       % only normal available
```

The QQ plot for the S&P 500 against the normal is shown in Figure 1.8(a).

The x-axis shows the standard normal while the y-axis measures outcomes from the data. The straight line is the normal prediction. We see that many observations seem to deviate from normality, both on the downside and on the upside, as the QQ plot has a clear S shape. The returns seem to have fatter tails than the normal but can we discover how fat the tails are?

Some idea of tail fatness can be obtained by comparing the data with a fat-tailed distribution. For example, the Student-t has fat tails, where the degrees of freedom indicate how fat the tails actually are.

In Figure 1.8(b) the Student-t with 5 degrees of freedom—that is, $t(5)$—is chosen as the reference distribution. The returns clearly seem to be fat relative to the $t(5)$ both on

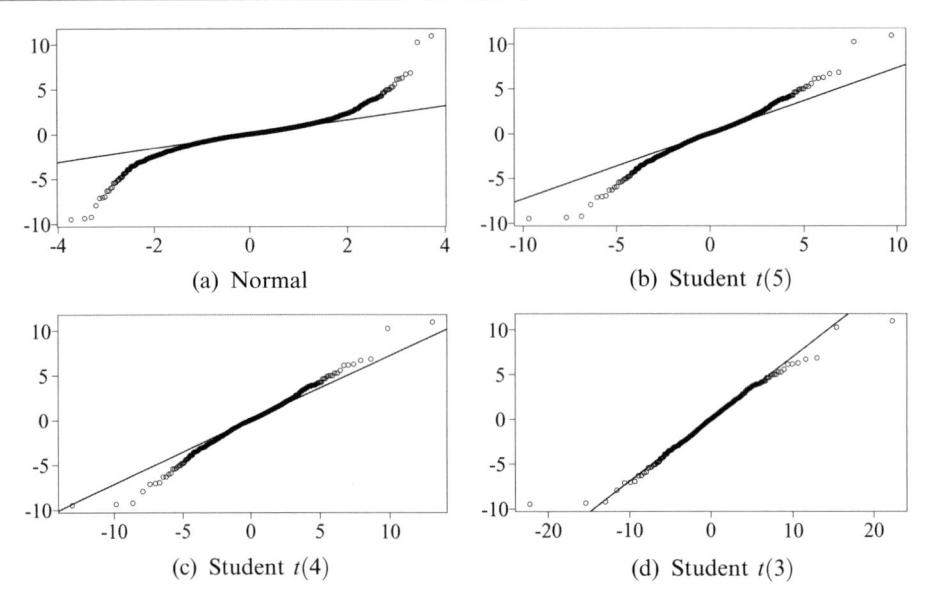

Figure 1.8. QQ plots for daily S&P 500 returns, 1989–2009.

the downside and the upside. Next we try the $t(4)$ in panel (c)—the data seem to be getting closer, the upside approximately matches the $t(4)$ while the downside is still quite fat. However, in looking at the $t(3)$ in panel (d), the data appear thin relative to the $t(3)$ both on the upside and downside. The conclusion is that S&P 500 returns have tails that are approximately equal to a $t(4)$, where the lower tail seems to be a tad thicker than the upper tail. We discuss later how we can estimate the degrees of freedom.

Sequential moments

An alternative graphical technique for detecting fat tails is a *sequential moments plot*. It is based on the formal definition of fat tails discussed in Chapter 9, which focuses on extreme value theory. There, the thickness of the tail of a distribution is measured by the tail index, indicated by ι. The lower the tail index the thicker the tails. In the special case of the Student-t distribution, the tail index corresponds to the degrees of freedom.

This suggests a simple graphical method of testing for tail thickness by using sample *moments* of data. The *m*th centered moment is given by:

$$E[(X - \mu)^m] = \int_{-\infty}^{\infty} (x - \mu)^m f(x) dx. \tag{1.1}$$

This integral does not have a finite solution for all m and all distributions. In particular, if the distribution is fat tailed, we can only compute the moments for $m < \iota$. The implication is that if the number of *bounded moments* is finite (i.e., we cannot calculate the moments in (1.1) for all $m > 0$), the data must have *fat tails*. In the case of the normal distribution we have $\iota = \infty$, so we can compute all moments in this case.

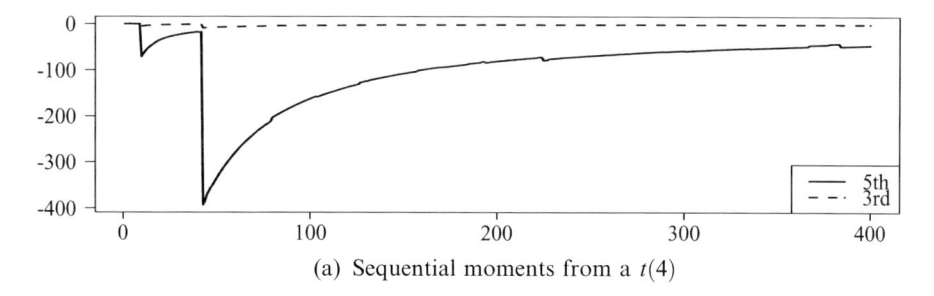

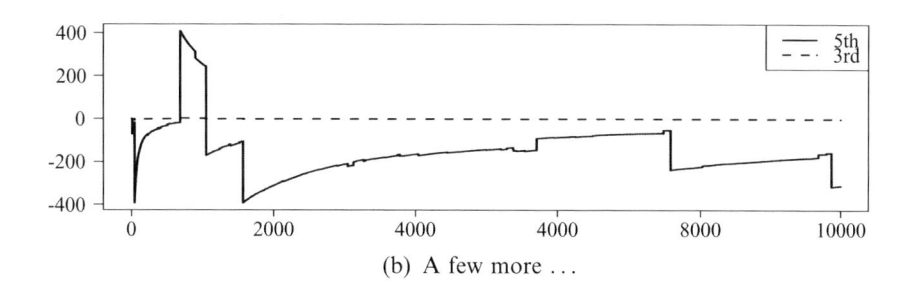

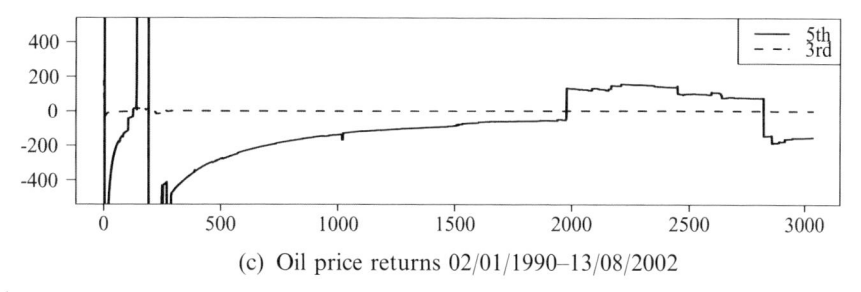

Figure 1.9. Sequential moments.
Data source: Datastream.

We can therefore measure tail thickness by graphically plotting the moments of a dataset as we add more and more observations:

$$\frac{1}{t}\sum_{i=1}^{t} x_t^m.$$

Such sequential moment plots are shown in Figure 1.9, where panels (a) and (b) show the fifth and third sequential moments for simulated data from a Student-$t(4)$ distribution. As expected, the third moment converges but the fifth does not. Panel (c) shows the third and fifth sequential moments for returns on oil prices. Here too we find that the fifth moment does not converge while the third does, indicating that the tail index of oil returns is between 3 and 5. More formal methods for estimating the tail index are presented in Chapter 9.

1.6.3 Implications of fat tails in finance

The fact that returns are non-normal has important consequences in finance. Many methods in portfolio theory and derivative pricing assume normality of returns, and break down in the absence of normality. It is, however, in the field of risk management where the normality of returns is crucially important. An assumption of normal distribution for risk calculations leads to a gross underestimation of risk. This has been widely recognized:

> "... as you well know, the biggest problems we now have with the whole evolution of risk is the fat-tail problem, which is really creating very large conceptual difficulties. Because as we all know, the assumption of normality enables us to drop off the huge amount of complexity in our equations ... Because once you start putting in non-normality assumptions, which is unfortunately what characterizes the real world, then these issues become extremely difficult."
>
> Alan Greenspan (1997)

Financial risk modeling is usually concerned with obtaining the probability of important but infrequent events, such as market crashes or how much money we may expect to lose in a worst case scenario. For such applications, the main concern is on the far left tail of the return distribution. Assuming normality will therefore lead to an underestimation of risk and may induce the wrong investment choice and perhaps leaving us underhedged, or overexposed.

Risk managers are in a difficult situation. If they assume normality, they are underestimating risk, often with dire consequences. However, the use of non-normal techniques is highly complicated, and unless correctly used, may lead to incorrect outcomes.

Option pricing is also crucially dependent on the underlying distribution. If the return distribution is indeed fat tailed, then using the Black–Scholes model will lead to underpricing.

The presence of fat tails has caused problems for many financial institutions. For example, in the beginning of the 2007–2009 crisis, several banks lost large amounts of money on their quantitative trading funds, such as Goldman Sachs as reported by the *Financial Times*:

> "For reasons that are still unclear, shares began to move in ways that were the opposite of those predicted by computer models. These moves triggered selling by the funds as they attempted to cover their losses and meet margin calls from banks. This in turn exacerbated the share price movements."
>
> *Financial Times* (2007)

This had a strong negative impact on Goldmans. Its GEO fund was down more than 30% and its flagship Global Alpha fund, a quant fund, lost 27% by that point in 2007.

> "We were seeing things that were 25-standard deviation moves, several days in a row," said David Viniar, Goldman's chief financial officer. "There have been issues in some of the other quantitative spaces. But nothing like what we saw last week."
>
> *Financial Times* (2007)

The *Wall Street Journal* notes the problems facing Lehmans, quoting Mr. Rothman, a University of Chicago Ph.D,

> "Wednesday is the type of day people will remember in quant-land for a very long time ... Events that models only predicted would happen once in 10,000 years happened every day for three days."
>
> *Wall Street Journal* (2007)

1.7 NONLINEAR DEPENDENCE

The final stylized fact of financial returns is nonlinear dependence (i.e., the observation that the dependence between different return series changes according to market conditions). For example, most of the time, the prices of assets move relatively independently of each other, but in a crisis they all drop together.

In practice, joint extreme outcomes are more likely to occur than predicted by multivariate normality and linear correlations. For example, the probability of the joint FTSE and S&P 500 crash in 1987 is 10^{-69} if measured by historical data and assumptions of bivariate normality.

Most statistical models assume that the relationship between different returns is linear. Suppose X and Y denote returns on two assets, then—if they are *linearly dependent*—the conditional expectation $E(Y|X)$ is a linear function of X. If this is true, we can measure the strength of their *linear* dependence by using correlations, such as Pearson's correlation coefficient ρ.

It is important to keep in mind that if $E[Y|X]$ cannot be expressed as a linear function of X, then ρ does not adequately capture the dependence structure between the two variables.

While it is tempting to conclude that the two data series are independent if the correlation coefficient is zero, in general this is not true, as illustrated by a simple example.

Example 1.1 *Consider a random variable X which is symmetrically distributed about zero, such as the normal, and let Y be another random variable defined as $Y = X^2$. In this case, Y is completely dependent on X while the correlation coefficient between them is zero, because the correlation coefficient only detects linear dependencies between two variables.*

Considerable recent research has shown that the assumption of linear dependence does not generally hold for asset returns, where correlations are usually lower in bull markets than in bear markets. Furthermore, if financial data were jointly normally distributed, correlations would decrease for extreme events whereas empirically we see that correlations tend to increase to one in a crisis, as demonstrated by the example in Section 1.7.1.

To capture such phenomena, models of nonlinear dependence allow the dependence structure to change according to market conditions. In this case, linear correlations overestimate dependence in non-crisis periods and underestimate correlations during crises.

Research such as Ang et al. (2001) and Patton (2002) has found that these nonlinear dependence structures command a premium in the market as investors require higher expected returns for portfolios where assets are highly correlated under bad market conditions. Aside from asset allocation, applications in risk analysis, economic capital and financial stability also focus on large outcomes. In such applications it is essential to address nonlinear dependence.

1.7.1 Sample evidence of nonlinear dependence

We illustrate nonlinear dependence with long-run correlations between the returns of three (former) investment banks, Morgan Stanley, Goldman Sachs and Bear Stearns, and one nonfinancial firm, Microsoft, for the time period May 5, 1999–September 12, 2007 (see Table 1.6). Unsurprisingly, financials are relatively highly correlated, while Microsoft is less correlated with financials at around 40%.

During the first round of the 2007–2009 crisis (August 2007), the correlations of all stocks increased dramatically. For example, Table 1.6(b) shows the correlations between Morgan Stanley and Goldman Sachs increasing from 81% to 94%. Such a high correla-

Table 1.6. Return correlations and means for Microsoft (MSFT), Morgan Stanley (MS), Goldman Sachs (GS) and Bear Stearns (BSC)

(a) Daily return correlations (May 5, 1999–September 12, 2007)

	MSFT	MS	GS
MS	44%		
GS	44%	81%	
BSC	38%	74%	71%

(b) Daily return correlations (1 August 2007–15 August 2007) during the opening events of the 2007 crisis

	MSFT	MS	GS
MS	93%		
GS	82%	94%	
BSC	82%	92%	89%

(c) Daily mean returns

	MSFT	MS	GS	BSC
1999/5/5–2007/9/12	−0.007%	0.028%	0.049%	0.050%
2007/8/1–2007/8/15	−0.252%	−1.094%	−1.208%	−1.468%

Data source: CRSP.

tion indicates that the two stocks almost move in lockstep. Even Microsoft was affected by this and its correlation with financials increased substantially.

Furthermore, Table 1.6(c) shows how actual stock prices were affected by the crisis. The effect on Microsoft is relatively insignificant, but all the financials saw their mean daily return of about 0.05% fall to -1.5%. It is an empirical fact that very high correlations are usually associated with very negative returns.

It is straightforward to write an R or Matlab program to download stock prices automatically and calculate correlations. We start by modifying Listings 1.1 and 1.2. We want to calculate correlations during the period of the financial crisis (i.e., from 2007/6/1 to 2009/12/31). Bear Stearns went into bankruptcy in 2008 so we exclude it from the sample. First, we show the R code in Listing 1.9, which is then followed by the Matlab code in Listing 1.10.

Listing 1.9. Download stock prices in R

```
price1 = get.hist.quote(instrument = "msft",start = "2007-06-01",
    end = "2009-12-31",quote="AdjClose")
price2 = get.hist.quote(instrument = "ms", start = "2007-06-01",
    end = "2009-12-31",quote="AdjClose")
price3 = get.hist.quote(instrument = "GS", start = "2007-06-01",
    end = "2009-12-31",quote="AdjClose")
p=cbind(price1,price2,price3)    # combine price vectors into a
                                   matrix
y=diff(log(p))
cor(y)                           # calculate correlation matrix
```

Listing 1.10. Download stock prices in Matlab

```
price = hist_stock_data('01062007','31122009','msft','ms','gs');
price=[price(1).AdjClose(end:-1:1),price(2).AdjClose(end:-1:1),
    price(3).AdjClose(end:-1:1)]
y=diff(log(price))
corr(y)    % calculate correlation matrix
```

1.7.2 Exceedance correlations

One method for documenting the presence of nonlinear dependence is by using *exceedance correlations* as proposed by Longin and Solnik (2001) and Ang and Chen (2002).

Consider two stock returns X and Y which have been standardized (mean zero and variance one). Exceedance correlations show the correlations of the two stocks as being conditional on exceeding some threshold, that is:

$$\tilde{\rho}(p) \equiv \begin{cases} \text{Corr}[X, Y | X \leq Q_X(p) \text{ and } Y \leq Q_Y(p)], & \text{for } p \leq 0.5 \\ \text{Corr}[X, Y | X > Q_X(p) \text{ and } Y > Q_Y(p)], & \text{for } p > 0.5, \end{cases} \quad (1.2)$$

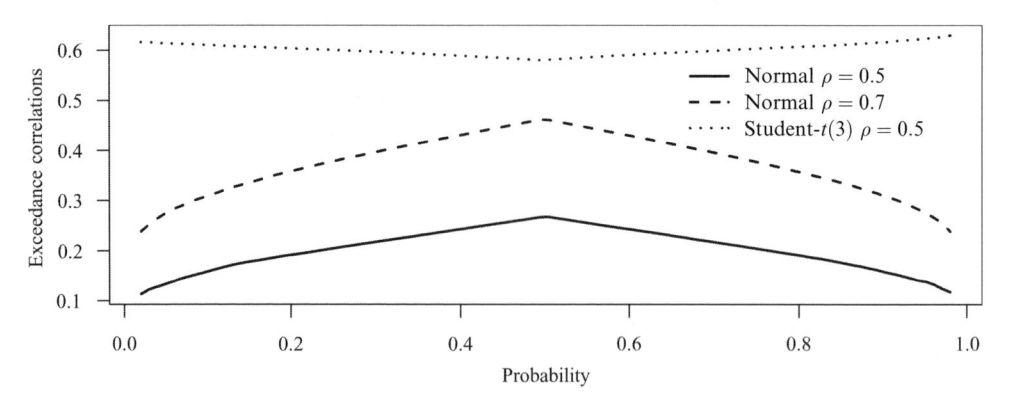

Figure 1.10. Exceedance plot for the bivariate normal and the Student-*t*.

where $Q_X(p)$ and $Q_Y(p)$ are the *p*th quantiles of X and Y, respectively, given a distributional assumption. The shape of the exceedance correlation plot depends on the underlying distribution of data.

Exceedance correlations for the standard bivariate normal and the Student-*t* distributions are shown in Figure 1.10. The horizontal axis shows the probability (we go from 0 to 0.5, and then from 1 to 0.5) and the vertical axis shows the correlation between the two returns given that both exceed that quantile (i.e., exceedance correlations). The plot is nonlinear in *p* but symmetric. Exceedance correlations decrease for the normal as we go out towards extreme quantiles, while they increase for the Student-*t*.

Figure 1.11 shows the empirical exceedance correlations for daily returns on Disney and IBM over 24 years, superimposed with exceedance correlations for the bivariate normal and the bivariate Student-*t*(3) distributions with the same correlation coefficient. The exceedance correlations exhibit substantial asymmetry. The stock returns become highly correlated at the left extreme, with correlations steadily decreasing when we move to the right of the distribution. This is precisely the type of dependence structure that risk-averse investors dislike.

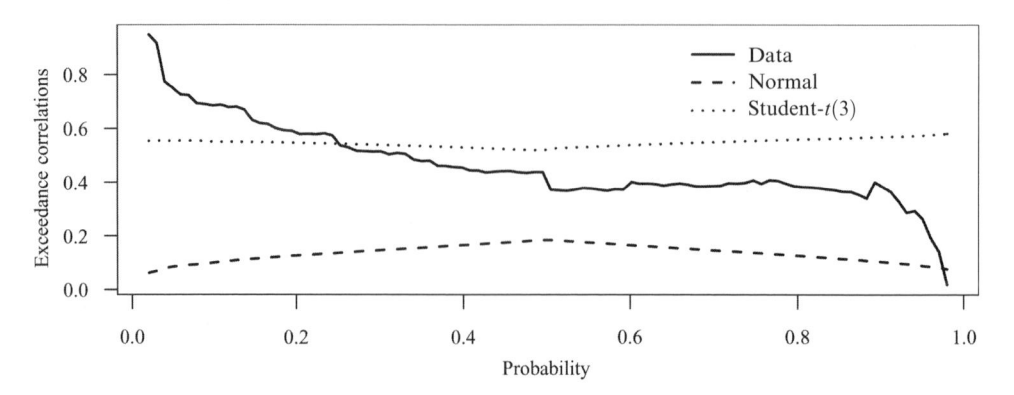

Figure 1.11. Exceedance plot for Disney and IBM returns (January 1, 1986–November 3, 2009). *Data source*: Yahoo Finance.

1.8 COPULAS

The correlation analysis shown in Table 1.6 along with the exceedance plots help in identifying the nature of nonlinear dependence (NLD). However, this still leaves the question of how to model NLD more formally. One approach is discussed in Chapter 3 (i.e., multivariate volatility models), but an alternative method is to use *copulas*. For more on the application of copulas in finance, see, for example, Patton (2009).

Copulas provide the means to create a multivariate distribution with a range of types of dependence. We start by taking the returns on each return series separately (called marginal returns), and transform them to the uniform distribution using the probability integral transformation discussed below.

Armed with returns transformed to a uniform random variable, we then proceed by modeling the dependence structure between these uniforms using a copula. Since the probability integral transform is invertible, the copula also describes the dependence between the original variables (returns).

In other words, we separate out the distribution of individual assets from the distribution that links them together. For example, each asset can have a normally distributed return, but taken jointly the portfolio is much more correlated in adverse market situations than in bull markets. The copula provides information about how assets behave together.

1.8.1 The Gaussian copula

Recall the normal (or Gaussian) distribution, where $\Phi(\cdot)$ is the normal distribution, and $\Phi^{-1}(\cdot)$ is the inverse normal distribution. U and V are uniform ($U, V \in [0,1]$) random variables, and $\Phi_\rho(\cdot)$ is the bivariate normal distribution with correlation coefficient ρ. The function $C(\cdot)$ in

$$C(u,v) = \Phi_\rho(\Phi^{-1}(u), \Phi^{-1}(v)))$$

is then known as the *Gaussian copula function*, made famous by Li (2000), whose work on the Gaussian copula enabled the pricing of structured credit products (like subprime CDOs) which subsequently got blamed for the 2007–2009 crisis. The copula provides the information that links the two univariate (also known as marginal) random variables together.

For an example of a Gaussian copula see Figure 1.12(a), which shows a cross plot (scatter plot) from a bivariate normal distribution, while panel (c) shows the joint distribution and panel (e) the contours.

1.8.2 The theory of copulas

The joint distribution of multiple random variables is composed of information about each variable separately, as well as information about how the various random variables are linked together. Suppose X and Y are two random variables representing the returns of two different stocks,

$$X \sim f$$
$$Y \sim g.$$

26 Financial markets, prices and risk

(a) Gaussian scatterplot

(b) Crossplot of Disney against IBM

(c) Fitted Gaussian copula

(d) Fitted Student-t copula

(e) Contour of the Gaussian copula

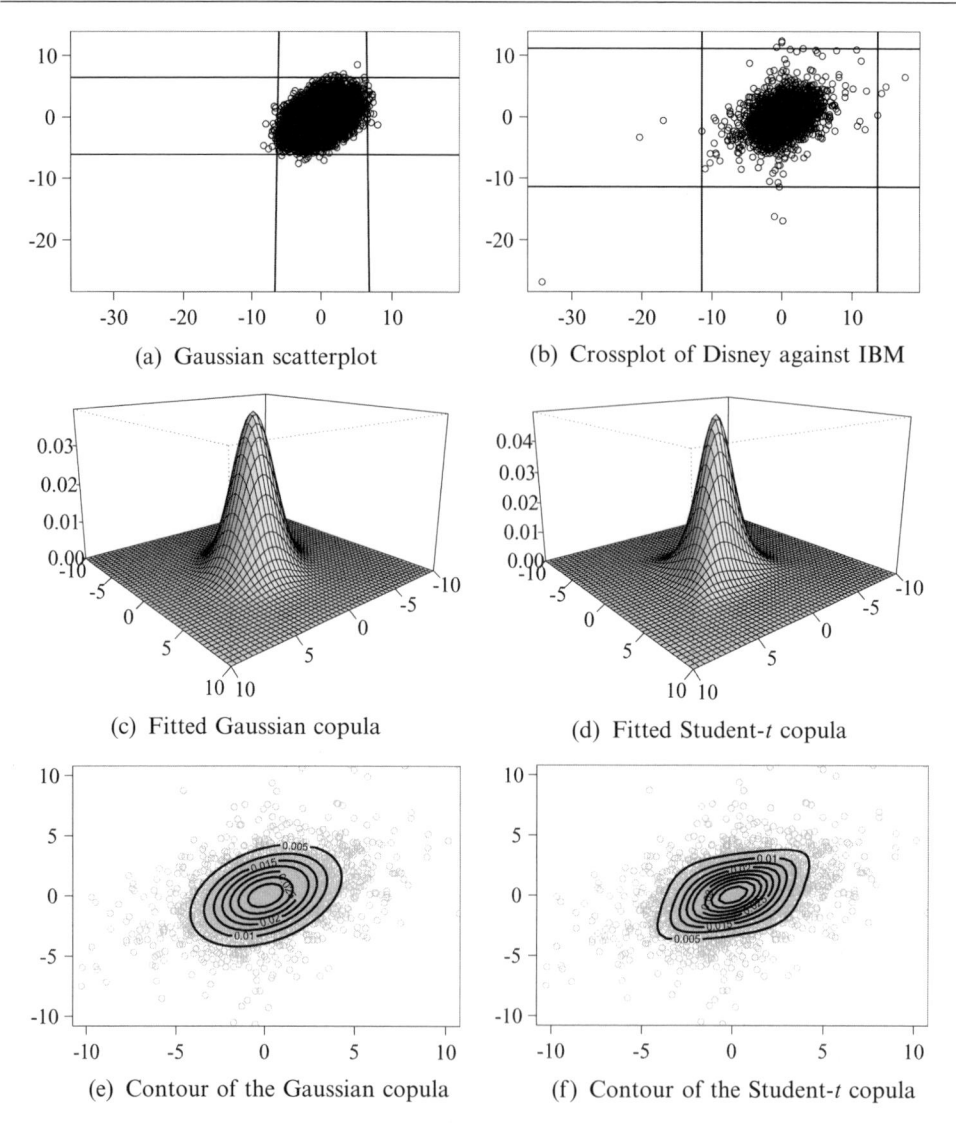

(f) Contour of the Student-t copula

Figure 1.12. Copula plots for daily Disney and IBM returns, 1986–2009.

Together, the joint distribution and the marginal distributions are represented by the joint density:

$$(X, Y) \sim h.$$

The idea behind the copula approach is that that we focus separately on marginal distributions (F, G) and the function that combines them into the joint distribution, H. That function is the *copula*. In other words, the copula extracts information on the dependence structure from the joint distribution.

The probability integral transformation

The first step in applying copulas is to transform X and Y into random variables that are distributed *uniformly* between zero and one, which removes individual information from the bivariate density h. The *probability integral transformation* due to Fisher (1925) states that:

Theorem 1.1 *Let a random variable X have a continuous distribution F, and define a new random variable U as:*
$$U = F(X).$$
Then, regardless of the original distribution F, $U \sim \text{Uniform}(0, 1)$.

The theorem says that any continuous distribution can be transformed into a uniform variable; therefore, knowing the distribution of the uniform random variable does not imply anything about the original distribution. The probability integral transformation is a strictly increasing transformation hence it is invertible. This means that we can identify the dependence between two variables with the dependence between their transforms.

On to copulas

Apply Theorem 1.1 to the two returns, X and Y, to obtain two uniform variables:
$$U = F(X)$$
$$V = G(Y).$$

A copula is a probability distribution on a unit cube for which every marginal distribution is uniform on the interval $[0, 1]$. The copula contains all the dependence information in the original bivariate density h, but none of the individual information. Sklar (1959) provides the main theory for copulas.

Theorem 1.2 *Let F be the distribution of X, G the distribution of Y and H the joint distribution of (X, Y). Assume that F and G are continuous. Then there exists a unique copula C such that:*
$$H(X, Y) = C(F(X), G(Y)). \tag{1.3}$$

In applications we are more likely to use densities; Sklar's theorem allows us to decompose joint density by:
$$h(X, Y) = f(X) \cdot g(Y) \cdot c(F(X), G(Y)).$$

Nelsen (1999) provides a corollary to the above theorem that allows us to extract the copula from any given multivariate distribution and use it independently of the original marginal distributions. In other words, we can construct a joint distribution from *any* two marginal distributions and *any* copula, and extract the implied copula and the marginal distributions from any joint distribution.

1.8.3 An application of copulas

We illustrate the application of copulas using the same Disney and IBM data as in Figure 1.11. Recall that the data showed greater dependence in the negative quadrant.

(a) Clayton's copula, $\theta = 1$

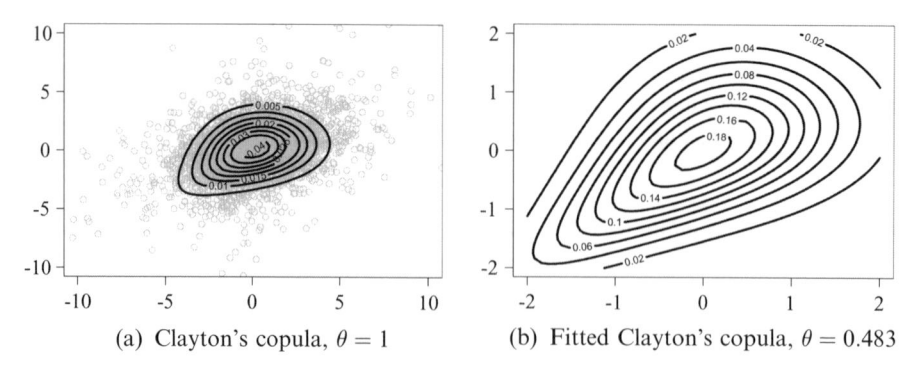

(b) Fitted Clayton's copula, $\theta = 0.483$

Figure 1.13. More examples of copulas, same data as in Figure 1.12.

The results are shown in Figure 1.12. Panel (b) shows a cross plot of stock returns along with their 0.05% and 99.95% quantiles. The vast majority of data points seem to be centered around zero, but there are a few outliers from both stocks that lie outside their sample quantiles.

We can analyze the dependence by comparing simulated data from the bivariate normal distribution with stock returns where both have the same covariance matrix. Panel (a) shows that simulated bivariate normal data do not have the same joint extremes as stock returns.

We estimated both a Gaussian and a Student-t copula for the data. The estimated parameter for the normal copula is the correlation coefficient, ρ, while for Student-t, the estimated parameters are the correlation coefficient and the degrees of freedom, ν. Fitted copula densities are shown in panels (c) and (d). It is hard to compare distributions from three-dimensional graphs, and the corresponding contour plots in panels (e) and (f) provide a clearer picture. The t-copula clearly has more correlated extremes, on both the upside and downside, as the plot is more stretched towards the top right and bottom left corners.

There are a number of copulas available; we present here the Clayton copula, which is often used in financial applications of return dependence (see Figure 1.13). The Clayton copula is from the Archimedean class of copulas and, unlike the normal and the Student-t, is asymmetric, exhibiting greater dependence in the negative tail than in the positive tail, with parameter θ a measure of the strength of dependence. Panel (a) shows the Clayton copula with $\theta = 1$, while panel (b) shows the estimated copula with the same Disney and IBM data as above.

1.8.4 Some challenges in using copulas

The main problem with copulas—demonstrated in the example to an extent—is that we can specify any type of dependence structure we want, where the copula need not be affected by the marginal densities we choose. In the example above, marginal densities were assumed to be the normal distribution. Currently, goodness-of-fit tests for copulas are not common and it is unclear whether a copula that has a good fit yields a good fit for the distribution of data.

One example of the possible misuse of copulas is when the rating agencies used Gaussian copulas to estimate the default correlation in a pool of mortgages, with damaging consequences, as shown in the 2007–2009 crisis.

No economic theory of copulas exists; hence, there is little guidance in choosing copulas. In turn, this means we have the freedom to choose any type of dependence structure we want.

1.9 SUMMARY

Many applications in finance are based on the assumption that returns on financial assets are IID normally distributed. This assumption has been analyzed in detail in this chapter. By using a sample of stocks of the most important stock market index in the world, the S&P 500, as well as a selection of stocks on the New York Stock Exchange, we have demonstrated that IID normality does not hold. Furthermore, it is straightforward to show similar results for most financial assets.

It is well known that financial returns follow a complicated and ever-changing probability distribution function where we can only hope to statistically model a very small part of the distribution of returns at any one time. Often, the underlying application dictates which part of the statistical distribution of returns we focus on.

The stylized facts of financial markets we have examined are

Volatility clusters

Fat tails

Nonlinear dependence

These stylized facts seem to hold for most if not all basic (i.e., non-derived) financial assets regardless of asset type, sampling frequency, observation period or market.

Other empirical results only hold some of the time. For example, return distributions are usually skewed either to the left or to the right. Returns often have a strong positive autocorrelation over long periods of time during bull markets such as the internet bubble, or negative autocorrelation during prolonged bear markets such as the Japanese stock market since 1990. At the highest frequencies, returns tend to have negative autocorrelations, but positive autocorrelations at the lowest frequencies. However, no regular first-moment or third-moment patterns about returns exist and the overwhelming conclusion is that we cannot profitably forecast prices in a systematic way using simple methods.

The focus in this chapter has been on empirically identifying these stylized facts using a range of statistical techniques. In subsequent chapters we focus on statistically modeling financial returns, primarily for the purpose of forecasting risk.

2
Univariate volatility modeling

One of the most important developments in empirical finance has been the modeling and forecasting of volatility. It has been spurred on by applications such as the rapid growth of financial derivatives, quantitative trading and risk modeling.

A key modeling difficulty is that market volatility is not directly observable—unlike market prices it is a *latent variable*. Volatility must therefore be *inferred* by looking at how much market prices move. If prices fluctuate a lot, we know volatility is high, but we cannot ascertain precisely how high. One reason is that we cannot distinguish whether a large shock to prices is transitory or permanent.

The latent nature of volatility means that it must be forecast by a statistical model, a process that inevitably entails making strong assumptions. Indeed, volatility modeling is quite demanding, and often seems to be as much an art as a science because of the challenges posed by the presence of issues such as nonnormalities, volatility clusters and structural breaks.

The presence of volatility clusters suggests that it may be more efficient to use only the most recent observations to forecast volatility, or perhaps assign a higher weight to the most recent observations. Indeed, that is how most of the methods discussed in this chapter work.

The focus of this chapter is on volatility forecasting for a single return series or *univariate volatility*. In Chapter 3 we discuss the forecasting of covariance matrices or *multivariate volatility*. In addition to presenting the most common volatility models, we demonstrate how to implement them in R and Matlab with a sample from the S&P 500. For a recent survey on volatility models see, for example, Francq and Zakoian (2010).

The most important specific notation used in this chapter is:

W_E Estimation window
λ Decay factor in EWMA
Z_t Residuals
α, β Main model parameters
ζ, δ Other model parameters
L_1, L_2 Lags in volatility models

2.1 MODELING VOLATILITY

A large number of methods for forecasting volatility exist, of which only a small number are in regular use. In model choice, there is a tradeoff between various factors such as tractability and robustness. We can classify the most commonly used models in the following way:

1. Moving average (MA).
2. Exponentially weighted moving average (EWMA) a.k.a. RiskMetrics™.
3. GARCH and its extension models.
4. Stochastic volatility.
5. Implied volatility.
6. Realized volatility.

In addition, there are many hybrid models that combine different model characteristics, such as implied volatility in GARCH-type models, or GARCH features in stochastic volatility models.

We usually assume that mean return is zero. While this is obviously not correct, the daily mean is orders of magnitude smaller than volatility and therefore can usually be safely ignored for the purpose of volatility forecasting.

Conditional volatility, σ_t, is typically, but not always, obtained from application of a statistical procedure to a sample of previous *return* observations, making up the *estimation window*. Such methodologies provide conditional volatility forecasts, represented by:

$$\sigma_t | \text{past returns and a model} = \sigma(y_{t-1}, \ldots, y_{t-W_E})$$

where various methods are used to specify the function $\sigma(\cdot)$.

2.2 SIMPLE VOLATILITY MODELS

The most obvious and easy way to forecast volatility is simply to calculate the sample standard error from a sample of returns. Over time, we would keep the sample size constant, and every day add the newest return to the sample and drop the oldest. This method is called the moving average (MA) model.

Since the MA model is known to perform badly, it can be improved by exponentially weighing returns, so that the most recent returns have the biggest weight in forecasting volatility. The best known such model is the exponentially weighted moving average (EWMA) model.

The distinguishing feature of these models compared with the others discussed in this chapter is that there is no parameter or model to be estimated; they are also very simple in construction.

2.2.1 Moving average models

Possibly the simplest volatility forecast model is the moving average (MA) model:

$$\hat{\sigma}_t^2 = \frac{1}{W_E} \sum_{i=1}^{W_E} y_{t-i}^2 \qquad (2.1)$$

where y_t is the observed return on day t; $\hat{\sigma}_t$ is the volatility forecast for day t; and W_E is the length of the estimation window (i.e., the number of observations used in the calculation, usually of an arbitrary length for the MA volatility model). Note that only lagged observations are used in the forecast (i.e., the most recent return used to forecast day t volatility is for day $t-1$).

One key shortcoming of MA models is that observations are equally weighted, which is problematic when financial returns exhibit volatility clusters, since the most recent data are more indicative of whether we are in a high-volatility or low-volatility cluster.

In practice, this method should not be used. It is very sensitive to the choice of estimation window length and will generate volatility forecasts that jump around and that are generally systematically too high or too low. Furthermore, when used for value-at-risk, their risk forecasts are usually on average too low.

2.2.2 Exponentially weighted moving average model

The moving average model can be improved by assigning greater weights to more recent observations. One of the easiest ways to specify the weights is to use an exponentially weighted moving average (EWMA) model.[1]

The EWMA model is based on modifying the MA so that weights λ exponentially decline into the past:

$$\hat{\sigma}_t^2 = \frac{1-\lambda}{\lambda(1-\lambda^{W_E})} \sum_{i=1}^{W_E} \lambda^i y_{t-i}^2$$

where the first part of the equation ensures the sum of the weights is one.

We demonstrate below that we can rewrite the EWMA model as the weighted sum of the previous period's volatility forecast and squared returns, where the sum of the weights is one:

$$\hat{\sigma}_t^2 = (1-\lambda) y_{t-1}^2 + \lambda \hat{\sigma}_{t-1}^2. \quad (2.2)$$

where $0 < \lambda < 1$ is the decay factor; and $\hat{\sigma}_t^2$ the conditional volatility forecast on day t.

An example of the weights can be seen in Figure 2.1 which contains exponentially declining weights and fixed weights for a 20-day observation window. The exponential weights decline to zero very quickly, which is presumably one reason EWMA is not permitted under the Basel Accords for the purposes of calculating VaR. However, on the whole, the EWMA model performs well compared with the more complicated models discussed later in this chapter.

Deriving the EWMA model

Since

$$(1-\lambda) \sum_{i=1}^{W_E} \lambda^i = (1-\lambda)(\lambda^1 + \cdots + \lambda^{W_E}) = \lambda - \lambda^{W_E+1}$$

it is straightforward to check that the sum of the weights is one.

---

[1] This model was originally proposed by J.P. Morgan (1993) and given the name RiskMetrics™, but subsequently J.P. Morgan spun off a part of its modeling arm under the same name, so it is preferable to use the more generic designation EWMA. See, for example, Alexander (2001, section 7.3) and Tsay (2005, section 7.2) for more background on EWMA.

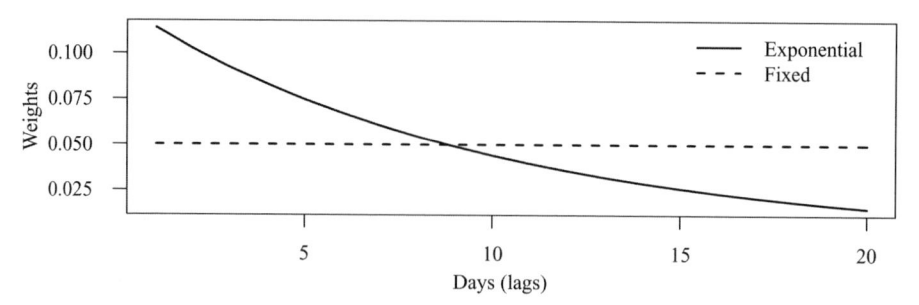

Figure 2.1. MA and EWMA weights, $\lambda = 0.94$ over time.

The exponential is a function that decreases rapidly, which means that for W_E large enough (but not necessarily very large) the terms λ^n are negligible for all $n \geq W_E$. Hence, we can approximate this model by its limit as W_E tends to infinity:

$$\hat{\sigma}_t^2 = \frac{1-\lambda}{\lambda} \sum_{i=1}^{\infty} \lambda^i y_{t-i}^2$$

knowing that from a certain i on, the terms can be considered equal to zero. In order to simplify the model, take the first term out of the sum and get

$$\hat{\sigma}_t^2 = (1-\lambda)y_{t-1}^2 + \frac{1-\lambda}{\lambda} \sum_{i=2}^{\infty} \lambda^i y_{t-i}^2.$$

Now rearrange the indices and the λs in the second part of the expression

$$\hat{\sigma}_t^2 = (1-\lambda)y_{t-1}^2 + (1-\lambda) \sum_{i=1}^{\infty} \lambda^i y_{t-1-i}^2.$$

This expression is similar to the conditional volatility at time $t-1$:

$$\frac{\lambda(1-\lambda^{W_E})}{1-\lambda}\hat{\sigma}_{t-1}^2 = \sum_{i=1}^{W_E} \lambda^i y_{t-1-i}^2.$$

Substituting this equality we obtain the main EWMA equation, (2.2).

Applying the EWMA

When the model was first proposed by J.P. Morgan it was suggested that λ be set at 0.94 for daily returns, and to this day this is the most common assumption. By making distributional assumptions about residuals it is straightforward to estimate λ.

The main disadvantage of the EWMA model is the fact that λ is constant and identical for all assets. This implies that it is not optimal for any asset in the sense that the GARCH models discussed below are optimal. However, it is clearly not realistic to expect λ to be the same for all assets and time periods.

As a result, the EWMA model by definition gives inferior forecasts compared with GARCH models, even though the difference can be very small in many cases.

The EWMA model, however, has two key advantages: first, it can be implemented much more easily than most alternatives. Second, multivariate forms can be applied in a straightforward fashion. Coupled with the fact that it often gives reasonable forecasts, EWMA is often the method of choice.

EWMA unconditional volatility

The conditional volatility of the EWMA model is given by (2.2), but it is often of interest to calculate the *unconditional* volatility as well. The EWMA model is a special version of the GARCH model discussed in the next section, where we show in (2.9) how to calculate its unconditional variances.

By considering the EWMA model as a special case of the GARCH model, the EWMA unconditional variance is

$$\sigma^2 = \frac{0}{0}$$

that is, it is undefined—meaning that the EWMA model is *covariance nonstationary*. Therefore, the EWMA unconditional variances cannot be calculated and if a EWMA process is allowed to run for a while it will explode. We can verify this by simulating the EWMA model in R and Matlab.

2.3 GARCH AND CONDITIONAL VOLATILITY

The majority of volatility forecast models in regular use belong to the GARCH family of models. The first such model was the autoregressive conditional heteroskedasticity (ARCH) model proposed by Engle (1982), but the generalized ARCH model (GARCH) of Bollerslev (1986) is the common denominator for most volatility models. Subsequently, a rich family of GARCH models has emerged, most of which see limited use.

The GARCH family of models belong to the category of *conditional volatility* models and are based on using optimal exponential weighting of historical returns to obtain a volatility forecast. Returns on day t are a function of returns on previous days, where older returns have a lower weight than more recent returns. The parameters of the model are typically estimated with maximum likelihood.

We want to study the statistical properties of returns given information available at time $t-1$ and create a model of how statistical properties or returns evolve over time. Lowercase letters y_t indicate sample observations and uppercase letters Y_t denote random variables (RVs).

The main object of interest is the conditional volatility of Y_t (i.e., σ_t); however, we need to address the mean somehow. It is generally more efficient to separate estimation of the mean from volatility estimation, and consequently most volatility models are based on using returns that have been *de-meaned* (i.e., the unconditional mean has been subtracted from the returns). In what follows we assume that $E(Y_t) = 0$, unless otherwise indicated, while the returns used in the applications below are de-meaned.

The innovation in returns is driven by random shocks (i.e., a sequence of IID mean 0, variance 1 RVs, denoted by $\{Z_t\}$). The return on day t can then be indicated by

$$Y_t = \sigma_t Z_t.$$

We don't need to make any further assumptions about the distribution of Z_t. In most cases it is assumed to be normal, but other distributions are frequently used, such as the Student-*t*.

An important feature of GARCH-type models is that unconditional volatility σ depends on the entire sample—while conditional volatilities σ_t are determined by model parameters and *recent* return observations.

2.3.1 ARCH

The first model designed to capture volatility clusters was ARCH

$$\sigma_t^2 = \omega + \sum_{i=1}^{L_1} \alpha_i Y_{t-i}^2 \qquad (2.3)$$

where L_1 is the number of lags.[2] Setting the lag to one in (2.3) will result in the ARCH(1) model which states that the conditional variance of today's return is equal to a constant, plus yesterday's return squared; that is:

$$\sigma_t^2 = \omega + \alpha Y_{t-1}^2. \qquad (2.4)$$

ARCH(1) unconditional volatility

The moments of any order m are given by:

$$E(Y^m) = E(E_t(Y^m)) = E(Y_t^m)$$

for all t. Therefore:

$$E(Y^2) = \sigma^2 = E(Y_t^2) = E(\sigma_t^2 Z_t^2) = E(\sigma_t^2).$$

Then

$$\sigma^2 = E(\omega + \alpha Y_{t-1}^2) = \omega + \alpha \sigma^2.$$

So, the unconditional volatility of the ARCH(1) model is given by:

$$\sigma^2 = \frac{\omega}{1-\alpha}. \qquad (2.5)$$

ARCH(1) fat tails

The most common distributional assumption for residuals Z is standard normality; that is:

$$Z_t \sim \mathcal{N}(0,1).$$

In this case, conditional returns are conditionally normal. However, the unconditional distribution of the returns will be fat, easily demonstrated by showing that unconditional excess kurtosis exceeds zero:

$$\text{Kurtosis} = \frac{E(Y^4)}{(E(Y^2))^2}.$$

For the 4th moment:

$$E(Y^4) = E(Y_t^4) = E(\sigma_t^4 Z_t^4) = 3E(\sigma_t^4)$$

---

[2] The convention in the literature on volatility models is to use p or P for L_1 and q or Q for L_2.

due to the independence of the variables and the normality of Z_t. Substituting we get:

$$E(Y^4) = 3E\left((\omega + \alpha Y_{t-1}^2)^2\right) = 3\omega^2 + 2\alpha\omega\sigma + \alpha^2 E(Y^4).$$

Substituting the value of σ, we get an expression for $E(Y^4)$,

$$E(Y^4) = \frac{3\omega^2(1+\alpha)}{(1-\alpha)(1-3\alpha^2)}.$$

We can now compute the unconditional kurtosis:

$$\text{Kurtosis} = \frac{3(1-\alpha^2)}{1-3\alpha^2} > 3 \quad \text{if } 3\alpha^2 < 1. \tag{2.6}$$

A more formal demonstration of the unconditional fat tails of the ARCH(1) model is shown in Chapter 9, which focuses on extreme value theory. It is demonstrated there that we can directly relate α to the tail index ι.

For example, the following table from Section 9.5.2 shows that the higher the α the fatter the tails (lower tail index ι implies fatter tails):

Table 2.1. Tail index and ARCH(1) parameter.

α	0.10	0.50	0.90	0.99
ι	26.48	4.73	2.30	2.02

Parameter restrictions

There are two main restrictions that are often imposed on the parameters of the ARCH model:

1. To ensure positive volatility forecasts:

$$\forall\, i = 1, \ldots, L_1, \quad \alpha_i, \omega > 0.$$

2. To ensure covariance stationarity so that unconditional volatility is defined, impose:

$$\sum_{i=1}^{L_1} \alpha_i < 1.$$

It is only the nonnegativity constraint that always has to be imposed and, depending on the final application, we may or may not want to impose covariance stationarity. In the case of the ARCH(1) model, if $\alpha \geq 1$ the unconditional volatility is no longer defined, as is clear from (2.5).

This does not, however, imply that the covariance stationarity restriction should be imposed in every case. If the model is correctly specified it may be a good idea to impose the restriction, but every model is flawed. As a result, allowing the parameters to be free may provide a better approximation to the true process.

If the restriction is binding, it is as if the top part of the likelihood function were sliced off, often resulting in more than one parameter combination satisfying the constraint. This means that the estimated parameters and hence the resulting volatility forecast are subject to a degree of arbitrariness. In repeated sequential estimation (e.g., in backtesting where a moving data window is used) the parameter estimates would then jump around from one day to the next, causing inconsistency and contributing to the *volatility of volatility*.

Usefulness of ARCH

On balance, ARCH models are not well suited for capturing volatility. Consider Figure 1.5(b) which shows the ACF plot of squared S&P 500 returns, where we see that about 600 lags of squared returns are statistically significant, implying that we would need to estimate an ARCH(600) model to capture the entire volatility structure. This is infeasible, as no estimation package could get even close to estimating an ARCH(600) model; a more practical upper limit might be ARCH(20). A similar problem also exists with autoregressive (AR) models, where it is often solved by introducing a moving average (MA) component. In the context of ARCH, a comparable solution is given by the GARCH model.

2.3.2 GARCH

One of the biggest problems with the ARCH model concerns the long lag lengths required to capture the impact of historical returns on current volatility. By including lagged volatility during ARCH model creation we have the potential to incorporate the impact of historical returns. This results in the GARCH(L_1, L_2) model:

$$\sigma_t^2 = \omega + \sum_{i=1}^{L_1} \alpha_i Y_{t-i}^2 + \sum_{j=1}^{L_2} \beta_j \sigma_{t-j}^2. \tag{2.7}$$

The most common version of (2.7) only employs one lag, resulting in the GARCH(1,1) model:

$$\sigma_t^2 = \omega + \alpha Y_{t-1}^2 + \beta \sigma_{t-1}^2. \tag{2.8}$$

GARCH(1,1) unconditional volatility

Unconditional volatility can be calculated similarly to the way it is done in the ARCH model, utilizing the same assumptions. Focusing on the GARCH(1, 1) model:

$$\sigma^2 = \mathrm{E}(\omega + \alpha Y_{t-1}^2 \beta \sigma_{t-1}^2) = \omega + \alpha \sigma^2 + \beta \sigma^2.$$

where

$$\sigma^2 = \omega + \alpha \sigma^2 + \beta \sigma^2.$$

So, the unconditional volatility is given by:

$$\sigma^2 = \frac{\omega}{1 - \alpha - \beta}. \tag{2.9}$$

GARCH(1,1) parameter restrictions

Similar to the ARCH model, there are two types of restrictions placed on parameters in the GARCH(1,1) model:

1. To ensure positive volatility forecasts:
$$\omega, \alpha, \beta > 0.$$

2. To ensure covariance stationarity:
$$\alpha + \beta < 1.$$

Therefore, unconditional variance is infinite when $\alpha + \beta = 1$ and undefined when $\alpha + \beta > 1$. Similar to the ARCH model, we should not impose the constraint when all we need is a forecast of conditional volatility, but it is necessary to predict unconditional volatility.

2.3.3 The "memory" of a GARCH model

The unconditional volatility of the GARCH model was given by (2.9), but oftentimes a very small or very large shock to the return process can cause conditional volatility to differ greatly from that number. It is often of interest to identify how long it takes for the impact of the shock to subside.

The "memory" of a GARCH model measures how long a shock to the process takes to subside. A measure of memory can be developed by looking at multistep-ahead conditional variance, where $\sigma^2_{t+2,t}$ is the volatility on day $t+2$ given information on day t. Another approach is to look at the *half-life* of a shock (i.e., the number of periods, n^*, it takes for conditional variance to revert back halfway towards unconditional variance).

Multiperiod volatility

First, it is helpful to rewrite the GARCH(1,1) model as a function of unconditional volatility σ rather than of the constant ω. Recall (2.9) and rewrite the GARCH(1,1) model as:

$$\begin{aligned}\sigma^2_{t+1} = \mathrm{E}_t(Y^2_{t+1}) &= \omega + \alpha Y^2_t + \beta \sigma^2_t \\ &= \omega + (\alpha + \beta)\sigma^2 + \alpha(Y^2_t - \sigma^2) + \beta(\sigma^2_t - \sigma^2) \\ &= \sigma^2 + \alpha(Y^2_t - \sigma^2) + \beta(\sigma^2_t - \sigma^2),\end{aligned}$$

where $\mathrm{E}_t(\sigma^2_{t+1})$ indicates volatility on day $t+1$ given information on day t. This shows that the GARCH(1,1) forecast can be thought of as a weighted average of unconditional variance, the deviation of last period's forecast from unconditional variance and the deviation of last period's squared returns from unconditional variance. We can now derive two-step-ahead volatility:

$$\begin{aligned}\sigma^2_{t+2,t} &\equiv \mathrm{E}_t(Y^2_{t+2}) \\ &= \mathrm{E}_t\big(\mathrm{E}_{t+1}(Y^2_{t+2})\big) \\ &= \mathrm{E}_t\big(\sigma^2 + \alpha(Y^2_{t+1} - \sigma^2) + \beta(\sigma^2_{t+1} - \sigma^2)\big) \\ &= \sigma^2 + \alpha\big(\mathrm{E}_t(Y^2_{t+1}) - \sigma^2\big) + \beta(\sigma^2_{t+1} - \sigma^2) \\ &= \sigma^2 + (\alpha + \beta)(\sigma^2_{t+1} - \sigma^2).\end{aligned}$$

Following similar arguments, the general formula for n periods is given as:

$$\sigma_{t+n,t}^2 = \sigma^2 + (\alpha + \beta)^{n-1}\left(\sigma_{t+1}^2 - \sigma^2\right), \quad n \geq 1. \tag{2.10}$$

The above expression shows that the forecast of one-period volatility n periods from now is a weighted average of unconditional variance and the deviation of the one-step forecast from unconditional variance. If $\alpha + \beta < 1$, the second term above goes to zero as $n \to \infty$, which implies that the longer the forecast horizon, the closer the forecast will get to unconditional variance. The size of $(\alpha + \beta)$ determines how quickly the predictability of the process subsides: if $(\alpha + \beta)$ is close to zero, predictability will die out very quickly. If $(\alpha + \beta)$ is close to one, predictability will die out slowly.

Half-life

An alternative way to think about volatility predictability is by considering the "half-life" of the deviation of conditional variance from unconditional variance. The half-life is the number of periods, n^*, it takes for conditional variance to revert back halfway towards unconditional variance:

$$\sigma_{t+n^*,t}^2 - \sigma^2 = \tfrac{1}{2}\left(\sigma_{t+1,t}^2 - \sigma^2\right). \tag{2.11}$$

For the GARCH(1,1) process:

$$(\alpha + \beta)^{n^*-1}\left(\sigma_{t+1}^2 - \sigma^2\right) = \tfrac{1}{2}\left(\sigma_{t+1}^2 - \sigma^2\right)$$

$$n^* = 1 + \frac{\log\left(\tfrac{1}{2}\right)}{\log(\alpha + \beta)}.$$

As $(\alpha + \beta) \to 1$, the process approaches a noncovariance-stationary process and the half-life diverges to infinity. With daily asset returns, it is common to see values of $(\alpha + \beta)$ near one; this prompted the development of "long memory" volatility models.

2.3.4 Normal GARCH

The most common conditional distribution in the GARCH model is the normal; that is, the shocks Z_t follow the distribution

$$Z_t \sim \mathcal{N}(0, 1).$$

We denote this model the normal GARCH.

2.3.5 Student-*t* GARCH

It is often the case that observed returns have fatter tails than would be implied by the normal GARCH model. This suggests that the normal GARCH model could be improved by replacing the conditional normal distribution with a conditionally fat distribution, where the parameters determining fatness are to be estimated along with other model parameters.

Several distributional proposals have been made; the most common was the Student-*t* which resulted in the Student-*t* GARCH model or simply the *t*-GARCH:

$$Z_t \sim t_{(\nu)}. \tag{2.12}$$

The degrees of freedom, ν, of the Student-t distribution are here estimated as an extra parameter. In practice, the degrees of freedom are often estimated to be around 6 to 10. This value is obviously very different from the normal distribution, which implies that $\nu = \infty$. However, the confidence bounds around ν are often quite wide.

The left and right tails of return distributions are different in many cases (i.e., the return distribution is asymmetric or skewed). In this case it may be useful to allow the conditional distribution to be skewed, such as the so–called skewed Student-t which resulted in the skew t-GARCH model.

2.3.6 (G)ARCH in mean

A central idea in finance is that the return on a risky security should be positively related to its risk. This was the motivation that led Engle et al. (1987) to develop the "ARCH in mean" or "ARCH-M" model which posits that the conditional mean of a return is dependent on some function of its conditional variance or standard deviation:

$$Y_t = \mu_t + \sigma_t Z_t$$

where μ_t is often a constant or follows an AR process. For example, a common specification is:

$$\mu_t = \delta \sigma_t^2$$

where δ is the parameter describing the impact volatility has on the mean. Many applications of the ARCH-M model find that the volatility term in the mean equation is not significant, perhaps due to the imprecision with which the ARCH model estimates conditional variance.

The conditional mean is of key importance to many applications such as portfolio allocation and trading. For most risk applications it is not all that important and, since estimating the mean can complicate the estimation process considerably, it is usually better ignored. In all applications in this chapter we assume the mean to be zero, but it is straightforward to incorporate ARCH-M effects in the estimation procedures discussed.

2.4 MAXIMUM LIKELIHOOD ESTIMATION OF VOLATILITY MODELS

The nonlinear nature of the volatility models discussed so far rules out estimation by standard linear regression methods such as ordinary least squares.

Bollerslev and Wooldridge (1992) demonstrate that using the normal distribution in maximum likelihood estimation will give consistent parameter estimates if the sole aim is estimation of conditional variance, even if the true density is nonnormal. This estimator is known as the quasi-maximum likelihood (QML) estimator. However, QML is not efficient unless the true density actually is normal.

A broad outline of maximum likelihood (ML) can be found in Appendix D, but we consider here some of the issues of ML estimation as they pertain to GARCH model estimation.

We can avoid having to make the distributional assumptions required by ML by estimating the model using the generalized method of moments, but this is not a common approach for volatility models.

2.4.1 The ARCH(1) likelihood function

Suppose the errors, Z_t, in an ARCH(1) model are standard normally distributed:

$$Y_t = \sigma_t Z_t$$
$$\sigma_t^2 = \omega + \alpha Y_{t-1}^2$$
$$Z_t \sim \mathcal{N}(0,1).$$

The presence of lagged returns means that the density function for $t = 1$ is unknown since we do not know y_0. The $t = 2$ density is given by:

$$f(y_2) = \frac{1}{\sqrt{2\pi(\omega + \alpha y_1^2)}} \exp\left(-\frac{1}{2}\frac{y_2^2}{\omega + \alpha y_1^2}\right).$$

Higher period densities are derived in a similar way. The joint density of y is:

$$\prod_{t=2}^{T} f(y_t) = \prod_{t=2}^{T} \frac{1}{\sqrt{2\pi(\omega + \alpha y_{t-1}^2)}} \exp\left(-\frac{1}{2}\frac{y_t^2}{\omega + \alpha y_{t-1}^2}\right).$$

The log-likelihood follows:

$$\log \mathcal{L} = \underbrace{-\frac{T-1}{2}\log(2\pi)}_{\text{Constant}} - \frac{1}{2}\sum_{t=2}^{T}\left(\log(\omega + \alpha y_{t-1}^2) + \frac{y_t^2}{\omega + \alpha y_{t-1}^2}\right).$$

We can derive the likelihood function for other distributions such as the Student-t in an analogous fashion. Aside from the Student-t distribution, common choices in finance for the density include the generalized error distribution and the skewed Student-t.

2.4.2 The GARCH(1,1) likelihood function

The normal GARCH(1,1) model is

$$\sigma_t^2 = \omega + \alpha Y_{t-1}^2 + \beta \sigma_{t-1}^2.$$

The same issue as before arises with the presence of lagged returns; therefore, the density function starts at $t = 2$. However, the presence of the extra lagged volatility term presents more difficulties, since there is no estimate of σ_1. There are two ways to obtain it.

We could estimate σ_1 as an additional parameter along with ω, α and β. This may be the theoretically preferred approach, but the parameter σ_1 is not likely to be estimated with much precision.

Another way is to set σ_1 to an arbitrary value, usually the sample variance of $\{y_t\}$. This is of course not theoretically correct and, depending on the application, may not be recommended, especially if the sample size is small, but for large sample sizes adverse impacts should not be significant in most cases.

Following the latter approach and assuming the normal distribution, the $t=2$ density is given by:

$$f(y_2) = \frac{1}{\sqrt{2\pi(\omega + \alpha y_1^2 + \beta \hat{\sigma}_1^2)}} \exp\left(-\frac{1}{2}\frac{y_2^2}{\omega + \alpha y_1^2 + \beta \hat{\sigma}_1^2}\right).$$

The log-likelihood function is then:

$$\log \mathcal{L} = \underbrace{-\frac{T-1}{2}\log(2\pi)}_{\text{Constant}} - \frac{1}{2}\sum_{t=2}^{T}\left(\log(\omega + \alpha y_{t-1}^2 + \beta \hat{\sigma}_{t-1}^2) + \frac{y_t^2}{\omega + \alpha y_{t-1}^2 + \beta \hat{\sigma}_{t-1}^2}\right).$$

2.4.3 On the importance of σ_1

The value that σ_1 is set to can in some cases make a large difference. For example, global volatility started picking up with the advent of the 2007 crisis, peaking in 2008. In such cases where there is a clear structural break in volatility, the GARCH model will experience difficulties, since it is based on the assumption of average volatility being constant. Unfortunately, it is likely to be difficult to modify the GARCH model to take this into account.

The impact of the choice of σ_1 is easily demonstrated by a sample from the S&P 500 spanning the second part of the 2000s. If we use a procedure that sets σ_1 to unconditional volatility, such as those demonstrated in Section 2.6, we will get very different values than from procedures using EWMA to set initial volatility.[3]

2.4.4 Issues in estimation

Volatility models, whether univariate or multivariate, are estimated by maximum likelihood (ML) where parameter estimates are obtained by numerically maximizing the likelihood function with an algorithm called an *optimizer*. This can lead to numerical problems that adversely affect maximization.

Some likelihood functions have multiple local minima—as in Figure D.1(b)—or long flat areas. In such cases, finding the maximum is analogous to finding Mount Everest in the Himalayas when the only way would be to climb up a number of peaksin the hope of finding the highest. Eventually, we would find Mount Everest, but it could take considerable time.

We may also encounter problems with numerical instability. While it may be possible to evaluate the likelihood function at the peak, we are searching for a solution and need to evaluate the likelihood for a large number of other combinations of parameters first. Some of these parameters may cause problems such as dividing two zeros by each other, resulting in an undefined result called a NaN or *not a number*.

While such problems might not exist at the peak of the likelihood function, they can for other parameter sets. Even more disconcertingly, if we run the optimization again

---
[3] For example, tarch from the *Oxford MFE Toolbox* (see footnote 5 on p. 53).

with different starting values we might not encounter these problem parameters and all will be fine—or we might even find new problems elsewhere in the parameter space.

These problems are rare for smaller models such as GARCH(1,1), but become increasingly likely as models become richer.[4] One way to guard against this is to try multiple starting values for the optimization.

Other problems may arise when we impose a binding covariance stationarity constraint such as $\alpha + \beta < 1$ in a GARCH(1,1) model; this can lead to multiple parameter combinations satisfying the constraint, often with serious consequences. Not only will the parameter solution and hence the volatility forecast be non-unique, but as we add new observations to the sample and perhaps drop old ones (as in backtesting) the parameter estimates will bounce around the solutions, causing volatility forecasts to jump around over time.

Often, one may not even be aware there is a problem, especially if a local minimum is found, no solution is found or the optimizer provides obscure error messages.

2.5 DIAGNOSING VOLATILITY MODELS

Is there a way of choosing the "best" volatility model? In practice, model choice should depend on the intended use of the model. For example, if a model is to be used for out-of-sample volatility forecasting, it should be chosen by considering the out-of-sample forecast performance of real life applications.

If this is not possible, several statistical methods are available for comparing models. One could look at the significance of model parameters, test for the significance of a group of parameters in nested models or evaluate the statistical properties of the residuals. These methods can also be used to assess the quality of estimation and, more importantly, the quality of forecasts.

2.5.1 Likelihood ratio tests and parameter significance

If we estimate a model and obtain parameter estimates along with their standard errors, we can simply use standard methods such as the *t*-test to see whether the parameters are statistically significantly different from zero or not. When one model *nests* inside another model, tests such as the likelihood ratio test can be used.

If models are nested, then the nested model is strictly a subset of the other. For example, the GARCH(1,1) nests the ARCH(1)—but not the ARCH(2) model.

Consider two models, M_R and M_U, where M_U is the unrestricted or larger model and M_R is the restricted or smaller model. Suppose the unrestricted model M_U has U parameters and the restricted model has R parameters. The restricted log-likelihood minus the unrestricted log-likelihood, doubled, follows the chi-squared distribution, with the degrees of freedom equaling the number of restrictions. If M_U is the ARCH(4) model and M_R is the ARCH(1) model, the degrees of freedom of the chi-squared statistic

---
[4] Examples include the APARCH models discussed in Section 2.7 and even the Student-*t* GARCH models. For multivariate GARCH models, as the number of assets increases, we are more likely than not to experience such problems.

Table 2.2. Likelihood ratio tests

Null	Alternative	Test
ARCH(1)	ARCH(4)	$H_0: \alpha_2 = \alpha_3 = \alpha_4 = 0$
GARCH(1,1)	ARCH(1)	$H_0: \beta = 0$
GARCH(2,2)	GARCH(1,1)	$H_0: \beta_2 = \alpha_2 = 0$
GARCH	EWMA	$H_0: \beta + \alpha = 1, \omega = 0$

equal 3. We can then form a likelihood ratio (LR) test:

$$\text{LR} = 2(\mathcal{L}_U - \mathcal{L}_R) \sim \chi^2_{(\text{number of restrictions})}.$$

This test can be applied to more complicated models provided they are nested. Some examples of nested models and parameter restrictions are shown in Table 2.2.

In out-of-sample forecast comparisons, it is often the case that the more parsimonious models perform better, even if a more flexible model is significantly better in sample. If the more flexible model is not significantly better in sample, it is very unlikely to do better out of sample.

2.5.2 Analysis of model residuals

A different approach is to analyze model residuals. Consider the normal ARCH(1) model. If the model is correct, the residuals are IID normal. This suggests that if estimated parameters and forecast volatility $\left(\hat{\alpha}, \hat{\beta}, \hat{\sigma}_t^2\right)$ are obtained, the estimated or fitted residuals

$$\hat{z}_t = \frac{y_t}{\hat{\sigma}_t}$$

can be tested for normality and clustering, providing an assessment of how well the model captured stylized facts in the data.

2.5.3 Statistical goodness-of-fit measures

Competing models can be ranked by goodness-of-fit measures, such as mean squared error (MSE). Normally, in order to judge the accuracy of a model, one requires knowledge of the realized value of the variable of interest—in our case, conditional variance. But the conditional variance is not observable even ex post, and hence *volatility proxies* are required. A volatility proxy is some variable that is useful for estimating the value of the true volatility. The simplest volatility proxy is the squared return, which can be justified as a volatility proxy because it is a conditionally unbiased estimator of true conditional variance and is *on average* correct.

If we denote a volatility proxy by s_t, then two possible goodness-of-fit measures for a volatility forecast are:

$$\text{Squared error:} \quad \sum_{t=1}^{T}(\hat{s}_t^2 - \hat{\sigma}_t^2)^2$$

$$\text{QLIKE:} \quad \sum_{t=1}^{T}\left(\log \hat{\sigma}_t^2 + \frac{\hat{s}_t^2}{\hat{\sigma}_t^2}\right).$$

Hansen and Lunde (2005) used these two goodness-of-fit measures to compare numerous out-of-sample ARCH-type models; they concluded that the APARCH(2,2) model performed the best.

2.6 APPLICATION OF ARCH AND GARCH

We estimate the ARCH and GARCH models discussed above by taking a sample of daily observations from the S&P 500 index between 2005 and 2009; we evaluate the estimates using both likelihood ratio tests and residual analysis.

The models compared are the ARCH(1), the ARCH(4), and the GARCH(4,1), as well as three GARCH(1,1) models with either a normal, a Student-*t* or a skew Student-*t* conditional distribution.

The computer code for the calculations is shown in Listings 2.1 and 2.2.

2.6.1 Estimation results

Estimation results are presented in Table 2.3. Standard errors, or *t*-tests, are not shown in the interest of space; instead, we use likelihood ratio (LR) tests to compare the

Table 2.3. ARCH and GARCH models estimated using daily S&P 500 returns from January 1, 2005 to December 31, 2009

	ARCH(1)	ARCH(4)	GARCH(4,1)	GARCH(1,1)		
Conditional distribution	Normal	Normal	Normal	Normal	Student-t	Skew Student-t
Log-likelihood	−2,208.4	−1,912.7	−1,825.9	−1,836.9	−1,812.6	−1,804.4
ω	1.366	0.332	0.024	0.012	0.007	0.008
α_1	0.555	0.058	0.000	0.081	0.084	0.087
α_2		0.292	0.017			
α_3		0.286	0.057			
α_4		0.297	0.067			
β_1			0.842	0.910	0.915	0.912
ν					6.813	6.706
Skew						0.871

Data source: Yahoo Finance.

Table 2.4. Likelihood ratio tests for the results in Table 2.3

Unrestricted model	Restricted model	LR statistic	Restrictions	p-value
ARCH(4)	ARCH(1)	591.4	3	0.000
GARCH(4,1)	ARCH(4)	173.5	1	0.000
GARCH(4,1)	GARCH(1,1)	21.9	3	0.000
t-GARCH(1,1)	GARCH(1,1)	48.5	1	0.000
Skew-t-GARCH(1,1)	t-GARCH(1,1)	16.4	1	0.000

models. Such a procedure is equivalent to comparing the significance of one parameter with a t-test, but has the advantage of allowing testing of the significance of multiple parameters.

The ARCH models are comfortably stationary, while the normal GARCH(1,1) has $\alpha + \beta = 0.991 < 1$, and the Student-$t$ variants have $\alpha + \beta = 0.999$. This suggests that the estimation procedure imposed a covariance stationarity restriction on the parameters, at least for the nonnormal variants.

For the GARCH(1,1) models, the three common coefficients are quite similar. The degree-of-freedom parameters are 6.8 and 6.7, and the skew parameter is 0.9.

2.6.2 Likelihood ratio tests

Results from likelihood ratio tests of the estimated models are shown in Table 2.4. The ARCH(4) model is significantly better than ARCH(1), which is not surprising since we would expect volatility dependence to last many days. By adding lagged volatility to get the GARCH(4,1) model, the fit continues to improve, and when GARCH(4,1) is compared with GARCH(1,1), GARCH(4,1) is significantly better.

Using the Student-t as a conditional distribution significantly improves on the normal version, while the skew Student-t is better than the symmetric Student-t.

Further testing would enable us to better identify the best model; for example, would a skew Student-t GARCH(1,1) be equivalent to a skew Student-t GARCH(4,1) or even a skew Student-t GARCH(2,1)? Furthermore, we did not explore whether more lags of volatility would improve the model; for example, whether a GARCH(1,2) is better than a GARCH(1,1).

2.6.3 Residual analysis

Another way of comparing the models is by analyzing the residuals

$$\hat{z}_t = \frac{y_t}{\hat{\sigma}_t}$$

of the models using methods such as the Jarque–Bera test for normality and the Ljung–Box test for autocorrelations.

We show the residual analysis for the four Gaussian models in Table 2.5. The ARCH(1) and ARCH(4) models fail to capture volatility clusters and fail the normality

Table 2.5. Analysis of residuals for results in Table 2.3—p-values

Model	Jarque–Bera test	Ljung–Box test (20 squared lags)
ARCH(1)	0.00	0.00
ARCH(4)	0.00	0.00
GARCH(4,1)	0.00	0.99
GARCH(1,1)	0.00	0.53

tests for the residuals. We do not find significant autocorrelations in the residuals of the GARCH models, but they still failed the test for normality of the residuals. This indicates that for applications where the tails of the distribution are of importance, such as value-at-risk, better models are to be preferred, perhaps the Student-t GARCH model.

2.6.4 Graphical analysis

Figure 2.2 shows graphical analysis of results for the normal GARCH(1,1) model. Panels (a) and (b) show index values and returns, panel (c) shows conditional volatility and panel (d) the returns with the doubled positive and negative volatility superimposed.

Superficial graphical inspection indicates that we seem to have done a good job capturing the salient features of the data. This is confirmed by panel (e) which shows the ACF of squared residuals, demonstrating that there is little evidence of volatility clusters in the residuals, which indicates that the model has captured the clustering phenomenon well. However, panel (f) shows that the residuals are still fat tailed in the QQ plot. This is consistent with the residual analysis in Table 2.4.

The QQ plot further seems to indicate that deviation from conditional normality is stronger on the downside, which is consistent with the Student-t skew parameter being significant. These results suggest that tail thickness is asymmetric, with the lower tail thicker than the upper tail. This is also consistent with results from Section 1.5.

2.6.5 Implementation

It is straightforward to estimate GARCH models in R and Matlab; Listing 2.1 shows the former and Listing 2.2 the latter. We start by loading the data into vector y. In both cases the mean is subtracted from the returns, which are also multiplied by 100.

The R function for GARCH estimation is `garchFit` from the `fGarch` library, while Matlab uses the `garchfit` function from the GARCH toolbox. Other functions exist for both languages. These functions have a lot of options, and it is advisable to consult the manual for the functions before using them.

Financial Risk Forecasting 49

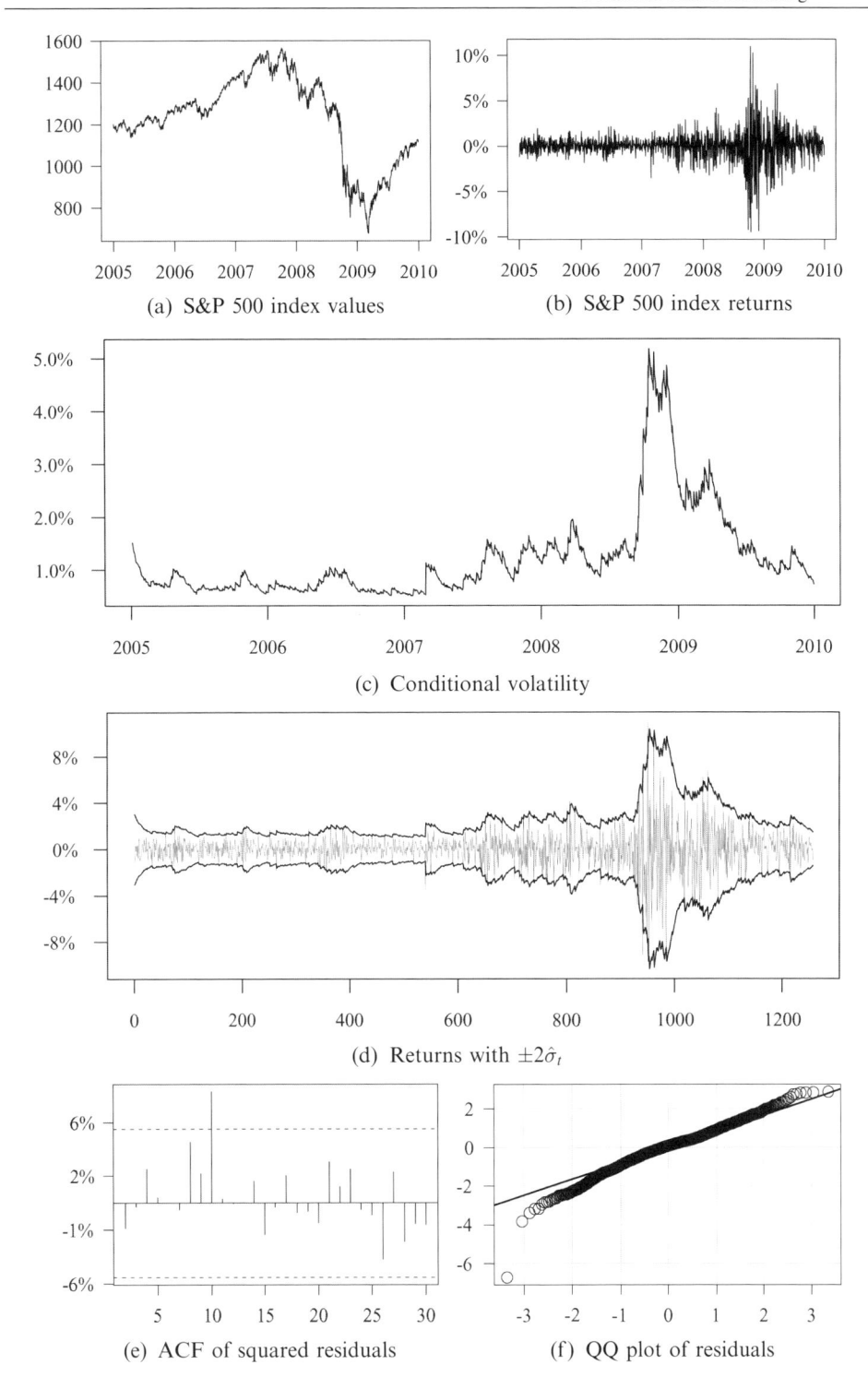

(a) S&P 500 index values

(b) S&P 500 index returns

(c) Conditional volatility

(d) Returns with $\pm 2\hat{\sigma}_t$

(e) ACF of squared residuals

(f) QQ plot of residuals

Figure 2.2. Analysis of the GARCH(1,1) results in Table 2.3.

Listing 2.1. ARCH and GARCH estimation in R

```
p = get.hist.quote(instrument = "^gspc", start = "2005-01-01",
    end="2009-12-31",quote="AdjClose",quiet=T)
                        # download the prices
y=diff(log(p))*100      # get returns and multiply them by 100 (so
                          they are expressed in returns)
y=y-mean(y)             # de-mean (set mean to zero)

library(fGarch)
garchFit(~ garch(1,0), data = y,include.mean=FALSE)
garchFit(~ garch(4,0), data = y,include.mean=FALSE)
garchFit(~ garch(4,1), data = y,include.mean=FALSE)
garchFit(~ garch(1,1), data = y,include.mean=FALSE)
garchFit(~ garch(1,1), data = y,include.mean=FALSE,
    cond.dist="std",trace=F)
res=garchFit(~ garch(1,1), data =
y,include.mean=FALSE,cond.dist="sstd",trace=F)
                        # saves output to res
plot(res)               # shows various graphical analysis
```

Listing 2.2. ARCH and GARCH estimation in Matlab

```
stocks = hist_stock_data('01012005','31122009','^gspc');
p=stocks.AdjClose(end:-1:1);
y=diff(log(p))*100;     % get returns and multiply them by 100 (so
                          they are expressed in returns)
y=y-mean(y)             % de-mean (set mean to zero)

                        % GARCH toolbox
                        % ARCH(1)
spec = garchset('P', 0, 'Q', 1,'C',NaN)
garchfit(spec,y)        % estimate the model, show estimation
                          progress and plots
                        % ARCH(4)
spec = garchset('P', 0, 'Q', 4,'C',NaN)
garchfit(spec,y)
                        % GARCH(4,1).
spec = garchset('P', 1, 'Q', 4,'C',NaN,'Display','off');
                        % Surpess plot and progress reports
garchfit(spec,y);
                        % GARCH(1,1)
spec = garchset('P', 1, 'Q', 1,'C',NaN,'Display','off');
[coeff, errors, LLF, innovations, sigmas,
```

```
summary]=garchfit(spec,y);  % Save all output

% t-GARCH(1,1)
spec = garchset('P', 1, 'Q',
1,'C',NaN,'Distribution','T','Display','off');
p=garchfit(spec,y) ;
```

2.7 OTHER GARCH-TYPE MODELS

A large number of extensions to the GARCH model have been proposed, most of which have seen very limited application. There are, however, two types of extensions that are sometimes found in models in practical use: asymmetry in the impact of positive and negative lagged returns (leverage effects) and allowing power in the volatility calculation to be flexible. These effects are combined in the APARCH model.

2.7.1 Leverage effects and asymmetry

It has been empirically noted that stock returns are sometimes negatively correlated with changes in volatility: volatility tends to rise following bad news and fall following good news. This is called the "leverage effect", as it could be explained by firms' use of leverage. The leverage effect is not easily detectable in stock indices and is not expected to be significant in foreign exchange.

Consider the relationship between the stock price and volatility of a corporation that has high debt. As the stock price of the firm falls, its debt-to-equity ratio rises. This will raise equity return volatility if the firm's cash flows are constant.

In this case, one might expect negative returns today to lead to higher volatility tomorrow, and vice versa for positive returns. This behavior cannot be captured by a standard GARCH(1,1) model, since from (2.8) tomorrow's volatility is quadratic in today's return, and the sign of today's return does not matter. We need to introduce asymmetry to capture leverage effects (i.e., the impacts of negative and positive shocks have to be different).

A straightforward way to incorporate leverage effects in the GARCH model is to use the model of Glosten et al. (1993) (GJR-GARCH, also known as threshold-GARCH).

Another widely used GARCH model allowing for leverage effects is the exponential GARCH (EGARCH) model proposed by Nelson (1991). In this model, volatility depends on the sign of lagged residuals. It can be written as:

$$\log(\sigma_{t+1}^2) = \omega + \alpha(Z_t) + \beta \log(\sigma_t^2) + \delta(|Z_t| - \mathrm{E}(|Z_t|))$$

where δ is a parameter to be estimated along with α and β. This equation contains the difference between absolute residuals and the expectation of absolute residuals, which gives rise to leverage effects. Another advantage of EGARCH over standard GARCH is that by modeling $\log \sigma_t$ rather than σ_t, a positive estimate of volatility is ensured. EGARCH is also attractive because it has direct connections with continuous time finance.

2.7.2 Power models

In studying the ACF of absolute returns and returns squared, sometimes absolute returns have stronger autocorrelations than squared returns. Since the main reason for past squared returns being included in the volatility equation is to capture the magnitude of market movements, there is no reason to believe that absolute returns would not serve the same function, or indeed any power of the absolute returns. This is captured by the power GARCH models proposed by Taylor (1986) and Schwert (1989).

2.7.3 APARCH

Ding et al. (1993) combine these two effects in the same model, the so-called asymmetric power GARCH or APARCH model:

$$\sigma_{t+1}^{\delta} = \omega + \sum_{i=1}^{L_1} \alpha_i (|Y_{t-i}| - \zeta_i Y_{t-i})^{\delta} + \sum_{j=1}^{L_2} \beta_j \sigma_{t-j}^{\delta}. \qquad (2.13)$$

The APARCH model is one of the most complicated models in use. It allows for leverage effects when $\zeta \neq 0$ and power effects when $\delta \neq 2$.

2.7.4 Application of APARCH models

Unfortunately, it is not all that straightforward to estimate APARCH models since they often suffer from the problems discussed in Section 2.4.4. In many cases estimation will fail if the data sample is too short or exhibits structural breaks.

This is the case for the sample used in Section 2.6; the structural break in volatility during the 2007–2009 crisis causes problems for estimation of APARCH models using daily S&P 500 returns, and the sample size (1,258 observations) is too short. Consequently, we extended the sample back to 1990 giving a total of 5,042 observations.

If we restrict the asymmetry parameter ζ to a fixed value, perhaps zero, or set the power parameter δ to, say, 2, estimation is feasible with a smaller sample. If we impose both restrictions we just get the GARCH model back. If, however, we use a nonnormal conditional distribution, like the Student-t, we need to estimate more parameters, further complicating estimation.

We estimate four versions of the APARCH model: a model with one lag of past returns and volatility as well as a conditionally normal distribution, a restricted version of that with $\delta = 2$ thus ruling out power effects, a model with a Student-t conditional distribution, and finally a model with two lags.

Table 2.6 shows estimation results and Table 2.7 likelihood ratio test results. The Student-t version of APARCH(1,1) is preferred over other one-lag variants, while the conditionally normal APARCH(2,2) significantly improves upon APARCH(1,1) at the 5% but not the 1% level. It would be of interest to estimate and compare other versions of the model, such as one where $\zeta = 0$ and another with a skew Student-t conditional distribution for both the one-lag and two-lag variants.

Table 2.6. APARCH estimation with daily S&P 500 returns from January 1, 1990 to December 31, 2009

	GARCH(1,1)	APARCH(1,1)			APARCH(2,2)
Conditional distribution	Normal	Normal	$\delta = 2$ normal	Student-t	Normal
Log-likelihood	−6,832.8	−6,750.6	−6,762.1	−6,674.1	−6,746.1
ω	0.007	0.014	0.011	0.010	0.026
α_1	0.063	0.056	0.036	0.051	0.039
β_1	0.931	0.937	0.932	0.941	0.164
ζ_1		0.856	0.762	0.912	1.000
δ		1.231		1.323	1.210
ν				8.328	
α_2					0.070
ζ_2					0.634
β_2					0.717

Table 2.7. Likelihood ratio tests for results in Table 2.6

Unrestricted model	Restricted model	LR statistic	Restrictions	p-value
APARCH(1,1)	GARCH(1,1)	164.4	2	0.000
APARCH(1,1)	APARCH(1,1), $\delta = 2$	22.9	1	0.000
t-APARCH(1,1)	APARCH(1,1)	153.1	1	0.000
APARCH(2,2)	APARCH(1,1)	9.1	3	0.028

2.7.5 Estimation of APARCH

It is straightforward to estimate APARCH models in R and Matlab. Start by taking a look at Listings 2.1 and 2.2. The R `garchFit` function from Listing 2.1 has an option for APARCH. In Matlab we can use the `garchfit` function from the GARCH toolbox, but that only supports the GJR variant. The `multigarch` function from the UCSD GARCH toolbox[5] can be used for APARCH estimation.

Listing 2.3. Advanced ARCH and GARCH estimation in R

```
# normal APARCH(1,1)
garchFit(~ aparch(1,1),data=y,include.mean=FALSE,trace=F)
# fix delta at 2 (or to any value)
```

---

[5] See http://www.kevinsheppard.com. We could have used the aparch() function from version 4.0 of the *Oxford MFE Toolbox* available from the same website.

```
garchFit(~ aparch(1,1),data=y,include.mean=FALSE,trace=F,
   include.delta=F,delta=2)
# Student-t conditional distribution
garchFit(~ aparch(1,1),data=y,include.mean=FALSE,cond.dist="std",
   trace=F)
# normal APARCH(2,2)
garchFit(~ aparch(2,2),data=y,include.mean=FALSE,trace=F)
```

Listing 2.4. Advanced ARCH and GARCH estimation in Matlab

```
% GJR GARCH(1,1)
spec = garchset('P',1,'Q',1,'C',NaN,'VarianceModel','GJR')
garchfit(spec,y)
```

2.8 ALTERNATIVE VOLATILITY MODELS

While the volatility models discussed above are a common way to produce volatility forecasts, several alternatives have been proposed: primarily, implied volatility, realized volatility and stochastic volatility. Of these the most frequently used is implied volatility, which is the primary volatility measure in many applications and is used for firmwide value-at-risk calculations in many financial institutions.

2.8.1 Implied volatility

Since the Black–Scholes (BS) formula for pricing European options is a function of the volatility of the underlying asset, one can calculate *implied volatility* by taking the actual transaction prices of options traded on an exchange and using the BS equation to back out the volatility that *implied* the option price.

One of the attractions of implied volatilities is that they are based on current market prices rather than historical data, and thus are sometimes termed "forward-looking" estimators of volatility. The biggest drawback is that they hinge critically on the accuracy of the BS model, which relies on an assumption of constant conditional volatility and normal innovations, something obviously not consistent with using implied volatilities for forecasting time-varying volatility. This is associated with the observed volatility "smile" or "smirk" in options markets.

If we plot implied volatilities from a range of options on the same underlying asset with the same expiry date, differing only by their strike prices, we would find that deep out-of-the-money options have implied volatilities that are much higher than at-the-money options.[6] If the BS model were correct, the plot should be a straight horizontal line. Using implied volatilities for risk analysis also suffers from lack of reliable data, since some options, especially long-dated ones, are very illiquid and their prices can be hard to obtain.

---

[6] This is usually taken as being further evidence that the true distribution of asset returns has fatter tails than the normal.

The VIX volatility index for the S&P 500 index is obtained from implied volatility models.

2.8.2 Realized volatility

Realized volatility measures what actually happened in the past and is based on taking intraday data, sampled at regular intervals (e.g., every 10 minutes), and using the data to obtain the covariance matrix. The main advantage is that it is purely data driven and there is no reliance on parametric models. The downside is that intraday data need to be available; such data are often difficult to obtain, hard to use, not very clean and frequently very expensive.

In addition, it is necessary to deal with diurnal patterns in volume and volatility when using realized volatility (i.e., address systematic changes in observed trading volume and volatility throughout the day). Moreover, the particular trading platform in use is likely to impose its own patterns on the data. All these issues complicate the implementation of realized volatility models.

2.8.3 Stochastic volatility

In the GARCH class of models, conditional volatility σ_t is known if the parameters $[\omega, \alpha, \beta]$ are specified. In the stochastic volatility[7] (SV) model the volatility process is a function of an exogenous shock as well as past volatilities, so the process σ_t is itself random, with an innovation term that is not known at time t.

A common way to express the SV model is:

$$Y_t = Z_t \sigma_t$$

$$Z_t \sim \mathcal{N}(0, 1)$$

$$\sigma_t^2 = \exp(\delta_0 + \delta_1 \log \sigma_{t-1}^2 + \delta_2 \eta_t)$$

where the distribution of shocks is:

$$\begin{pmatrix} Z_t \\ \eta_t \end{pmatrix} \sim \mathcal{N}\left(\mathbf{0}, \begin{pmatrix} 1 & \varsigma \\ \varsigma & 1 \end{pmatrix}\right).$$

The SV model has *two* innovation terms: Z_t for the return itself and η_t for the conditional variance of the return. The parameter on the latent shock, δ_2, provides a testable hypothesis of the validity of the stochastic component of the SV model, and ς provides correlation between returns and volatility, giving rise to the leverage effect.

The presence of the additional innovation term in SV models makes both estimation and forecasting much more difficult than for GARCH models. This is because the volatility process follows a separate distribution and cannot, therefore, be estimated by past observations of returns.

Stochastic volatility models have several advantages over GARCH-type models. They are more closely integrated with financial theory and can be written quite naturally in a continuous time form, which is useful for option-pricing purposes. Volatility flow can be interpreted as an exogenous information flow to the markets, and SV models allow for

---

[7] For more on the SV model, see, for example, Clark (1973), Tauchen and Pitts (1983), Taylor (1986), and Danielsson (1994).

Table 2.8. SV estimation results. Log-likelihood $= -1,814.8$

Parameter	Estimate	Standard error
δ_0	0.000	0.004
δ_1	0.994	0.000
δ_2	0.130	0.016

easy integration of volume into the model. However, SV models are not as common for forecasting as GARCH models, and there is little evidence that they produce superior volatility forecasts than simple GARCH models.

We estimated the SV model—where the leverage term (ζ) was set at zero—using the simulated maximum likelihood method proposed by Daníelsson (1994) from S&P 500 data used in the application in Section 2.6. The results are reported in Table 2.8, where $\delta_0, \delta_1, \delta_2$ are the mean, AR1 parameter and standard deviation of the SV model, respectively. The results from the GARCH(1,1) model in Table 2.3 are similar—here, $\omega = 0.024$, $\alpha = 0.00$ and $\beta = 0.91$ with a log-likelihood of $-1,836.9$. The SV log-likelihood is higher than the GARCH(1,1) log-likelihood, but since the two models are not nested it does not mean that the SV model is significantly better.

2.9 SUMMARY

This chapter has focused on univariate volatility forecasting. There are a large number of competing methods available for volatility forecasting. We have identified the main categories of volatility models and put a special focus on models that are relevant for practical risk forecasting.

The univariate models the reader is most likely to encounter in practical applications are EWMA, GARCH(1,1) and implied volatility models.

Some of the other models may be used in more specialized cases. For example, because the APARCH model allows for more fine-grained modeling of volatility, it may be used where more accuracy and sensitivity to particular volatility characteristics is important, such as in portfolio analysis. Similarly, the realized volatility models may be used in applications involving intraday data if both relevant data feeds and modeling expertise are available. The reader is most likely to encounter stochastic volatility models in applications involving derivative pricing.

The emphasis in this chapter has been on univariate models. The next chapter focuses on multivariate volatility models, while Chapter 5 focuses on implementing risk forecast models and Chapter 8 on model evaluation. Both Chapters 5 and 8 address the practical application of models discussed in this chapter.

3
Multivariate volatility models

The models in Chapter 2 addressed the volatility of a single asset. However, most applications deal with portfolios where it is necessary to forecast the entire covariance matrix of asset returns. The covariance matrix is important for applications such as asset allocation, risk management, contagion, systemic risk and portfolio selection. In risk management, multivariate volatility is an input into the value-at-risk calculation of a portfolio of assets.

When forecasting a covariance matrix, we need to forecast both covariances and variances, and at the same time take clustering into account. Furthermore, the returns of one asset can be expected to affect the future volatilities of other assets in the portfolio as well as correlations. This means that multivariate volatility models are generally much more complicated than their univariate counterparts. For a recent survey of volatility models see Francq and Zakoian (2010).

Because of the complications that arise in the implementation of multivariate volatility models, most models preferred in theory have serious problems in practical implementation. The emphasis in this chapter is on the more practical models, with the more theoretically elegant models relegated to the end of the chapter.

The most important notation used in this chapter is:

Σ_t	Conditional covariance matrix
$Y_{t,k}$	Return on asset k at time t
$y_{t,k}$	Sample return on asset k at time t
$y_t = \{y_{t,k}\}$	Vector of sample returns on all assets at time t
$y = \{y_t\}$	Matrix of sample returns on all assets and dates
A and B	Matrices of parameters
R	Correlation matrix

3.1 MULTIVARIATE VOLATILITY FORECASTING

Consider the univariate volatility model:

$$Y_t = \sigma_t Z_t$$

where Y_t are returns; σ_t is conditional volatility; and Z_t are random shocks. If there are $K > 1$ assets under consideration, it is necessary to indicate which asset and parameters are being referred to, so the notation becomes more cluttered:

$$Y_{t,k} = \sigma_{t,k} Z_{t,k}$$

where the first subscript indicates the date; and the second subscript the asset.

The convention in the literature on multivariate volatility models is to refer to multivariate returns (and covariance matrices) by asset followed by time (i.e., $Y_{k,t}$), and not time followed by asset as in $Y_{t,k}$. This means the matrix of returns must be of dimensions $K \times T$ and not $T \times K$. However, the latter would seem more natural where returns on each asset separately compose the columns, while the rows are all returns on a given day. Here we set $Y_{t,k} = Y_{\text{time,asset}}$.

The conditional covariance matrix of returns is denoted by Σ_t and the conditional covariance between two assets i and j is indicated by:

$$\text{Cov}(Y_{t,i}, Y_{t,j}) \equiv \sigma_{t,ij}.$$

The number of volatility terms (own volatility and covariances) in the covariance matrix increase more rapidly than the number of assets. There are three unique terms in the two-asset case (two volatilities and one covariance), six unique terms in the three-asset case (three volatilities and three covariances), ten unique terms in the four-asset case (four volatilities and six covariances), etc.

In the three-asset case, the conditional covariance matrix takes the following form (note that $\sigma_{t,ij} = \sigma_{t,ji}$):

$$\Sigma_t = \begin{pmatrix} \sigma_{t,11} & \sigma_{t,12} & \sigma_{t,13} \\ \sigma_{t,12} & \sigma_{t,22} & \sigma_{t,23} \\ \sigma_{t,13} & \sigma_{t,23} & \sigma_{t,33} \end{pmatrix}.$$

The explosion in the number of volatility terms, as the number of assets increases, is known as "the curse of dimensionality". It complicates the estimation of multivariate volatility models and is the main reason much fewer such models exist than univariate volatility models.

A difficult problem that often arises in multivariate volatility models is the lack of *positive semi-definiteness*. For a single-asset volatility we need to ensure that the variance is not negative and, similarly, a covariance matrix should be positive semi-definite.

This ensures that portfolio variance will always be nonnegative regardless of the underlying portfolio. Unfortunately, ensuring positive semi-definiteness can be challenging for many, otherwise good, models.

3.1.1 Application

We demonstrate implementation of some of the models presented in this chapter from two daily stock returns, Microsoft and IBM, from January 1, 2000 to December 31, 2009.

Listings 3.1 and 3.2 show how prices can be downloaded into R and Matlab, respectively, and then transformed into vector y. We subtract the mean from the returns, which are also multiplied by 100.

Listing 3.1. Download stock prices in R

```
library("tseries")           # the two prices are downloaded
                               separately
p1 = get.hist.quote(instrument = "msft",start = "2000-01-01",
    end = "2009-12-31",quote="AdjClose")
p2 = get.hist.quote(instrument = "ibm", start = "2000-01-01",
    end = "2009-12-31",quote="AdjClose")
p = cbind(p1,p2)             # prices combined in one vector
y = diff(log(p))*100         # convert prices to returns
y[,1] = y[,1]-mean(y[,1])    # subtract mean
y[,2] = y[,2]-mean(y[,2])
T = length(y[,1])
```

Listing 3.2. Download stock prices in Matlab

```
stocks = hist_stock_data('01012000','31122009','msft','ibm')
p1 = stocks(1).AdjClose(end:-1:1);   % use the adjusted closing
                                        prices
p2 = stocks(2).AdjClose(end:-1:1);
p = [p1 p2];                          % combine the two prices in one
                                        vector
y = diff(log(p))*100;                 % convert prices to returns
y(:,1)=y(:,1)-mean(y(:,1));           % subtract mean
y(:,2)=y(:,2)-mean(y(:,2));
T = length(y);
```

It is assumed in the listings that follow that the return vector y has already been loaded (i.e., that the code in Listings 3.1 and 3.2 has been run).

3.2 EWMA

Perhaps the easiest multivariate volatility model to implement is EWMA. The univariate form of the model from (2.2) is:

$$\hat{\sigma}_t^2 = \lambda \hat{\sigma}_{t-1}^2 + (1-\lambda)y_{t-1}^2,$$

where the weight λ is assumed to be known—often set at 0.94 for daily returns. The multivariate form of the model is essentially the same:

$$\hat{\Sigma}_t = \lambda \hat{\Sigma}_{t-1} + (1-\lambda)y'_{t-1}y_{t-1} \quad (3.1)$$

with an individual element given by:

$$\hat{\sigma}_{t,ij} = \lambda \hat{\sigma}_{t-1,ij} + (1-\lambda)y_{t-1,i}y_{t-1,j}, \quad i,j = 1,\ldots,K. \quad (3.2)$$

The covariance matrix can be forecast by applying (3.2) separately to each asset and pair of assets in the portfolio. Implementing the EWMA model is thus straightforward, even

Multivariate volatility models

for a large number of assets. Coupled with the fact that the covariance matrix is guaranteed to be positive semi-definite, it is not surprising that EWMA is often the chosen method.

The downside is its restrictiveness, both because of the simple structure and the assumption of a single and usually non-estimated λ. In applications, this often means that covariances seem to move excessively (as suggested by Figure 3.1, see p. 66). It is of course not hard to estimate λ with QML.

It is simple to implement EWMA in R and Matlab. Σ_1 is usually set as the unconditional volatility of the data and some 30 days of data are used to update the volatility forecast before it is used. This is sometimes called *burn time*, and takes into account the error induced into the model by setting the value of Σ_1 to an arbitrary value.

Listing 3.3. EWMA in R

```
EWMA = matrix(nrow=T,ncol=3)     # create a matrix to hold the
                                   covariance matrix for each t
lambda = 0.94
S = cov(y)                        # initial (t=1) covariance matrix
EWMA[1,] = c(S)[c(1,4,2)]         # extract the variances and
                                   covariance
for (i in 2:T){                   # loop though the sample
   S = lambda * S + (1-lambda) * t(y[i]) %*% y[i]
   EWMA[i,] = c(S)[c(1,4,2)]      # convert matrix to vector
}
EWMArho = EWMA[,3]/sqrt(EWMA[,1]*EWMA[,2])
                                  # calculate correlations
```

Listing 3.4. EWMA in Matlab

```
EWMA = nan(T,3);                  % create a matrix to hold the covariance
                                    matrix for each t
lambda = 0.94
S = cov(y)                        % initial (t=1) covariance matrix
EWMA(1,:) = S([1,4,2]);           % extract the variances and covariance
for i = 2:T                       % loop though the sample
   S = lambda * S + (1-lambda) * y(i,:)' * y(i,:)
   EWMA(i,:) = S([1,4,2]);        % convert matrix to vector
end
EWMArho = EWMA(:,3) ./ sqrt(EWMA(:,1) .* EWMA(:,2))
                                  % calculate correlations
```

The three commands

```
  .*      ./     .^
```

are used for element-by-element operations rather than matrix multiplication.

Note that the EWMA matrix is initialized as EWMA = nan(T,3) in Matlab. It is important for reasons of efficiency to predefine the matrix holding the volatilities. However, we could have set it to ones or zeros but instead chose nan. In both R and Matlab this stands for *not a number* (NaN). The main difference between R and Matlab is that in the former matrix() creates a matrix of NaNs by default. The reason we prefer to initialize the matrix of volatilities by NaN is so that we know which entries of the matrix contain the result of a calculation (i.e., those elements of EWMA not set to NaN after the procedure has run). Ultimately, this helps debugging and ensuring the code runs correctly. We use the same device throughout this book.

Dimension issues

When doing matrix multiplication, we need to make sure the dimensions of the matrices match up. In R we use matrix() to transform data into a matrix and can use the transpose function t() to obtain the correct dimensions. It is necessary that the % sign precedes and follows the * sign for matrix multiplications in R (i.e., %*% multiplies matrices). In Matlab when we write x=[2;3] it becomes a column matrix, while y=[2 3] is a row vector.

Suppose the row matrix a contains returns

$$a = (-0.0140, 0.0054).$$

Depending on the transpose, when multiplied into itself, it either yields a 2-by-2 matrix or a scalar. First, an example in R:

```
> a %*% t(a)
[1,]    0.0001958697    -7.625740e-05
[2,]   -0.0000762574     2.968908e-05
#
> t(a) %*% a
              [,1]
[1,]    0.0002255588
```

and then Matlab:

```
>> a
a =    -0.0140      0.0054
%
>> a* a'
ans =
         2.2556e-04
>> a'* a
ans =
         1.0e-03 *
         0.1959    -0.0763
        -0.0763     0.0297
```

If we did the calculation incorrectly with the matrices wrongly transposed—such as t(a) %*% a or a*a'—we get an incorrect value, but we would not receive any warning. However, if a was a column vector, we would have to reverse the transpose. Hence, it is advisable to verify matrix multiplication manually.

3.3 ORTHOGONAL GARCH

This section, and the next, present practical multivariate-volatility-forecasting models where the forecasting of univariate volatility is separated from correlation forecasting. The reason is that it is usually very hard to estimate multivariate GARCH models, suggesting that in practice alternative methodologies for obtaining the covariance matrix are needed.

The reason one needs to estimate the entire conditional covariance matrix of returns in one go is that the correlations are not zero. The orthogonal approach addresses this problem by linearly transforming the observed returns matrix into a set of portfolios with the key property that they are *uncorrelated*, implying we can forecast their volatilities separately. This makes use of principal components analysis (PCA).

This approach is known as orthogonal GARCH, or OGARCH, because it involves transforming correlated returns into uncorrelated portfolios and then using GARCH to forecast the volatilities of each uncorrelated portfolio separately.[1]

3.3.1 Orthogonalizing covariance

The first step in the OGARCH approach is to transform the return matrix y into uncorrelated portfolios u. Denote the sample correlation matrix of y by $\hat{R}$. We then calculate the $K \times K$ matrix of eigenvectors of $\hat{R}$, denoted by Λ. Then u is defined by:

$$u = \Lambda \times y.$$

u has the same dimensions as y and possesses the property that different rows are uncorrelated so we can run a univariate GARCH or a similar model on each row in u separately to obtain its conditional variance forecast, denoted by D_t. We then obtain the forecast of the conditional covariance matrix of the returns by:

$$\hat{\Sigma}_t = \Lambda \hat{D}_t \Lambda'.$$

This implies that the covariance terms can be ignored when modeling the covariance matrix of u, and the problem has been reduced to a series of univariate estimations.

3.3.2 Implementation

It is simple to implement OGARCH in R and Matlab. R uses the gogarch library whilst Matlab uses the UCSD GARCH toolbox.

---
[1] This method was first applied by Ding (1994) and Alexander and Chibumba (1994).

Listing 3.5. OGARCH in R

```
library(gogarch)
res = gogarch(y,formula = ~garch(1,1),garchlist =
   c(include.mean=FALSE))
OOrho = ccor(res)     # gets a vector of correlations
```

Listing 3.6. OGARCH in Matlab

```
% UCSD GARCH
[par, Ht] = o_mvgarch(y, 2,1,1);
Ht = reshape(Ht,4,T)';0     % Ht comes from o_mvgarch as a 3D matrix,
                              this transforms it into a 2D matrix
OOrho = - Ht(:,3) ./ sqrt(Ht(:,1) .* Ht(:,4));
                            % gets a vector of correlations
```

3.3.3 Large-scale implementations

In the procedure outlined above all the principal components (PCs) were used to construct the conditional covariance matrix. However, it is possible to use just a few of the columns (i.e., those PCs that correspond to most of the variation in y). The highest eigenvalue corresponds to the most important principle component—the one that explains most of the variation in the data.

Such approaches are in widespread use because it is possible to construct the conditional covariance matrix for a very large number of assets. In a highly correlated environment, just a few principal components are required to represent system variation to a very high degree of accuracy. This is much easier than forecasting all volatilities directly in one go.

This method also allows estimates for volatilities and correlations of variables to be generated even when data are sparse (e.g., in illiquid markets). Moreover, the use of PCA guarantees the positive definiteness of the covariance matrix.

PCA also facilitates building a covariance matrix for an entire financial institution by iteratively combining the covariance matrices of the various trading desks, simply by using one or perhaps two principal components. For example, one can create the covariance matrices of small caps and large caps separately and use the first principal component to combine them into the covariance matrix of all equities. This can then be combined with the covariance matrix for fixed income assets, etc.

3.4 CCC AND DCC MODELS

A related approach is to separate out correlation modeling from volatility modeling within a GARCH-type framework. We can divide the estimation into two parts: one for the correlation matrix and the other for the variances. We discuss two such models below: the CCC and DCC.

3.4.1 Constant conditional correlations (CCC)

Bollerslev (1990) proposes the constant conditional correlations (CCC) model where time-varying covariances are proportional to the conditional standard deviation.

In the CCC model the conditional covariance matrix $\hat{\Sigma}_t$ consists of two components that are estimated separately: sample correlations $\hat{R}$ and the diagonal matrix of time-varying volatilities $\hat{D}_t$. Then, the covariance forecast is given by:

$$\hat{\Sigma}_t = \hat{D}_t \hat{R} \hat{D}_t, \tag{3.3}$$

where

$$\hat{D}_t = \begin{pmatrix} \hat{\sigma}_{t,1} & 0 & 0 \\ 0 & \ddots & 0 \\ 0 & 0 & \hat{\sigma}_{t,K} \end{pmatrix}.$$

The volatility of each asset $\hat{\sigma}_{t,k}$ follows a GARCH process or any of the univariate models discussed in the last chapter.

This model guarantees the positive definiteness of $\hat{\Sigma}_t$ if $\hat{R}$ is positive definite. The CCC is a very simple model and easy to implement. Since matrix $\hat{D}_t$ has only diagonal elements, we can estimate each volatility separately.

However, simplicity does not come without cost. In particular, the assumption of correlations being constant over time is at odds with the vast amount of empirical evidence supporting nonlinear dependence. Consequently, the DCC model below is preferred to the CCC model.

3.4.2 Dynamic conditional correlations (DCC)

Engle (2002) and Tse and Tsui (2002) propose the dynamic conditional correlations (DCC) model as an extension to the CCC model to correct the latter's main defect: constant correlations. The Engle (2002) model is described below.

Let the correlation matrix from (3.3) be time dependent, so $\hat{R}_t$ is composed of a symmetric positive definite autoregressive matrix $\hat{Q}_t$:

$$\hat{R}_t = \hat{Q}'_t \hat{Q}_t$$

with $\hat{Q}_t$ given by:

$$\hat{Q}_t = (1 - \zeta - \xi)\overline{Q} + \zeta Y'_{t-1} Y_{t-1} + \xi \hat{Q}_{t-1}$$

where $\overline{Q}$ is the $(K \times K)$ unconditional covariance matrix of Y; and ζ and ξ are parameters such that $\zeta, \xi > 0$ and $\zeta + \xi < 1$ to ensure positive definiteness and stationarity, respectively.

One advantage of the DCC model is that it can be estimated in two steps. When the model is estimated by maximum likelihood, we can "break" the log-likelihood function into two parts: one for parameters determining univariate volatilities and another for parameters determining the correlations. This is known as the DCC two-step estimation technique. Large covariance matrices can be consistently estimated using this technique without requiring too much computational power.

One shortcoming of the DCC model is that parameters ζ and ξ are constants, which implies that the conditional correlations of all assets are driven by the same underlying dynamics—often an unrealistic assumption.

3.4.3 Implementation

It is simple to implement DCC in R and Matlab. R uses the `dcc.estimation` function from the ccgarch library whilst Matlab uses the `dcc_mvgarch` function from the UCSD GARCH library. The `dcc.estimation` function is a bit cumbersome to use because all starting parameters need to be specified before estimation. It is better to first estimate a univariate GARCH model in order to use its parameter estimates as starting values.

Listing 3.7. DCC in R

```
library(ccgarch)
# estimate univariate GARCH models to get starting values
f1 = garchFit(~ garch(1,1), data=y[,1],include.mean=FALSE)
f1 = f1@fit$coef
f2 = garchFit(~ garch(1,1), data=y[,2],include.mean=FALSE)
f2 = f2@fit$coef
# create vectors and matrices of starting values
a = c(f1[1], f2[1])
A = diag(c(f1[2],f2[2]))
B = diag(c(f1[3], f2[3]))
dccpara = c(0.2,0.6)

# estimate the model
dccresults = dcc.estimation(inia=a, iniA=A, iniB=B,
   ini.dcc=dccpara,dvar=y, model="diagonal")
# Parameter estimates and their robust standard errors
   dcc.results$out
DCCrho = dccresults$DCC[,2]
```

Listing 3.8. DCC in Matlab

```
% UCSD GARCH
[p, lik, Ht] = dcc_mvgarch(y,1,1,1,1)
Ht = reshape(Ht,4,T)';
DCCrho = Ht(:,3) ./ sqrt(Ht(:,1) .* Ht(:,4));     % correlations
```

3.5 ESTIMATION COMPARISON

The above listings demonstrate estimation of the EWMA, OGARCH and DCC models using data discussed in Section 3.1.1.

Instead of showing model parameters or likelihood values—which would not be very informative since the three models are not nested—we simply show correlations.

Figure 3.1 shows a plot of the stock prices (scaled to start at $100) in panel (a), the two returns in panel (b) and finally the correlation forecasts in panel (c), which also shows

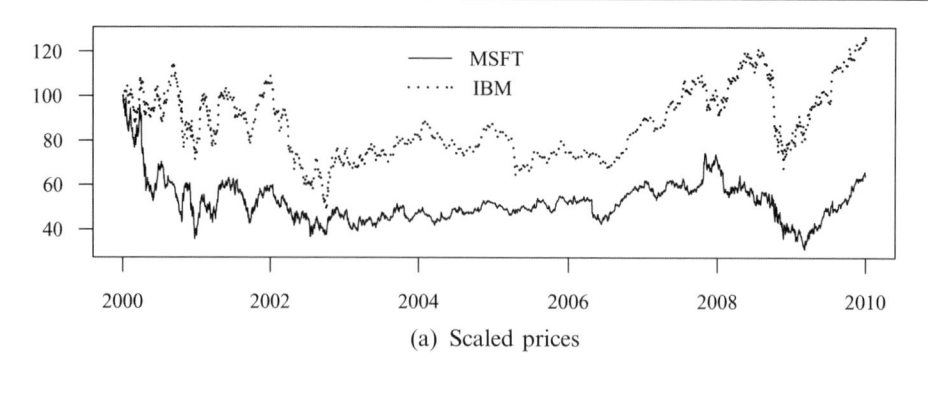

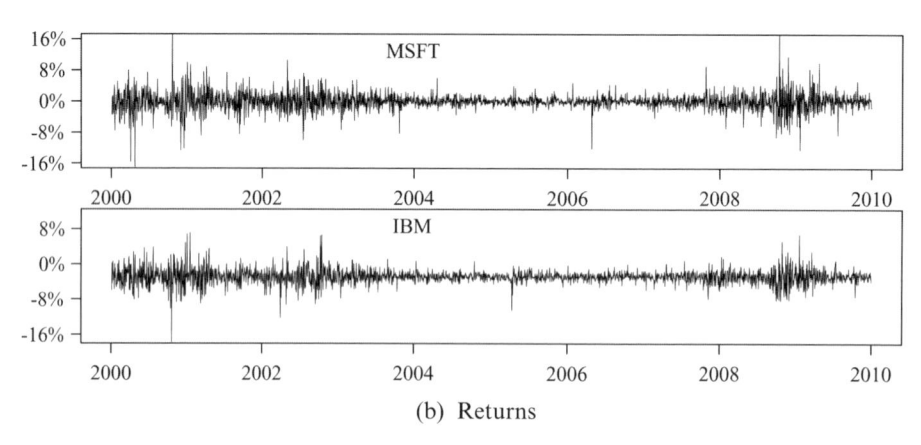

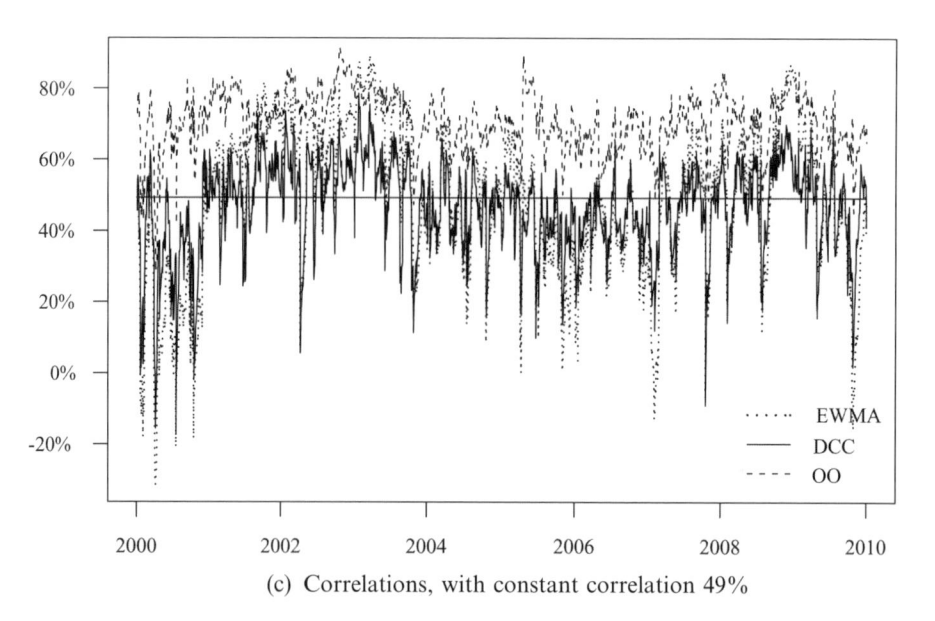

Figure 3.1. Multivariate volatility analysis for daily Microsoft and IBM returns from 2000 to 2009.

the unconditional correlation of the data (49%). We focus on the main year of the crisis (i.e., 2008) in Figure 3.2, where it is easier to identify individual correlations and their drivers. Listings 3.9 and 3.10 show how we combine correlations from the three models—Listings 3.3 to 3.8—into one variable, which is then plotted.

Listing 3.9. Correlation comparison in R

```
matplot(cbind(EWMArho,DCCrho,OOrho),type='l')
legend('bottomright',c("EWMA","DCC","OOrho"),lty=1:3)
```

Listing 3.10. Correlation comparison in Matlab

```
plot([EWMArho,DCCrho,OOrho])
legend('EWMA','DCC','OOrho','Location','SouthWest')
```

The correlation forecasts for EWMA seem to be most volatile, which is not surprising considering how the correlations are directly modeled in (3.1). A time period of a few days where one stock appreciates while the other falls in price such that their return product $y_{t,1} y_{t,2}$ is negative sharply drives correlations down—even to the point of becoming negative.

Not surprisingly, both DCC and OGARCH models have more stable correlations, with the OGARCH having the lowest fluctuations. The large swings in EWMA correlations might be an overreaction, but significant compromises are the price paid for tractability by all three models, and all three correlation forecasts reflect these compromises.

It is easier to see individual correlations in Figure 3.2 which focuses on 2008. For example, IBM is on an upward trend in July and August, while Microsoft is mostly falling in price, with both having relatively low volatility during that period. All three correlation measures fall sharply with EWMA going from about 70% to about 10% in just a few days in July. The correlations then reach their previous level by August. Throughout the year, EWMA exhibits the biggest swings and OGARCH the smallest, with OGARCH having the highest average correlations.

3.6 MULTIVARIATE EXTENSIONS OF GARCH

It is conceptually straightforward to develop multivariate extensions of the univariate GARCH-type models discussed in the last chapter—such as multivariate GARCH (MVGARCH). Unfortunately, it is more difficult in practice because the most obvious model extensions result in the number of parameters exploding as the number of assets increases. It is sometimes possible to simplify the model structure.[2] All such simplifications come at some cost to model flexibility.

---
[2] See, for example, the survey by Bauwens et al. (2006).

68   Multivariate volatility models

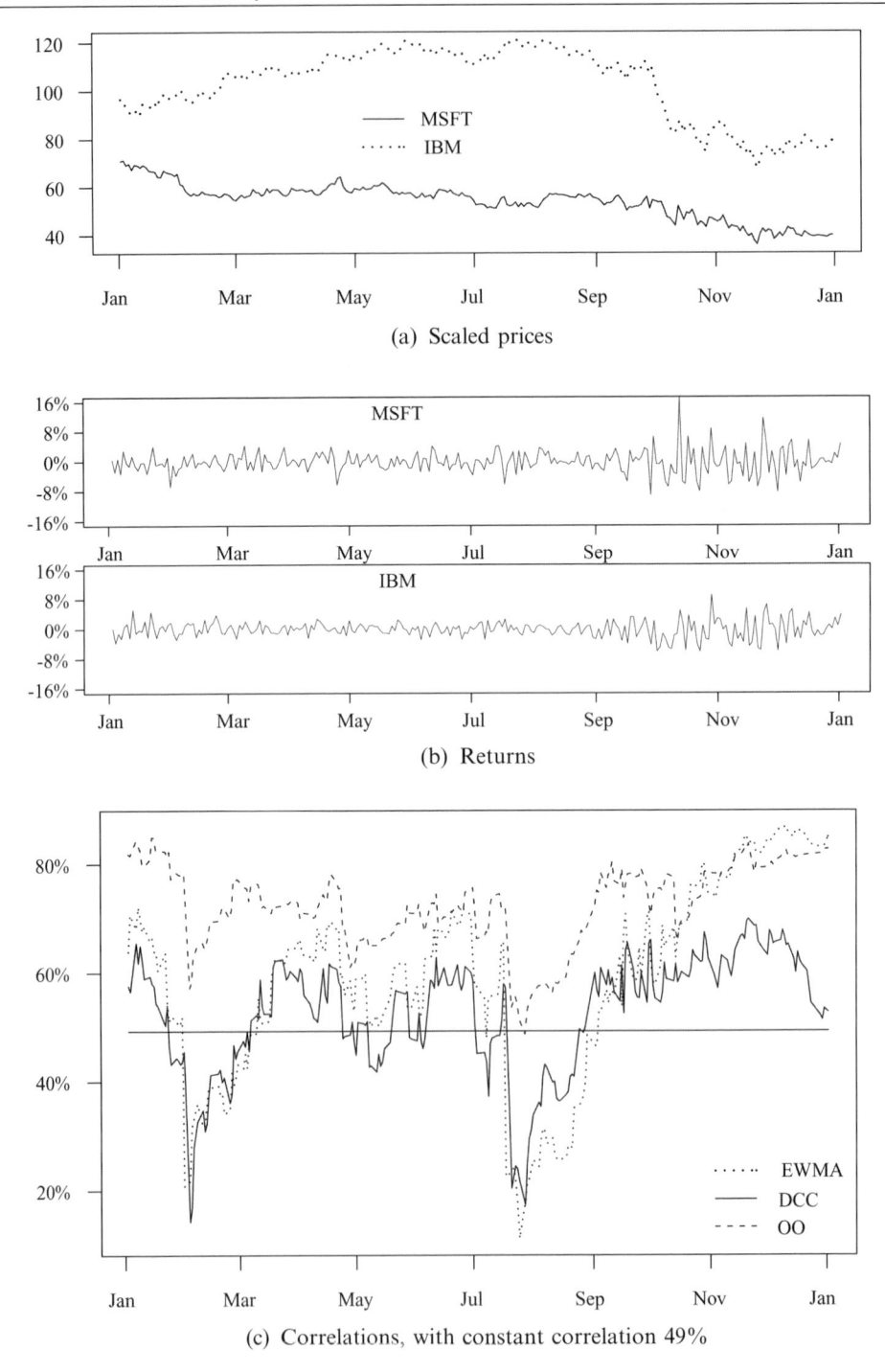

Figure 3.2. Focus on the crisis: Microsoft and IBM in 2008.

(a) Scaled prices

(b) Returns

(c) Correlations, with constant correlation 49%

3.6.1 Numerical problems

Estimating MVGARCH models is usually quite challenging because of a range of numerical problems that arise in estimation—we are much more likely to encounter numerical problems for multivariate models than for univariate models. Programming the likelihood function is usually quite straightforward, while addressing all the subsequent numerical problems is not.

Multivariate stationarity constraints are much more important for MVGARCH models than in the univariate case. When estimating a univariate GARCH model, even if covariance stationarity is violated, the estimation proceeds without hindrance with no numerical problems encountered. This means that we still obtain a volatility forecast even if $\alpha + \beta > 1$. This is generally not the situation for the MVGARCH models discussed in this section. The conditions for covariance stationarity for these models are much more complicated than for univariate models; moreover, a parameter set resulting in violation of covariance stationarity might also lead to unpleasant numerical problems. For example, when covariant stationarity conditions are violated, Σ_t may no longer be invertible leading to a NaN when evaluating the likelihood.

Numerical algorithms need to address these problems, thus complicating the programming process considerably. Furthermore, for end-users to be aware of them they will need to be relatively expert. We could not find any reliable implementations of multivariate GARCH models in either Matlab or R, and for these reasons we simply show the models, but do not implement them. Perhaps the best implementation is the G@RCH package for the Ox language, see Laurent (2009) and http://www.garch.org/.

3.6.2 The BEKK model

There are a number of alternative MVGARCH models available, but the BEKK model is probably the most widely used.

In the BEKK[3] model, proposed by Engle and Kroner (1995), the matrix of conditional covariances is a function of the outer product of lagged returns and lagged conditional covariances, each pre-multiplied and post-multiplied by a parameter matrix. This results in a quadratic function that is guaranteed to be positive semi-definite.

The BEKK model has several useful features besides positive semi-definiteness. It allows for interactions between different asset returns and volatilities, and is relatively parsimonious in terms of parameters required.

The two-asset, one-lag BEKK(1,1,2) model is defined as:

$$\Sigma_t = \Omega\Omega' + A'Y'_{t-1}Y_{t-1}A + B'\Sigma_{t-1}B$$

---

[3] The acronym comes from the names of authors proposing this model: Baba, Engle, Kraft and Kroner.

or:

$$\Sigma_t = \begin{pmatrix} \sigma_{t,11} & \sigma_{t,12} \\ \sigma_{t,12} & \sigma_{t,22} \end{pmatrix}$$

$$= \begin{pmatrix} \omega_{11} & 0 \\ \omega_{21} & \omega_{22} \end{pmatrix} \begin{pmatrix} \omega_{11} & 0 \\ \omega_{21} & \omega_{22} \end{pmatrix}'$$

$$+ \begin{pmatrix} \alpha_{11} & \alpha_{12} \\ \alpha_{21} & \alpha_{22} \end{pmatrix}' \begin{pmatrix} Y_{t-1,1}^2 & Y_{t-1,1}Y_{t-1,2} \\ Y_{t-1,2}Y_{t-1,1} & Y_{t-1,2}^2 \end{pmatrix} \begin{pmatrix} \alpha_{11} & \alpha_{12} \\ \alpha_{21} & \alpha_{22} \end{pmatrix}$$

$$+ \begin{pmatrix} \beta_{11} & \beta_{12} \\ \beta_{21} & \beta_{22} \end{pmatrix}' \begin{pmatrix} \sigma_{t-1,11} & \sigma_{t-1,12} \\ \sigma_{t-1,12} & \sigma_{t-1,22} \end{pmatrix} \begin{pmatrix} \beta_{11} & \beta_{12} \\ \beta_{21} & \beta_{22} \end{pmatrix}.$$

The general BEKK(L_1,L_2,K) model is given by:

$$\Sigma_t = \Omega\Omega' + \sum_{k=1}^{K}\sum_{i=1}^{L_1} A'_{i,k} Y'_{t-i} Y_{t-i} A_{i,k} + \sum_{k=1}^{K}\sum_{j=1}^{L_2} B'_{j,k} \Sigma_{t-j} B_{j,k}. \qquad (3.4)$$

The number of parameters in the BEKK(1,1,2) model is $K(5K+1)/2$ (i.e., 11 in the two-asset case).

One drawback of the BEKK model is that it contains too many parameters that do not directly represent the impact of lagged squared returns or lagged volatility forecasts on elements of the covariance matrix. This implies its parameters may be hard to interpret. Furthermore, many parameters are often found to be statistically insignificant, which suggests the model may be overparameterized.

The overwhelming difficulty with estimating BEKK models is the high number of parameters, leading to the conclusion that the number of assets needs to be quite small for estimation to be feasible.

3.7 SUMMARY

Estimating multivariate volatility models is considerably more difficult than estimating univariate models. Consequently, any implementation of multivariate volatility inevitably implies a number of compromises.

At one end of the scale, we have multivariate extensions to univariate GARCH models such as general and sophisticated models like the BEKK. They promise relatively accurate covariance forecasts, but have practical limitations that prevent their use in most applications, especially when the number of assets is not very small. Essentially, such models are almost impossible to estimate in most cases.

At the other end we have the EWMA model which is easily implemented, but is very limited in the type of volatility and correlation dynamics it can capture. The weaknesses of EWMA become especially apparent in correlation forecasting as manifested in Section 3.5.

The OGARCH and DCC models sit in between, and are based on separating univariate estimation from correlation estimation. OGARCH is based on estimating a constant correlation matrix prior to univariate estimations, similar to the CCC model. The DCC model allows the correlation matrix to be dynamic and therefore is more general. However, this limits the number of assets whose covariance matrix can be forecast at any one time.

One advantage of the OGARCH approach is that it is well suited to large-scale problems, such as obtaining the covariance matrix for an entire financial institution. This is because we can use a principal components analysis (PCA) approach to build up the covariance matrix iteratively, like a house of Lego blocks, and use the first principal components (PCs) to join them up. However, it would be straightforward to combine a PCA approach with other methods. For example, one could use DCC for a desk with many assets and BEKK for a smaller desk whose assets have complicated interactions, and finally use PCA to create a combined covariance matrix.

4
Risk measures

There is no universal definition of what constitutes risk. On a very general level, financial risk could be defined as "the chance of losing part or all of an investment", but a large number of such statements could equally be made, most of which would be contradictory. When using the concept of risk within financial institutions, a more formal definition is required as one of their key functions is to actively manage financial risks.

The objective of this chapter is to introduce theoretical definitions of the most common measures of risk: volatility, value-at-risk (VaR) and expected shortfall (ES). Here, we make the simplifying assumption that the underlying statistical distributions are known so as to focus on the concepts. The issue of estimating risk is dealt with elsewhere: volatility models are addressed in Chapters 2 and 3 and historical simulation in Section 5.2.

Furthermore, this chapter focuses on risk in basic assets, while Chapters 6 and 7 are concerned with risk in options and bonds.

The specific notation used in this chapter is:

p	Probability
Q	Profit and loss
q	Observed profit and loss
w	Vector of portfolio weights
X and Y	Refer to two different assets
$\varphi(\cdot)$	Risk measure
ϑ	Portfolio value

4.1 DEFINING AND MEASURING RISK

Consider Figure 4.1 which plots simulated returns on three different types of assets, all with the same volatility and mean. Panel (a) shows observations from a normal distribution, panel (b) is from a Student-$t(3)$ distribution which resembles typical financial returns. Panel (c) shows returns that are zero most of the time but have occasional large declines commonly associated with fixed exchange rates subject to sporadic devaluations, defaultable bonds or certain derivative portfolios.

Standard mean variance analysis indicates that all three assets are equally risky and preferable because their means and volatilities are the same. However, in reality market participants view the risk in them quite differently and are likely to have a preference for one of these assets. This suggests that some objective way to compare the risk in assets with different distributions is desirable.

74   Risk measures

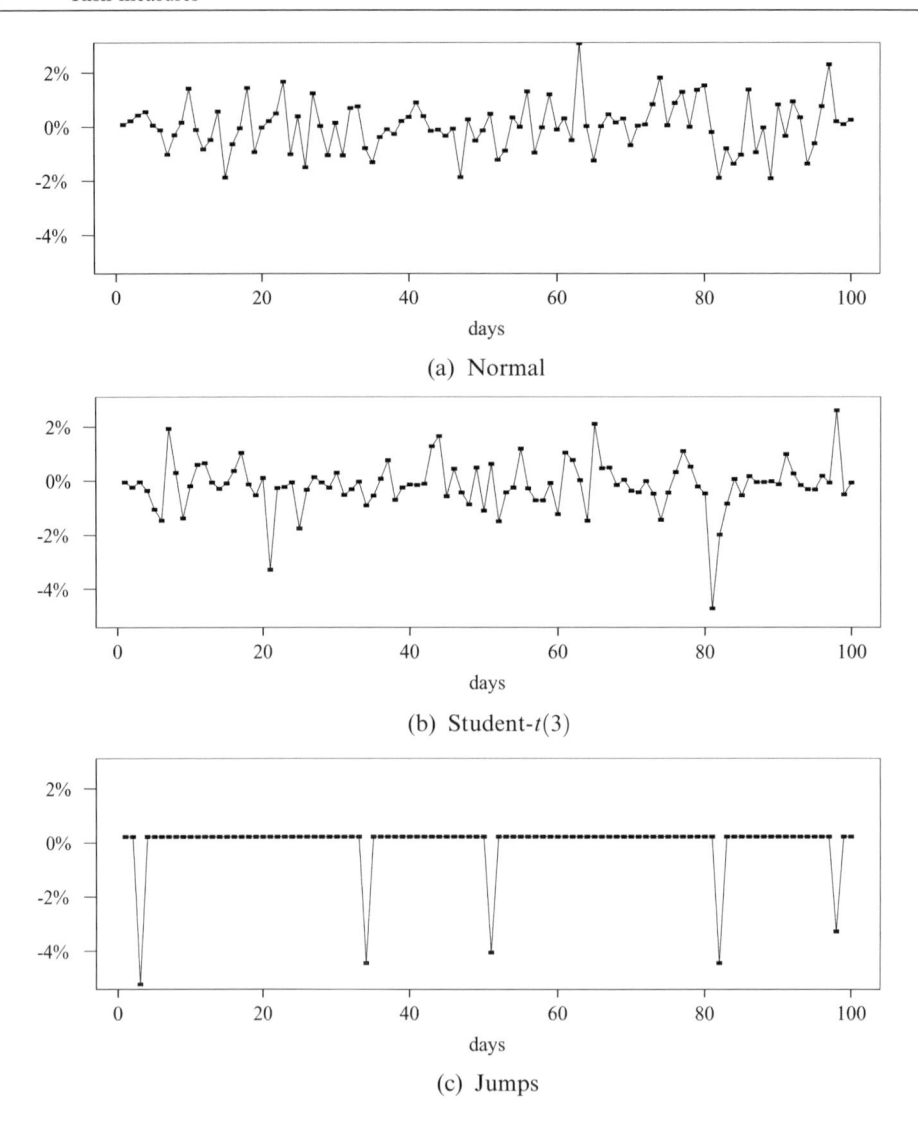

Figure 4.1. Random returns with volatility one and mean zero.

(a) Normal

(b) Student-$t(3)$

(c) Jumps

There is no obvious way to discriminate between the assets in Figure 4.1. We could try to model the underlying distributions, but even if that could be done successfully it is unlikely to help in decision-making. After all, each of these distributions has different parameters and shapes making comparisons difficult.

In practice, the problem of risk comparisons is harder because the underlying distribution of market prices and returns for various assets is unknown. One can try to identify the distribution by maximum likelihood methods, or test the distributions against other distributions by using methods such as the Kolmogorov–Smirnov test, but generally such methods are not very robust. Practically, it is impossible to accurately identify the distribution of financial returns.

The task of forecasting financial risk is further complicated by the fact that financial risk cannot be measured directly, but has to be *inferred* from the behavior of observed market prices. This means financial risk cannot be measured in the same manner as temperature is measured by a thermometer: risk is a *latent variable*. For example, at the end of a trading day, the day's return is known while the day's risk is unknown. All we can say is that risk is probably high if prices have fluctuated wildly during the day. Consequently, measuring risk requires statistical modeling, which inevitably entails making some assumptions.

Even if we knew the distribution of returns, as long as each asset was distributed differently the comparison of risk between assets would be challenging.

The most common approach to the problem of comparing the risk of assets having different distributions is to employ a risk measure that represents the risk of an asset as a single number that is comparable across assets.

A subtle difference exists between the terms *risk measure* and *risk measurement*. The former applies to definition of the method, the latter to a number.

Definition 4.1 (Risk measure) *A risk measure is a mathematical method for computing risk.*

We discuss three risk measures below: volatility, value-at-risk and expected shortfall.

Definition 4.2 (Risk measurement) *A number that captures risk. It is obtained by applying data to a risk measure.*

The objective of risk measures is to aid decision-making. As a consequence, the best way to evaluate such measures is by discovering how well they perform at the intended task. If different risk measures give the same outcome we choose the one that is easiest to work with. If, on the other hand, they give different rankings of investment choices, we have to think more carefully about which one to use.

4.2 VOLATILITY

Volatility, or the standard deviation of returns, is the main measure of risk in most financial analysis. It is sufficient as a risk measure only when financial returns are normally distributed. The reason is that all statistical properties of the normal distribution are captured by the mean and variance. However, as discussed in Chapter 1, an assumption of normality for returns is violated for most if not all financial returns. For that reason the use of volatility as a risk measure can lead to misleading conclusions.

This is demonstrated in Figure 4.1. If volatility were to be used to determine riskiness, we would be indifferent between all three assets, as the volatility and mean are the same in each case. Each asset would be at the same place on a mean–variance diagram.

However, it is clear from the figures that the risk profiles of the three assets are quite distinct, and in practice different investors would prefer different assets.

The level of inaccuracy from using volatility depends in practice on specific applications. In many cases, extreme outcomes are not the concern and the use of volatility might be relatively innocuous in such cases. The same cannot be said for most applications in financial risk where volatility is likely to systematically underestimate risk.

4.3 VALUE-AT-RISK

The most common risk measure after volatility is value-at-risk (VaR). It is a single summary statistical measure of risk, it is distribution independent and it is a measure of losses as a result of "typical" market movements.

While VaR has well-documented flaws (discussed below) it has remained the risk measure of choice in the financial industry. When one considers its theoretical properties, issues in implementation and ease of backtesting, the reason becomes clear. VaR provides the best balance among the available risk measures and therefore underpins most practical risk models.

Definition 4.3 (Value-at-risk) *The loss on a trading portfolio such that there is a probability p of losses equaling or exceeding VaR in a given trading period and a $(1-p)$ probability of losses being lower than the VaR.*

We may write it as VaR(p) or VaR$^{100 \times p\%}$ to make the dependence on probability explicit—for example, VaR(0.05) or VaR$^{5\%}$. The most common probability levels are 1% or 5%, but numbers higher and lower than these are often used in practice.

VaR is a *quantile* on the distribution of profit and loss (P/L). We indicate profit and loss P/L on an investment portfolio by the random variable Q, with a particular realization indicated by q. If we hold one unit of an asset, P/L would be indicated by:

$$Q = P_t - P_{t-1}.$$

More generally, if the portfolio value is ϑ:

$$Q = \vartheta Y.$$

That is, the P/L is the portfolio value multiplied by the returns. The density of P/L is denoted by $f_q(\cdot)$. VaR is then given by:

$$\Pr[Q \leq -\text{VaR}(p)] = p \tag{4.1}$$

or

$$p = \int_{-\infty}^{-\text{VaR}(p)} f_q(x) dx. \tag{4.2}$$

We use a minus sign because VaR is a positive number and we are dealing with losses— that is, the probability of losses being larger (more negative) than negative VaR.

Example 4.1 *The commodities' trading book is worth £1 billion and daily $VaR^{1\%} = £10$ million. This means we expect to lose £10 million or more once every 100 days, or about once every 5 months.*

Figure 4.2 demonstrates how VaR is defined. Panel (a) shows the entire density of P/L, while panel (b) zooms in on the left tail, where the shaded areas identify the 1% and 5% probabilities (the area under the curve from negative infinity to negative VaR equals 0.01 and 0.05, respectively). Panel (c) shows the entire distribution of P/L. Finally, panel (d) shows the left part of the distribution.

4.3.1 Is VaR a negative or positive number?

VaR can be alternatively presented as a negative or a positive number and, equivalently, probabilities can be stated as close to one or close to zero—for example, VaR(0.95) or VaR(0.05). This does not imply any inconsistency, it is simply how VaR is dealt with in the real world.

VaR represents potential losses, but in informal speech both profits and losses can be referred to as positive numbers. This convention can be confusing in places. Does a VaR

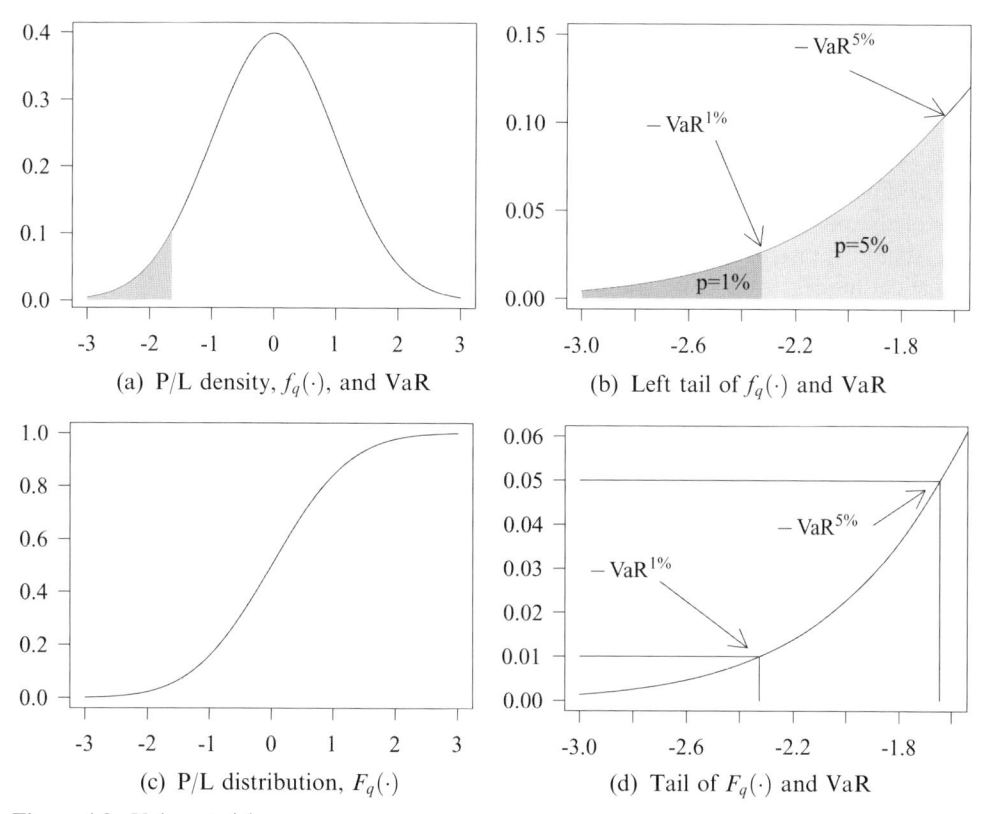

Figure 4.2. Value-at-risk.

increase mean a change from −$10 to −$5 or $10 to $15, and if the VaR probability increases does it mean a change from 10% to 5% or 95% to 99%? Thus, it is safer to say the numbers become smaller or more extreme implying, respectively, movement into the distribution or out to the tails.

There is no convention in the literature on how to represent the sign of VaR. In this book we take the more common approach of referring to VaR as a positive number using low-probability terminology (e.g., 5%).

4.3.2 The three steps in VaR calculations

There are three steps in VaR calculations. First, the *probability* of losses exceeding VaR, p, needs to be specified, with the most common probability level being 1%. Theory provides little guidance about the choice of p; it is mainly determined by how the user of the risk management system wishes to interpret the VaR number. Is a "large" loss one that occurs with a probability of 1% or 5% or even 0.1%? VaR levels of 1%–5% are very common in practice, but less extreme higher numbers (e.g., 10%) are often used in risk management on the trading floor and more extreme lower numbers (e.g., 0.1%) may be used for applications like economic capital, survival analysis or long-run risk analysis for pension funds.

The second step is the *holding period* (i.e., the time period over which losses may occur). This is usually one day, but can be more or less depending on particular circumstances. Those who actively trade their portfolios may use a one-day holding period, but longer holding periods are more realistic for institutional investors and nonfinancial corporations. Many proprietary trading desks focus on intraday VaR, perhaps from one hour to the next. The longer the holding period, the larger the VaR. The one-day holding period is the easiest to use.

The third and final step is identification of the *probability distribution* of the profit and loss of the portfolio. This is the most difficult and important aspect of risk modeling. The standard practice is to estimate the distribution by using past observations and a statistical model.

4.3.3 Interpreting and analyzing VaR

In interpreting and comparing VaR numbers, it is crucial to keep the probability and holding period in mind since, without them, VaR numbers are meaningless. For example, an identical portfolio could produce two different VaR estimates if risk managers choose different values of p and holding periods. Obviously, a loss suffered with a probability of only 1% exceeds a loss suffered with a probability of 5%.

Whether the VaR of a firm's portfolio of positions is a relevant measure of the risk of financial distress over a short period depends on the liquidity of portfolio positions and the risk of extreme cash outflows. Adverse liquidity conditions lead to high transaction costs such as wide spreads and large margin calls. VaR is unlikely to capture these effects.

In risk management, VaR is a significant step forward with respect to traditional measures based on sensitivities to market variables (e.g., the "greeks"[1]). VaR is a

---
[1] The greeks measure the sensitivities of options to underlying risk factors (e.g., delta and gamma).

universal concept and can be applied to most financial instruments. It summarizes in a single number all the risks of a portfolio including interest rate risk, foreign exchange risk, and so on, where we would need many greeks—one for each type of risk. It also facilitates comparisons between different asset classes. The VaR measure combines loss (quantile) and probability, whereas the greeks are essentially "what if" scenarios that say nothing about the probabilities of the "if".

4.3.4 VaR and normality

A common misunderstanding among many commentators is that VaR implies normality of returns. This is, of course, untrue; we can use any distribution in calculating VaR provided the mean is defined.

Perhaps the most common distributional assumption for returns in the calculation of VaR is normality—either conditional or unconditional.

In this case, volatility provides the same information as VaR, since in that case VaR is simply a constant multiplied by volatility. We demonstrate this formally in the next chapter.

4.3.5 Sign of VaR

In all the discussion on VaR so far, we have implicitly assumed that VaR is positive. A manifestation of this implicit assumption is shown in Figure 4.2 where VaR is comfortably positive.

However, there is no intrinsic reason for this to hold in generality. If the mean of the density of P/L is sufficiently large, the probability p quantile, corresponding to VaR, might easily end up on the other side of zero. This might happen, say, for very long holding periods, For example, we demonstrate in Section 5.4 that over time the mean return grows at rate T while the volatility grows at rate $\sqrt{T}$. This means that as the holding period increases eventually the mean will become so large as to make the VaR switch signs.

One example of this is shown in Figure 4.3. In this case the VaR is meaningless. VaR is meant to capture potential losses but here relevant losses have become profits. Consequently, in such situations we need different approaches: either making the probability

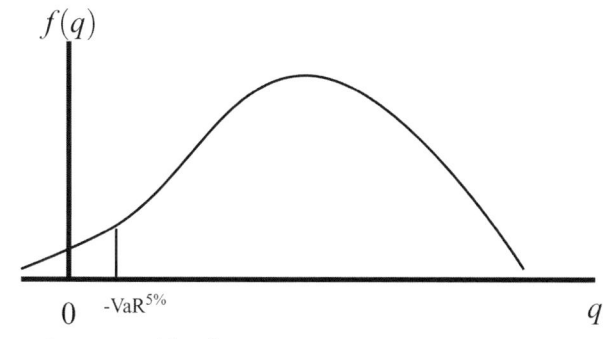

Figure 4.3. VaR on the wrong side of zero.

more extreme and hence keeping VaR on the right side of zero or using a different measure of risk.

Since this can happen for very long holding periods, the usefulness of VaR as a risk measure for annual, even quarterly, holding periods is very much in doubt.

4.4 ISSUES IN APPLYING VaR

There are three main issues that arise in the implementation of VaR:

1. VaR is only a quantile on the P/L distribution.
2. VaR is not a coherent risk measure.
3. VaR is easy to manipulate.

4.4.1 VaR is only a quantile

VaR is the *minimum* potential loss that a portfolio can suffer in an adverse outcome. But, this raises the question: Why should we be interested in such a loss regardless of how serious all the other losses are? VaR gives the "best of worst case scenarios" and, as such, it inevitably underestimates the potential losses associated with a probability level.

For example, daily VaR at the 5% confidence level means that for 95 days out of 100 downward asset price movements are expected to be less than the VaR and for 5 days out of 100 they are expected to exceed the VaR. As a consequence, 5% VaR is incapable of capturing the risk of extreme movements that have a probability of less than 5%.

Indeed, because VaR is only a quantile on the distribution of P/L, the shape of the tail before and after VaR need not have any bearing on the actual VaR number. For a demonstration of this see Figure 4.4 and Example 4.2.

Figure 4.4 shows three possible, but unusual, asset return distributions. In panel (a) density is bimodal: there is a small bump to the left of the VaR number, which would mean a concentration of outcomes around that point. Panel (b) shows the uniform distribution with its bounded tails, where we cannot get outcomes much below the VaR number. By contrast, panel (c) shows a super-fat tail, where we may observe much more negative outcomes.

Example 4.2 (A VaR paradox) *Consider a portfolio X that consists of long option positions that have a maximum downside of $100 where the worst 1% of cases over a week all result in maximum loss. Another portfolio Y, which has the same face value as X, consists of short futures positions that allow for an unbounded maximum loss. We can choose Y such that its VaR is $100 over a week.*

- *In portfolio X, the 1% worst case losses are all $100.*
- *In portfolio Y, the 1% worst case losses range from $100 to some unknown high value.*

According to 1% VaR, however, both portfolios bear the same risk!

f(q)   *f(q)*

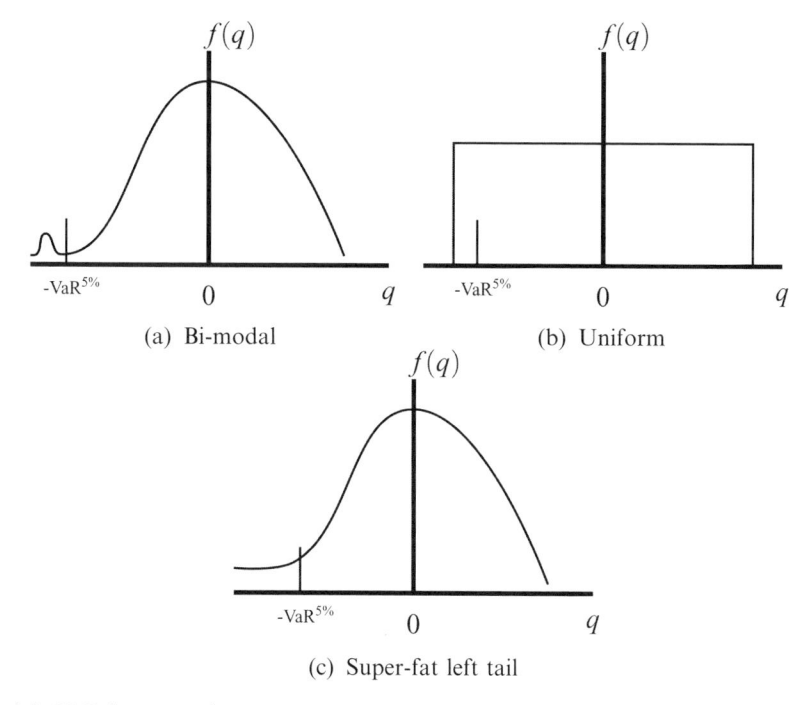

-VaR$^{5\%}$ 0   q   -VaR$^{5\%}$ 0   q

(a) Bi-modal   (b) Uniform

f(q)

-VaR$^{5\%}$ 0   q

(c) Super-fat left tail

Figure 4.4. VaR in unusual cases.

4.4.2 Coherence

Artzner et al. (1999) study the properties a risk measure should have in order to be considered a sensible and useful risk measure; they identify four axioms that risk measures ideally should adhere to. A risk measure that satisfies these four axioms is termed *coherent*. Let a risk measure be denoted by $\varphi(\cdot)$, which could be volatility, VaR, or something else.

Definition 4.4 (Coherent risk measures) *Consider two real-valued random variables (RVs): X and Y. A function $\varphi(\cdot): X, Y \to \mathbb{R}$ is called a coherent risk measure if it satisfies for X, Y and constant c.*

1. **Monotonicity**

$$X, Y \in V, \quad X \leq Y \quad \Rightarrow \quad \varphi(X) \geq \varphi(Y).$$

If portfolio X never exceeds the values of portfolio Y (i.e., is always more negative, hence its losses will be equal or larger), the risk of Y should never exceed the risk of X.

2. **Subadditivity**

$$X, Y, X + Y \in V \quad \Rightarrow \quad \varphi(X + Y) \leq \varphi(X) + \varphi(Y).$$

The risk to the portfolios of X and Y cannot be worse than the sum of the two individual risks—a manifestation of the diversification principle.

> **3. Positive homogeneity**
> $$X \in V,\ c > 0 \quad \Rightarrow \quad \varphi(cX) = c\varphi(X).$$
> For example, if the portfolio value doubles ($c = 2$) then the risk doubles.
>
> **4. Translation invariance**
> $$X \in V,\ c \in \mathbb{R} \quad \Rightarrow \quad \varphi(X + c) = \varphi(X) - c.$$
> Adding c to the portfolio is like adding cash, which acts as insurance, so the risk of $X + c$ is less than the risk of X by the amount of cash, c.

The axiom of positive homogeneity is sometimes violated in practice. If it holds, risk is directly proportional to the value of the portfolio. For example, suppose a portfolio is worth \$1,000 with risk \$10, then doubling the portfolio size to \$2,000 will double the risk to \$20. This will generally hold for small positions in liquid stocks, but as relative shareholdings increase and/or the liquidity of a stock decreases, we may end up in a situation where risk increases more rapidly than the portfolio size. If we try to sell the stock and hence realize the profits or losses, we would exert a significant price impact. That is, because we are trying to sell, the price of the stock will fall and the eventual selling price will therefore be lower than the initial market price. In such a situation positive homogeneity is violated; that is:

$$\varphi(cX) > c\varphi(X).$$

Of the four axioms, the most relevant for our discussion is subadditivity. If it holds, a portfolio of assets is measured as less risky than the sum of the risks of individual assets. For risk measures that violate this axiom, one may erroneously reach the conclusion that diversification results in an increase in risk.

VaR is not a coherent risk measure, since it does not always satisfy the axiom of subadditivity (as demonstrated in Example 4.4). VaR is, however, subadditive under the normal distribution where VaR is proportional to volatility, which is subadditive (as demonstrated in Example 4.3).

> **Example 4.3 (Volatility is subadditive)** Recall how portfolio variance is calculated when we have two assets, X and Y, with volatilities σ_X and σ_Y, respectively, correlation coefficient ρ and portfolio weights w_X and w_Y:
>
> $$\sigma_{\text{port}}^2 = w_X^2 \sigma_X^2 + w_Y^2 \sigma_Y^2 + 2 w_X w_Y \rho \sigma_X \sigma_Y.$$
>
> Rewriting, we get
>
> $$\sigma_{\text{port}}^2 = (w_X \sigma_X + w_Y \sigma_Y)^2 - 2 w_X w_Y \sigma_X \sigma_Y + 2 w_X w_Y \rho \sigma_X \sigma_Y$$
> $$= (w_X \sigma_X + w_X \sigma_Y)^2 - 2 w_X w_Y (1 - \rho) \sigma_X \sigma_Y$$
>
> where the last term is positive. Volatility is therefore subadditive because:
>
> $$\sigma_{\text{port}} \leq w_X \sigma_X + w_Y \sigma_Y.$$

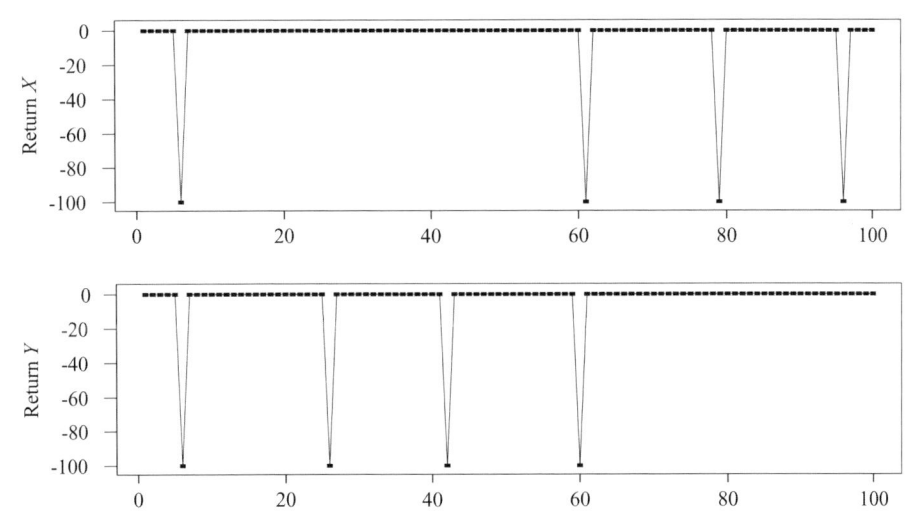

Figure 4.5. Two independent asset returns over 100 days.

Example 4.4 *Consider an asset X such that there is a 4.9% chance of a return of -100 and a 95.1% chance of a return of zero. In this case $VaR^{5\%} = 0$ and $VaR^{1\%} = 100$. An example of this asset can be seen in Figure 4.5.*

Suppose we hold an equally weighted portfolio of assets X and Y, where both have the same distribution and are independent of each other. In this case the 5% VaR of the portfolio is approximately 50. We therefore have the result:

$$VaR^{5\%}(0.5X + 0.5Y) \approx 50 > VaR^{5\%}(X) + VaR^{5\%}(Y) = 0 + 0.$$

In this example, the portfolio appears to have more risk than if all funds were invested in a single asset because the probability of a loss is slightly below the VaR probability for one asset (4.9% compared with 5%), but when we hold two assets the probability of one asset losing money is higher than the VaR probability:

$$\Pr(\text{at least one asset losing money}) = 1 - (0.951 \times 0.951) \approx 0.096.$$

4.4.3 Does VaR really violate subadditivity?

VaR is subadditive in the special case of normally distributed returns. Daníelsson et al. (2010a) study the subadditivity of VaR further and find that VaR is indeed subadditive provided the tail index exceeds 2 (i.e., when the second moment, or variance, is defined under a condition of multivariate regular variation).[2] In other words, subadditivity for the VaR is only violated when the tails are *super fat*. For example, in Figure 4.1 the assets in panels (a) and (b) would not lead to violations of subadditivity of the VaR, while the asset in panel (c) would.

---
[2] See Section 9.2 for a detailed discussion on the meaning of these terms.

In practice, it is important to know whether particular portfolios suffer from subadditivity violations. Most assets do not have tails that are so fat that subadditivity may be violated. This includes most equities, exchange rates and commodities.

There are several assets that may suffer from subadditivity violation: those that are subject to occasional very large negative returns such that their returns are similar to those in Figure 4.1(c). Examples of such assets include exchange rates in countries that peg their currency but are subject to occasional devaluations, electricity prices subject to very extreme price swings and defaultable bonds where most of the time the bonds deliver a steady positive return but may on occasion default and thus be subject to a large negative return.

Subadditivity violation may also happen in "protection seller"-type portfolios—those that earn small amounts with a high level of probability and suffer very large losses with very small probability—such as carry trades. This can also happen in certain derivatives portfolios—such as those containing short options. Finally, insurance contracts provide a steady return to the insurer, but occasionally a large loss happens making such contracts typical of assets that suffer from subadditivity violation.

4.4.4 Manipulating VaR

An important weakness of VaR is how easily it can be manipulated. Because it is only a quantile on the distribution of profit and loss, a financial institution will often find it easy to move the quantile around and hence manipulate the VaR.

A simple way to lower the VaR is to reduce holdings of risky assets, but it can equally well be lowered by using simple trading strategies involving options. In this case, VaR could be lowered at the expense of overall profitability and even by increasing downside risk. Hence, the risk reduction implied by lower VaR is illusionary: reported risk (VaR(p)) is reduced, but actual risk increases and profits decrease.

One example of how this could be done is provided by Daníelsson (2002) who demonstrates how judicious use of put options can deliver any VaR desired.

Example 4.5 (VaR manipulation) *Suppose the VaR before any manipulation is VaR_0 and that a bank would really like the VaR to be VaR_1 where $0 > VaR_1 > VaR_0$ (as in Figure 4.6). One way to achieve this is to write a put option with a strike price below VaR_0 and buy one with a strike above VaR_1. The effect of this will be to lower expected profit and increase downside risk.*

Manipulation (as in Example 4.5) only succeeds in lowering the VaR at the target probability; the VaR may actually increase for most other probability levels. Because the price of the long put is higher than the price of the short put, the strategy will lead to lower overall profits.

Generally, a bank is perfectly within its rights to execute such trading strategies as a part of its normal activities; it might not be obvious to an outside observer that the objective of the trading strategy is manipulation of reported risk.

While it is clear in Example 4.5 that manipulation has occurred, in most real-world cases it would be almost impossible to identify such manipulation.

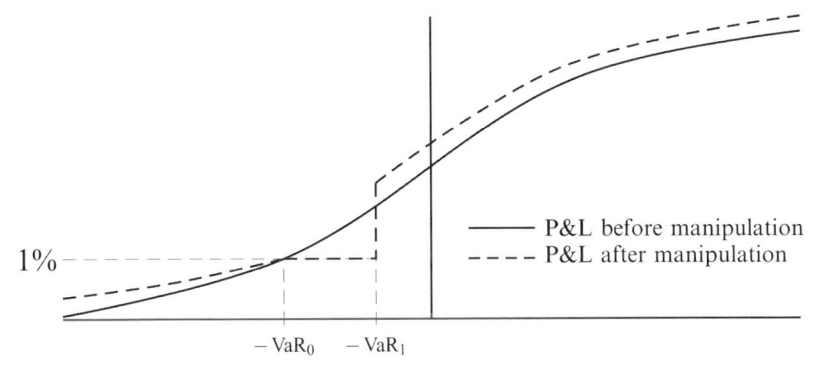

Figure 4.6. Manipulation of the distribution of profit and loss.

4.5 EXPECTED SHORTFALL

A number of alternative risk measures have been proposed to overcome the problem of lack of subadditivity in the VaR and/or provide more information about the tail shape. Such measures typically summarize the entire tail of the distribution as a single-risk measurement. The most common alternative risk measure is *expected shortfall* (ES), also known as tail VaR, expected tail loss, among others. Artzner et al. (1999) demonstrate that ES is subadditive. ES answers the question:

> What is *expected* loss when losses exceed VaR?

Assuming the distribution function of the portfolio is continuous, the answer to the question is given by a conditional expected value below the quantile associated with probability p. Consequently, ES can distinguish between the levels of riskiness in the manipulated and non-manipulated assets in Example 4.5. The fact that we are taking an expectation means that *ES is aware of the shape of the tail distribution while VaR is not.*

> **Definition 4.5 (Expected shortfall)** *Expected loss conditional on VaR being violated (i.e., expected profit/loss, Q, when it is lower than negative VaR):*
> $$\mathrm{ES} = -\mathrm{E}[Q|Q \leq -\mathrm{VaR}(p)].$$

A mathematical expectation is defined by:
$$\mathrm{E}(X) = \int_{-\infty}^{\infty} x f(x) dx.$$

In the case of ES, we are not taking expectation from $-\infty$ to ∞, but from $-\infty$ to $-\mathrm{VaR}(p)$. The area under $f_q(\cdot)$ in the interval $[-\infty, -\mathrm{VaR}(p)]$ is less than one, implying $f_q(\cdot)$ is not a proper density function in this case. This can be overcome by defining a new

86   Risk measures

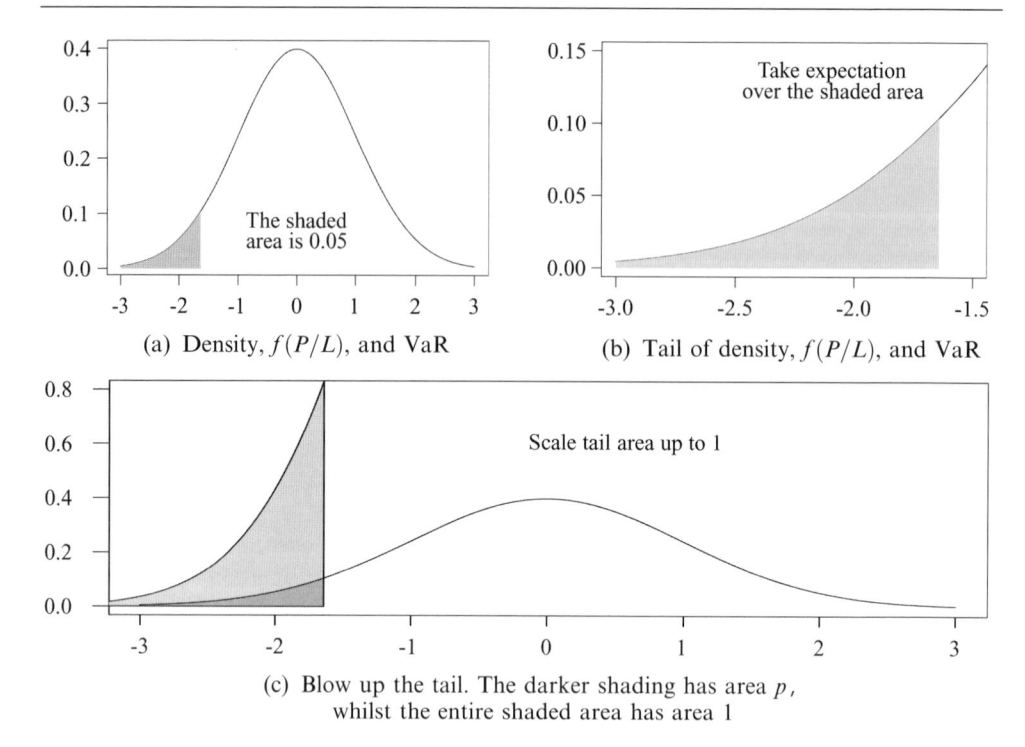

(a) Density, $f(P/L)$, and VaR

(b) Tail of density, $f(P/L)$, and VaR

(c) Blow up the tail. The darker shading has area p, whilst the entire shaded area has area 1

Figure 4.7. ES and VaR for profit/loss outcomes.

density, $f_{\text{VaR}}(\cdot)$, obtained by scaling $f_q(\cdot)$ up so the area under it becomes one (as can be seen in Figure 4.7).

To derive a mathematical expression for ES, we first identify the correct density to use:

$$1 = \int_{-\infty}^{\infty} f_q(x)\,dx$$

$$p = \int_{-\infty}^{-\text{VaR}(p)} f_q(x)\,dx$$

so the tail density, $f_{\text{VaR}}(\cdot)$, is given by:

$$1 = \int_{-\infty}^{-\text{VaR}(p)} f_{\text{VaR}}(x)\,dx = \frac{1}{p}\int_{-\infty}^{-\text{VaR}(p)} f_q(x)\,dx.$$

The ES is then the negative expected value of P/L over the tail density $f_{\text{VaR}}(\cdot)$:

$$\text{ES} = -[Q|Q \leq -\text{VaR}(p)]$$

$$= -\int_{-\infty}^{-\text{VaR}(p)} x f_{\text{VaR}}(x)\,dx. \qquad (4.3)$$

Table 4.1. VaR and ES for a standard normal distribution

p	0.5	0.1	0.05	0.025	0.01	0.001
VaR	0	1.282	1.645	1.960	2.326	3.090
ES	0.798	1.755	2.063	2.338	2.665	3.367

In Table 4.1, the VaR for different levels of confidence is computed along with the corresponding ES for a portfolio with a face value of $1 and normally distributed P/L with mean zero and volatility one. Equation (5.6) shows the formal derivation of ES under normality. If the portfolio value and volatility equal one, then:

$$ES = -\frac{\phi(\Phi^{-1}(p))}{p}$$

where ϕ and Φ are the normal density and distribution, respectively.

Table 4.1 makes it clear that ES is not much lower than VaR itself far away in the tails. This reflects the fact that the tails of a normal distribution decrease at a very rapid rate. The ES to VaR ratio actually converges to one as the confidence level increases for the normal distribution. For other distributions, the ES value can be far removed from the VaR.

The code that R and Matlab use to compute the VaR and ES values in Table 4.2 is given in Listings 4.1 and 4.2, respectively, where the normal density and inverse distribution in R is dnorm and pnorm, respectively, and normpdf and norminv in Matlab.

Listing 4.1. ES in R

```
p = c(0.5,0.1,0.05,0.025,0.01,0.001)
VaR = qnorm(p)
ES = dnorm(qnorm(p))/p
```

Listing 4.2. ES in Matlab

```
p = [0.5,0.1,0.05,0.025,0.01,0.001]
VaR = norminv(p)
ES = normpdf(norminv(p))./p
```

We further compare VaR and ES in terms of subadditivity in Example 4.6.

Example 4.6 Consider two different bonds X and Y where we expect at most one of them to default. The face value of both bonds is 100. If a bond defaults, there are two possible outcomes with recovery values 70 and 90 as well as probabilities of 3% and 2%, respectively. All in all, the two bonds can have five possibles outcomes, the first being when bond X has a loss of 30 and bond Y has no losses. The probability of this outcome is $0.95 \times 0.03 = 0.0285$. The five possible outcomes are:

Outcome	X	Y	X + Y	Probability
1	70	100	170	3%
2	90	100	190	2%
3	100	70	170	3%
4	100	90	190	2%
5	100	100	200	90%

Let us suppose that the initial value of each bond is the expected value of the payoff $100 \times 0.95 + 70 \times 0.03 + 90 \times 0.02 = 98.9$ and $VaR^{5\%}$ is $-(90 - 98.9) = 8.9$. For the portfolio, $VaR^{5\%}$ is $-(170 - 2*98.9) = 27.8$. The other values are:

	X	Y	X + Y
Initial value	98.9	98.9	197.8
VaR 5%	8.9	8.9	27.8
ES 5%	20.9	20.9	27.8

where the ES calculation for X and Y is:

$$\frac{(98.9 - 70) \times 0.03 + (98.9 - 90) \times 0.02}{0.05} = 20.9.$$

Given the first five outcomes, $\Pr(portfolio = 190) = 0.04$, $\Pr(portfolio = 170) = 0.06$ and $\Pr(portfolio = 200) = 0.9$. So, at $p = 0.05$ we expect the portfolio value to be 170 and the loss to be $170 - 2 \times 98.9 = 27.8$.

In Example 4.6, the VaR of the portfolio ($27.8) is bigger than the sum of individual VaRs (2 × $8.9 = $17.8) violating subadditivity, while the ES for the portfolio ($27.8) is smaller than the sum of individual ESs ($41.8) and does not violate subadditivity.

ES shares many advantages with VaR. It is universal and can be applied to almost any instrument and almost any underlying source of risk. It is perhaps an even simpler concept than VaR and any bank that has a VaR-based risk management system could implement ES without much additional effort. At the same time, ES is subadditive while VaR is not.

In spite of this theoretical advantage, in practice the vast majority of financial institutions employ VaR and not ES. Essentially, there are two reasons for this:

1. ES is measured with more uncertainty than VaR. The first step in ES estimation is ascertaining the VaR and the second step is obtaining the expectation of tail observations. This means that there are at least two sources of error in ES.
2. More importantly, ES is much harder to backtest than VaR because the ES procedure requires estimates of the tail expectation to compare with the ES forecast. Therefore, in backtesting, ES can only be compared with the output from a model while VaR can be compared with actual observations.

Many more risk measures have been proposed, with most summarizing the tail in some way or another. Fundamentally, though, a similar comparison could be made between these risk measures, resulting in the same conclusion being reached.

4.6 HOLDING PERIODS, SCALING AND THE SQUARE ROOT OF TIME

4.6.1 Length of holding periods

In practice, the most common holding period is daily, but many other holding periods are in widespread use.

Shorter holding periods are common for risk management on the trading floor where risk managers use hourly, 20-minute and even 10-minute holding periods. The reason is they don't want to see individual traders take on too much risk in a short period of time. The focus here is often on 90% risk. Such intraday modeling of VaR is considerably more difficult than daily risk because we have to take into account intraday patterns in prices requiring high-frequency data feeds, which can be very costly and/or contain mistakes. Furthermore, intraday modeling requires specially trained, and expensive, risk modelers.

Modelling VaR with holding periods exceeding one day is also demanding. Nonetheless, financial institutions often need to obtain multi-day VaR forecasts, mainly because the Basel Accords require financial institutions to model risk using 10–day holding periods.

The reason multi-day VaR forecasting is more difficult than single-day forecasting is we are estimating events that occur rarely. With 1% VaR we only have one observation of the event of interest out of a hundred. Most techniques need at least a few hundred observations to estimate risk accurately. For a 10-day holding period, this means at least 3,000 trading days, or about 12 years.

In some special cases we can use data from 12 years ago (especially for large stock market indices such as the S&P 500), but in most cases such data are fairly useless even if available. For annual VaR we would need at least 300 years, and very few assets have been traded that long. When more extreme probabilities are needed (e.g., 0.1%), data requirements also increase accordingly.

Consequently, in applications requiring long holding periods and/or extreme probabilities, different approaches are called for. The majority of risk managers employ *scaling laws* to obtain such risk levels. Scaling laws are based on the assumption that as observations are added together (e.g., going from daily to multi-day returns under continuous compounding), statistical theory governs how interest properties change as data are added. The best known scaling law is the central limit theorem, which says that the estimated sample mean approaches a normal distribution as the sample size increases. The central limit theorem does not apply to quantiles, such as VaR, where more specialized methods are required.

4.6.2 Square-root-of-time scaling

Suppose we observe an IID random variable $\{X_t\}$ with variable σ^2 over time. The variance of the sum of two consecutive Xs is then:

$$\text{Var}(X_t + X_{t+1}) = \text{Var}(X_t) + \text{Var}(X_{t+1}) = 2\sigma^2.$$

This implies that volatility scales up by $\sqrt{2}$.

> **Definition 4.6 (Square-root-of-time rule)** *Under this rule the statistical measurements of a random variable, such as volatility or VaR, are obtained by multiplying a higher frequency measurement by the square root of the number of observations in the holding period.*

The square-root-of-time rule applies to volatility regardless of the underlying distribution of the data provided returns are IID. It does not apply to VaR unless we make an additional assumption (i.e., that the returns are normally distributed). This result is demonstrated in Section 9.4. Therefore, using the square-root-of-time rule to aggregate VaR is only correct when the returns are IID normal. The problem is we don't know whether the square-root-of-time rule is too high or too low. Daníelsson et al. (1998) and Daníelsson and Zigrand (2006) present conflicting opinions on the matter. For a comprehensive treatment of these topics see Cheng et al. (2010).

Moreover, the aggregation of data over time changes data's dynamic properties. For example, daily data exhibit strong volatility clustering, while monthly data have less clustering. At the same time, the level of clustering depends on the risk level (see Daníelsson and Morimoto, 2000). Overall, accurate calculations of risk for longer holding periods such as 10 days or more require the use of specialist techniques if at all possible.

For these reasons, multi-day VaR forecasts—obtained by scaling up daily VaR using the square-root-of-time rule as a proper multi-day VaR—should not be considered. Instead, it is best to use daily VaR multiplied by a constant. Note that this applies to the 10-day VaR holding periods in the Basel Accords, the 1996 amendment of which explicitly recommends the square-root-of-time approach.

4.7 SUMMARY

The underlying distribution of financial returns is unknown and impossible to identify accurately with current technology. This suggests that the use of *distribution-free* risk measures is the best way to forecast risk in most cases.

In this chapter we have discussed the three most common risk measures: volatility, value-at-risk (VaR) and expected shortfall (ES).

Volatility is the appropriate risk measure as long as returns are normally distributed, a property that rarely holds in practice. Assuming normality of returns and using volatility as a risk measure may be justifiable in many cases; however, in most risk applications it is likely to lead to an underrepresentation of risk. Volatility is the most common risk measure in practical use.

The second most common risk measure is VaR, which often provides the best balance between theoretical strength and feasibility of implementation. Its biggest weakness is the lack of subadditivity for some asset classes, but for most assets VaR remains subadditive.

Finally, ES is the best known subadditive risk measure and is both theoretically and intuitively preferable to VaR. However, severe practical deficiencies prevent its widespread use in real world applications. Not only is it estimated with more uncertainty than VaR, but, even more seriously, backtesting ES requires much larger data samples than backtesting VaR.

An important conclusion from this chapter is that VaR is most relevant for short holding periods, especially one day. As holding periods lengthen, we run into time-scaling problems and the possibility of VaR switching signs. At the other end of the scale, as holding periods get shorter so issues about the intraday dynamics of financial markets become increasingly problematic. Consequently, the preferred holding period is one day, and any other holding period should only be implemented after careful consideration.

5
Implementing risk forecasts

The theoretical discussion of risk measures in Chapter 4 was based on the assumption that the distribution of profit and loss (P/L) was known. However, in practice, one needs to estimate the P/L distribution using historical observations of the asset returns of interest, where different assumptions inevitably lead to different forecasts of risk.

The focus in this chapter is on implementing two of the risk measures discussed in Chapter 4: VaR and ES. The third, volatility, was covered earlier in the book.

There are two main methods for forecasting VaR and ES: nonparametric and parametric. In some special cases we might see a combination of the two. Nonparametric risk forecasting generally refers to historical simulation (HS), which uses the empirical distribution of data to compute risk forecasts. No statistical models are assumed nor are any parameter estimates required for nonparametric methods.

By contrast, parametric methods are based on estimating the underlying distribution of returns and then obtaining risk forecasts from the estimated distribution. For most applications, the first step in the process is forecasting the covariance matrix.

The methods used for forecasting the covariance matrix typically include MA, EWMA or GARCH (as seen in Chapters 2 and 3). They are frequently used with the normal distribution and occasionally with the Student-t, but other conditional distributions may also be used. The parametric approach is often referred to as the variance–
covariance (VCV) method.

In this chapter we only implement risk-forecasting methods, leaving evaluation of the quality of risk forecasts, typically backtesting, to Chapter 8.

The most important specific notation used in this chapter is:

$\gamma(p)$ Significance level as a function of probability

μ Mean

5.1 APPLICATION

We demonstrate implementation of the models presented in this chapter by using two daily stock returns, Microsoft and IBM, from January 1, 2000 to December 31, 2009. These are the same dates as used in Chapter 3 on multivariate volatility; a description on loading the data can be found in Section 3.1.1.

For one of the methods discussed below—historical simulation (HS)—we forecast risk by the $(p \times T)$th observation. Therefore, $p \times T$ needs to be an integer. For example, if the sample size is 250 and we want 1% VaR, we would need to use the 2.5th observation, which of course does not exist. Interpolating between the 2nd and 3rd observations might seem the answer, but unfortunately there is no correct way to do such an interpolation because of the nonlinearity of the distribution. A possible solution is to discard the first 50 observations to obtain a sample size of 200.

Over the time period under consideration we have 2,515 price observations and hence 2,514 returns. To ensure that $p \times T$ is an integer, the first 14 observations are discarded. In R this is done by `y1=tail(y1,T-14)` and in Matlab by `y1=y1(15:end,:)`.

One potential complication that arises in R is that `get.hist.quote()` returns a *time series object*, meaning that each observation is linked to a specific calendar day. So, if we plot the prices in R we will get dates on the *x*-axes. In Matlab we just get the index of the observations. Usually, this does not cause problems and is often an advantage, but unfortunately if a time series object is sorted, the sort order is by date—not size. For historical simulation (HS) we need to sort by size. For this reason we remove the time series information in R with the function `coredata()`.

VaR is denoted in monetary units and we therefore have to specify the size of the portfolio. We opted for $1,000, which is specified by `value = 1000` in the code. Finally, the probability level is set at 1%, or `p = 0.01`. The returns on Microsoft and IBM are in vectors `y1` and `y2`, respectively, with the matrix of both returns `y`. Univariate applications use Microsoft returns. See Section 3.1.1 for more information about the code.

Listing 5.1. Download stock prices in R

```
library("tseries")                    # time series library
                                      # the two prices are downloaded
                                      separately
p1 = get.hist.quote(instrument = "msft",start = "2000-01-01",
    end = "2009-12-31",quote = "AdjClose")
p2 = get.hist.quote(instrument = "ibm", start = "2000-01-01",
    end = "2009-12-31",quote = "AdjClose")
y1=coredata(diff(log(p1)))            # convert prices to returns
y2=coredata(diff(log(p2)))
y1=tail(y1,T-14)                      # length adjustment
y2=tail(y2,T-14)
T = length(y1)
value = 1000                          # portfolio value
y=cbind(y1,y2)                        # combine returns in one matrix
p = 0.01                              # probability
```

Listing 5.2. Download stock prices in Matlab

```
stocks = hist_stock_data('01012000','31122009','msft','ibm')
p1=stocks(1).AdjClose(end:-1:1);
p2=stocks(2).AdjClose(end:-1:1);
y1 = diff(log(p1));    % convert prices to returns
y2 = diff(log(p2));
```

```
y1 = y1(15:end,:);      % length adjustment
y2 = y2(15:end,:);
y = [y1 y2];
T = length(y1)
value = 1000;           % portfolio value
p = 0.01;               % probability
```

For all following listings in this chapter it is assumed that the code above has been run and that all variables in the above code are present.

5.2 HISTORICAL SIMULATION

Historical simulation (HS) is a simple method for forecasting risk and relies on the assumption that history repeats itself, where one of the observed past returns is expected to be the next period return.

Each historical observation carries the same weight in HS forecasting. This can be a disadvantage, particularly when there is a structural break in volatility. However, in the absence of structural breaks, HS tends to perform better than alternative methods. It is less sensitive to the odd outlier and does not incorporate estimation error in the same way as parametric methods. The advantages of HS become especially clear when working with portfolios because it directly captures nonlinear dependence in a way that other methods cannot.

Univariate HS

The VaR at probability p is simply the negative $(T \times p)$th value in the sorted return vector multiplied by the monetary value of the portfolio.

Listing 5.3. Univariate HS in R

```
ys = sort(y1)           # sort returns
op = T*p                # p % smallest
VaR1 = -ys[op]*value    # VaR number
```

Listing 5.4. Univariate HS in Matlab

```
ys = sort(y1);          % sort returns
op = T*p;               % p % smallest
VaR1 = -ys(op)*value    % VaR number
```

Both languages give a `VaR1` value of $64.78.

HS is further illustrated in Figure 5.1 where we show how HS works for an estimation window of 400 days. Panel (a) shows returns along with a solid line identifying the observation corresponding to the 99% VaR. Panel (b) shows sorted returns—from the smallest to the largest—and panel (c) focuses on the 40 most negative observations, where observations corresponding to the 1% and 5% VaR members are specially identified (i.e., the 5th and 25th, respectively).

Multivariate HS

HS is only slightly more complicated in the case of multiple assets. First, form a portfolio of historical returns using current portfolio weights:

$$y_{\text{port}} = \sum_{k=1}^{K} w_k y_k \qquad (5.1)$$

where K is the number of assets in the portfolio; port indicates the portfolio; $y_k = \{y_{t,k}\}_{t=1}^{T}$ is the matrix of returns on asset k; w_k is the weight on asset k; and y_{port} the historical portfolio return vector.

It is neater to use matrix algebra. Let y be the $T \times K$ matrix of historical returns and w the $K \times 1$ matrix of portfolio weights, then (5.1) could be written as:

$$y_{\text{port}} = yw.$$

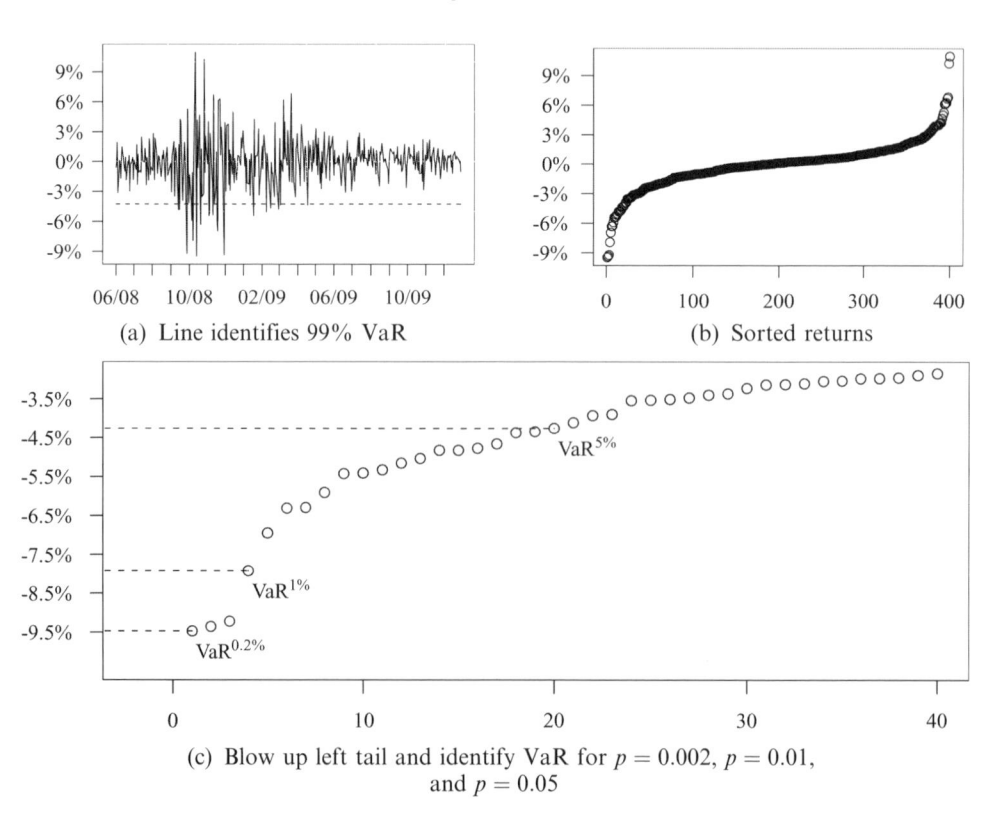

(a) Line identifies 99% VaR

(b) Sorted returns

(c) Blow up left tail and identify VaR for $p = 0.002$, $p = 0.01$, and $p = 0.05$

Figure 5.1. VaR and 400 daily Microsoft returns, 2008–2009.

Listing 5.5. Multivariate HS in R

```
w = matrix(c(0.3,0.7))      # vector of portfolio weights
yp = y %*% w                # obtain portfolio returns
yps = sort(yp)
VaR2 = -yps[op]*value       # VaR number
```

Listing 5.6. Multivariate HS in Matlab

```
w = [0.3; 0.7]              % vector of portfolio weights
yp = y*w;                   % portfolio returns
yps = sort(yp);
VaR2 = -yps(op)*value       % VaR number
```

Here the VaR is $51.10.

5.2.1 Expected shortfall estimation

It is straightforward to obtain expected shortfall (ES) by HS. First, VaR is obtained by HS, then ES is calculated by taking the mean of all observations equal to or more negative than $-$VaR.

The downside to this approach is that the sample size needs to be large. For example, if a sample of 300 observations is used to forecast the 1% VaR, which is the third smallest observation in the sample, then the ES is forecast by taking the mean of the three smallest observations, which is clearly not a large sample. A minimum of 10 observations are recommended to calculate ES with HS, which implies a sample size of 1,000 for 1% ES. It is easy to extend Listings 5.3 and 5.4 to calculate ES.

Listing 5.7. Univariate ES in R

```
ES1 = -mean(ys[1:op]) * value
```

Listing 5.8. Univariate ES in Matlab

```
ES1 = -mean(ys(1:op)) * value
```

Both languages give an `ES1` value of $91.51.

5.2.2 Importance of window size

In the example above we used all 2,500 observations to estimate the VaR. In other words, the estimation window size, W_E, was 2,500. If we had used a smaller window size,

Table 5.1. HS daily VaR at 1% for Microsoft

W_E	VaR forecast for date			
	January 17, 2004	January 12, 2006	January 9, 2008	January 1, 2010
300	$30.2	$12.2	$22.4	$42.3
400	$34.1	$13.6	$20.4	$53.9
600	$36.3	$14.6	$20.1	$37.9
800	$41.5	$20.1	$18.0	$33.7
1,000	$42.5	$29.2	$18.0	$31.4

the VaR forecast most likely would have been different. The VaR corresponds to a particular return, but observations closer to the extremes are more likely to move by larger amounts from one day to the next than observations closer to the center of return distribution; so, the smaller the window size, the bigger the movements in HS.

Bigger window sizes therefore have both advantages and disadvantages. The advantage is that they are less sensitive to one-off extreme observations, while the disadvantage is that VaR forecasts take longer to adjust to structural changes in risk. Furthermore, very old data are unlikely to be representative of current market conditions.

Since we expect the value equaling or exceeding the VaR to change only in one out of every $1/p$ observations, we expect forecast VaR to be constant most of the time. As a general rule, the minimum recommended sample size for HS is $3/p$.

Table 5.1 shows VaR forecasts for four dates spaced 500 days apart and estimation window sizes ranging from 300 to 1,000. Two observations are immediately clear from the table. First, the VaRs are highest for the first and last dates. Second, window size can make a considerable difference to the magnitude of the VaR. In order to make a decision as to the optimal window size, we would need to backtest the model.

Figure 5.2 provides more detailed information for two window sizes, 300 and 1,000 days, from 2006 until the end of 2009. As expected, forecasts from the smaller window size move around a lot more and adjust much more sharply to increasing volatility during the financial crisis. Note how the large volatility cluster in the second part of 2008 takes considerable time to affect the VaR forecasts.

5.3 RISK MEASURES AND PARAMETRIC METHODS

In contrast to nonparametric HS, the first step in parametric methods is estimation of the covariance matrix.

The primary focus in this section is the derivation of VaR and ES given the distributional assumptions that are the most common: normality and the Student-t. For the remainder of this section we assume returns have volatility that is not time varying so that we can drop the time subscript on variance. We demonstrate in the subsequent section how the various conditional volatility models can be used for risk forecasting.

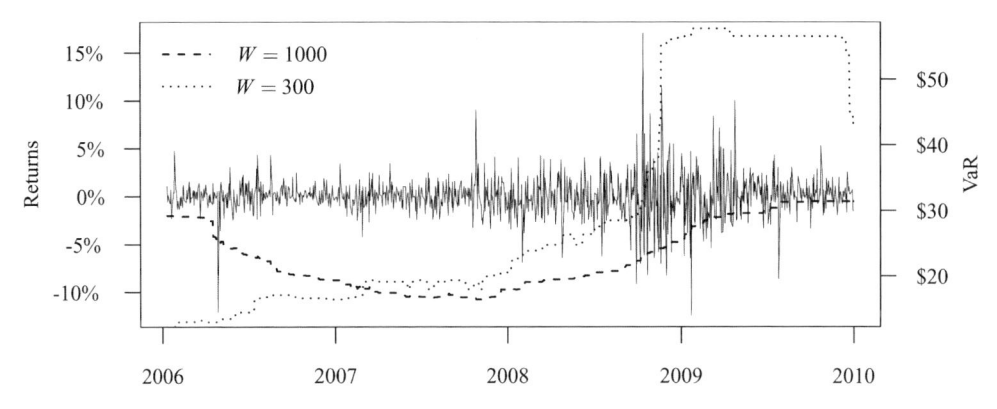

Figure 5.2. HS daily VaR at 1% for Microsoft.

5.3.1 Deriving VaR

Recall the definition of VaR from (4.1) and (4.2):

$$p = \Pr[Q \leq -\text{VaR}(p)]$$
$$= \int_{-\infty}^{-\text{VaR}(p)} f_q(x)dx.$$

where Q is the profit/loss (P/L).

We now turn to deriving the VaR for both the return notions discussed in Chapter 1: simple returns and continuously compounded returns. We start with the former.

VaR for simple returns

We assume initially that we hold one unit of the asset (i.e., the current portfolio value is P_t). We then derive the VaR for simple returns from Definition 1.2:

$$R_t = \frac{P_t - P_{t-1}}{P_{t-1}}$$

where—following the discussion in Section 5.4—we assume mean return is zero. Volatility is indicated by σ. Let us start with the definition of VaR from (4.1):

$$\Pr[Q_t \leq -\text{VaR}(p)] = p.$$

VaR is then obtained from:

$$p = \Pr(P_t - P_{t-1} \leq -\text{VaR}(p))$$
$$= \Pr(P_{t-1}R_t \leq -\text{VaR}(p))$$
$$= \Pr\left(\frac{R_t}{\sigma} \leq -\frac{\text{VaR}(p)}{P_{t-1}\sigma}\right).$$

Let us denote the distribution of standardized returns (R_t/σ) by $F_R(\cdot)$ and the inverse distribution by $F_R^{-1}(p)$. Then it follows that the VaR for holding one unit of the asset is:

$$\text{VaR}(p) = -\sigma F_R^{-1}(p) P_{t-1}.$$

We denote the significance level by $\gamma(p) = F_R^{-1}(p)$, so the VaR equation can be written as
$$\text{VaR}(p) = -\sigma\gamma(p)P_{t-1}. \tag{5.2}$$

VaR for continuously compounded returns

However, if we use the continuously compounded returns from Definition 1.3:
$$Y_t = \log P_t - \log P_{t-1}$$
then
$$p = \Pr(P_t - P_{t-1} \leq -\text{VaR}(p))$$
$$= \Pr(P_{t-1}(e^{Y_t} - 1) \leq -\text{VaR}(p))$$
$$= \Pr\left(\frac{Y_t}{\sigma} \leq \log\left(-\frac{\text{VaR}(p)}{P_{t-1}} + 1\right)\frac{1}{\sigma}\right)$$

since $-\text{VaR}(p)/P_{t-1} \leq 1$. Denoting the distribution of standardized returns (Y_t/σ) by $F_y(\cdot)$ and the inverse distribution by $\gamma(p) = F_y^{-1}(p)$, we have:
$$\text{VaR}(p) = -\left(\exp(F_y^{-1}(p)\sigma) - 1\right)P_{t-1}$$
and for small $F_y^{-1}(p)\sigma$, the VaR for holding one unit of the asset is given by:
$$\text{VaR}(p) \approx -\sigma\gamma(p)P_{t-1}.$$

So, the VaR for continuously compounded returns is approximately the same as the VaR using simple returns (5.2).

VaR when there is more than one asset

This analysis can be easily extended to a multivariate framework. In the two-asset case:
$$\sigma_{\text{port}}^2 = \begin{pmatrix} w_1 & w_2 \end{pmatrix} \begin{pmatrix} \sigma_{11} & \sigma_{12} \\ \sigma_{12} & \sigma_{22} \end{pmatrix} \begin{pmatrix} w_1 \\ w_2 \end{pmatrix}$$
or
$$\sigma_{\text{port}}^2 = w_1^2\sigma_1^2 + w_2^2\sigma_2^2 + 2w_1w_2\rho\sigma_1\sigma_2.$$

Note that $\sigma_{11} = \sigma_1^2$ is the variance and $\sigma_{12} = \rho\sigma_1\sigma_2$ is the covariance. Generally, let w be a $K \times 1$ matrix of portfolio weights and Σ a $K \times K$ covariance matrix, then portfolio variance is:
$$\sigma_{\text{port}}^2 = w'\Sigma w.$$
So, the VaR is:
$$\text{VaR}(p) = -\sigma_{\text{port}}\gamma(p)P_{t-1}.$$

Portfolio value, ϑ

In the discussion above, we held one unit of asset, i.e., the portfolio value is P_{t-1}. More generally, it is better to have notation for an arbitrary portfolio value; in this book we use ϑ.

A more general form of (5.2) is therefore:
$$\text{VaR}(p) = -\sigma\gamma(p)\vartheta \tag{5.3}$$
where dependence on portfolio value is made explicit.

5.3.2 VaR when returns are normally distributed

We did not specify the distribution of returns in the derivations above. Let us suppose returns are (conditionally) normally distributed. The normal distribution is indicated by $\Phi(\cdot)$.

Univariate

Suppose $\vartheta = \$1$ and $\sigma = 1$, where returns are normally distributed. If $p = 0.05$, we get $\text{VaR} = -\Phi^{-1}(0.05) = 1.64$. If σ does not equal one, then the VaR is simply:

$$\text{VaR}^{5\%} = \sigma 1.64$$

and if the portfolio value does not equal one, then:

$$\text{VaR}^{5\%} = \sigma 1.64 \vartheta.$$

We can either look the inverse distribution up in statistical tables to get the quantile from the probability or simply use an R or Matlab function, qnorm(p) and norminv(p), respectively.

The following two listings show how to forecast VaR using (5.3) for the Microsoft returns used in the HS estimation above. We use the sample covariance matrix.

Listing 5.9. Normal VaR in R

```
sigma = sd(y1)                  # estimate the volatility
VaR3 = -sigma * qnorm(p) * value    # calculate the VaR
```

Listing 5.10. Normal VaR in Matlab

```
sigma = std(y1)                 % estimate the volatility
VaR3 = -sigma * norminv(p) * value  % calculate the VaR
```

For both languages, the VaR is $52.70.

Multivariate normal VaR

Multivariate calculations are similarly straightforward to implement; we proceed as in the univariate case.

Listing 5.11. Portfolio normal VaR in R

```
sigma = sqrt(w' %*% cov(y) %*% w)   # portfolio volatility
VaR4 = -sigma * qnorm(p)*value
```

Listing 5.12. Portfolio normal VaR in Matlab

```
sigma = sqrt(w' * cov(y) * w);        % portfolio volatility
VaR4 = -sigma * norminv(p) * value
```

For both languages the VaR is $41.36.

5.3.3 VaR under the Student-t distribution

Let us suppose returns are Student-t distributed with degrees of freedom ν. The advantage of the Student-t over the normal for VaR forecasting is that it is fat tailed, where ν indicates how fat the tails are. When $\nu = \infty$ the Student-t becomes the normal.

Adjusting for variance

The variance implied by ν of a Student-t distribution is given by:

$$\frac{\nu}{\nu-2}. \tag{5.4}$$

The variance of a Student-t-distributed random variable is not defined when $\nu \leq 2$, as is clear from (5.4). The variance of a standard Student-t is not equal to one but the value from (5.4). If we generate data from, say, a $t(4)$, its sample variance will be around 2. If we then used that sample variance in the calculation of VaR along with the inverse $t(4)$ distribution, the VaR would be overestimated. Volatility effectively shows up twice—both in $\gamma(p)$ and $\hat{\sigma}$. Consequently, in that case we need to scale the volatility estimate by ν. Define:

$$\sigma^2 \equiv \frac{\nu}{\nu-2}\tilde{\sigma}^2 \tag{5.5}$$

that is, $\tilde{\sigma}^2$ is the variance in excess of that implied by the standard Student-t.

Estimation

We want to estimate the Student-t parameters for the Microsoft returns used above using a maximum likelihood approach. There is a lower chance of numerical problems in such optimization when the data are scaled so that data volatility is close to one, than if we run the optimization on unscaled returns. Consequently, we pre-multiply the returns by 100, and define a variable `scy1` for the scaled `y1`.

The results from both R and Matlab yield parameter estimates of $\sigma = 1.301$ and $\nu = 2.56$. Since we pre-multiplied the returns by 100, we should divide σ by 100 after estimation.

In R we can use the `fit.st()` function from the `QRMlib` library to estimate ν while `mle()` is the equivalent in Matlab.

Listing 5.13. Student-t VaR in R

```
library(QRMlib)
scy1=(y1)*100                    # scale the returns
res=fit.st(scy1)                 # estimate the distribution
                                   parameters
sigma=res$par.ests[3]/100        # rescale the volatility
nu=res$par.ests[1]               # extract the degrees of
                                   freedom
VaR5 = -sigma * qt(df=nu,p=p) * value    # calculates the VaR
```

Listing 5.14. Student-t VaR in Matlab

```
scy1=y1*100;                              % scale the returns
res=mle(scy1,'distribution','tlocationscale')
sigma = res(2)/100                        % rescale the volatility
nu = res(3)
VaR5 = - sigma * tinv(p,nu) * value       % VaR calculation
```

For R the VaR is $67.94 and for Matlab it is $67.87.

5.3.4 Expected shortfall under normality

The derivation of expected shortfall (ES) is more involved than the derivation of VaR because we need, first, to obtain the VaR and then calculate the conditional expectation.

Recall the definition of expected shortfall (ES) from (4.3):

$$\mathrm{ES} = -\int_{-\infty}^{-\mathrm{VaR}(p)} x f_{\mathrm{VaR}}(x)\,dx.$$

When returns are normally distributed and the portfolio value is one, we have:

$$\mathrm{ES} = \frac{1}{p}\int_{-\infty}^{-\mathrm{VaR}(p)} x \frac{1}{\sqrt{2\pi\sigma^2}} \exp\left[-\frac{1}{2}\frac{x^2}{\sigma^2}\right] dx.$$

Therefore:

$$\mathrm{ES} = \frac{1}{p}\left[-\frac{\sigma^2}{\sqrt{2\pi\sigma^2}} \exp\left[-\frac{1}{2}\frac{x^2}{\sigma^2}\right]\right]_{-\infty}^{-\mathrm{VaR}(p)}$$

that is, the term in brackets only needs to be evaluated at the boundaries. Since the lower bound is zero, and noting that standard normal density is $\phi(x) = \frac{1}{\sqrt{2\pi}} \exp\left[-\frac{x^2}{2}\right]$, we get:

$$\mathrm{ES} = -\frac{\sigma^2 \phi(-\mathrm{VaR}(p))}{p}.$$

If the portfolio value is ϑ we get:

$$\text{ES} = -\vartheta \frac{\sigma^2 \phi(-\text{VaR}(p))}{p}. \tag{5.6}$$

Listings 5.9 and 5.10 can easily be extended to obtain the ES.

Listing 5.15. Normal ES in R

```
ES2 = sigma*dnorm(qnorm(p))/p * value
```

Listing 5.16. Normal ES in Matlab

```
ES2=sigma*normpdf(norminv(p))/p * value
```

For both the ES is $60.37.
We could also use direct integration, which might be useful generally.

Listing 5.17. Direct integration ES in R

```
VaR = -qnorm(p)
integrand = function(q){q * dnorm(q)}
ES = -sigma * integrate(integrand,-Inf,-VaR)$value/p * value
```

Listing 5.18. Direct integration ES in Matlab

```
VaR = -norminv(p)
ES = -sigma * quad(@(q) q.* normpdf(q),-6,-VaR)/p * value
```

Since we cannot specify $-\infty$ in quad in Matlab, we pick a sufficiently negative number, here -6.

5.4 WHAT ABOUT EXPECTED RETURNS?

It is frequently assumed that expected return is zero even if we know that the distribution of returns has a nonzero mean. Is there any justification for assuming $\mu = 0$? Recall Table 1.2, which shows that the daily mean for the S&P 500 was 0.021% and the daily volatility was 1.1% (i.e., volatility is about 50 times larger than the mean). In VaR calculations like (5.3), after we multiply the significance level by the volatility, the volatility component of the equation might be a hundred times larger than the mean component. Given that statistical uncertainty in most VaR calculations is probably more than 10%, the VaR calculation is only significant to one digit and the mean is smaller than that.

Let us start with the VaR definition from (4.1), stated in terms of returns, and assume in the remainder of this subsection that the portfolio value is one:

$$\Pr[(Q + E(Q)) \leq -\text{VaR}(p)] = p.$$

For VaR at probability p, this would mean rewriting (5.3) as:

$$\text{VaR}(p) = -\sigma\gamma(p) - \mu.$$

Under an assumption of IID, both the mean and variance aggregate at the same rates. However, volatility aggregates at the rate of the square root of time. The T-period VaR is therefore:

$$\text{VaR}(T \text{ day}) = -\sigma(T \text{ day})\gamma(p) - \mu(T \text{ day})$$
$$= -\sqrt{T}\sigma\gamma(p) - T\mu. \quad (5.7)$$

Example 5.1 *The daily distribution of an asset return is given by:*

$$Y \sim \mathcal{N}(0.0033, 0.006) \quad (5.8)$$

where returns are assumed to be IID. The annual distribution (assuming 252 trading days) is therefore:

$$Y_{\text{annual}} \sim \mathcal{N}(0.832, 1.512).$$

The daily 1% VaR for a portfolio of value one is:

$$\text{VaR}^{1\%} = 2.33 \times \sqrt{0.006} - 0.0033 \approx 2.33 \times \sigma.$$

The assumption $\mu = 0$ is relatively harmless as the error is small at the daily level. Such an assumption is justified because it simplifies all the calculations and removes the need to specify the mean, which is not a trivial undertaking.

Figure 5.3 shows the impact of including and excluding the mean when calculating VaR using time aggregation—assuming the portfolio value is one, of course. The discrepancy between mean included and mean excluded is not wide below 50 days; for market risk, VaR is usually calculated for a horizon of at most 10 days.

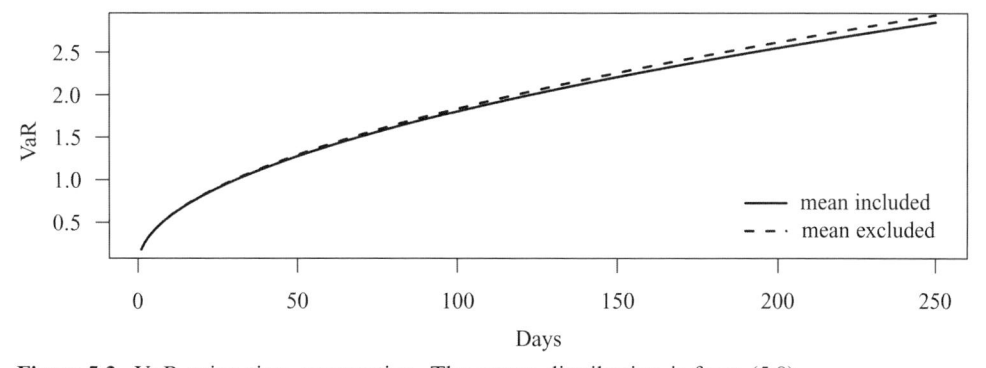

Figure 5.3. VaR using time aggregation. The return distribution is from (5.8).

5.5 VAR WITH TIME-DEPENDENT VOLATILITY

We argued in Chapter 1 that returns exhibit volatility clusters and assumed in Section 5.3 that returns are IID. In the following sections we discuss several alternative implementations of risk forecasting using time-dependent volatility models: moving average (MA), exponentially weighted moving average (EWMA) and GARCH.

5.5.1 Moving average

The easiest way to forecast time-dependent volatility is to use the MA volatility model, and plug the sample variance of data into the analytical formula for VaR (5.3). MA VaR should not be implemented in practice as it provides very poor VaR forecasts.

Let us modify Listings 5.9 and 5.10, indicate the estimation window by W_E—set at 20 days—and forecast VaR for Microsoft for the last 5 days in the sample.

Listing 5.19. MA normal VaR in R

```
WE=20
for (t in seq(T-5,T)){
   t1= t-WE+1
   window = y1[t1:t]     # estimation window
   sigma = sd(window)
   VaR6 = -sigma * qnorm(p) * value
}
```

Listing 5.20. MA normal VaR in Matlab

```
WE=20
for t = T-5:T
   t1 = t-WE+1;
   window = y1(t1:t);    % estimation window
   sigma = std(window);
   VaR6 = -sigma * norminv(p) * value
end
```

We get results for days 2,496 to 2,501 (recall it is a one-day-ahead forecast):

```
VaR(2496) = 24.9
VaR(2497) = 24.7
VaR(2498) = 21.7
VaR(2499) = 21.8
VaR(2500) = 21.4
VaR(2501) = 22.7
```

5.5.2 EWMA

The MA model assumes that each day in the sample gets the same weight, but we can improve volatility forecasts by applying more weight to the most recent dates. This can be done using the EWMA model (3.2) and (3.1):

$$\hat{\sigma}_{t,ij} = \lambda \hat{\sigma}_{t-1,ij} + (1-\lambda) y_{t-1,i} y_{t-1,j},$$

and

$$\hat{\Sigma}_t = \lambda \hat{\Sigma}_{t-1} + (1-\lambda) y'_{t-1} y_{t-1}$$

where $\lambda < 1$ is known as the decay factor (e.g., 0.94). It is straightforward to implement both univariate and multivariate forms of the EWMA model. The main issue that arises relates to initialization of the model.

The volatility on the first day, σ_1, is usually set as the unconditional volatility of the data. About 30 days need to pass, whilst the volatility is updated, before using the volatility forecast. This is sometimes called *burn time*, and takes into account the error induced into the model by setting the value of Σ_1 to an arbitrary value.

Univariate implementation

For a single asset, the EWMA for day T can be calculated by Listings 5.21 and 5.22.

Listing 5.21. EWMA VaR in R

```
lambda = 0.94;           # weight
s11 = var(y1[1:30]);     # initial variance
for (t in 2:T){
   s11 = lambda * s11 + (1-lambda) * y1[t-1]^2
}
VaR7 = -sqrt(s11) * qnorm(p) * value
```

Listing 5.22. EWMA VaR in Matlab

```
lambda = 0.94;
s11 = var(y1(1:30));     % initial variance
for t = 2:T
   s11 = lambda * s11 + (1-lambda) * y1(t-1)^2;
end
VaR7 = -sqrt(s11) * norminv(p) * value
```

The univariate EWMA VaR is $25.27.

Multivariate implementation

Let us combine Listings 5.11 and 5.12 with Listings 5.21 and 5.22. A two-asset case can be given by Listings 5.23 and 5.24.

Listing 5.23. Two-asset EWMA VaR in R

```
s = cov(y)                           # initial covariance
for (t in 2:T) {
    s = lambda * s + (1-lambda) * y[t-1,] %*% t(y[t-1,])
}
sigma = sqrt(t(w) %*% s %*% w)       # portfolio vol
VaR8 = -sigma * qnorm(p) * value
```

Listing 5.24. Two-asset EWMA VaR in Matlab

```
s = cov(y);                          % initial covariance
for t = 2:T
    s = lambda * s + (1-lambda) * y(t-1,:)' * y(t-1,:);
end
sigma = sqrt(w' * s * w);            % portfolio vol
VaR8 = -sigma * norminv(p) * value
```

The bivariate EWMA VaR is $17.48.

5.5.3 GARCH normal

The EWMA model has a very simple structure. The value of the only parameter, λ, is assumed and not estimated. By contrast, the GARCH family of models allows for richer specifications of the dynamic properties of volatilities, while at the same time estimating model parameters for each dataset. Consequently, the GARCH model promises to provide better volatility forecasts—and hence VaR forecasts—than the other parametric models discussed in this chapter.

The GARCH(1,1) model from (2.8) is:

$$\sigma_{t+1}^2 = \omega + \alpha Y_t^2 + \beta \sigma_t^2. \tag{5.9}$$

The most common conditional distribution in the GARCH model is the normal; that is, the shocks Z_t follow the distribution

$$Z_t \sim \mathcal{N}(0, 1)$$

so that returns are given by $Y_t \sim \mathcal{N}(0, \sigma_t^2)$. We denote this model as the normal GARCH.

VaR implementation is the same as in Section 2.6.5, but there are some additional steps to obtain volatility forecasts. When implementing VaR forecasts from a GARCH model, one needs to take the last volatility estimate $\hat{\sigma}_t$ and the parameter vector to obtain the VaR forecast for day $t + 1$. In effect, we have to *manually* calculate $\hat{\sigma}_{t+1}^2$.

Listing 5.26. GARCH in R

```
library(fGarch)
g = garchFit(~garch(1,1),y1,cond.dist = "norm",include.mean =
   FALSE,trace = FALSE)      # parameter estimates
omega = g@fit$matcoef[1,1]
alpha = g@fit$matcoef[2,1]
beta = g@fit$matcoef[3,1]
sigma2 = omega + alpha * y[T]^2 + beta * g@h.t[T]
                             # compute sigma2 for t+1
VaR9 = -sqrt(sigma2) * qnorm(p) * value
```

Listing 5.26. GARCH in Matlab

```
spec = garchset('P', 1, 'Q', 1,'C',NaN,'Display','off');
[parameters, errors, LLF, innovations, ht, summary] =
   garchfit(spec,y1);
omega = parameters.K
alpha = parameters.ARCH
beta = parameters.GARCH
sigma2 = omega + alpha * y1(end)^2 + beta * ht(end)^2
                             % compute sigma2 for t + 1
VaR9 = -sqrt(sigma2) * norminv(p) * value
```

The VaR from R is $30.22, while that from Matlab is $30.21. This discrepancy is simply because GARCH estimation involves numerical maximization, which is only done to a certain numerical precision, so parameter estimates are not completely identical. Were the difference in VaRs much larger than 0.01 it would be a cause for concern.

5.5.4 Other GARCH models

We demonstrated a number of different GARCH-type models in Chapters 2 and 3. It is straightforward to obtain VaR forecasts from those models by combining the implementation in Section 5.5.3 with the listings in those two chapters. All it entails is estimating the model and using the last day's return and volatility along with the model structure and parameters to obtain the one-step-ahead volatility forecast. It makes little difference if the model is univariate or multivariate, normal or Student-t. In every case, the implementation is essentially the same as in Section 5.5.3.

5.6 SUMMARY

This chapter has focused on implementing the risk measures discussed previously in this book, primarily VaR but also ES. We have discussed two categories of estimation methods: nonparametric and parametric.

In nonparametric methods (usually, HS) no model is specified and no parameters estimated; however, we do have to assume a window length for estimation. The advantage of HS is that it uses observed data directly, is not subject to estimation error and can directly capture nonlinear dependence. The disadvantage is that it is based on fixed weights on returns so that it reacts slowly to structural changes in asset risk.

By contrast, parametric methods are based on estimating some distribution of the data, from which a VaR forecast is obtained. This inevitably means that estimation error and model risk become a serious concern, often making the choice of model difficult. Some parametric models perform quite badly, like the moving window method, but other methods have the potential to provide better forecasts, albeit at the expense of increased complexity.

Ultimately, we will need to compare the performance of the various models by backtesting; this is done in Chapter 8.

The focus in this chapter was basic assets. For options and bonds, the first step is usually a volatility forecast, followed by either analytical calculation of VaR or, more typically, Monte Carlo simulation. The following two chapters implement such methods.

6
Analytical value-at-risk for options and bonds

The implementation of value-at-risk (VaR) in Chapter 5 was for assets where we could directly calculate the VaR from the asset distribution. This is not possible in the case of assets such as bonds and options, because their intrinsic value changes with the passing of time.

For example, the price of a bond converges to a fixed value as time to maturity elapses, and therefore its inherent risk decreases. This means that when we observe the same bond over time, we are looking at an asset whose risk characteristics are constantly changing. A 5-year bond is not the same as a 4-year bond. The same applies to options. This means that it is not possible to model risk in such assets directly by the methods discussed so far in Chapters 4 and 5.

The main difficulty arises from the fact that the standard deviation of the returns of a bond or an option cannot be easily estimated, and we have to rely on a transformation—or mapping—from a risk factor like interest rates or stock prices to the risk in the bond or option.

There are two main approaches for such a risk transformation: the analytical methods discussed in this chapter and the Monte Carlo methods discussed in Chapter 7. For most applications the Monte Carlo approach is preferred.

The discussion in this chapter is essentially theoretical, focused on the mathematical derivation and implementation of the various methods. Because the variety of derived assets is almost infinite, it is hard to provide specific examples with real-world data while treating the subject matter comprehensively. Consequently, the approach taken in this chapter is to use a typical, or representative, instrument from which risk is obtained.

The specific notation used in this chapter is:

T	Delivery time/maturity
r	Annual interest rate
σ_r	Volatility of daily interest rate increments
σ_a	Annual volatility of an underlying asset
σ_d	Daily volatility of an underlying asset
τ	Cash flow
D^*	Modified duration
C	Convexity
Δ	Option delta
Γ	Option gamma
$g(\cdot)$	Generic function name for pricing equation

6.1 BONDS

A bond is a fixed income instrument where the bond issuer is obliged to pay interest (the coupon) at regular intervals and repay the principal at the maturity date to the bond holder. The price of a bond is given by the sum of its discounted future cash flows.

We assume in this chapter that the yield curve is flat so that the interest rates, r, for all maturities are the same. The price of a bond, P, is given by the present value of the cash flow, $\{\tau_t\}_{t=1}^T$ (i.e., the coupon payments), where the last payment, τ_T, also includes the principal:

$$P = g(r, t) = \sum_{t=1}^{T} \frac{\tau_t}{(1+r)^t}. \tag{6.1}$$

We denote (6.1) as the bond-pricing equation, $g(\cdot)$, which is a function of both interest rates and time. As we only consider interest rates here, we therefore write it as $g(r)$. The R and Matlab codes to price a bond by (6.1) can be seen in Listings 7.5 and 7.6.

Our interest is in mapping the randomness in interest rates to the risk in a bond. Generally, we would also need to consider the default risk of the bond, but here we assume the bond is issued by a risk-free entity (e.g., certain governments such as the US government).

The main problem in bond risk analysis arises because a *symmetric* change in interest rates results in an *asymmetric* change in bond prices. This is illustrated by Example 6.1.

Example 6.1 *Consider a bond with face value $1,000, a maturity of 50 years and an annual coupon of $30. Assuming we have a flat yield curve with interest rates presently at 3%, then the current price is $484. Consider parallel shifts in the yield curve either to 5% or 1%:*

Interest rate	Price	Change in price
1%	$892	$408
3%	$484	
5%	$319	$165

The change from 3% to 1% makes the bond price increase by $408, while a same magnitude but positive change in interest rates to 5% makes the bond price fall by only $165. A symmetric change in interest rates results in an asymmetric change in bond prices. This is shown graphically in Figure 6.1.

6.1.1 Duration-normal VaR

We need to find a way to approximate the risk in the bond as a function of the risk in interest rates. There are several ways to do this; for example, we could use Ito's lemma, or follow the derivation for options VaR in Section 6.2.2. Regardless of the approach, we would arrive at the same answer. Here we only present the result, as the derivation would just repeat that in Section 6.2.2.

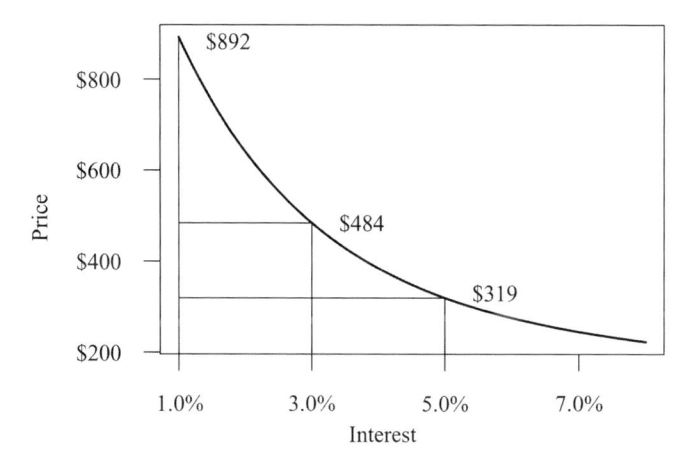

Figure 6.1. Bond convexity in Example 6.1.

A common way to ascertain the sensitivity of bond prices as a function of the sensitivity in interest rates is modified duration, D^*. Start with the bond pricing function from (6.1), $g(r)$, where we consider the impact of a small change in r (i.e., dr). We can then express the impact of the change in r as a function of the first $g'(r)$ derivatives:

$$g(r+dr) \approx g(r) + (dr)g'(r).$$

The negative of the first derivative, $g'(r)$, divided by prices is known as modified duration, D^*, so:

$$D^* = -\frac{1}{P}g'(r)$$

The first step in calculating the VaR for the bond is to identify the distribution of interest rate changes, dr. Here we assume they are given by

$$r_t - r_{t-1} = dr \sim N(0, \sigma_r^2)$$

but we could have used almost any distribution.

The next step is mapping the distribution of dr onto the bond prices. Regardless of whether we use Ito's lemma or follow the derivation in Section 6.2.2, we arrive at the duration-normal method to get bond VaR. Here we find that the bond returns are simply modified duration times the interest rate changes, so the distribution of bond returns is:

$$R_{\text{Bond}} \overset{\text{Approx}}{\sim} N(0, (D^*\sigma_r)^2)$$

The VaR follows directly:

$$\text{VaR}_{\text{Bond}}(p) \approx D^* \times \sigma_r \times \gamma(p) \times \vartheta \qquad (6.2)$$

where the significance level is the inverse normal distribution for probability p, $\gamma(p) = \Phi^{-1}(p)$.

6.1.2 Accuracy of duration-normal VaR

The accuracy of these approximations depends on the magnitude of duration and the VaR time horizon. The main sources of error are the assumptions of linearity and a flat yield curve.

We demonstrate these issues in Figures 6.2 and 6.3. First, Figure 6.2 shows the price–yield relationship for two bonds, both with a face value of $1,000 and coupon payment of $50. The bond in panel (a) has a maturity of one year while the bond in panel (b) has a maturity of 50 years. It is clear from the figure that duration approximation is quite accurate for the short-dated bond while it is very poor for long-dated bonds. For the purpose of VaR calculations using duration-normal methods, maturity is a key factor in calculation accuracy.

The second factor in the accuracy of duration-normal VaR approximation is interest rate change volatility. Figure 6.3 shows the error in duration-normal VaR calculations, measured by the ratio of true VaR—denoted as VaR(true) and calculated using Monte Carlo simulation—to duration-normal VaR, which is denoted as VaR(duration). We let the maturity increase from one year to 60 years while volatility ranged from 0.1% to 2%.

The figure shows that duration-normal VaR approximation is quite good for low volatilities, but quality declines sharply with increasing volatility.

This suggests that the accuracy of duration-normal VaR methods is generally highest for low-maturity, low-volatility bonds.

6.1.3 Convexity and VaR

It is conceptually straightforward to improve the duration approximation by also incorporating a second-order term (i.e., convexity). In this case the interest rate change, dr, appears twice, the second time squared. This means that even if dr is normally distributed, R_{bond} is not. The distribution of $(dr)^2$ is the chi–squared, and it would be straightforward to derive a VaR equation with convexity.

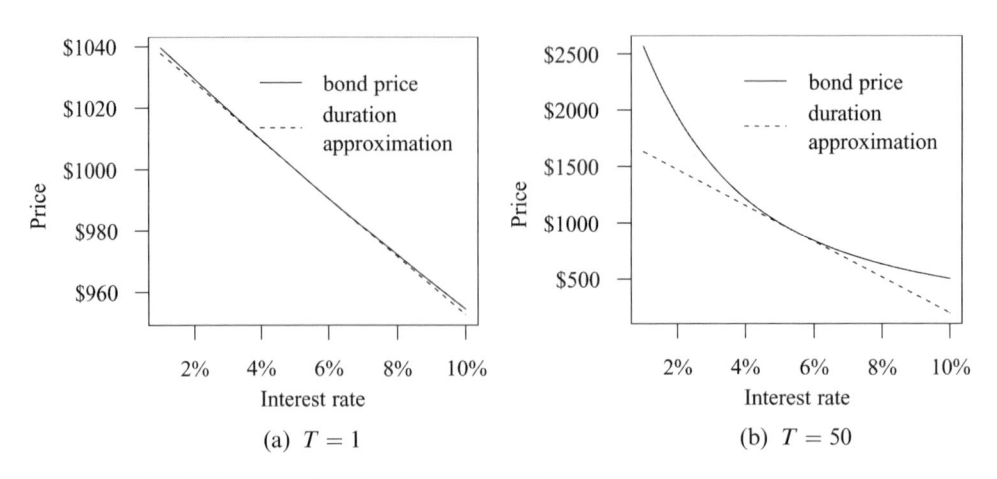

(a) $T = 1$

(b) $T = 50$

Figure 6.2. Bond prices and duration for two maturities.

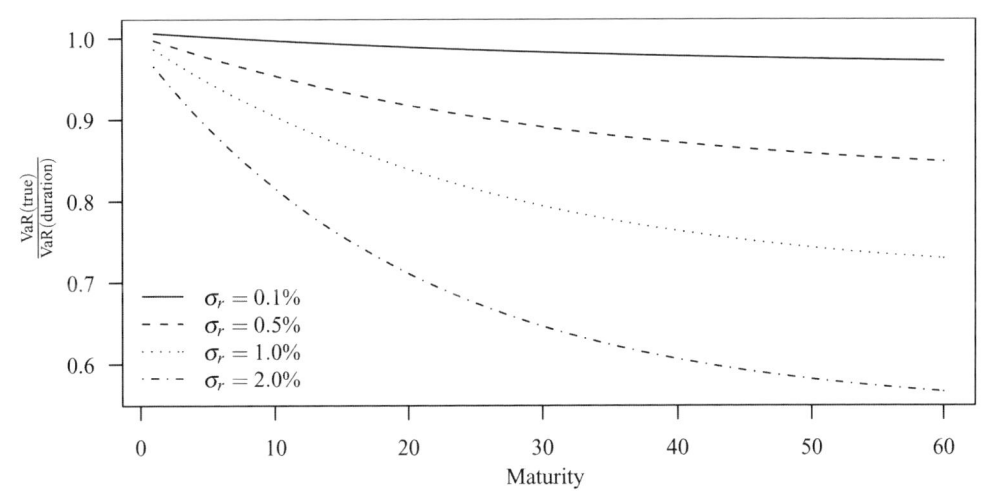

Figure 6.3. Error in duration-normal VaR for various volatilities.

As a practical matter, even incorporating convexity can leave considerable bias in VaR calculations. We could of course incorporate even higher order terms. This would, however, further increase mathematical complexity. In addition, if we have a portfolio of bonds, the presence of these nonlinear transformations of the normal distribution is likely to make the calculation of portfolio VaR very cumbersome. For this reason, the Monte Carlo methods in Chapter 7 are generally preferred.

6.2 OPTIONS

An option gives the owner the right but not the obligation to buy (call) or sell (put) an underlying asset at a fixed date in the future known as the expiry date at a predetermined price called the strike price.

European options can only be exercised at the expiry date, while American options can be exercised at any point up to the expiry date at the discretion of the holder. Here we focus on the simplest options (i.e., European), but the basic analysis can be extended to many other variants.

European options can be priced using the Black and Scholes (1973) equation:

$$\text{put}_t = Xe^{-r(T-t)} - P_t + \text{call}_t$$

$$\text{call}_t = P_t\Phi(d_1) - Xe^{-r(T-t)}\Phi(d_2)$$

where

$$d_1 = \frac{\log(P_t/X) + (r + \sigma_a^2/2)(T-t)}{\sigma_a\sqrt{T-t}}$$

$$d_2 = \frac{\log(P_t/X) + (r - \sigma_a^2/2)(T-t)}{\sigma_a\sqrt{T-t}} = d_1 - \sigma_a\sqrt{T-t}$$

where P_t is the price of the underlying asset at time t, which is measured in years; X is the strike price; r is the annual risk-free interest rate; $T - t$ is the time until expiration; σ_a is the annual volatility of the underlying asset; and Φ is the standard normal distribution. We refer to the pricing function by the function name $g(\cdot)$ and use the term g to denote both a call and a put.

The Black–Scholes (BS) equation is often stated using S for prices and K for strike prices, but since these letters are used for other variables in this book, we have opted to use P for prices and X for strike prices.

The value of an option is affected by many underlying factors. Nevertheless, under standard BS assumptions, the underlying asset has continuous IID-normal returns, with a flat nonrandom yield curve; so, for VaR the only risk factor that matters is P. The risk in all the other variables can be ignored.

The objective then is to map the risk in the underlying asset onto an option (i.e., the risk in P). This can be done using the option delta and gamma.

Delta

The first-order sensitivity of an option with respect to the underlying price is called delta, which is defined as:

$$\Delta = \frac{\partial g(P)}{\partial P} = \begin{cases} \Phi(d_1) > 0 & \text{call} \\ \Phi(d_1) - 1 < 0 & \text{put.} \end{cases}$$

Delta is equal to ± 1 for deep in-the-money options, depending on whether it is a call or a put, close to ± 0.5 for at-the-money options and 0 for deep out-of-the-money options.

For small changes in P, the option price will change approximately by Δ. The approximation is reasonably good for asset prices close to the price at which delta was calculated, but it gets gradually worse for prices that deviate significantly from that price (as Figure 6.4 illustrates).

Figure 6.4 shows the price of a call option for a range of strike prices. Both panels show the price at expiration, while panel (a) shows the price one month to expiration and panel (b) the price six months to expiration. In both panels we calculate delta when the option is at the money and show the tangent at that point. Delta approximation is more accurate for longer maturity options and when the option is deep in or out of the money.

Gamma

The second-order sensitivity of an option with respect to the price is called gamma, which is defined as:

$$\Gamma = \frac{\partial^2 g}{\partial P^2} = e^{-r(T-t)} \frac{\phi(d_1)}{P_t \sigma_a \sqrt{(T-t)}}.$$

Gamma for the option payoff in panel (a) of Figure 6.4 can be seen in Figure 6.5. Note that gamma is highest when an option is a little out of the money, and dropping as the underlying price moves away from the strike price. This is not surprising since the price plot increasingly becomes a straight line for deep in-the-money and out-of-the-money options.

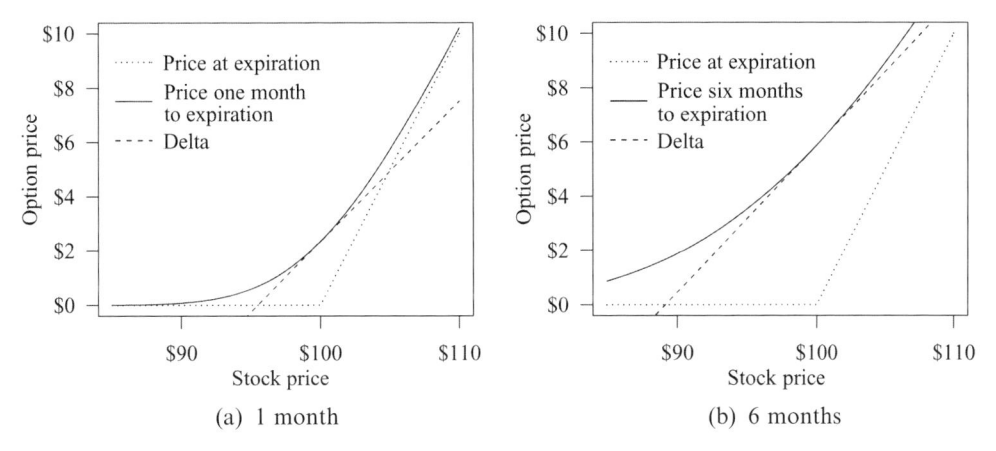

Figure 6.4. Call option and delta. $X = 100$, $r = 0.01$, $\sigma = 0.2$.

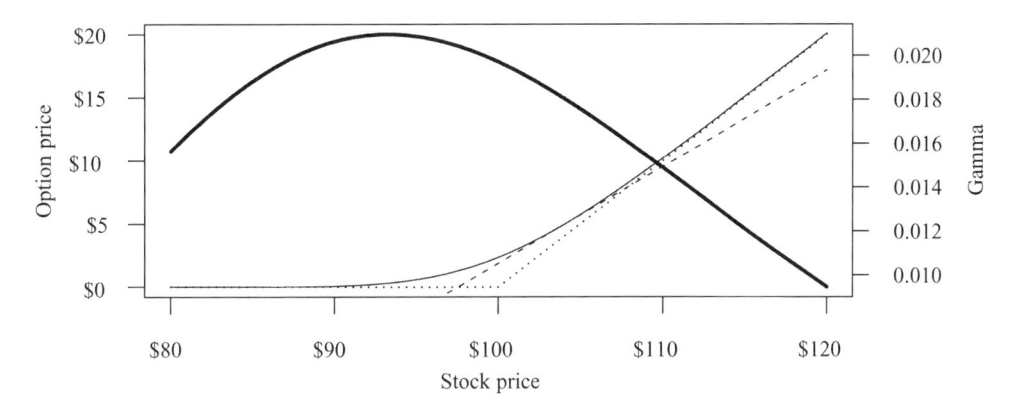

Figure 6.5. Gamma for the option payoff in panel (a) of Figure 6.4.

6.2.1 Implementation

We implement the Black–Scholes equation and calculation of delta and gamma as a function in R and Matlab called bs. This function takes (X, P, r, sigma, T) as arguments and returns a structure that holds the call and put prices as well as delta and gamma. In R this is done by the list command and in Matlab by creating a structure.

Listing 6.1. Black–Scholes function in R

```
bs = function(X, P, r, sigma, T){
    d1 = (log(P/X) + (r + 0.5 * sigma^2)*(T))/(sigma * sqrt(T))
    d2 = d1 - sigma * sqrt(T)

    Call = P * pnorm(d1, mean = 0, sd = 1) - X * exp(-r * (T)) * pnorm(d2,
```

118   Analytical value-at-risk for options and bonds

```
    mean = 0, sd = 1)
Put = X * exp(-r *(T)) * pnorm(-d2, mean = 0, sd = 1) - P * pnorm(-d1,
    mean = 0, sd = 1)

Delta.Call = pnorm(d1, mean = 0, sd = 1)
Delta.Put = Delta.Call - 1
Gamma = dnorm(d1, mean = 0, sd = 1)/(P * sigma * sqrt(T))

return(list(Call = Call, Put = Put, Delta.Call = Delta.Call,
    Delta.Put = Delta.Put, Gamma = Gamma))
}
```

Listing 6.2. Black–Scholes function in Matlab

```
function res = bs(K,P,r,sigma,T)
    d1 = (log(P./K)+(r+(sigma^2)/2) * T)./(sigma * sqrt(T));
    d2 = d1 - sigma * sqrt(T);
    res.Call = P.* normcdf(d1,0,1)-K.* exp(-r*T).* normcdf(d2,0,1);
    res.Put = K.* exp(-r*T).* normcdf(-d2,0,1)-P.*
        normcdf(-d1,0,1);
    res.Delta.Call = normcdf(d1,0,1);
    res.Delta.Put = res.Delta.Call -1;
    res.Gamma = normpdf(d1,0,1)./(P * sigma * sqrt(T));
end
```

By using the element-by-element operators ./ and .* we can pass a vector to the function in Matlab.

We demonstrate how to use this code in Listings 6.3 and 6.4 where the strike price is 90, the price is 100, the risk-free rate is 5%, volatility is 20% and expiry is half a year.

Listing 6.3. Black–Scholes in R

```
source('bs.r')
f = bs(90,100,0.05,0.2,0.5)
> f
$Call
[1] 13.49852
$Put
[1] 1.276410
$Delta.Call
[1] 0.8395228
$Delta.Put
[1] -0.1604772
$Gamma
[1] 0.01723826
```

Listing 6.4. Black–Scholes in R

```
>> f = bs(90,100,0.05,0.2,0.5)
f =
   Call:     13.4985
   Put:      1.2764
   Delta:    [1x1 struct]
   Gamma:    0.0172
>> f.Delta
ans =
   Call:      0.8395
   Put:      -0.1605
```

6.2.2 Delta-normal VaR

We can use delta to approximate changes in the option price as a function of changes in the price of the underlying.

Let us denote the daily change in stock prices as:

$$dP = P_t - P_{t-1}.$$

The price change dP implies that the option price will change approximately by

$$dg = g_t - g_{t-1} \approx \Delta dP = \Delta(P_t - P_{t-1}),$$

where Δ is the option delta at time $t-1$; and g is either the price of a call or put.

The simple returns on the underlying are as in Definition 1.2:

$$R_t = \frac{P_t - P_{t-1}}{P_{t-1}}.$$

Following the BS assumptions, the returns are IID-normally-distributed:

$$R_t \sim N(0, \sigma_d^2)$$

with daily volatility σ_d. The derivation of the VaR for options parallels the VaR derivation for simple returns in Section 5.3.1.

Let us denote the VaR on the option by $\text{VaR}_o(p)$, where p is probability:

$$\begin{aligned}
p &= \Pr(g_t - g_{t-1} \leq -\text{VaR}_o(p)) \\
&= \Pr(\Delta(P_t - P_{t-1}) \leq -\text{VaR}_o(p)) \\
&= \Pr(\Delta P_{t-1} R_t \leq -\text{VaR}_o(p)) \\
&= \Pr\left(\frac{R_t}{\sigma_d} \leq -\frac{1}{\Delta}\frac{\text{VaR}_o(p)}{P_{t-1}\sigma_d}\right).
\end{aligned}$$

The distribution of standardized returns (R_t/σ_d) is the standard normal, $\Phi(\cdot)$, so the significance level is given by $\gamma(p) = F_R^{-1}(p)$. Then, it follows that the VaR for holding an option on one unit of the asset is:

$$\text{VaR}_o(p) \approx -|\Delta| \times \sigma_d \times \gamma(p) \times P_{t-1}.$$

This means that the option VaR is simply delta multiplied by the VaR of the underlying, VaR_u:

$$VaR_o(p) \approx |\Delta|VaR_u(p).$$

We need the absolute value of Δ because we may either have put or call options, while VaR is always positive.

The quality of the approximation here depends on the extent of nonlinearities, which are a function of the type of option, their maturities, the volatility of underlying market factors and the VaR horizon. The shorter the VaR horizon, the better delta-normal approximation is. For risk management purposes, poor approximation of delta to the true option price for large changes in the price of the underlying is clearly a cause of concern.

6.2.3 Delta and gamma

We can also approximate the option price by the second-order expansion, Γ. While dP is normal, $(dP)^2$ is not normal, but chi-squared. This means the same issues apply here as for the bonds in Section 6.1.4.

6.3 SUMMARY

VaR forecasting for assets such as options and bonds is much more complicated than VaR forecasting for basic assets like stocks and foreign exchange. We need to employ a two-step process: first, model the underlying risk factor and, then, use the pricing equation and a function expansion to obtain the VaR for the option or bond.

In the cases discussed in this chapter, where we only have one derived asset, the mathematical complexity is not very high, but the accuracy of the approximations is still low in many cases. To obtain higher accuracy the mathematics become much more complicated, and in a portfolio situation more complicated still. Expansions have to be derived for each different type of asset, which is tedious and prone to errors. For these reasons, in most practical applications the Monte Carlo approaches discussed in the next chapter are preferred.

7
Simulation methods for VaR for options and bonds

The limitations of the analytical VaR methods discussed in the last chapter, together with advances in computing power, have made Monte Carlo simulation the method of choice for VaR forecasting for portfolios containing assets like options and bonds.

Numerical methods that make use of random numbers are called Monte Carlo (MC) simulation methods—after the city state with the well-known casinos. The terms Monte Carlo and simulations are used interchangeably, either together or separately.

The idea behind MC simulations is that we replicate market outcomes on the computer, based on some model of the evolution of the market. By doing a sufficient number of simulations, we get a large sample of market outcomes enabling us to calculate accurately some quantities of interest, such as option prices, bond prices or VaR. This works because the object of interest (e.g., the price of an option or VaR) is based on a mathematical expectation of an underlying statistical process. If we observe a sufficiently large sample from the statistical process and calculate the average, we can then arrive at a number that approximately equals the mathematical expectation.

There are two important limitations to this approach. First, it is always based on some model and the quality of the results is inevitably limited by the quality of the model. Second, we often need a very large simulation size to do the calculations accurately, in some cases resulting in significant computation time. However, in the applications in this chapter, the computation should take no more than a couple of seconds.

Creating a large sample of high-quality *random numbers* (RNs) is a demanding task. In the past, RNs were generated by drawing numbers out of a hat, an approach only feasible for very small applications. Now computers use an algorithm known as a *pseudo random number generator* (RNG) to create outcomes that appear to be random.

The notation used in this chapter will become more cluttered than the notation in other chapters because here we have to denote variables by time period, asset and simulation while in other chapters we need no more than the first two. The first subscript is time, followed by asset and then simulation. For example:

$$X_{\text{time,asset,simulation}} = X_{t,k,s}.$$

We may skip one or more subscripts when there is only one asset or the quantity is not simulated.

We assume in this chapter that the covariance matrix of returns is known and that returns are normally distributed.

The specific notation used in this chapter is:

F Futures price

g Derivative price

S Number of simulations

x^b Portfolio holdings (basic assets)

x^o Portfolio holdings (derivatives)

7.1 PSEUDO RANDOM NUMBER GENERATORS

The fundamental input into MC analysis is a long sequence of random numbers (RNs). A deterministic machine such as a computer uses a *pseudo random number generator* (RNG) to produce numbers that, for all practical purposes, are random.

RNGs generally create *integer* numbers between 0 and some large number from the uniform distribution. The length of the sequence of unique RNs is called a period, and if we generate more RNs than the period the numbers repeat themselves.

They are usually generated by a function like $u_{i+1} = h(u_i)$, where u_i represents the ith RN and $h(\cdot)$ is the RNG, so that the next random number is a function of the previous random number.

Definition 7.1 (Period of a random number generator) *Random number generators can only provide a fixed number of different random numbers, after which they repeat themselves. This fixed number is called a period.*

Building high-quality RNGs is a formidable task. While it is easy to create an algorithm that generates something resembling a random number, getting that number to be properly random is quite difficult. It is essential that the unconditional distribution of random numbers be IID-uniform. Symptoms of low-quality RNGs include a low period, serial dependence or subtle deviations from the uniform distribution.

7.1.1 Linear congruental generators

No numerical algorithm can generate a truly random sequence of numbers; nonetheless, algorithms exist that generate repeating sequences of integers that are, to a fairly good approximation, randomly distributed within a range. The best known RNGs are the so-called *linear congruental generators* (LCGs), where the formula linking the ith and $(i+1)$th integer in the sequence of RNs is given by:

$$u_{i+1} = (a \times u_i + c) \bmod m \quad (7.1)$$

where a is known as the multiplier; c is the increment; m is the modulus where all are integers; and mod is the modulus function (i.e., the remainder after division).

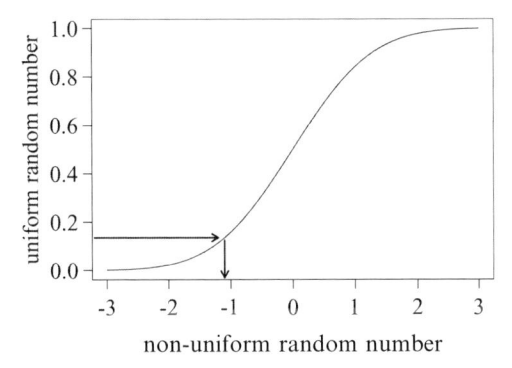

Figure 7.1. Normal inverse distribution.

The first random number in the sequence is called the *seed*, usually chosen by the user. It is good practice when doing simulation estimation to set the seed to a fixed value prior to estimation. This ensures that we always get the same sequence of random numbers and hence the same estimation outcome.

Serial correlation is generally the main flaw of LCGs and cannot be easily eliminated. As a result, more complicated RNGs, which introduce nonlinearities, are generally preferred. The default RNG in R and Matlab is the Mersenne twister.[1] Its name comes from the fact it has a period of $2^{19,937} - 1$, a Mersenne prime number. RNGs with a bigger period do exist, but they are much slower.

7.1.2 Nonuniform RNGs and transformation methods

Most RNGs generate uniform random numbers, (u), which in most cases are scaled to be in the interval $[0, 1]$ while most practical applications require random numbers drawn from a different distribution. Transformation methods convert the uniform (i.e., uniform number) into an RN drawn from the distribution of interest. The inverse distribution is the obvious candidate for such a transformation, although this approach is not recommended since such transformations are often slow and not very accurate, particularly for the tails.

For an example of an inverse distribution see Figure 7.1, which shows how the inverse distribution can be used to transform a uniform (on the y-axis) onto some other distribution (on the x-axis). The figure is easily created in R and Matlab (see Listings 7.1 and 7.2).

Listing 7.1. Transformation in R

```
x = seq(-3,3,by = 0.1)
plot(x,pnorm(x),type = "l")
```

---

[1] The Mersenne twister is a pseudorandom number generator developed by Matsumoto and Nishimura whose name derives from the period being Mersenne prime. See http://www.math.sci.hiroshima-u.ac.jp/~m-mat/MT/emt.html for more information.

Listing 7.2. Transformation in Matlab

```
x = -3:0.1:3;
plot(x,normcdf(x))
```

The most common method for generating normal random numbers is the *Box–Muller method*. It was developed as a more computationally efficient alternative to the inverse distribution method. If we generate two uniforms (u_1, u_2) then we can transform this pair into a pair of IID normals (n_1, n_2) by:

$$n_1 = \sqrt{-2\log u_1} \sin(2\pi u_2)$$
$$n_2 = \sqrt{-2\log u_1} \cos(2\pi u_2).$$

The Box–Muller method is elegant, reasonably fast and fine for casual computations, but it may not be the best method. In some circumstances the two normals are not fully independent, which becomes apparent in the extreme tails.

We generally do not need to worry about transformation methods as both R and Matlab provide a range of RNGs and transformation methods in the same function. For example, Listings 7.3 and 7.4 show the R and Matlab code to generate 10 random numbers from a uniform, a normal and a Student-$t(4)$. Note that each time the code is run it will generate different answers unless we set the seed first. Also R and Matlab will not provide the same RNs.

Listing 7.3. Various RNs in R

```
set.seed(12)         # the seed
S = 10
runif(S)
rnorm(S)
rt(S,4)
```

Listing 7.4. Various RNs in Matlab

```
randn('state',12);   % the seed
S = 10
rand(S,1)
randn(S,1)
trnd(4,S,1)
```

7.2 SIMULATION PRICING

There are several methods available to price assets such as options and bonds. For relatively simple assets we can use an analytical solution (e.g., the present value formula for a standard nondefaultable bond and the Black–Scholes model for a European option). More complicated derivatives are commonly priced with MC simulations.

The theory underlying the simulation approach is that the price of an asset is the expectation taken under risk neutrality of its final payoff function. The payoff of a derivative depends on the price movements of its underlying asset. Therefore, if we simulate a sufficient number of price paths of the underlying, we can often obtain a very good estimate of the true price.

7.2.1 Bonds

The price and risk of fixed income assets, such as bonds, is based on market interest rates. By using a model of the distribution of interest rates, we can simulate random yield curves from that model and use them to obtain the distribution of bond prices. In other words, we map the distribution of interest rates on to the distribution of bond prices.

Pricing

We indicate annual interest rates by r_j (i.e., the zero-coupon rate used to discount a payment received at time j in the future). We can use a modified pricing equation (6.1), when we *do not* assume the yield curve is flat (i.e., that all r are the same):

$$P = \sum_{j=1}^{T} \frac{\tau_j}{(1+r_j)^j},$$

where P is the price of the bond; and τ_j is the cash flow from the bond, including the par value in τ_T.

Suppose we have a bond with 10 years to expiration, a par value of $10, and annual interest of 7%, where the current market interest rates are $\{r_t\} = (5.00, 5.69, 6.09, 6.38, 6.61, 6.79, 6.94, 7.07, 7.19, 7.30) \times 0.01$.

The code to price the bond is given in Listing 7.5 for R and Listing 7.6 for Matlab.

Listing 7.5. Price bond in R

```
yield = c(5.00,5.69,6.09,6.38,6.61,6.79,6.94,7.07,7.19,7.30)
                                           # yield curve
T = length(yield)
r = 0.07                                   # initial yield rates
Par = 10                                   # par value
coupon = r * Par                           # coupon payments
cc = 1:10 * 0 + coupon                     # vector of cash flows
cc[10] = cc[10] + Par                      # add par to cash flows
P = sum(cc/((1 + yield/100)^(1:T)))        # calculate price
```

Note that all three vectors—yield, cash flow and time—need to have the same dimensions in Matlab.

Listing 7.6. Price bond in Matlab

```
yield = [5.00 5.69 6.09 6.38 6.61 6.79 6.94 7.07 7.19 7.30];
                                   % initial yield curve
T = length(yield);
r = 0.07;                          % initial yield
Par = 10;                          % par value
coupon = r * Par;                  % coupon payments
cc = zeros(1,T)+coupon;            % vector of cash flows
cc(10) = cc(10)+Par;               % add par to cash flows
P = sum(cc./((1+yield./100).^(1:T)))   % calculate price
```

We get the current value of the bond as $9.91 in both R and Matlab.

Simulation

We now make a simplifying assumption that the yield curve is restricted so that it can only shift up and down, not change shape. This simplifies the implementation below; however, one would generally want to allow yield to change shape as well.

Changes in yields, ϵ_i, are normally distributed with standard deviation, σ; that is,

$$\epsilon_i \sim N(0, \sigma^2).$$

Figure 7.2 shows eight simulated yield curves with the initial, or true, curve the one in Listings 7.5 and 7.6.

The following R and Matlab code demonstrates how we can do the simulation. Note that for the figure to be legible, it is necessary to keep the number of simulations, S, quite small, while to actually calculate prices by simulations it needs to be much larger.

In both listings we set the seed before the simulation. The matrix of simulated yields is ysim. Figure 7.2 shows eight simulated yield curves, simply obtained by setting S=8 and plotting ysim. See the last line of Listings 7.7 and 7.8 for the plot command.

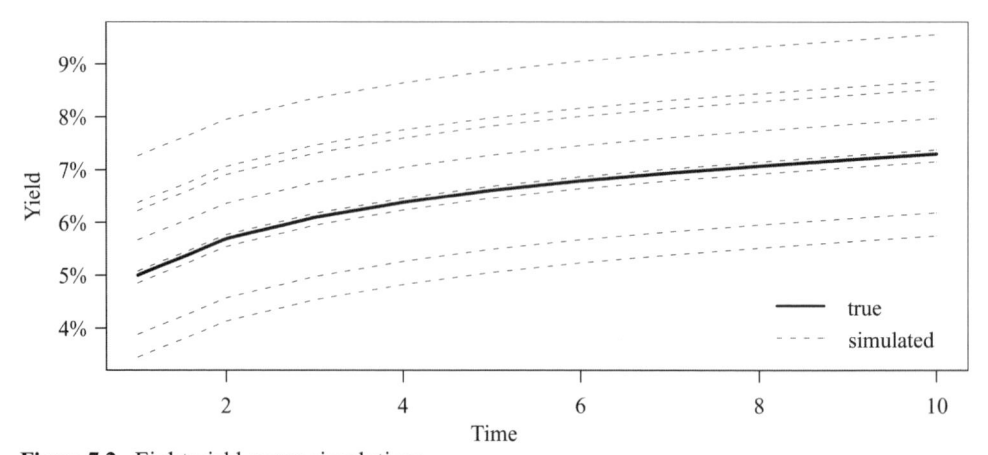

Figure 7.2. Eight yield curve simulations.

There are at least two different methods to get ysim: a loop over each simulated yield curve, or a more complicated statement which calculates ysim with built-in matrix operators, where the vector of yields and random numbers is duplicated S times into a matrix. This is done for the yields in R as matrix(matrix(y,T,S),ncol=S) and repmat(yield,1,S) in Matlab. We show both the loop method and the matrix approach in the code.

Listing 7.7. Simulate yields in R

```
set.seed(12)              # set seed
sigma = 1.5               # daily yield volatility
S = 8                     # number of simulations
r = rnorm(S,0,sigma)      # generate random numbers
                          # There are 2 ways to get matrix of simulated
                            yields in a loop
ysim = matrix(nrow = T,ncol = S)
for (i in 1:S) ysim[,i] = yield+r[i]
                          # this way is likely to be much faster
ysim = matrix(matrix(yield,T,S),ncol=S) + matrix(t(matrix(r,S,T)),
   ncol=S)
matplot(ysim,type = 'l')
```

Listing 7.8. Simulate yields in Matlab

```
S = 8                         % number of simulations
sigma = 1.5                   % daily yield volatility
randn('state',123);           % set the seed
r = randn(1,S)* sigma;        % generate random yield changes in a loop
ysim=nan(T,S);
for i = 1:S
   ysim(:,i) = yield + r(i);
end
ysim = repmat(yield',1,S) + repmat(r,T,1);
                              % get matrix of random yields
plot(ysim)
```

The pricing equation is similar to (6.1). The ith simulated price, P_i, is the present value of cash flows, using simulated interest rates ϵ_i:

$$P_i = \sum_{j=1}^{T} \frac{\tau_j}{(1+r_j+\epsilon_i)^i}, \quad i = 1,\ldots,S$$

where $r_j + \epsilon_i$ is the ith simulated interest rate at time j.

After simulating the prices, they are plotted in Figure 7.3 with the histogram of prices in Figure 7.4, where S=50000, along with the normal distribution with the same mean

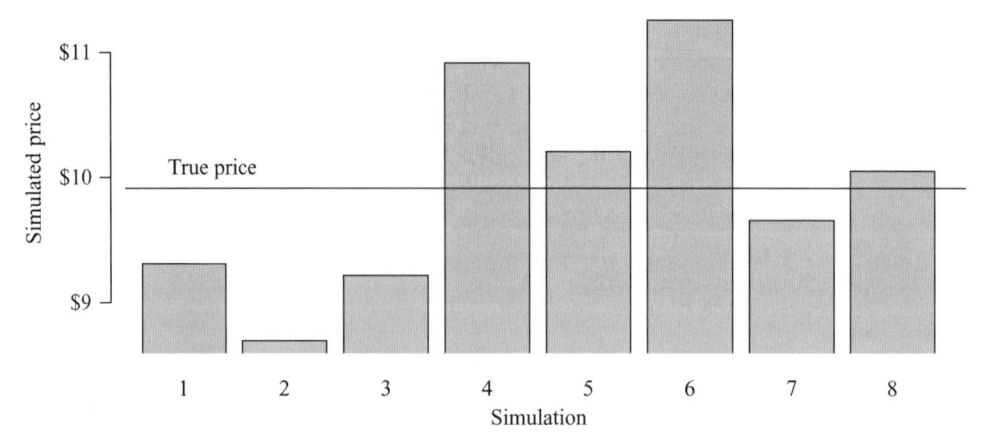

128   Simulation methods for VaR for options and bonds

Figure 7.3. Eight bond simulations with yields from Figure 7.2.

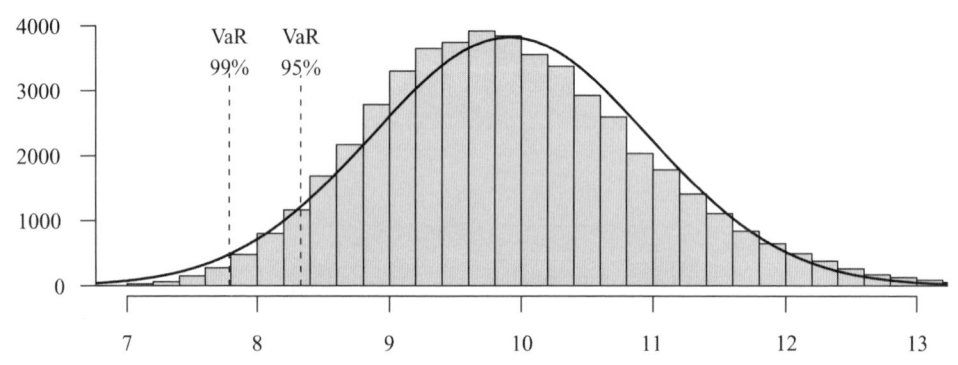

Figure 7.4. Distribution of 50,000 bond simulations, with the normal distribution superimposed.

and variance as the simulated prices. Note the slight asymmetry in the simulated distribution.

The relevant plot commands are indicated in the code. Simulated prices are indicated by SP.

Listing 7.9. Simulate bond prices in R

```
SP = vector(length = S)
for (i in 1:S) {                # S simulations
    SP[i] = sum(cc/((1 + ysim[,i]/100)^(T)))
}
SP = SP - (mean(SP) - P)        # correct for mean

barplot(SP)                     # Figure 7.3
                                # next 3 lines to make Figure 7.4
hist(SP, probability = TRUE)
x = seq(6, 16, length = 100)
lines(x, dnorm(x, mean = mean(SP), sd = sd(SP)))
```

Listing 7.10. Simulate bond prices in Matlab

```
SP = nan(S,1);            % vector for sim prices
for s = 1:S               % do S simulations
   SP(s) = sum(cc./(1 + ysim(:,s)'./100).^((1:T)));
end
SP = SP - (mean(SP) - P); % correct for mean
bar(SP)                   % Figure 7.3
histfit(SP)               % Figure 7.4
```

Allowing the yield curve to change shape

In the application above, we made the simplifying assumption that the yield curve can only shift up and down, where the random shock was normally distributed. This is unrealistic in practice, as yield curves do change shape over time, and the distribution of interest rate changes may not be the normal.

It would be relatively straightforward to modify the approach above to incorporate such effects. For example, if we want to allow the yield curve to change shape, it might be useful to use principal components analysis (PCA) and simulate the first two or three principal components in the simulation. This would provide an efficient way to model the dynamics of the yield curve.

7.2.2 Options

We want to use MC to obtain the price of a European option on a non-dividend-paying stock, where all of the Black–Scholes (BS) assumptions hold.

There are two primitive assets in the BS pricing model. A money market account whose value appreciates at the risk-free rate and the underlying stock which follows a normally distributed random walk with drift r (i.e., the annual risk-free rate). The latter is called geometric Brownian motion when in continuous time, which is one of the underlying assumptions in the Black–Scholes equation.

The no-arbitrage futures price of stock for delivery at time T, at the annual risk-free rate r, is given by:

$$F = Pe^{rT}.$$

Analytical pricing

We use a European call option as an example below, where the current stock price is $50, annual volatility is 20%, the annual risk-free rate is 5%, there are 6 months to expiration and the strike price is $40.

We use results from the analytical calculations in Listings 6.1 and 6.2 for comparison with the Monte Carlo results below; it is assumed that files containing the code are present under filenames `bs.r` and `bs.m` for R and Matlab, respectively.

Listing 7.11. Black–Scholes valuation in R

```
source('bs.r')              # input the Black Scholes pricing function
P0 = 50                     # initial spot price
sigma = 0.2                 # annual volatility
r = 0.05                    # annual interest
T = 0.5                     # time to expiration
X = 40                      # strike price
f = bs(X,P0,r,sigma,T)      # analytical call price
```

Listing 7.12. Black–Scholes valuation in Matlab

```
P0 = 50;                    % initial spot price
sigma = 0.2;                % annual volatility
r = 0.05;                   % annual interest
T = 0.5;                    % time to expiration
X = 40;                     % strike price
f = bs(X,P0,r,sigma,T);     % analytical price
```

The price of the call is $11.0873 in both R and Matlab.

Monte Carlo

We first simulate the returns over the period until expiration and use these values to calculate the simulated futures prices. Once we have a sufficient sample of futures prices, it is straightforward to compute the set of payoffs of the option; for example, $\max(0, F - X)$ for the call option. The MC price of the option is then given by the mean of these payoffs. The only complexity that arises from this procedure is due to the expectation of a log-normal random variable; that is, if

$$O \sim N(\mu, \sigma^2)$$

then

$$E[\exp(O)] = \exp\left(\mu + \tfrac{1}{2}\sigma^2\right). \tag{7.2}$$

Therefore, we have to apply a log-normal correction (i.e., subtract $\tfrac{1}{2}\sigma^2$ from the simulated stock return) to ensure that the expectation of the simulated futures price is the same as the theoretical value.

We price a European call by simulation using the R and Matlab code in Listings 7.13 and 7.14.

Listing 7.13. Black–Scholes simulation in R (*cont.*)

```
S = 1e6                      # number of simulations
set.seed(12)                 # set seed
F = P0 * exp(r*T)            # futures price
ysim = rnorm(S,-0.5 * sigma * sigma * T,sigma * sqrt(T))
                             # simulated returns with the log normal
                                correction
F = F * exp(ysim)            # futures price
SP = F - X                   # payoff
SP[SP < 0] = 0               # set negative outcomes to zero
fsim = SP * exp(-r*T)        # discount
```

Listing 7.14. Black–Scholes simulation in Matlab (*cont.*)

```
randn('state',0);            % set seed
S = 1e6;                     % number of simulations
F = P0 * exp(r*T);           % futures price
ysim = randn(S,1) * sigma * sqrt(T) - 0.5 * T * sigma^2;
                             % random return, mean corrected
F=F * exp(ysim);
SP = F-X;                    % simulated future payoff
SP(find(SP < 0)) = 0;        % set negative outcomes to 0
fsim = SP * exp(-r*T);       % MC call price
```

We can measure the accuracy of the simulation by how close the MC price is to the Black–Scholes price, which is $11.0873. R gives $11.08709 and Matlab $11.0996, close enough for most practical purposes.

Density plots

Figures 7.5 and 7.6 show the density of simulated future prices and option payoffs. Note the asymmetry in the density in Figure 7.5, as a result of the fact that the prices are lognormally distributed. Listings 7.15 and 7.16 show how to create the figures.

Listing 7.15. Option density plots in R (*cont.*)

```
hist(F,probability = TRUE,ylim = c(0,0.06))    # make Figure 7.5
                                                # make Figure 7.6
x = seq(min(F),max(F),length = 100)
lines(x, dnorm(x, mean = mean(F), sd = sd(SP)))
hist(fsim,nclass = 100,probability = TRUE)
```

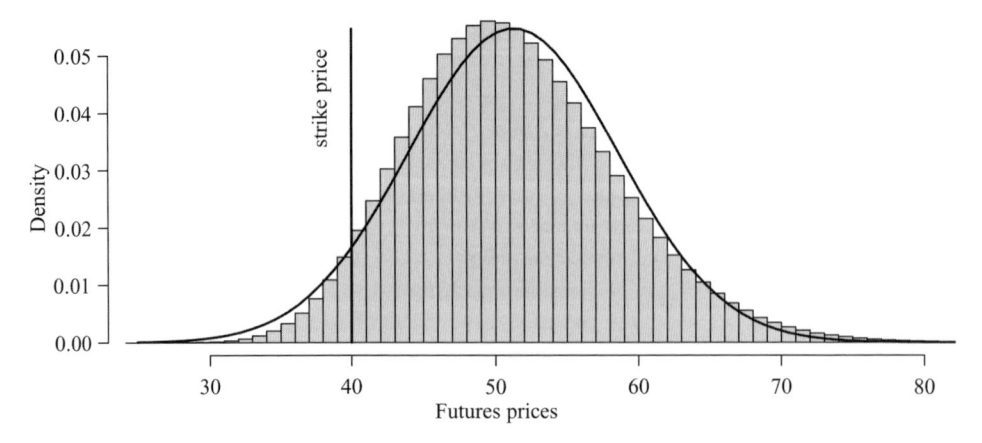

Figure 7.5. Distribution of 10^6 simulated futures prices, $P = 50$, $\sigma = 0.2$, $r = 0.05$, $T = 0.5$, $X = 40$, with the normal superimposed.

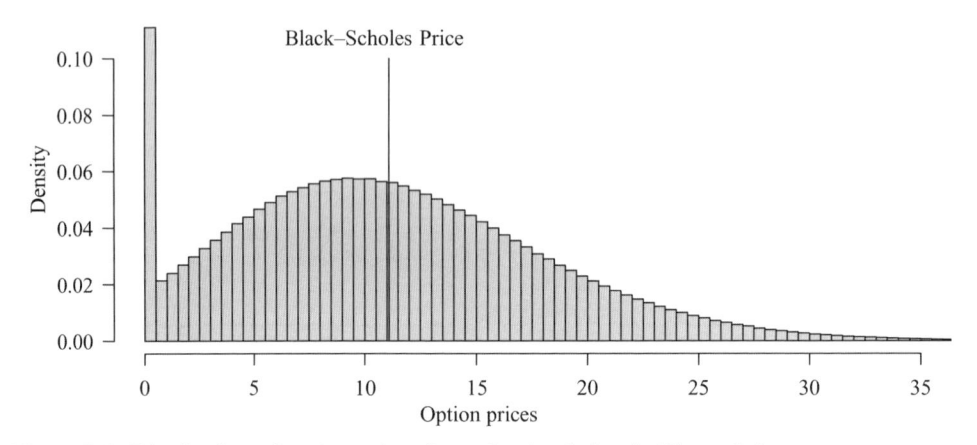

Figure 7.6. Distribution of option prices from the simulation in Figure 7.5.

Listing 7.16. Option density plots in Matlab *(cont.)*

```
histfit(F);           % make Figure 7.5
hist(fsim,100);       % make Figure 7.6
```

To calculate the VaR, we simply read off the 1% smallest value from the distribution to obtain the 99% VaR.

7.3 SIMULATION OF VAR FOR ONE ASSET

The methods discussed in Section 7.2 can be used to obtain the VaR, but they are not the most convenient methods for the purpose. A better approach is to simulate the one-day return of an asset and then apply analytical pricing formulas to the simulated future price. The difference between tomorrow's simulated future values and today's known value represents the simulated P/L in our portfolio, from which we can calculate the MC VaR.

Consider an asset with price P_t and IID-normally-distributed returns, with one-day volatility σ, and where the annual risk-free rate is r.

The number of units of the basic asset held in a portfolio is denoted by x^b, while x^o indicates the number of options held.

In the following, *calendar time* (365 days a year) is used for interest rate calculations. For volatility scaling we use *trading time* (typically 250 days a year).

7.3.1 Monte Carlo VaR with one basic asset

The procedure for obtaining the MC VaR is summarized in the following steps.

1 Compute the initial portfolio value:
$$\vartheta_t = x^b P_t.$$

2 Simulate S one-day returns, $y_{t+1,t}$, from:
$$N(0, \sigma^2), \quad i = 1, \ldots, S.$$

3 Calculate the one-day future price by:
$$P_{t+1,i} = P_t e^{r(1/365)} \times e^{y_{t+1,i}} \times e^{-0.5\sigma^2}, \quad i = 1, \ldots, S.$$

$P_{t+1,i}$ is the ith simulated value. The last term is the log-normal correction from (7.2).

4 Calculate the simulated futures value of the portfolio by:
$$\vartheta_{t+1,i} = x^b P_{t+1,i}.$$

5 The ith simulated profit and loss value is then:
$$q_{t+1,i} = \vartheta_{t+1,i} - \vartheta_t.$$

6 VaR can be obtained directly from the vector of simulated P/L, $\{q_{t+1,i}\}_{i=1}^{S}$. For example, VaR(0.01) is the 1% smallest value.

It is important to realize that it is the $t+1$ price of the basic asset that is being simulated. This is calculated by multiplying the exponential of the simulated return by the future price, then applying a log-normal correction. We use risk-free return because that is what the Black–Scholes equation assumes, but we can use any number we want. Since it will be very small, it could simply be set at zero.

Example 7.1 *We own one stock with a price of 100, where returns have daily volatility $\sigma = 0.01$. The annual risk-free rate is 5%. The MC one-day VaR is calculated in R and Matlab using 10 million simulations with the code given in Listings 7.17 and 7.18.*

Listing 7.17. Simulate VaR in R

```
set.seed(1)                                  # set seed
S = 1e7                                      # number of simulations
s2 = 0.01^2                                  # daily variance
p = 0.01                                     # probability
r = 0.05                                     # annual risk free
P = 100                                      # today's price
ysim = rnorm(S,r/365-0.5 * s2,sqrt(s2))      # sim returns
Psim = P * exp(ysim)                         # future prices
q = sort(Psim - P)                           # simulated P/L
VaR1 = -q[p*S]                               # get VaR
```

Listing 7.18. Simulate VaR in Matlab

```
randn('state',0);                            % set seed
S = 1e7;                                     % number of simulations
s2 = 0.01^2;                                 % daily variance
p = 0.01;                                    % probability
r = 0.05;                                    % risk free
P = 100;                                     % today's price
ysim = randn(S,1)* sqrt(s2)+r/365-0.5*s2;    % simulate return
Psim = P * exp(ysim);                        % future prices
q = sort(Psim - P);                          % sort sim P/L
VaR1 = -q(S * p)
```

R and Matlab give $2.285 and $2.291, respectively. The answers will be more equal if more simulations are done.

7.3.2 VaR of an option on a basic asset

For options, the extra step is to apply the Black–Scholes equation to current and simulated future prices, where we have x^o options. $g()$ denotes the Black–Scholes equation, but could refer to any derivative-pricing equation.

From the list of steps in Section 7.3.1, replace items **1** and **4** with:

1′ The initial portfolio value is

$$\vartheta_t = x^o g(P_t, X, T, \sqrt{250}\sigma, r).$$

4′ The *i*th simulated future value of the portfolio is then

$$\vartheta_{t+1,i} = x^o g(P_{t+1,i}, X, T - 1/365, \sqrt{250}\sigma, r).$$

The other steps are the same.

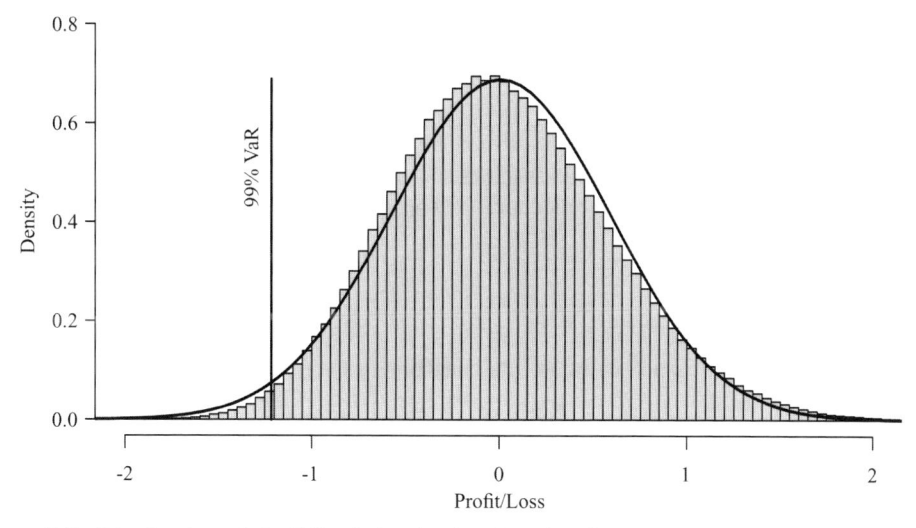

Figure 7.7. Distribution of the P/L of the simulated option from Example 7.2 with the normal distribution superimposed.

Example 7.2 *(continuing from Example 7.1)* We own one call option with strike price 100 and an expiration date in 3 months' time. The MC one-day VaR for the option is calculated in R and Matlab using the code given in Listings 7.19 and 7.20. The distribution of the P/L of the simulated option is shown in Figure 7.7.

Listing 7.19. Simulate option VaR in R

```
T = 0.25;                              # time to expiration
X = 100;                               # strike price
sigma = sqrt(s2 * 250);                # annual volatility
f = bs(X,P,r,sigma,T)                  # analytical call price
fsim = bs(X,Psim,r,sigma,T - (1/365))  # simulate option prices
q = sort(fsim$Call - f$Call)           # simulated P/L
VaR2 = -q[p * S]                       # get VaR
```

Listing 7.20. Simulate option VaR in Matlab

```
T = 0.25;                              % time to expiration
X = 100;                               % strike price
sigma = sqrt(s2*250);                  % annual volatility
f = bs(X,P,r,sigma,T);                 % analytical call price
fsim = bs(X,Psim,r,sigma,T - (1/365)); % sim call price
q = sort(fsim.Call - f.Call);          % sorted sim P/L
VaR2 = -q(p*S)                         % p% VaR
```

The VaR in both R and Matlab is $1.21.

7.3.3 Options and a stock

This methodology extends directly to a situation where we have a portfolio with both a stock and an option or even multiple options (put and call and/or many strike prices) on the same stock. The notation will get messy, so suppose for now that we only have one type of option. Example 7.3 has two options.

From the list of steps in Section 7.3.2, replace items **1'** and **4'** with:

1" Initial portfolio value is:

$$\vartheta_t = x^b P_t + x^o g(P_t, X, T, \sqrt{250}\sigma, r).$$

4" The ith simulated future value of the portfolio is then:

$$\vartheta_{t+1,i} = x^b P_{t+1,i} + x^o g(P_{t+1,i}, X, T - 1/365, \sqrt{250}\sigma, r).$$

The other steps are the same.

Example 7.3 *(continuing from Example 7.2)* We own one call option with strike price 100 and a put with strike 110 along with the underlying stock. The MC one-day VaR for the option is calculated in R and Matlab using the code in Listings 7.19 and 7.20.

Listing 7.21. Example 7.3 in R *(continuing from Listing 7.19)*

```
X1 = 100                              # call strike
X2 = 110                              # put strike
f1 = bs(X1,P,r,sigma,T)               # analytical price
f2 = bs(X2,P,r,sigma,T)
f2sim = bs(X2,Psim,r,sigma,T - (1/365))
f1sim = bs(X1,Psim,r,sigma,T - (1/365))
q = sort(f1sim$Call + f2sim$Put + Psim - f1$Call - f2$Put - P);
VaR3 = -q[p * S]
```

Listing 7.22. Example 7.3 in Matlab *(continuing from Listing 7.20)*

```
X1 = 100;                             % call strike
X2 = 110;                             % put strike
f1 = bs(X1,P,r,sigma,T);              % analytical price
f2 = bs(X2,P,r,sigma,T);
f1sim = bs(X1,Psim,r,sigma,T-(1/365));
f2sim = bs(X2,Psim,r,sigma,T-(1/365));
q = sort(f1sim.Call + f2sim.Put + Psim - f1.Call - f2.Put - P);
VaR3 = -q(p * S)
```

In both R and Matlab we get $1.50.

7.4 SIMULATION OF PORTFOLIO VaR

The main difference in the multivariate case is that, instead of simulating the return of one asset, we need to simulate *correlated* returns for all assets. This ensures that the dependence structure is maintained for the portfolio. Simulated future prices are calculated in the same way as before, and we obtain the portfolio value by summing up individual simulated asset holdings.

Suppose there are two non-derivative assets in our portfolio, with the daily return distribution

$$\mathcal{N}\left(\mu = \begin{pmatrix} 0.05/365 \\ 0.05/365 \end{pmatrix}, \Sigma = \begin{pmatrix} 0.01 & 0.0005 \\ 0.0005 & 0.02 \end{pmatrix}\right).$$

The statement in R to simulate multivariate normals is `mvrnorm(S,mu,Sigma)`, where S is the number of simulations, mu is a vector of means and Sigma is a $K \times K$ covariance matrix. In order to use this function, the MASS library is required.

Listing 7.23. Simulated two-asset returns in R

```
library (MASS)
mu = c(r/365,r/365)                              # return mean
Sigma = matrix(c(0.01, 0.0005, 0.0005, 0.02),ncol = 2)
                                                 # covariance matrix
set.seed(12)                                     # set seed
y = mvrnorm(S,mu,Sigma)                          # simulated returns
```

The equivalent statement in Matlab is `mvnrnd(mu,Sigma,S)`.

Listing 7.24. Simulated two-asset returns in Matlab

```
mu = [r/365 r/365]';                             % return mean
Sigma = [0.01 0.0005; 0.0005 0.02];              % covariance matrix
randn('state',12)                                % set seed
y = mvnrnd(mu,Sigma,S);                          % simulated returns
```

In this case each row of y represents a vector of simulated returns on the assets in the portfolio.

7.4.1 Simulation of portfolio VaR for basic assets

The multivariate version of the method presented in Section 7.3.1 is now given. Here x^b is the vector of holdings, i the simulation index number and k the asset index number, such that $P_{t,k,i}$ denotes the ith simulated price of asset k at time t.

1 The initial portfolio value is:

$$\vartheta_t = \sum_{k=1}^{K} x_k^b P_{t,k}.$$

138   Simulation methods for VaR for options and bonds

2. We simulate a vector of one-day returns from today until tomorrow, denoted by $y_{t+1,i}$, from:
$$N\left(\mu - \tfrac{1}{2}\text{Diag } \Sigma, \Sigma\right)$$
where Diag Σ extracts the diagonal elements of Σ because of the log-normal correction.

3. The ith simulated future price of asset k is:
$$P_{t+1,k,i} = P_{t,k} \exp(y_{t+1,k,i}).$$

4. The ith simulated futures value of the portfolio is given by:
$$\vartheta_{t+1,i} = \sum_{k=1}^{K} x_k^b P_{t+1,k,i}.$$

5. The ith simulated profit and loss (P/L) value (q) is then:
$$q_{t+1,i} = \vartheta_{t+1,i} - \vartheta_t.$$

6. VaR can be obtained directly from the vector of simulated P/L, $\{q_{t+1,i}\}_{i=1}^{S}$, as before.

Let us suppose we hold one unit of each asset. The R and Matlab codes to compute the P/L of the simulated portfolio is given in Listings 7.25 and 7.26 (i.e., as continuations from Listings 7.23 and 7.24).

Listing 7.25. Two-asset VaR in R

```
K=2
P = c(100,50)                              # prices
x = c(1,1)                                 # number of assets
Port = P %*% x                             # portfolio at t
Psim = matrix(t(matrix(P,K,S)),ncol=K) * exp(y)
PortSim = Psim %*% x                       # simulated portfolio
q = sort(PortSim-Port[1,1])                # simulated P/L
VaR4 = -q[S * p]
```

Note the Port[1,1] from the penultimate line. As Port is a one-by-one matrix, it cannot be subtracted from a matrix of a different dimension. Port[1,1] extracts the only element as a real.

Listing 7.26. Two-asset VaR Matlab

```
K = 2;                                     % 2 assets
P = [100 50]';                             % prices
x = [1 1]';                                % number of assets
Port = P'* x;                              % portfolio at t
Psim = repmat(P,1,S)' .* exp(y);           % sim prices
PortSim = Psim * x;                        % sim portfolio
q = sort(PortSim - Port);                  % simulated P/L
VaR4 = -q(S * p)
```

The VaR in both R and Matlab is $25.97.

7.4.2 Portfolio VaR for options

If there are options in the portfolio, some modifications to the previous procedure along the lines of the univariate implementation above are required. For simplicity suppose there is only one option type per stock. Items **1** and **4** from Section 7.4.1 are then replaced by:

1' The initial portfolio value is:

$$\vartheta_t = \sum_{k=1}^{K} \left(x_k^b P_{t,k} + x_k^o g(P_{t,k}, X_k, T, \sqrt{250}\sigma_k, r) \right).$$

4' The *i*th simulated future value of the portfolio is then given by:

$$\vartheta_{t+1,i} = \sum_{k=1}^{K} \left(x_k^b P_{t+1,k,i} + x_k^o g(P_{t+1,k,i}, X_k, T - \tfrac{1}{365}, \sqrt{250}\sigma_k, r) \right).$$

The other steps remain unchanged.

Suppose we hold one at-the-money call option on the second stock in the example above, while being long one of the first stock. We can then modify the previous two listings to Listings 7.27 and 7.28.

Listing 7.27. A two-asset case in R with an option

```
f = bs(P[2],P[2],r,sigma,T)       # analytical price
fsim = bs(P[2],Psim[,2],r,sigma,T-(1/365))
q = sort(fsim$Call + Psim[,1] - f$Call - P[1]);
VaR5 = -q[p*S]
```

Listing 7.28. A two-asset case in Matlab with an option

```
f = bs(P(2),P(2),r,sigma,T);      % analytical price
fsim=bs(P(2),Psim(:,2),r,sigma,T-(1/365));
q = sort(fsim.Call+Psim(:,1)-f.Call-P(1));
VaR5 = -q(p*S)
```

The VaR in R is $20.78 and the VaR in Matlab is $20.81.

7.4.3 Richer versions

We kept the examples above relatively simple because, otherwise, the notation would have got quite cluttered. However, it is straightforward to incorporate much more complicated examples.

For example, we could have a number of stocks and multiple options on each stock. The examples above used European options but they could just as easily have been American or more exotic options. It would be simple to combine fixed income assets with the stocks and options used here. The general framework is quite flexible.

Furthermore, instead of simulating from a multivariate normal, we could simulate from a different distribution such as the Student-t, or even use historical simulation to get future prices.

7.5 ISSUES IN SIMULATION ESTIMATION

There are several issues that need to be addressed in all Monte Carlo simulation exercises; the most important are the quality of the RNG and the transformation method as well as the number of simulations.

7.5.1 The quality of the RNG

Monte Carlo simulations are based on replicating the real world on the computer. As such, the quality of MC simulation is not only dependent on the quality of the underlying stochastic model, but also the quality of the actual RNG used.

The properties of the RNG drive the entire result; if a low-quality generator is used, biased or inaccurate results will result. For example, if the period of the RNG is 10 and we run a simulation of size 100, the same calculation is repeated 10 times.

The desired quality and period of the generator depend on the underlying application. While simple calculations involving one asset do not make big demands on the generator, a large number of random numbers is necessary for portfolios consisting of many exotic options.

Similarly, the quality of the transformation method also plays a key role. Many transformation methods are only optimally tuned for the center of the distribution; this can become problematic when simulating extreme events. It is not uncommon for some transformation methods to use linear approximations for the extreme tails, which will lead to extreme uniforms being incorrectly transformed.

7.5.2 Number of simulations

It is important to choose the number of simulations correctly. If we choose too few simulations the resulting answer will be inaccurate; if we choose too many we are wasting valuable computer resources. Considering that simulations can take quite a long time to run, even on very-high-end hardware, the choice of simulation size is often vital.

There are no set rules regarding the number of simulations needed for an accurate answer. In special cases there are formal statistical tests for the number of simulations but, for the most part, more informal methods have to be relied upon. Common proposals stating that the accuracy of simulation is related to the inverse simulation size are not recommended, because they are based on an assumption of linearity, which is not correct in the applications in this chapter.

As most MC VaR applications are based on nonlinear transformation of a random variable and only use a quantile of the outcomes, determination of the number of simulations is even more complex. The best way, in many cases, is to simply increase the number of simulations and see how the MC estimate converges. When numbers have

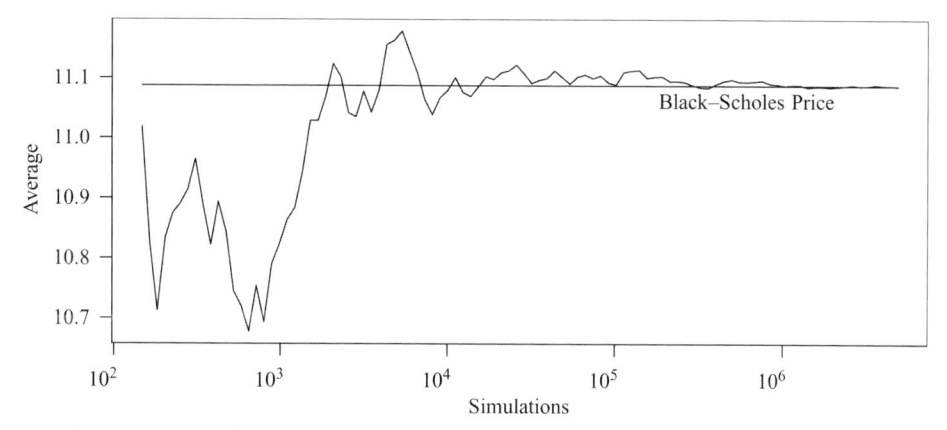

Figure 7.8. Cumulative MC estimate, from the simulation in Figure 7.5.

stopped changing up to three significant digits, the number of simulations is probably sufficient.

As an example of how to choose the number of simulations, consider MC pricing of a European option. To determine the optimal number of simulations, we can compare the true (analytical) price to the MC estimate.

In Figure 7.8 the x-axis shows the number of simulations, ranging from 100 to 5,000,000, on a log scale, while the y-axis shows the simulation estimate of the option price for the corresponding number of simulations.

The true value is around 11.09; it takes about 5,000 simulations to get that number up to three significant digits. There are still fluctuations in the estimate for 5 million simulations. Of course, in most practical applications such precision is unnecessary.

Figure 7.9 shows the MC VaR for a stock with daily volatility 1% as the number of simulations increases from 100 to hundreds of thousands, along with the 1% and 99% confidence bounds, where the true VaR is 100.

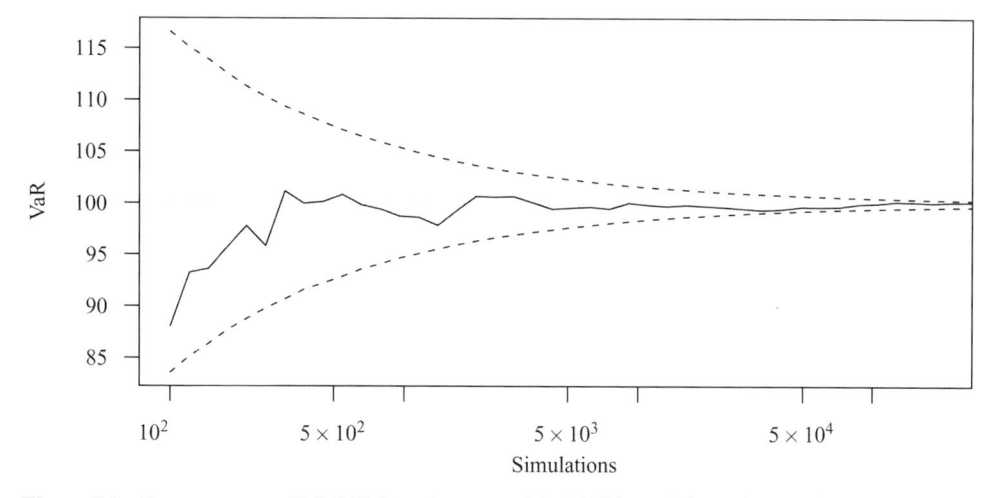

Figure 7.9. Convergence of MC VaR estimates, with ±99% confidence intervals.

For the lowest number of simulations, the confidence interval is quite wide but rapidly narrows. At $S = 10^3$ it is (98.54, 101.57) and at $S = 10^4$ it is (99.57, 100.52); so, in 99% of cases, MC estimates are equal to three significant digits. In light of the fact that accuracy in the volatility forecast is considerably lower than that, the conclusion is that 100,000 simulations are more than enough here.

7.6 SUMMARY

The starting point in all risk analysis is getting hold of a statistical model of the underlying risk factors—be they equities, foreign exchange, commodities, interest rates or something else. With such a model in hand, we can obtain measures of risk, like VaR, by methods such as those discussed in Chapter 5. However, if we hold options or bonds, it is necessary to first forecast the risk in the risk factor, and then somehow map that on to the risk in the bond or option.

Traditionally, this was done using mathematical expansions—such as the methods in Chapter 6—but nowadays Monte Carlo simulations are much more common. The reason is that they enable us to outsource most of the heavy calculations to a computer instead of tediously deriving the risk properties of the myriad derived assets one by one.

In this chapter, we first demonstrated how MC could be used to obtain the price of a bond or an option. The examples chosen were sufficiently simple such that the analytical price was known and could therefore be compared with the price obtained by simulations, providing easy verification of the results.

We then implemented a straightforward way to obtain risk by the MC method whereby we simulated the prices of an underlying asset, applied the analytical pricing equations where appropriate and from this obtained simulated profit and loss (P/L). Then, it was an easy matter to obtain the VaR as a probability p quantile of simulated P/L, similar to historical simulation.

8
Backtesting and stress testing

How do we choose the best model for forecasting risk? Unfortunately, there is no single correct answer to this question. We can diagnose individual models, perhaps by testing for parameter significance or analyzing residuals, but these methods often do not properly address the risk-forecasting property of the models under consideration.

Backtesting is a procedure that can be used to compare the various risk models. It aims to take ex ante value-at-risk (VaR) forecasts from a particular model and compare them with ex post realized return (i.e., historical observations). Whenever losses exceed VaR, a *VaR violation* is said to have occurred.

Backtesting is useful in identifying the weaknesses of risk-forecasting models and providing ideas for improvement, but is not informative about the causes of weaknesses. Models that do not perform well during backtesting should have their assumptions and parameter estimates questioned. However, backtesting can prevent underestimation of VaR and, hence, ensure that a bank carries sufficiently high capital. At the same time backtesting can reduce the likelihood of overestimating VaR, which can lead to excessive conservatism.

In this chapter, we introduce the procedure of backtesting, statistical techniques for testing the significance of VaR violations and several common procedures for evaluating the quality of risk forecasts. Towards the end of the chapter we discuss the backtesting of expected shortfall (ES) and, finally, stress testing. For a good overview of backtesting see Campbell (2005).

The specific notation used in this chapter is:

W_T Testing window size
$T = W_E + W_T$ Number of observations in a sample
$\eta_t = 0, 1$ Indicates whether a VaR violation occurs (i.e., $\eta_t = 1$)
$v_i, i = 0, 1$ Number of violations ($i = 1$) and no violations ($i = 0$) observed in $\{\eta_t\}$
v_{ij} Number of instances where j follows i in $\{\eta_t\}$

8.1 BACKTESTING

Assessment of the accuracy of VaR forecasts should ideally be done by tracking the performance of a model in the future using operational criteria. However, as violations are only observed infrequently, a long period of time would be required. To eliminate the waiting time, *backtesting* evaluates VaR forecasts by checking how a VaR forecast model performs over a period in the past.

Definition 8.1 (Estimation window) *The estimation window (W_E) is the number of observations used to forecast risk. If different procedures or assumptions are compared, the estimation window is set to whichever one needs the highest number of observations.*

Definition 8.2 (Testing window) *The testing window (W_T) is the data sample over which risk is forecast (i.e., the days where we have made a VaR forecast).*

Typically, the entire sample size T is equal to the sum of W_E and W_T:

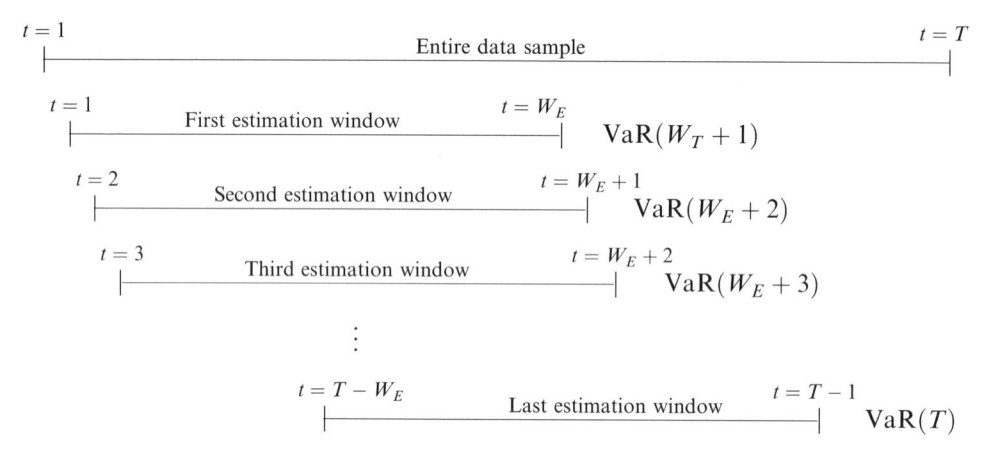

```
t = 1                                                                        t = T
|————————————————— Entire data sample ————————————————|

t = 1                              t = W_E
|————— First estimation window ————|  VaR(W_T + 1)

  t = 2                              t = W_E + 1
  |————— Second estimation window ————|  VaR(W_E + 2)

    t = 3                              t = W_E + 2
    |————— Third estimation window ————|  VaR(W_E + 3)

                       ⋮

           t = T - W_E                          t = T - 1
           |————— Last estimation window ————|  VaR(T)
```

Example 8.1 *We have a 10-year sample of daily data from 1999 until the end of 2009. The first two years, 1999 and 2000, are used to forecast daily VaR for the first day of 2001. The 500 trading days in 1999 and 2000 therefore constitute the first estimation window. The estimation window is then moved up by one day to obtain the risk forecast for the second day of 2001, etc. We assume here for simplicity that there are 250 trading days in the year:*

Estimation window in dates

Start	End	VaR forecast
1/1/1999	31/12/2000	VaR(1/1/2001)
2/1/1999	1/1/2001	VaR(2/1/2001)
⋮	⋮	⋮
31/12/2007	30/12/2009	VaR(31/12/2009)

As the daily returns from 2001–2009 are already known, VaR forecasts can be compared with the actual outcome.

Example 8.2 *(continuing from Example 8.1)* However, instead of referring to calendar dates (e.g., 1/1/2004), we refer to days by indexing the returns, so y_1 is the return on 1/1/1999 and $y_{2,500}$ the return on the last day, 31/12/2009, assuming 250 trading days per year. The estimation window W_E is set at 500 days, and the testing window W_T is therefore 2,000 days:

Estimation and testing windows

t	$t + W_E - 1$	$VaR(t + W_E)$
1	500	$VaR(501)$
2	501	$VaR(502)$
⋮	⋮	⋮
1,999	2,499	$VaR(2,500)$

In Example 8.2, we have 8 years (or 2,000 days) of VaR forecasts, which is the size of the testing window. If the actual return on a particular day exceeds the VaR forecast, then the *VaR limit is said to have been violated*. We can then make a judgment on the quality of the VaR forecasts by recording the relative number of violations—a technique called *violation ratios*—or use more sophisticated statistical techniques.

We record the violations as η_t, which takes the value 1 when a violation occurs and 0 otherwise. The number of violations are collected in the variable v, where v_1 is the number of violations and v_0 is the number of days without violations. These two add up to make the testing period.

Definition 8.3 (VaR violation) *An event such that:*

$$\eta_t = \begin{cases} 1 & \text{if } y_t \leq -VaR_t \\ 0 & \text{if } y_t > -VaR_t. \end{cases} \quad (8.1)$$

v_1 *is the count of* $\eta_t = 1$ *and* v_0 *is the count of* $\eta_t = 0$, *which are simply obtained by:*

$$v_1 = \sum \eta_t$$
$$v_0 = W_T - v_1.$$

The main tools used in backtesting are *violation ratios*, where the actual number of VaR violations are compared with the expected value.

Definition 8.4 (Violation ratio) *The violation ratio is:*

$$VR = \frac{\text{Observed number of violations}}{\text{Expected number of violations}} = \frac{v_1}{p \times W_T}.$$

Intuitively, if the violation ratio is greater than one the VaR model *underforecasts risk* and if smaller than one the model *overforecasts risk*.

Backtesting is based on an important, but sometimes incorrect, assumption. When estimating daily VaR, it is assumed that the portfolio is "frozen" over the next trading day. This means that there is no change expected in the composition of the portfolio. Actual realized returns, however, may reflect revenue and transaction costs from intra-day trading, miscellaneous fee incomes, rebalancing and other items. Strictly speaking, the user should use a return for backtesting that represents a frozen portfolio obtained by applying daily price changes to fixed positions.

8.1.1 Market risk regulations

Financial institutions regulated under the Basel Accords are required to set aside a certain amount of capital due to market risk, credit risk and operational risk. The formula for determining the market risk capital was set by the 1996 Market Risk Amendment to the 1988 Basel I Accords. It is based on multiplying the maximum of previous day 1% VaR and 60 average VaR by a constant, Ξ, which is determined by the number of violations that happened previously:

$$\text{Market risk capital}_t = \Xi_t \max\left(\text{VaR}_t^{1\%}, \overline{\text{VaR}}_t^{1\%}\right) + \text{Constant}.$$

$\overline{\text{VaR}}_t^{1\%}$ is average reported 1% VaR over the previous 60 trading days. Importantly, the multiplication factor Ξ_t varies with the number of violations, v_1, that occurred in the previous 250 trading days—the required testing window length for backtesting in the Basel Accords. This is based on three ranges for the number of violations, named after the three colors of traffic lights:

$$\Xi_t = \begin{cases} 3 & \text{if } v_1 \leq 4 \quad \text{Green} \\ 3 + 0.2(v_1 - 4) & \text{if } 5 \leq v_1 \leq 9 \quad \text{Yellow} \\ 4 & \text{if } 10 \leq v_1 \quad \text{Red}. \end{cases} \quad (8.2)$$

A bank experiencing an excess number of violations will be penalized by having to set aside a larger amount of risk capital. Moreover, if v_1 is in the red zone, banks will have to take immediate action to reduce their risk or improve the VaR model; they may even lose their banking license.

Fundamentally, this approach is unchanged in Basel II and is not expected to change much in Basel III.

8.1.2 Estimation window length

The estimation window length is mainly determined by the choice of VaR model and probability level. Different methods have different data requirements (e.g., EWMA requires about 30 days, HS needs at least 300 for $\text{VaR}^{1\%}$, and GARCH even more). When making comparisons, the estimation window should be sufficiently large to accommodate the most stringent data criteria. Even within the same method, it may be helpful to compare different window lengths. For example, we may want to compare EWMA, 300-day HS and 500-day HS. In this case the estimation window should be 500 days.

8.1.3 Testing window length

VaR violations are, by definition, infrequent events. With a 1% VaR, a violation is expected once every 100 days, so that 2.5 violations are expected per year. Therefore, the actual sample size of violations is quite small, causing difficulties for statistical inference. We might need perhaps 10 violations for reliable statistical analysis, or 4 years of data. This means the size of the testing window needs to increase with the extremity of VaR levels. Furthermore, when using some of the formal statistical tests discussed below, the data requirements may increase even more.

8.1.4 Violation ratios

The question of how to interpret violation ratios remains. A VR value of one is expected, but how can we ascertain whether any value other than one is statistically significant? We discuss some formal tests below, but a useful rule of thumb is that if $VR \in [0.8, 1.2]$ it is a good forecast and if $VR < 0.5$ or $VR > 1.5$ the model is imprecise. Both bounds narrow with increasing testing window lengths. As a first attempt, one could plot the actual returns and VaR together, thereby facilitating a quick visual inspection of the quality of the VaR forecast.

Backtesting focuses on violation ratios, but it is possible that two different VaR methods can deliver the same violation ratios yet have major discrepancies in their VaR forecasts. In this case, it may be useful to consider the volatility of risk forecasts (i.e., the standard deviation of VaR estimates). Clearly, the model with the lower standard deviation is preferred. This is discussed in Danielsson (2002).

8.2 BACKTESTING THE S&P 500

We demonstrate backtesting by using many of the most common VaR forecast methods discussed in Chapter 5 and by taking a sample of daily S&P 500 returns from February 2, 1994 to December 31, 2009—4,000 observations in all.

We start by downloading the prices, converting them into returns, and saving them to vector y. In R we need to convert the *time series* object using coredata().

Listing 8.1. Load data in R

```
library("tseries")        # time series library
p = get.hist.quote(instrument = "^gspc", start = "1994-02-11",
    end = "2009-12-31",quote = "AdjClose",quiet = T)
                          # download the prices
y = diff(log(p))          # get returns
y = coredata(y)           # strip date information from returns
```

Listing 8.2. Load data in Matlab

```
stocks = hist_stock_data('11021994','31122009','^gspc');
price = stocks.AdjClose(end:-1:1);
y = diff(log(price));      % get returns
```

We then set up the probability (1%), window length (1,000 days) and carry out EWMA initialization. Finally, we create a matrix, VaR, with dimensions $T \times 4$ to hold the various forecasts, which are initially set to NaNs.

Listing 8.3. Set backtest up in R

```
T = length(y)                      # number of observations for return y
WE = 1000                          # estimation window length
p = 0.01                           # probability
l1 = WE * p                        # HS observation
value = 1;                         # portfolio
VaR = matrix(nrow=T,ncol=4)        # matrix to hold VaR forecasts for 4
                                     models
# EWMA setup
lambda = 0.94;
s11 = var(y[1:30]);
for(t in 2:WE) s11 = lambda * s11 + (1 - lambda) * y[t - 1]^2
library(fGarch)
```

Listing 8.4. Set backtest up in Matlab

```
T = length(y);            % number of observations for return y
WE = 1000;                % estimation window length
p = 0.01;                 % probability
value = 1;                % portfolio
l1 = WE * p ;             % HS observation
VaR = NaN(T,4);           % matrix to hold VaR forecasts for 4 models
% EWMA setup
lambda = 0.94;
s11 = var(y(1:30));       % initial variance
for t = 2:WE
    s11 = lambda * s11 + (1 - lambda) * y(t - 1)^2;
end
% GARCH specification
spec = garchset('P', 1, 'Q', 1,'C',NaN,'Display','off')
```

We implement four models: exponential moving average (EWMA), moving average (MA), historical simulation (HS) and GARCH(1,1). We need to manually update the GARCH volatility forecasts $\hat{\sigma}_{t+1}$ as discussed in Section 5.5.3.

A potentially important issue arises when GARCH is used for backtesting, since GARCH estimation takes a nontrivial amount of time. Of course, if we only need to estimate the model once, it does not matter whether estimation takes half a second or 3 seconds, but in backtesting the model for each different data window has to re-estimated, which can often involve thousands of estimations. In this case it is desirable to speed up estimation in some way.

We can achieve this by setting starting values efficiently. After the first estimation we obtain parameter estimates, which are not likely to change very much when we move the window through the sample. Therefore, it makes sense to recycle parameter estimates for the previous window as starting values in the next estimation. In one experiment using Matlab, this made the program run 2.5 times faster.

Listing 8.5. Running backtest in R

```
for (t in (WE + 1):T){
  t1 = t - WE;                     # start of the data window
  t2 = t - 1;                      # end of the data window
  window = y[t1:t2]                # data for estimation
  # EWMA
  s11 = lambda * s11 + (1 - lambda) * y[t - 1]^2
  VaR[t,1] = -qnorm(p) * sqrt(s11) * value
  # MA
  VaR[t,2] = -sd(window) * qnorm(p) * value
  # HS
  ys = sort(window)                # sort returns
  VaR[t,3] = -ys[11]* value        # VaR number
  # GARCH(1,1)
  g=garchFit(formula = ~ garch(1,1), window ,trace=FALSE,
  include.mean=FALSE)
  par=g@fit$matcoef                # put parameters into vector par
  s4=par[1]+par[2]* window[WE]^2+par[3]* g@h.t[WE]
  VaR[t,4] = -sqrt(s4) * qnorm(p) * value
}
```

Listing 8.6. Running backtest in Matlab

```
for t = WE + 1:T
  t1 = t - WE;                     % start of the data window
  t2 = t - 1;                      % end of data window
  window = y(t1:t2) ;              % data for estimation
  % EWMA
  s11 = lambda * s11 + (1 - lambda * y(t - 1)^2;
```

150   Backtesting and stress testing

```
    VaR(t,1) = -norminv(p) * sqrt(s11) * value ;
    % MA
    VaR(t,2) = -std(window)* norminv(p)* value;
    % HS
    ys = sort(window);
    VaR(t,3) = -ys(11)* value;
    % GARCH
    [par,errors,LLF,innovations,ht] = garchfit(spec,window);
    h = par.K + par.ARCH*window(end)^2 + par.GARCH*ht(end)^2;
    VaR(t,4) = -sqrt(h) * norminv(p) * value;
end
```

8.2.1 Analysis

We analyze the results from these VaR forecasts by means of violation ratios, VaR volatility and graphical methods. In Section 8.3 we consider more formal tests of violation ratios.

The code below shows how to calculate violation ratios and VaR volatility, how to print out the results and finally how to make a joint plot with returns and VaRs similar to the one in Figure 8.1.

Listing 8.7. Backtesting analysis in R

```
W1 = WE+1
for (i in 1:4){
   VR = sum(y[W1:T] < -VaR[W1:T,i])/(p*(T - WE))
   s = sd(VaR[W1:T,i])              # VaR volatility
   cat(i,"VR",VR,"VaR vol",s,"\n")   # print results
}
matplot(cbind(y[W1:T],VaR[W1:T,]),type='l')
```

Listing 8.8. Backtesting analysis in Matlab

```
for i = 1:4
    VR = length(find(y(WE + 1:T)<-VaR(WE + 1:T,i)))/(p *(T - WE));
                                     % violation ratio
    s = std(VaR(WE + 1:T,i));        % VaR volatility
    disp([i VR s])                   % print results
end
plot([y(WE + 1:T) VaR(WE + 1:T,:)])
```

Numerical results from the backtests are shown in Table 8.1. The two methods that apply equal weight to historical data, MA and HS, perform abysmally, while the conditional methods, EWMA and GARCH, are better, but still by no means good.

Financial Risk Forecasting 151

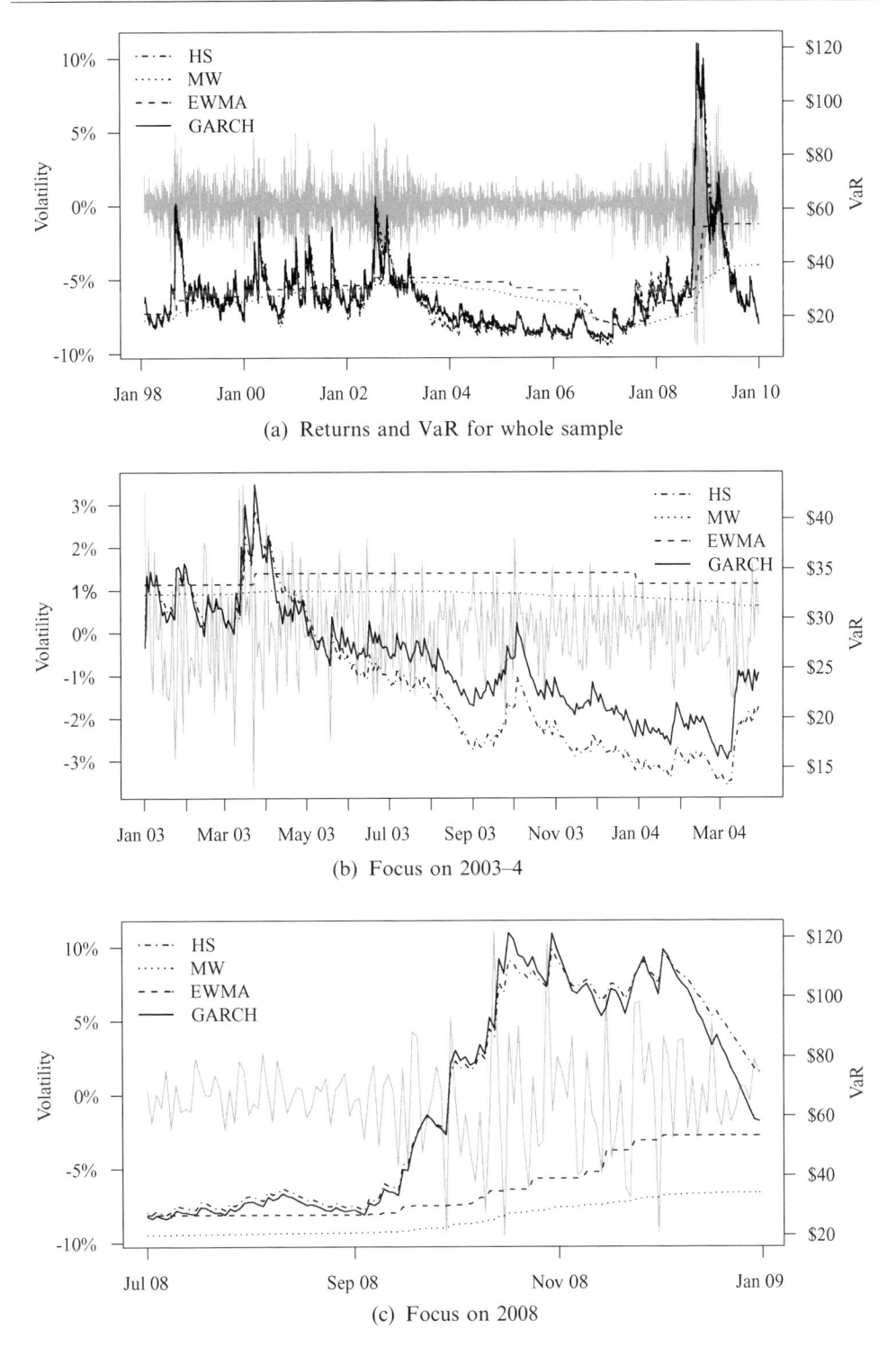

Figure 8.1. Backtesting a $1,000 portfolio of S&P 500 returns.

(a) Returns and VaR for whole sample

(b) Focus on 2003–4

(c) Focus on 2008

Table 8.1. Backtesting S&P 500 returns, January 30, 1998 to December 31, 2009 ($W_T = 3,000$).

Method	VR	VaR volatility
EWMA	1.87	0.016
MA	3.03	0.006
HS	2.03	0.009
GARCH	1.83	0.014

Table 8.2. Backtesting S&P 500 returns, January 30, 1998 to November 1, 2006 ($W_T = 2,000$).

Method	VR	VaR volatility
EWMA	1.40	0.010
MA	1.60	0.003
HS	1.05	0.003
GARCH	1.25	0.009

Not surprisingly, GARCH performs better than EWMA, but not by much. As expected, VaRs from conditional methods are much more volatile. The conclusion from this exercise is that none of these four methods should be used in this case.

To study these issues in more detail, we removed the last 1,000 observations from the sample and repeated the exercise. The results are presented in Table 8.2. The results here are much better—the MA method is the only one that can be considered unacceptable and both HS and GARCH perform quite well. This suggests there was a structural break at the onset of the 2007 crisis causing difficulties for all methods.

More information on what went wrong can be seen in Figure 8.1, which shows VaR forecasts on a $1,000 portfolio. Panel (a) shows that there seem to be three different regimes throughout the sample period. Volatility is relatively high from the beginning of the sample until around 2003, where it drops considerably. To explore this in more detail, panel (b) focuses on 2003 and the first part of 2004. In this case, volatility is steadily dropping with EWMA and GARCH VaRs following suit, while HS and MA VaRs stay high. In this time period, the number of violations for the last two methods seem to be much too low.

Volatility stays low until the beginning of the crisis in 2007. Then, volatility steadily increases until we hit a very large volatility cluster in 2008, after which volatility drops sharply. The most dramatic events happened at the height of the crisis in the second part of 2008, coinciding with the failure of Lehmans and AIG. After the main crisis events, volatility again dropped sharply. Here we see the opposite to what happened in 2003, HS and MA VaRs stay too low with an excessive number of violations, while EWMA and GARCH pick up on high volatility much faster and adjust VaR forecasts sharply upwards.

The abrupt changes in volatilities seen in 2003 and 2008 are likely to cause problems for most VaR models. The models tried here clearly fail during those structural breaks—some much more than others.

Let us consider the failure of the GARCH model in more detail. Of the four models used, it performed the best, but still its violation ratio exceeded 1.8 when the longer testing window was used. This suggests several changes to the procedure we have implemented here: first, use a fat-tailed conditional distribution such as the Student-t; second, make the estimation window smaller and study how GARCH model parameters change over time; and, third, it may turn out to be a bad idea to initialize the volatility of the GARCH using unconditional variance (as proposed in Section 2.4).

An alternative way to initialize the GARCH model can be done by implementing the `tarch()` function in the MFE toolbox, where GARCH volatility is initialized by EWMA implying that estimated parameters may be different from those here.

More ambitiously, the underlying model could be modified to take into account both long-run structural changes and short-run volatility dynamics.

8.3 SIGNIFICANCE OF BACKTESTS

The above analysis of VaR violations was conducted by graphical and rule-of-thumb methods, but ideally one should be able to employ formal statistical tests. Besides simple violation ratio analysis, a formal test of the significance of the violation ratio would be useful, as would a test of whether violations cluster, such as we see towards the end of 2008.

Violations over time in a backtest are a sequence of ones and zeros, often called a *hit sequence*, indicated by $\{\eta_t\}$, which is Bernoulli distributed. We focus on two issues, the number of violations and clustering, tested by the *unconditional coverage* and *independence* tests, respectively.

The unconditional coverage property ensures that the theoretical confidence level p matches the empirical probability of violation. For a 1% VaR backtest, we would expect to observe a VaR violation 1% of the time. If, instead, violations are observed more often, say 5% of the time, the VaR model is systematically underestimating risk at the 1% level. In other words, the 1% VaR produced from the model is in reality the 5% VaR. Graphical analysis and violation ratio analysis provide a quick means of checking this property.

The independence property is more subtle, requiring any two observations in the hit sequence to be independent of each other. Intuitively, the fact that a violation has been observed today should not convey any information about the likelihood of observing a violation tomorrow. If VaR violations cluster, we can predict a violation today if there was one yesterday, and therefore the probability of a loss exceeding 1% VaR today is higher than 1%. In this case, a good VaR model would have increased the 1% VaR forecast following a violation. As illustrated above, models that are not very responsive to changing volatility in the market, such as HS, generally do not satisfy this property.

Unfortunately, the form of clustering observed in VaR forecasts is more subtle. For example, panel (c) in Figure 8.1 shows there is clustering of violations, especially for HS and MA. However, we don't seem to observe many sequential violations. Instead, there seem to be one or more days between them. While this is still a clear example of clustering, it would not be detected by the independence test discussed here.

The two properties—unconditional coverage and independence—are distinct and it is entirely possible that a VaR model satisfying one of them would not satisfy the other. For example, a hit sequence produced from a 5% VaR can give violations exactly 5% of the time, but with all violations squeezed into a 3-week period. The risk of bankruptcy here is clearly much higher than if losses are spread out evenly over time.

The main downside of these tests is that they rely on asymptotic distributions. Given that violations are rare events, the effective sample size is relatively small and, therefore, tests may not be as robust as we would like. One may be better off obtaining confidence bounds by means of simulations.

8.3.1 Bernoulli coverage test

We indicate whether a violation occurred on day t by η_t, which takes values 1 or 0: 1 indicates a violation and 0 no violation. η_t is then a sequence of Bernoulli-distributed random variables.

We then use the Bernoulli coverage test to ascertain the proportion of violations. The null hypothesis for VaR violations is:

$$H_0 : \eta \sim B(p),$$

where B stands for the Bernoulli distribution. The Bernoulli density is given by:

$$(1-p)^{1-\eta_t}(p)^{\eta_t}, \quad \eta_t = 0,1.$$

Probability p can be estimated by:

$$\hat{p} = \frac{v_1}{W_T}. \tag{8.3}$$

The likelihood function is given by:

$$\mathcal{L}_U(\hat{p}) = \prod_{t=W_E+1}^{T} (1-\hat{p})^{1-\eta_t}(\hat{p})^{\eta_t} = (1-\hat{p})^{v_0}(\hat{p})^{v_1}.$$

We denote this as the unrestricted likelihood function because it uses estimated probability $\hat{p}$ in contrast to the likelihood function below where we restrict the probability value to p.

Note we are working with a framework where a data sample is split into a testing and estimation window. Since the first W_E days are reserved for estimation, testing starts on day $W_E + 1$.

Under the H_0, $p = \hat{p}$, so the restricted likelihood function is:

$$\mathcal{L}_R(p) = \prod_{t=W_E+1}^{T} (1-p)^{1-\eta_t}(p)^{\eta_t} = (1-p)^{v_0}(p)^{v_1}$$

and we can use a likelihood ratio test to see whether $\mathcal{L}_R = \mathcal{L}_U$ or, equivalently, whether $p = \hat{p}$:

$$LR = 2(\log \mathcal{L}_U(p) - \log \mathcal{L}_U(\hat{p}))$$

$$= 2\log \frac{(1-\hat{p})^{v_0}(\hat{p})^{v_1}}{(1-p)^{v_0}(p)^{v_1}}$$

$$\overset{\text{asymptotic}}{\sim} \chi^2_{(1)}. \tag{8.4}$$

Choosing a 5% significance level for the test, the null hypothesis is rejected if $LR > 3.84$, but in most cases we would simply calculate the p-value. The choice of significance level affects the power of the test. A low type I error implies a higher type II error and therefore a lower power for the test.

We implement the tests as functions and demonstrate their use later in this section.

Listing 8.9. Bernoulli coverage test in R

```
bern_test = function(p,v){
   a=p^(sum(v))*(1 - p)^(length(v) - sum(v))
   b = (sum(v)/length(v))^(sum(v))*(1 - (sum(v)/length(v)))^
      (length(v) - sum(v))
   return(-2*log(a/b))
}
```

Listing 8.10. Bernoulli coverage test in Matlab

```
function res=bern_test(p,v)
   a = p^(sum(v))*(1 - p)^(length(v)-sum(v));
   b = (sum(v)/length(v))^(sum(v))*(1-(sum(v)/length(v)))^
      (length(v)-sum(v));
   res = -2*log(a/b);
end
```

The Bernoulli coverage test is nonparametric in the sense that it does not assume a distribution for the returns and often provides good benchmarks for the assessment of accuracy of VaR models. However, it does not have much power when sample sizes are small, like the one-year size specified in the Basel Accords. Consequently, the expected number of violations should be at least 10.

8.3.2 Testing the independence of violations

The above analysis focused on unconditional coverage which ignores time variation in the data. It is also of interest to test whether violations cluster (i.e., whether all violations happen one after the other), indicating a sequence of losses since violations should theoretically spread out over time. This is important given the strong evidence for volatility clusters.

A conditional coverage test was developed by Christoffersen (1998). We need to calculate the probabilities of two consecutive violations (i.e., p_{11}) and the probability of a violation if there was no violation on the previous day (i.e., p_{01}); more generally, the probability that:

$$p_{ij} = \Pr(\eta_t = i | \eta_{t-1} = j)$$

where i and j are either 0 or 1.

The first-order transition probability matrix is defined as:

$$\Pi_1 = \begin{pmatrix} 1 - p_{01} & p_{01} \\ 1 - p_{11} & p_{11} \end{pmatrix}.$$

The restricted likelihood function—where the transition matrix from the null hypothesis is used since the hit sequence is Bernoulli distributed—is:

$$\mathcal{L}_R(\Pi_1) = (1 - p_{01})^{v_{00}} p_{01}^{v_{01}} (1 - p_{11})^{v_{10}} p_{11}^{v_{11}} \qquad (8.5)$$

where v_{ij} is the number of observations where j follows i. Maximum likelihood (ML) estimates are obtained by maximizing $\mathcal{L}_R(\Pi_1)$:

$$\hat{\Pi}_1 = \begin{pmatrix} \dfrac{v_{00}}{v_{00} + v_{01}} & \dfrac{v_{01}}{v_{00} + v_{01}} \\ \dfrac{v_{10}}{v_{10} + v_{11}} & \dfrac{v_{11}}{v_{10} + v_{11}} \end{pmatrix}.$$

Under the null hypothesis of no clustering, the probability of a violation tomorrow does not depend on today seeing a violation; then, $p_{01} = p_{11} = p$ and the estimated transition matrix is simply:

$$\hat{\Pi}_0 = \begin{pmatrix} 1 - \hat{p} & \hat{p} \\ 1 - \hat{p} & \hat{p} \end{pmatrix}$$

where

$$\hat{p} = \frac{v_{01} + v_{11}}{v_{00} + v_{10} + v_{01} + v_{11}}.$$

The unrestricted likelihood function according to null hypothesis uses the estimated transition matrix and is:

$$\mathcal{L}_U(\hat{\Pi}_0) = (1 - \hat{p})^{v_{00} + v_{10}} \hat{p}^{v_{01} + v_{11}}. \qquad (8.6)$$

The likelihood ratio test is implemented with likelihoods (8.5) and (8.6):

$$LR = 2\left(\log \mathcal{L}_U(\hat{\Pi}_0) - \log \mathcal{L}_R(\hat{\Pi}_1)\right) \overset{\text{asymptotic}}{\sim} \chi^2_{(1)}.$$

This test does not depend on true p and *only* tests for independence. The main problem with tests of this sort is that they must specify the particular way in which independence is breached. For example, let us assume independence is not satisfied if the probability of VaR violation today depends on whether or not there was VaR violation yesterday. However, there are many possible ways in which the independence property is not fulfilled. This test will have no power to detect departures from independence if the likelihood of VaR being violated today depends on whether VaR was violated 2 days ago—not on yesterday's VaR being violated.

Listing 8.11. Independence coverage test in R

```
ind_test = function(V) {
  J = matrix(ncol = 4, nrow = length(V))
  for (i in 2:length(V)) {
    J[i,1] = V[i - 1] == 0 & V[i] == 0
    J[i,2] = V[i - 1] ==0 & V[i] == 1
    J[i,3] = V[i - 1] == 1 & V[i] == 0
    J[i,4] = V[i - 1] == 1 & V[i] == 1
  }
  V_00 = sum(J[,1],na.rm = TRUE)
```

```r
    V_01 = sum(J[,2],na.rm = TRUE)
    V_10 = sum(J[,3],na.rm = TRUE)
    V_11 = sum(J[,4],na.rm = TRUE)
    p_00 = V_00/(V_00 + V_01)
    p_01 = V_01/(V_00 + V_01)
    p_10 = V_10/(V_10 + V_11)
    p_11 = V_11/(V_10 + V_11)
    hat_p = (V_01 + V_11)/(V_00 + V_01 + V_10 + V_11)
    a = (1 - hat_p)^(V_00 + V_10)*(hat_p)^(V_01 + V_11)
    b = (p_00)^(V_00)*(p_01)^(V_01)*(p_10)^(V_10)* p_11^(V_11)
    return(-2 * log(a/b))
}
```

Listing 8.12. Independence coverage test in Matlab

```matlab
function res = ind_test(V)
  T = length(V);
  J = zeros(T,4);
  for i = 2:T
    J(i,1) = V(i - 1) == 0 & V(i) == 0;
    J(i,2) = V(i - 1) == 0 & V(i) == 1;
    J(i,3) = V(i - 1) == 1 & V(i) == 0;
    J(i,4) = V(i - 1) == 1 & V(i) == 1;
  end
  V_00 = sum(J(:,1));
  V_01 = sum(J(:,2));
  V_10 = sum(J(:,3));
  V_11 = sum(J(:,4));
  p_00 = V_00/(V_00 + V_01);
  p_01 = V_01/(V_00 + V_01);
  p_10 = V_10/(V_10 + V_11);
  p_11 = V_11/(V_10 +V_11);
  hat_p = (V_01 + V_11)/(V_00 + V_01 + V_10 + V_11);
  a = (1 - hat_p)^(V_00 + V_10)*(hat_p)^(V_01 +V_11);
  b = (p_00)^(V_00)*(p_01)^(V_01)*(p_10)^(V_10)* p_11^(V_11);
  res = -2 * log(a/b);
end
```

8.3.3 Testing VaR for the S&P 500

We apply these tests to the VaR forecasts in Section 8.2 and collect the VaR forecasts in matrix VaR. Since the first WE days were reserved for the estimation window, the analysis starts on day WE+1. For simplicity, we create a new matrix VaRa and vector ya where we have simply removed the first W days.

Listing 8.13. Backtesting S&P 500 in R

```
W1 = WE + 1
ya = y[W1:T]
VaRa = VaR[W1:T,]
m = c("EWMA","MA","HS","GARCH")
for (i in 1:4){
   q = y[W1:T]< -VaR[W1:T,i]
   v = VaRa*0
   v[q,i] = 1
   ber = bern_test(p,v[,i])
   ind = ind_test(v[,i])
   cat(i,m[i],'Bernoulli',ber,1 - pchisq(ber,1),"independence",
      ind,1 - pchisq(ind,1),"\n")
}
```

Listing 8.14. Backtesting S&P 500 in Matlab

```
ya = y(WE + 1:T);
VaRa = VaR(WE + 1:T,:);
for i = 1:4
   q = find(y(WE + 1:T) < -VaR(WE + 1:T,i));
   v = VaRa * 0;
   v(q,i) = 1;
   ber = bern_test(p,v(:,i));
   ind = ind_test(v(:,i));
   disp([i,ber,1-chi2cdf(ber,1),ind,1-chi2cdf(ind,1)])
end
```

The results are reported in Table 8.3. Not surprisingly, a violation ratio of 1 is strongly rejected by both coverage tests for all models, while we also get rejection of independence for HS and MA at 5%—but not for EWMA or GARCH. These results are not that surprising since the violation ratios are quite high, clearly implying rejection. Conditional models adjust much more sharply to changes in volatility. After considering Figure 8.1, there is little surprise that independence tests do not reject conditional models.

Table 8.4 shows the results of discarding the last 1,000 observations (i.e., the 2007–2009 crisis). In this case we only reject the hypothesis of $VR = 1$ at 5% for MA—but not the other methods. We find no rejection in the independence tests.

It would be worthwhile to simulate the test statistic to get more accurate confidence bounds in order to evaluate rejection significance.

Table 8.3. Comparison of the four VaR models reported in Table 8.2

Model	Coverage test		Independence test	
	Test statistic	p-value	Test statistic	p-value
EWMA	18.1	0.00	0.00	0.96
MA	81.2	0.00	7.19	0.01
HS	24.9	0.00	4.11	0.04
GARCH	16.9	0.00	0.00	0.99

Table 8.4. Comparison of the four VaR models reported in Table 8.3

Model	Coverage test		Independence test	
	Test statistic	p-value	Test statistic	p-value
EWMA	2.88	0.09	0.68	0.41
MA	6.15	0.01	2.62	0.11
HS	0.05	0.82	1.52	0.22
GARCH	1.17	0.28	0.99	0.32

8.3.4 Joint test

We can jointly test whether violations are significantly different from those expected and whether there is violation clustering by constructing the following test statistic:

$$LR(\text{joint}) = LR(\text{coverage}) + LR(\text{independence}) \sim \chi_2^2.$$

The joint test is simply the sum of the two individual tests. At this point, it may seem that the joint test should be universally preferred to tests of either the coverage property or the independence property, but this is usually not the case. The joint test has less power to reject a VaR model which only satisfies *one* of the two properties. For example, if the hit sequence produced by a particular VaR model exhibits correct coverage but violates independence then an independence test has a greater ability to reject this model than a joint test. Intuitively, the fact that one of the two properties is satisfied makes it difficult for the joint test to detect inadequacy in the VaR model. Individual tests should be used if the user has some prior knowledge of weaknesses in the VaR model.

8.3.5 Loss-function-based backtests

Lopez (1998, 1999) suggests that an alternative backtest could be constructed based on a general loss function, $l(\text{VaR}_t(p), y_t)$, which would take into consideration the magnitude of VaR violation. An example of such a loss function is:

$$l(y, x) = 1 + (y - x)^2 \quad \text{for } y \leq x.$$

Otherwise, it takes the value zero. If y indicates returns and x negative VaR, then we would typically calculate sample average loss as:

$$\hat{L} = \frac{1}{W_T} \sum_{t=W_E+1}^{T} l(y_t, \text{VaR}_t(p)).$$

The functional form of the loss function is flexible and can be tailored to address specific concerns. The disadvantage is that—in order to determine whether $\hat{L}$ is "too large" relative to what is expected—an explicit assumption about P/L distribution needs to be made. A null hypothesis for $\hat{L}$ should be mandatory.

Given the uncertainty over the true P/L distribution, a finding that $\hat{L}$ is "too large" relative to what is expected could either be due to inaccuracy in the VaR model or an inaccurate assumed distribution. In other words, the test is a joint test of the VaR model and the P/L distribution. This is problematic. Recall that for coverage and independence, the hit sequence should be identically and independently distributed as a Bernoulli random variable regardless of the P/L distribution, as long as the VaR model is well designed. Loss-function-based backtests may consequently be better suited for discriminating among competing VaR models than judging the absolute accuracy of a single model.

8.4 EXPECTED SHORTFALL BACKTESTING

It is harder to backtest expected shortfall (ES) than VaR because we are testing an expectation rather than a single quantile. Fortunately, there exists a simple methodology for backtesting ES that is analogous to the use of violation ratios for VaR.

For days when VaR is violated, normalized shortfall NS is calculated as:

$$NS_t = \frac{y_t}{\text{ES}_t}$$

where ES_t is the observed ES on day t. From the definition of ES, the expected y_t—given VaR is violated—is:

$$\frac{E[Y_t | Y_t < -\text{VaR}_t]}{\text{ES}_t} = 1.$$

Therefore, average NS, denoted by $\overline{NS}$, should be one and this forms our null hypothesis:

$$H_0 : \overline{NS} = 1.$$

In what follows, we opted to implement just the EWMA and HS versions, since the other two (MA and GARCH) are quite similar.

We assume the code in Section 8.2 has already been run and modify Listings 8.5 and 8.6 to Listings 8.15 and 8.16, respectively.

Listing 8.15. Backtest ES in R

```
ES = matrix(nrow = T, ncol = 2)          # ES forecasts for 2 models
VaR = matrix(nrow = T, ncol = 2)         # VaR forecasts for 2 models
for (t in (WE + 1):T){
  t1 = t - WE;
  t2 = t - 1;
  window = y[t1:t2]
  # EWMA
  s11 = lambda * s11 + (1 - lambda * y[t - 1]^2
  VaR[t,1] = -qnorm(p) * sqrt(s11 * value
  ES[t,1] = sqrt(s11) * dnorm(qnorm(p)) / p
  # HS
  ys = sort(window)
  VaR[t,2] = -ys[11]* value
  ES[t,2] = -mean(ys[1:11] * value     # ES number
}
```

Listing 8.16. Backtest ES in Matlab

```
VaR = NaN(T,2);                         % VaR forecasts for 2 models
ES = NaN(T,2);                          % ES forecasts for 2 models
for t = WE + 1:T
  t1 = t - WE;
  t2 = t - 1;
  window = y(t1:t2) ;
  % EWMA
  s11 = lambda * s11 + (1-lambda) * y(t - 1)^2;
  VaR(t,1) = -norminv(p) * sqrt(s11) *value ;
  ES(t,1) = sqrt(s11) * normpdf(norminv(p)) / p;
  % HS
  ys = sort(window);
  VaR(t,2) = -ys(11) * value;
  ES(t,2) = -mean(ys(1:11)) * value;    % ES number
end
```

We then implement the normalized ES test by adapting Listings 8.13 and 8.14 to Listings 8.17 and 8.18.

Listing 8.17. Backtest ES in R

```
ESa = ES[W1:T,]
VaRa = VaR[W1:T,]
for (i in 1:2){
    q = ya <= -VaRa[,i]
    nES = mean(ya[q] / -ESa[q,i])
    cat(i,"nES",nES,"\n")
}
```

Listing 8.18. ES in Matlab

```
VaRa = VaR(WE + 1:T,:);
ESa = ES(WE + 1:T,:);
for i = 1:2
    q = find(ya <= -VaRa(:,i));
    nES = mean(ya(q) ./ -ESa(q,i));
    disp([i,nES])
end
```

Both R and Matlab give us 1.11 for EWMA and 1.08 for HS.

With ES, we are testing whether the mean of returns on days when VaR is violated is the same as average ES on these days. It is much harder to create formal tests to ascertain whether normalized ES equals one or not than the coverage tests developed above for VaR violations. The reason is that such a test would be a joint test of the accuracy of VaR and the expectation beyond VaR, so that errors in estimating VaR also have to be taken into account, implying inaccuracy in the ES backtest is necessarily much higher than that in a VaR backtest. This means that the reliability of any ES backtest procedure is likely to be much lower than that of VaR backtest procedures, such as coverage tests.

The conclusion is that backtesting ES requires many more observations than backtesting VaR. In instances where ES is obtained directly from VaR, and gives the same signal as VaR (i.e., when VaR is subadditive), it is better to simply use VaR.

8.5 PROBLEMS WITH BACKTESTING

There are at least two problems with the overall backtesting approach as outlined above. Backtesting assumes that there have been no structural breaks in the data throughout the sample period. Financial markets, on the other hand, are continually evolving, and new technologies, assets, markets and institutions affect the statistical properties of market prices. It is unlikely that the statistical properties of market data in the 1990s are the same as today, implying that a risk model that worked well then might not work well today. The reason the results in Section 8.2 were so poor is exactly because of the presence of two important structural breaks in the sample.

The second problem with backtesting is *data mining* and intellectual integrity. In theory, backtesting is only statistically valid if we have no ex ante knowledge of the data in the testing window (i.e., we create a risk model, run it once on test data we have never seen and make a decision regarding the model). If we iterate the process—continually refining the risk model with the same test data and thus learning about the events in the testing window—the model will be fitted to those particular outcomes, violating underlying statistical assumptions. Models created in this way are likely to perform poorly in predicting future risk.

8.6 STRESS TESTING

The purpose of stress testing is to create artificial market outcomes in order to see how risk management systems and risk models cope with the artificial event, and to assess the ability of a bank to survive a large shock. For example, suppose that all equity prices in a bank's portfolio drop by 10%. We would then look to see how the risk management system reacts to this. For example, did asset allocations change, does the system properly integrate the impact of this event on the various subsystems, does the bank fail and so on?

The gap that stress testing aims to fill is model failure to encounter rare situations that could cause a severe loss, since backtesting relies on recent historical data. A good example is devaluation of the Mexican peso in December 1994, when the peso/dollar exchange rate jumped to 5.64 from 3.45 (as shown in Figure 8.2). This devaluation was mostly unanticipated and a conventional VaR system would not have been able to predict the magnitude of the devaluation.

8.6.1 Scenario analysis

The main aim of stress testing is to come up with scenarios that are not well represented in historical data but are nonetheless possible and detrimental to portfolio performance. We then revalue the portfolio in this hypothetical environment and obtain an estimate of maximum loss. This procedure then allows the bank to set aside enough capital for such an eventuality.

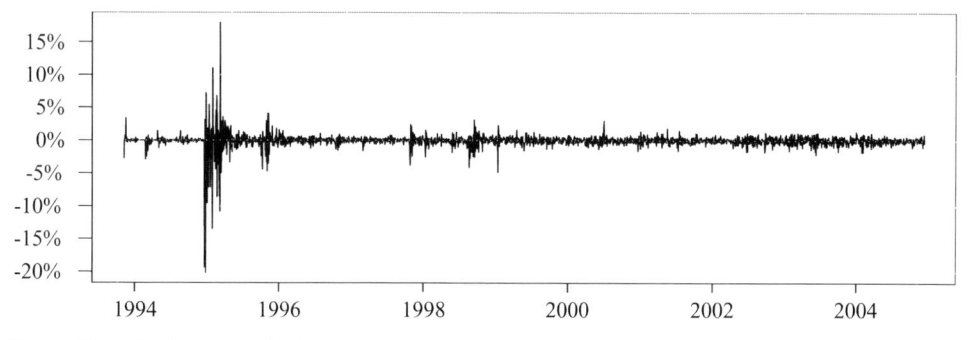

Figure 8.2. Mexican peso/dollar returns.

Table 8.5. Examples of historical scenarios

Scenario	Period
Stock market crash	October 1987
ERM crisis	September 1992
Bond market crash	April 1994
Asian currency crisis	Summer 1997
LTCM and Russia crisis	August 1998
Global crisis	Starting summer 2007

Berkowitz (2000) classifies scenarios into two broad types:

1. Simulating shocks that have never occurred or are more likely to occur than historical data suggest.
2. Simulating shocks that reflect permanent or temporary structural breaks—where historical relationships do not hold.

Stress test scenarios can either be simulated or based on actual historical events like those in Table 8.5. A simulated scenario is where we create our own customized crisis periods (e.g., the price of all equities drops by 10% or all the bonds in a portfolio suffer a downgrade in their credit rating). Given the infinite combinations possible, what are the most relevant scenarios? The Derivatives Policy Group recommends focusing on a set of specific movements:

- parallel yield curve shift by ± 100 bp;
- yield curve twisting by ± 25 bp;
- equity index values changing by $\pm 10\%$;
- swap spreads changing by ± 20 bp;
- currencies moving by 6% for major liquid ones and 20% for others.

The goal here is to provide comparable results across institutions. The relevant scenario should depend on the particular portfolio being stress-tested. A highly leveraged portfolio with a long position in corporate bonds hedged by a short position in treasuries will suffer a sharp loss if the yield curve steepens; therefore, the scenarios we are interested in should concentrate on different steepening situations.

The scenarios in the list above consist of movements in one underlying risk factor. Scenario analysis can become unmanageable if there are many factors, especially when portfolios are valued by Monte Carlo methods. In addition, extreme movements may not be appropriate for some portfolios, such as straddles, where the greatest loss will occur if the underlying does not move.

Furthermore, correlations between risk factors are ignored if we just pay attention to one factor or assign the same probability to different scenarios.

Correlations depend on market conditions, as noted in the discussion on nonlinear dependence in Section 1.7 where the correlations all increased with the onset of the 2007 crisis. The main advantage of using historical scenarios is that correlations are automatically taken into account. Ideally, simulated scenarios should also provide a realistic description of *joint* movements of market risk factors.

8.6.2 Issues in scenario analysis

An often-cited criticism of scenario analysis in stress tests is that the results indicate that banks should set aside a large amount of capital to absorb the worst case loss, which is usually not practical. Nevertheless, there are other actions that a bank can take such as buying insurance for the events in question and changing the composition of the portfolio to reduce exposure to a particular market variable.

There are two key problems with stress testing. The first is the lack of a mechanism to reliably judge the probability of a stress test scenario since they are both highly subjective and difficult to pinpoint. For example, it might sound interesting to create a scenario in which all bonds in a portfolio have their rating cut by two notches (e.g., from AAA to A). However, if we do not specify the probability of this happening it may not be a very useful exercise as it is not clear how the result should be interpreted. If this scenario only happens once every 10,000 years and we wrongly estimate the probability to be 5% and reduce our position accordingly, we are overreacting to the scenario. The problematic task of attributing the correct probability to historical or simulated scenarios limits the usefulness of stress testing as a tool to evaluate risk models.

The second problem is the potential for feedback effects, or endogenous risk since the focus is on institution-level risk, where feedback effects are disregarded. Institution-level stress testing does not address the core problem of endogenous risk or procyclicality. Ideally, supervisors should run systemwide stress tests. This has been considered by the Committee on the Global Financial System, but was ultimately dismissed, "The group concluded that, under ideal circumstances, aggregate stress tests could potentially provide useful information in a number of areas. ... However, the group also noted that it is as yet unclear whether such ideal circumstances prevail" (CGFS, 2000).

8.6.3 Scenario analysis and risk models

It is straightforward to integrate scenario analysis with risk models in use. Assume a risk manager has assigned a probability ξ to a particular scenario and the potential loss arising from it. The probability can be purely a subjective judgment from the manager's experience or could be derived from a model.

Berkowitz (2000) suggests that the most consistent method to incorporate stress tests is to construct a new return probability distribution f_{new} that attributes probability ξ to the scenario distribution and $(1 - \xi)$ to the distribution estimated from data. We draw a number u from a uniform(0,1) distribution. If the u is greater than ξ we draw from f, otherwise we draw from f_{stress}. By following this procedure, we are effectively creating a customized dataset that simultaneously reflects available historical data as well as gaps in the data filled by the scenarios:

$$f_{new} = \begin{cases} f & \text{with probability } (1 - \xi) \\ f_{stress} & \text{with probability } \xi. \end{cases}$$

If relevant scenario probabilities are well chosen, the new combined distribution will present a more accurate picture, and a better VaR or ES can be estimated. Knowing probability ξ also allows us to backtest the new VaR by using data drawn from f_{new}.

The scenario analysis described above can be undertaken using all VaR calculation methods. The use of actual historical scenarios lends itself particularly well to the use of historical simulation for calculating VaR.

Unlike the results of scenario analysis, which investigate the impact on portfolio value of a sudden and extreme move in market prices, stressing VaR inputs scrutinizes the consequences of changing the "status quo" as the covariance matrix is measured over a period of time, rather than a single day. A dramatic change in the covariance matrix is usually indicative of a structural break. Given that changes in volatilities and correlations are usually not instantaneous, the threat they pose is very different from that posed by a one-day extreme move.

8.7 SUMMARY

The objective of this chapter has been comparison of the main approaches for analyzing risk forecast quality. The starting point was backtesting and violation ratios, whereby the value-at-risk (VaR) methods under consideration were used to forecast VaR over a historical sample and these VaR forecasts compared with observed returns. On days when losses exceed the VaR, a violation is said to occur. By doing this for a sufficiently large sample, we can analyze the quality of the VaR method under consideration.

We focused on three different approaches for analyzing backtests: violation ratios, graphical analysis and statistical testing of the significance of violations (i.e., coverage and independence tests). As a practical example, the four most common VaR forecast methods and a sample from the S&P 500 were used to demonstrate implementation of the tests. We also studied backtesting of expected shortfall (ES).

Finally, we discussed different approaches for analyzing risk model quality—most importantly, stress testing—and focused on the pros and cons of such approaches.

9
Extreme value theory

Previous chapters have focused principally on events that occur with a 1% or 5% probability. This is fine for most day-to-day applications in financial institutions, and methods such as GARCH and historical simulation are well suited to provide VaR for these purposes. However, there are circumstances where we care about more extreme probability levels (e.g., pension fund risk management, economic capital applications and stress testing). We might be interested in a 0.1% VaR, the probability of a 25% drop in the stock market, the likelihood that a CDS spread exceeds 10% or other important but rare events. In these cases, we need more advanced techniques—usually extreme value theory (EVT).

Many statistical models are based on modeling the entire distribution of the quantity of interest, where observations in the center of the distribution dominate the estimation process given the scarcity of extreme observations. Accordingly, we may obtain a good approximation of the distribution of data for common events, but an inaccurate estimate of the distribution of the tails.

EVT, on the other hand, focuses explicitly on analyzing the tail regions of distributions (i.e., the probability of uncommon events); most EVT estimation methods make full use of extreme observations. An appealing aspect of EVT is that it does not require a prior assumption about the return distribution because the fundamental result of EVT identifies three possible distributions for extreme outcomes, but only one for fat-tailed returns, irrespective of the underlying return distribution.

EVT has a long and successful history in areas such as engineering, where it has been used to design flood walls and dikes. It was introduced to financial applications by Koedijk et al. (1990) and Jansen and de Vries (1991).

The theory of EVT is more complicated than the theory of the other methods discussed in this book; applications of EVT are more specialized. For this reason, the focus of this chapter is more on providing a basic introduction to the concept of EVT; however, any serious application of these methods requires more study.

Fortunately, there are many high-quality sources of material dealing with EVT, both free on the internet and in books. The most comprehensive treatment of EVT is Embrechts et al. (1997); there is also a condensed version in McNeil et al. (2005, ch. 7). There are excellent libraries in R for applying EVT while the choices in Matlab are much more limited.

The most important specific notation used in this chapter is:

ι Tail index

$\xi = 1/\iota$ Shape parameter

M_T Maximum of X
C_T Number of observations in the tail
u Threshold value
ψ Extremal index

9.1 EXTREME VALUE THEORY

All the applications we have seen in this book so far focus on relatively frequent and common events. Daily 1% VaR very much falls into that category.

However, many applications in finance depend on less common, or more extreme, outcome probabilities. For example, when doing a stress test, we may want to identify the expected worst outcome in the stock market in 10 years or identify the probability of credit spreads widening to 5%. Many investors want to know the probability of a CDS on government debt in the Eurozone widening to over 15% or the likelihood of the euro–dollar exchange rate appreciating by more than 20% in one week. Furthermore, one early indicator that the financial crisis was underfoot in 2007 was the widening of margins, so it would be of interest to identify the probability of a sharp increase in margins. All these questions, and many others, represent highly practical, if not specialized applications in finance; they have all been tackled using the method discussed in this chapter: extreme value theory (EVT).

Furthermore, aggregation of outcomes is often important. Because extreme outcomes aggregate differently from common outcomes, we can use EVT to identify how they aggregate.

Most statistical methods in applied finance focus on the entire distribution, like most of the methods discussed in this book so far, with the exception of historical simulation. For example, GARCH modeling is done with the entire distribution of returns. By contrast, EVT is explicitly concerned with the behavior of extreme outcomes. Consequently, it promises to be much more accurate for applications focusing on the extremes. The downside is that by definition we don't have that many extreme observations to estimate the quantities of interest, which necessarily limits the practicability of EVT.

9.1.1 Types of tails

EVT is usually presented in terms of the upper tail (positive observations), and we follow this convention here. Of course, in most risk analysis we are more concerned with the lower tail (negative observations), but this does not present much of a challenge since we can always reverse the distribution by pre-multiplying returns by -1.

Furthermore, there is no reason to believe the distribution of returns is symmetric; the upper and lower tails do not have the same thickness or shape. We saw one example of this asymmetry in Figure 1.8 where the upper tail of S&P 500 returns was thinner than the lower tail, and another in the rightmost column of Table 2.3 which dealt with the skew Student-t parameter. EVT can be useful in such situations as it enables us to explicitly identify the type of asymmetry in the extreme tails.

Financial returns follow an almost infinite variety of alternative distributions, making comparison between the risk properties of different returns challenging. However, in

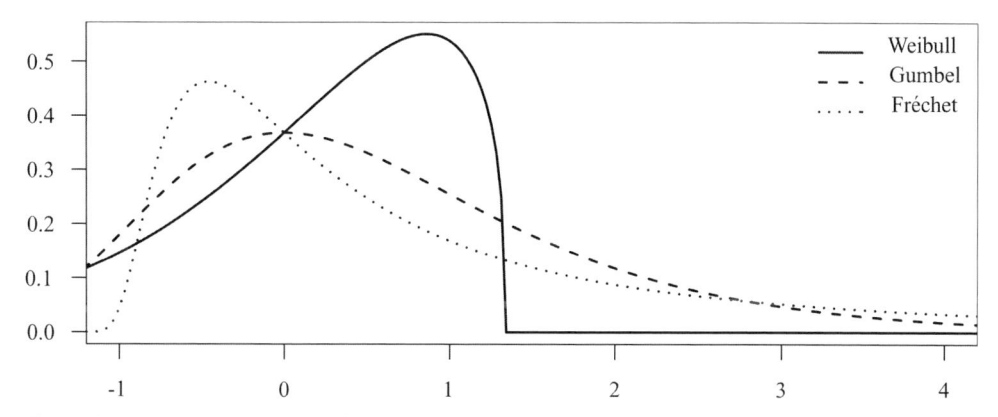

Figure 9.1. Extreme value distributions.

most risk applications we do not need to focus on the entire distribution of returns since all we care about are large losses, which usually belong in the tails. In that case, the main result of EVT states that, regardless of the overall shape of the distribution, the tails of all distributions fall into one of three categories as long as the distribution of an asset return series does not change over time. This means that for risk applications we only need to focus on one of these three categories:

Weibull   Thin tails where the distribution has a finite endpoint (e.g., the distribution of mortality and insurance/re-insurance claims).
Gumbel   Tails decline exponentially (e.g., the normal and log-normal distributions).
Fréchet   Tails decline by a power law; such tails are known as "fat tails" (e.g., the Student-*t* and Pareto distributions).

Figure 9.1 shows the three distributions. The Weibull clearly has a finite endpoint, and the Fréchet tail is thicker than the Gumbel's. In most applications in finance, we know the tails of returns are fat; therefore, we can limit our attention to the Fréchet case.

The key model parameter in EVT analysis is the *tail index* denoted by ι, or the inverse tail index denoted by $\xi = 1/\iota$, also known as the *shape parameter*—the lower the tail index, the thicker the tails. For the Student-*t* distribution, the tail index corresponds to the degrees of freedom.[1] As the degrees of freedom go to infinity, the Student-*t* becomes the normal distribution.

9.1.2 Generalized extreme value distribution

Let $X_1, X_2, \ldots, X_T$ denote IID random variables (RVs). We use the term M_T to indicate maxima in a sample of size T.

The Fisher and Tippett (1928) and Gnedenko (1943) theorems are the fundamental results in EVT stating that the maximum of a sample of properly normalized IID random variables converges in distribution to one of three possible distributions: the Gumbel, Fréchet or the Weibull.

---
[1] See Danielsson and de Vries (2003).

An alternative way of stating this is in terms of the maximum domain of attraction (MDA) which is the set of limiting distributions for properly normalized maxima as the sample size goes to infinity.

The theorems by Fisher–Tippet and Gnedenko then state that the distribution of standardized maxima, M_T, is:

$$\lim_{T \to \infty} \Pr\left\{\frac{M_T - a_T}{b_T} \leq x\right\} = H(x) \tag{9.1}$$

where the constants a_T and $b_T > 0$ exist and are defined as $a_T = T\mathrm{E}(X_1)$ and $b_T = \sqrt{\mathrm{Var}(X_1)}$. We then get the limiting distribution, $H(\cdot)$, of the maxima as the generalized extreme value (GEV) distribution:

$$H_\xi(x) = \begin{cases} \exp\left\{-(1+\xi x)^{-\frac{1}{\xi}}\right\}, & \xi \neq 0 \\ \exp(-\exp(-x)), & \xi = 0 \end{cases} \tag{9.2}$$

$H_\xi(\cdot)$ becomes the Fréchet if $\xi > 0$, the Weibull if $\xi < 0$ and the Gumbel if $\xi = 0$.

9.2 ASSET RETURNS AND FAT TAILS

It has been argued by many researchers that asset returns exhibit fat tails. Arguably, the earliest examples are Mandelbrot (1963) and Fama (1963, 1965).

The term "fat tails" is often used indiscriminately, where it can take on several meanings, the most common being "extreme outcomes occur more frequently than predicted by the normal distribution." While such a statement might make intuitive sense, it has little mathematical rigor as stated. A more formal definition of fat tails is required to facilitate the statistical modeling of risk.

The definition one most frequently encounters is kurtosis. Although a kurtosis higher than 3 may indicate the presence of fat tails, it is not always true. Kurtosis measures mass in the center relative to the non-center part of the distribution. In other words, it is more concerned with the sides of the distribution than the heaviness of tails.

The formal definition of fat tails comes from *regular variation*.

Definition 9.1 (Regular variation) *A random variable, X, with distribution $F(\cdot)$ has fat tails if it varies regularly at infinity; that is, there exists a positive constant ι such that:*

$$\lim_{t \to \infty} \frac{1 - F(tx)}{1 - F(t)} = x^{-\iota}, \quad \forall x > 0, \; \iota > 0.$$

We call ι the tail index.

In the fat-tailed case, therefore, the tail distribution is Fréchet:

$$H(x) = \exp(-x^{-\iota}).$$

Lemma 9.1 then follows.

Lemma 9.1 *A random variable X has regular variation at infinity (i.e., has fat tails) if and only if its distribution function F satisfies the following condition:*

$$1 - F(x) = \Pr\{X > x\} = Ax^{-\iota} + o(x^{-\iota}),$$

for positive constant A, when $x \to \infty$.

The expression $o(x^{-\iota})$ means that if we Taylor-expand $\Pr\{X > x\}$, the remaining terms will be of the type Dx^{-j} for constant D with $j > \iota$. In other words, in order to study the tails of the distribution the only term that matters is the first one, the others tend to zero more quickly.

This means that, as $x \to \infty$, the tails are asymptotically Pareto-distributed:

$$F(x) \approx 1 - Ax^{-\iota} \tag{9.3}$$

where $A > 0$; $\iota > 0$; and $\forall x > A^{1/\iota}$.

We demonstrate various tail thicknesses in Figure 9.2 as we change the tail index for two distributions: the Student-t and the Pareto.

The definition demonstrates that fat tails are defined by how rapidly the tails of the distribution decline as we approach infinity. As the tails become thicker, we detect increasingly large observations that impact the calculation of moments:

$$\mathrm{E}(X^m) = \int x^m f(x) dx. \tag{9.4}$$

The mth moment of X is the expectation of X^m. The mean is the first moment, while variance, skewness and kurtosis are all functions of the second, third and fourth moments, respectively.

If $\mathrm{E}(X^m)$ exists for all positive m, a complete set of moments exist, such as for the normal distribution. Definition 9.1 implies that moments $m \geq \iota$ are not defined for fat-tailed data. For example, if the tail index is 4, kurtosis is not defined; this explains the high kurtosis estimates sometimes obtained from financial data.

Many common models suggest returns are fat tailed (e.g., it is straightforward to derive the tail index of a GARCH process as a function of GARCH parameters). On the whole, returns on nonderivative financial assets seem to have a tail index between 3 and 5, even though many exceptions to this exist.

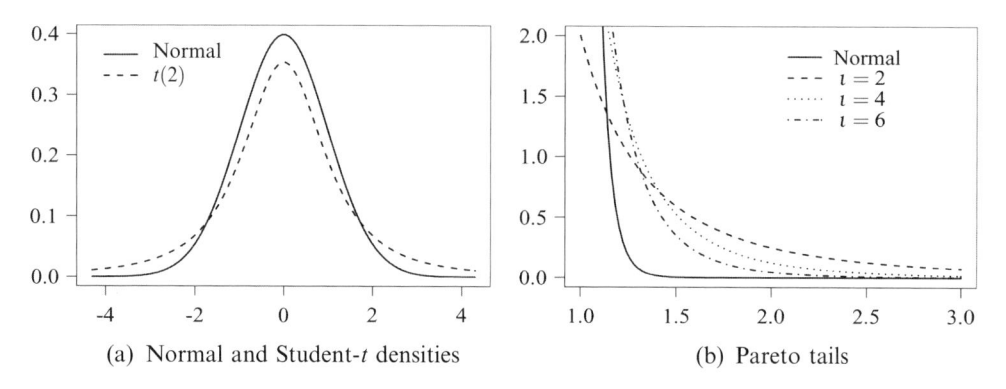

(a) Normal and Student-t densities

(b) Pareto tails

Figure 9.2. Normal and fat distributions.

9.3 APPLYING EVT

There are two main approaches to implementing EVT in practice: block maxima and peaks over thresholds (POT). The block maxima approach follows directly from (9.1) where we estimate the GEV by dividing the sample into blocks and using the maxima in each block for estimation. This procedure is rather wasteful of data and a relatively large sample is needed for accurate estimation.

Therefore, the POT approach is generally preferred and forms the basis of our approach below. It is based on models for all large observations that exceed a high threshold and hence makes better use of data on extreme values. There are two common approaches to POT:

- fully parametric models (e.g., the generalized Pareto distribution or GPD);
- semi-parametric models (e.g., the Hill estimator).

9.3.1 Generalized Pareto distribution

The generalized Pareto distribution (GPD) approach is based on the idea that EVT holds sufficiently far out in the tails such that we can obtain the distribution not only of the maxima but also of other extremely large observations.[2] Consider a random variable X, fix a threshold u and focus on the positive part of $X - u$ (recall we are focusing on the upper tail). This distribution—that is, $F_u(x)$—is:

$$F_u(x) = \Pr(X - u \leq x | X > u). \tag{9.5}$$

If u is the VaR, then (9.5) asks what is the probability that we exceed VaR by a particular amount (a shortfall) given that VaR is violated? The key result here is that as the threshold $u \to \infty$, $F_u(x)$ converges to the GPD $G_{\xi,\beta}(x)$:

$$G_{\xi,\beta}(x) = \begin{cases} 1 - \left(1 + \xi \dfrac{x}{\beta}\right)^{-\frac{1}{\xi}} & \xi \neq 0 \\ 1 - \exp\left(\dfrac{x}{\beta}\right) & \xi = 0 \end{cases} \tag{9.6}$$

where $\beta > 0$ is the scale parameter; and $x \geq 0$ when $\xi \geq 0$ and $0 \leq x \leq -(\beta/\xi)$ when $\xi < 0$.

We therefore need to estimate both shape (ξ) and scale (β) parameters when applying GPD. If the shape parameter is zero the distribution becomes the Gumbel, if it is negative it becomes the Weibull and when it is positive it becomes the Fréchet.

To reiterate, the GEV is the limiting distribution of normalized maxima, whereas the GPD is the limiting distribution of normalized data beyond some high threshold. The tail index is the same for both GPD and GEV distributions.

It is straightforward to estimate GEV parameters from the log-likelihood function of the GPD from (9.6).

---
[2] The main contributors are Balkema and de Haan (1974), Pickands (1975) and Davison and Smith (1990).

The VaR in the GPD case is:[3]

$$\text{VaR}(p) = u + \frac{\beta}{\xi}\left[\left(\frac{1-p}{F(u)}\right)^{-\xi} - 1\right].$$

9.3.2 Hill method

Alternatively, we could use the semi-parametric Hill (1975) estimator for the tail index in (9.3):

$$\hat{\xi} = \frac{1}{\hat{\iota}} = \frac{1}{C_T}\sum_{i=1}^{C_T} \log\frac{x_{(i)}}{u},$$

where C_T is the number of observations in the tail, $2 \leq C_T \leq T$, while $T, C_T \to \infty$, and $C_T/T \to 0$. The notation $x_{(i)}$ indicates sorted data, where the maxima is denoted by $x_{(1)}$, the second-largest observation by $x_{(2)}$, etc.

Obviously, we would expect the Hill estimator to be sensitive to the choice of threshold, u; this is discussed in more detail in Section 9.3.3. The Hill estimator attains the Cramér–Rao lower bound when data are Pareto-distributed, and hence is efficient and cannot be improved upon in this case.

Which method is chosen—GPD or Hill—depends on factors like how much knowledge one has of the data. GPD, as the name suggests, is more general than the Hill method as it can be applied to all three types of tails. By contrast, the Hill method is in the maximum domain of attraction (MDA) of the Fréchet distribution, and so is only valid for fat-tailed data—not in the normal or "relatively" fat-tailed distributions such as the log-normal.

Risk analysis

After estimation of the tail index, the next step is to apply a risk measure. Daníelsson and de Vries (1997) propose an estimator for the VaR. Note that while VaR is positive, it is applied to the left side of the distribution (returns less than zero) and thus applies to the lower tail, hence the minus.

The problem is finding $\text{VaR}(p)$ such that:

$$\Pr[X \leq -\text{VaR}(p)] = F_X(-\text{VaR}(p)) = p$$

for probability level p, where $F_X(u)$ is the probability of being in the tail (i.e., returns exceeding the threshold u).

Let G be the distribution of X since we are in the left tail (i.e., $X \leq -u$). By the Pareto assumption, (9.3), we have

$$G(-\text{VaR}(p)) = \left(\frac{\text{VaR}(p)}{u}\right)^{-\iota}.$$

By the definition of conditional probability:

$$G(-\text{VaR}(p)) = \frac{p}{F_X(u)}.$$

---

[3] See McNeil et al. (2005, p. 283) for details.

We equate the two relationships to obtain the expression for VaR(p):

$$\text{VaR}(p) = u\left(\frac{F_X(u)}{p}\right)^{\frac{1}{\iota}}.$$

$F_X(u)$ can be estimated by the proportion of data beyond the threshold u, C_T/T. The quantile or VaR estimator is thus:

$$\widehat{\text{VaR}(p)} = u\left(\frac{C_T/T}{p}\right)^{\widehat{1/\iota}}.$$

The estimator of VaR is driven by choosing the number of extremes C_T and the estimated tail index $\hat{\iota}$. The statistical properties of VaR(p) are, however, driven by $\hat{\iota}$, as it appears in the power. It is therefore sufficient to study the statistical properties of the Hill estimator.

9.3.3 Finding the threshold

Actual implementation of EVT is relatively simple and delivers good probability–quantile estimates where EVT holds. Unfortunately, EVT is often applied inappropriately. It should only be applied in the tails; as we move into the center of the distribution it becomes increasingly inaccurate. However, there are no rules that tell us when it becomes inaccurate, because it depends on the underlying distribution of the data. In some cases, it may be accurate up to 1% or even 5%, while in other cases it is not reliable even up to 0.1%.

The sample size and probability levels employed in estimation depend on the underlying distribution of data. As a rule of thumb, the sample size should be no smaller than 1,000 and the probability levels 0.4% or smaller, which corresponds to an annual event for daily data. For applications with smaller sample sizes or less extreme probability levels, other techniques—such as HS or fat-tailed GARCH—should be used.

It can be challenging to estimate EVT parameters given that the effective sample size is small (i.e., the number of extremes). This relates to choosing the number of observations in the tail, C_T. In general, we face two conflicting directions. As C_T become smaller, the tails become increasingly Pareto like, and hence estimation bias decreases along with C_T. On the other hand, estimation variance increases at the same time. We therefore reduce bias by lowering C_T and reduce variance by increasing C_T.

One specific case (demonstrated in Figure 9.3) is when we find the optimal threshold C_T^* at $C_T = 107$.

If we know the underlying distribution, then deriving the optimal threshold is easy, but of course in such a case EVT is superfluous.

Several methods have been proposed to determine the optimal threshold. The most common approach is the *eyeball method* where we look for a region where the tail index seems to be stable. More formal methods are based on minimizing the mean squared error (MSE) of the Hill estimator (i.e., finding the optimal point in Figure 9.3), but such methods are not easy to implement.[4]

---

[4] Daníelsson et al. (2001) and Daníelsson and de Vries (2003) propose a double-bootstrap technique for this purpose.

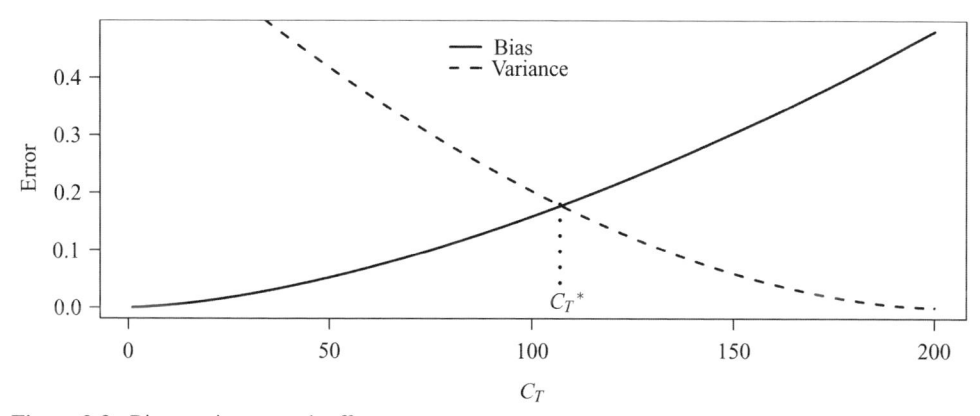

Figure 9.3. Bias–variance tradeoff.

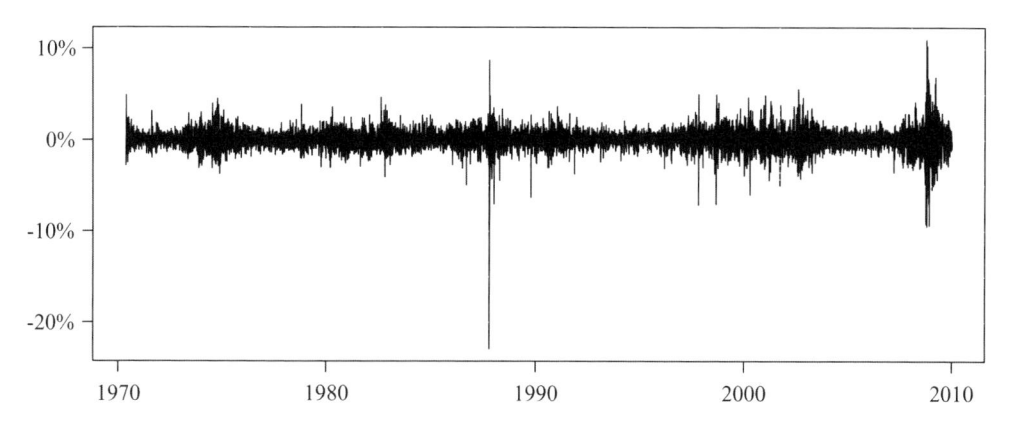

Figure 9.4. S&P 500 returns from 1970 to 2009.

9.3.4 Application to the S&P 500 index

We demonstrate application of EVT by using the Hill estimator with a sample of daily returns from the S&P 500 index from May 21, 1970 to the end of 2009—10,000 observations in all. The returns can be seen in Figure 9.4. When C_T is known, it is straightforward to implement EVT. In Listings 9.1 and 9.2 we have already loaded the return vector y.

Listing 9.1. Hill estimator in R

```
ysort = sort(y)                               # sort the returns
CT = 100                                      # set the threshold
iota = 1/mean(log(ysort[1:CT]/ysort[CT + 1])) # get the tail index
```

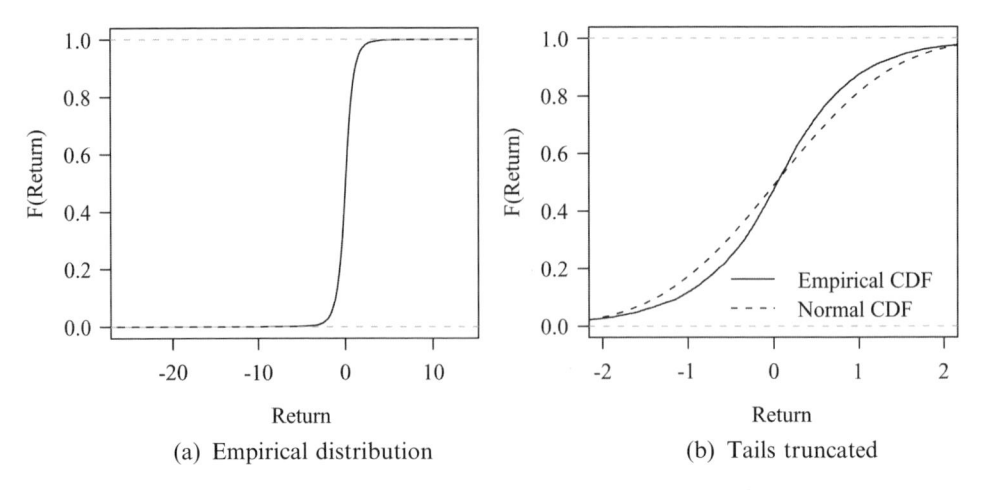

Figure 9.5. Empirical and normal distribution of daily S&P 500 returns from 1972 to 2009.

Listing 9.2. Hill estimator in Matlab

```
ysort = sort(y);                                        % sort the returns
CT = 100;                                               % set the threshold
iota = 1/mean(log(ysort(1:CT)/ysort(CT + 1)));          % get the tail index
```

Figure 9.5 shows the empirical distribution of returns where a normal distribution with the same mean and variance as the data is superimposed. Panel (a) shows the entire distribution while panel (b) cuts the tails off at 3.

The figure makes it clear how the normal distribution fails to capture the actual shape of the distribution of the S&P 500. This is exactly the same result we got in Section 1.5.

Figure 9.6 depicts both the tail index estimate ι obtained by the Hill estimator, and the VaR estimate as the threshold is varied from 5 to 500 in the sample from the S&P 500. Such plots are aptly known as *Hill plots*. In Figure 9.6 we find the optimal threshold in the region ranging from $C_T = 100$ to $C_T = 200$, giving a tail index estimate of about 3 and a VaR of about 2.7.

We estimated the lower and upper tails using the normal distribution and EVT where C_T was set at 70. These distributions are superimposed on the empirical distribution in Figure 9.7. It is obvious from the figure that the normal distribution underestimates both tails, where error increases as one moves towards the extremes. The distribution obtained by EVT, by contrast, runs smoothly through the empirical distribution.

9.4 AGGREGATION AND CONVOLUTION

The act of adding up observations, either across time (time aggregation) or across assets (portfolios) is termed *convolution*. From Feller (1971, theorem VIII.8) we get Theorem 9.1.

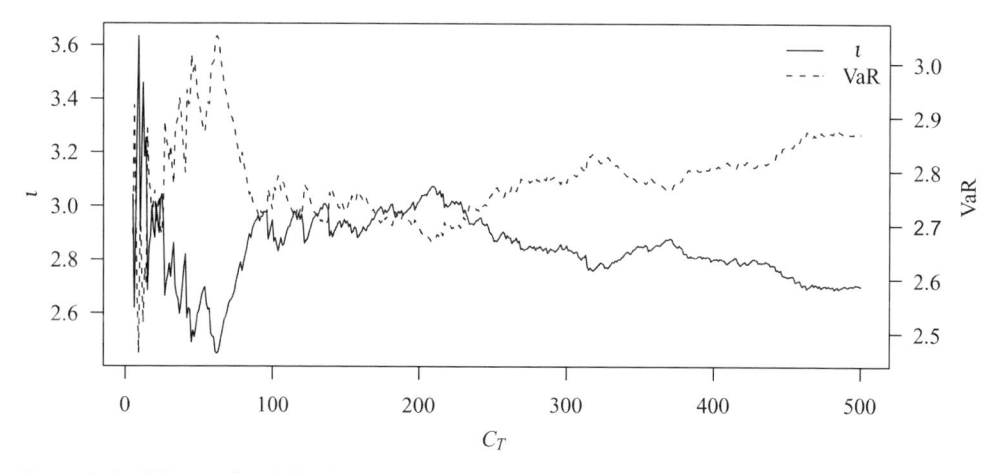

Figure 9.6. Hill plot for daily S&P 500 returns from 1970 to 2009.

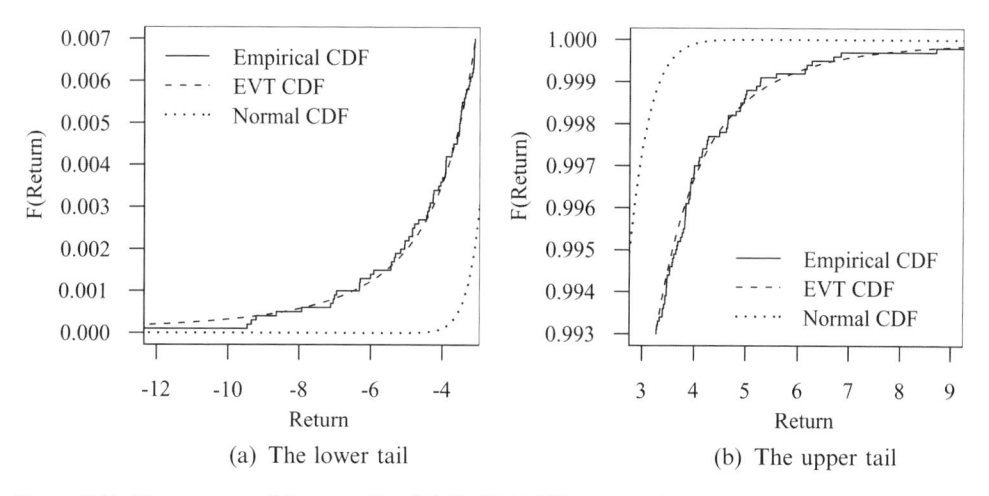

(a) The lower tail

(b) The upper tail

Figure 9.7. The upper and lower tails of daily S&P 500 returns from 1970 to 2009. Comparison of the empirical distribution, the EVT-estimated distribution with $C_T = 70$ and the normal distribution.

Theorem 9.1 *Let X_1 and X_2 be two independent random variables with distribution functions satisfying*

$$1 - F_i(x) = \Pr\{X_i > x\} \approx A_i x^{-\iota_i}$$

for $i = 1, 2$, when $x \to \infty$. Then, the distribution function F of the variable $X = X_1 + X_2$ in the positive tail can be approximated as follows.

Case 1 *When $\iota_1 = \iota_2$ we say that the random variables are first-order similar and we set $\iota = \iota_1$ and F satisfies*

$$1 - F(x) = \Pr\{X > x\} \approx (A_1 + A_2) x^{-\iota}.$$

Case 2 When $\iota_1 \neq \iota_2$ we set ι as the minimum of ι_1 and ι_2 and F satisfies

$$1 - F(x) = \Pr\{X > x\} \approx Ax^{-\iota}$$

where A is the corresponding constant.

As a consequence, if two random variables are identically distributed, the distribution function of the sum will be given by $\Pr\{X_1 + X_2 > x\} \approx 2Ax^{-\iota}$; hence, the probability doubles when we combine two observations from different days. But if one observation comes from a fatter tailed distribution than the other, then only the heavier tail matters.

If we are interested in obtaining quantiles (VaR) of fat tail data as we aggregate across time, then we can use Theorem 9.2 (de Vries, 1998).

Theorem 9.2 (de Vries, 1998) *Suppose X has finite variance with a tail index $\iota > 2$. At a constant risk level p, increasing the investment horizon from 1 to T periods increases the VaR by a factor:*

$$T^{1/\iota}.$$

This result has direct implications for aggregating risk over time. Financial institutions are required under the Basel Accords to calculate VaR for a 10-day holding period, where the rules allow the 10-day VaR to be calculated by scaling the one-day VaR by the square root of 10.

EVT distributions retain the same tail index for longer period returns, and Theorem 9.2 shows that the scaling parameter is slower than the square-root-of-time adjustment. Intuitively, as extreme values are more rare, they should aggregate at a slower rate than the normal distribution. For example, if $\iota = 4$, $10^{0.25} = 1.78$, which is less than $10^{0.5} = 3.16$.

VaR estimates across various risk levels and across days are compared in Table 9.1. For one-day horizons, EVT VaR is higher than VaR assuming the normal distribution, especially for more extreme risk levels. At the 0.05% level, EVT VaR is 3 compared with a normal VaR of 2. This is balanced by the fact that the 10-day EVT VaR is 5.1 which is now less than the normal VaR of 6.3. This seems to suggest that the square-root-of-time rule may be sufficiently prudent for longer horizons.

It is important to keep in mind that the ι root rule in Theorem 9.2 only holds asymptotically (i.e., for probability levels very close to 0%) and that for any other

Table 9.1. VaR and time aggregation of fat tail distributions

Risk level	5%	1%	0.5%	0.1%	0.05%	0.005%
Extreme value						
1 day	0.9	1.5	1.7	2.5	3.0	5.1
10 day	1.6	2.5	3.0	4.3	5.1	8.9
Normal						
1 day	1.0	1.4	1.6	1.9	2.0	2.3
10 day	3.2	4.5	4.9	5.9	6.3	7.5

From Danielsson and de Vries' (2000) 10-day VaR prediction on December 30, 1996 in millions of US dollars for a $100 million trading portfolio.

probability the appropriate scaling factor is somewhere between $\sqrt{T}$ and $\sqrt[2]{T}$, and even exceeds the latter—as in the model of Daníelsson and Zigrand (2006)—where returns have a jump component. For a comprehensive treatment of these topics see Cheng et al. (2010). A simulation experiment shows that for 1% VaR the $\sqrt[2]{T}$ is almost correct, while for probabilities of 0.001% the $\sqrt{T}$ is almost correct in the case of Student-t. This issue is further explored by Daníelsson et al. (1998).

9.5 TIME DEPENDENCE

When we discussed the theory of EVT in Section 9.1.2, we made the assumption that returns were IID, suggesting that EVT may not be relevant for financial data. Fortunately, we do not need an IID assumption.

Not only are EVT estimators consistent and unbiased in the presence of higher moment dependence, we can also explicitly model extreme dependence using the *extremal index*.

Example 9.1 *Let us consider extreme dependence in a MA(1) process:*

$$Y_t = X_t + \alpha X_{t-1}, \quad |\alpha| < 1. \tag{9.7}$$

Let X_t and X_{t-1} be IID such that $\Pr\{X_t > x\} \to A x^{-\iota}$ as $x \to \infty$. Then by Theorem 9.1:

$$\Pr\{Y_t \geq x\} \approx (1 + \alpha^\iota) A x^{-\iota} \quad \text{as } x \to \infty.$$

Dependence enters "linearly" by means of the coefficient α^ι. But the tail shape is unchanged.

Example 9.1 suggests that time dependence has the same effect as having an IID sample with fewer observations. If we record each observation twice:

$$Y_1 = X_1, Y_2 = X_1, Y_3 = X_2, \ldots$$

it increases the sample size to $D = 2$. Define $M_D \equiv \max(Y_1, \ldots, Y_D)$. Evidently:

$$\Pr\{M_D \leq x\} = F^T(x) = F^{\frac{D}{2}}(x),$$

supposing $a_T = 0$ and $b_T = 1$. The important result here is that *dependence increases the probability that the maximum is below threshold x*.

9.5.1 Extremal index

Dependence in the extremes is measured by the *extremal index*, $0 < \psi \leq 1$. If the data are independent then we get from (9.1) and (9.6):

$$\Pr\{M_T \leq x\} \to e^{-x^{-\iota}} \quad \text{as } T \to \infty,$$

when $a_T = 0$ and $b_T = 1$.

However, if the data are dependent, the limit distribution changes to:

$$\Pr\{M_D \leq x\} \to \left(e^{-x^{-\iota}}\right)^{\psi} = e^{-\psi x^{-\iota}}$$

where $0 \leq \psi \leq 1$ is the extremal index (i.e., a measure of tail dependence); and $1/\psi$ is a measure of the *cluster size* in large samples.

For double-recorded data $\psi = 1/2$. For the MA process in (9.7) we obtain:

$$\Pr\{T^{-\frac{1}{\iota}}M_D \leq x\} \to \exp\left(-\frac{1}{1+\alpha^{\iota}}x^{-\iota}\right)$$

where $\psi = \dfrac{1}{1+\alpha^{\iota}}$.

9.5.2 Dependence in ARCH

Consider the normal ARCH(1) process from Section 2.3.1:

$$Y_t = \sigma_t Z_t$$
$$\sigma_t^2 = \omega + \alpha Y_{t-1}^2$$
$$Z_t \sim \mathcal{N}(0,1).$$

Subsequent returns are uncorrelated, $\mathrm{Cov}[Y_t, Y_{t-1}] = 0$. Nevertheless, they are not independent since $\mathrm{Cov}[Y_t^2, Y_{t-1}^2] \neq 0$.

Even when Y_t is conditionally normally distributed, we noted in Section 2.3.1 that the unconditional distribution of Y is fat tailed. de Haan et al. (1989) show that the unconditional distribution of Y is given by

$$\Gamma\left(\frac{\iota}{2} + \frac{1}{2}\right) = \sqrt{\pi}(2\alpha)^{-\iota/2}.$$

From which we can easily solve the extremal index for the ARCH(1) process. For example:

α	0.10	0.50	0.90	0.99
ι	26.48	4.73	2.30	2.02
ψ	0.99	0.72	0.46	0.42

Therefore, the higher the α, the fatter the tails and the level of clustering. Similar results can be obtained for GARCH.[5]

9.5.3 When does dependence matter?

The importance of extreme dependence and the extremal index ψ depends on the underlying application. Extreme dependence can be ignored when dealing with *unconditional* probabilities. For example, suppose you are building a flood wall to protect against a storm, your concern is the water level on the worst day of the storm—not the

---
[5] See McNeil et al. (2005, p. 297).

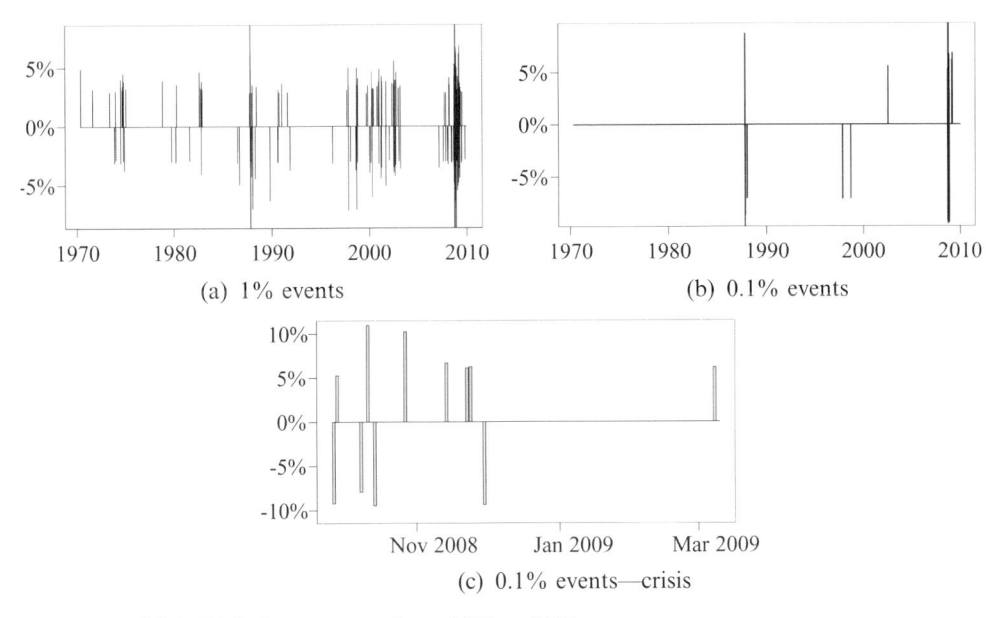

Figure 9.8. S&P 500 index extremes from 1970 to 2009.

number of days the storm lasts. The extremal index matters when calculating *conditional* probabilities. For example, if you are experiencing heavy rain causing floods, cumulative rain matters as much as the rain in any given day.

For many stochastic processes, including GARCH, the time between tail events becomes increasingly independent. This means that the strength of dependence decreases as we move into the tails even if the returns are highly dependent in the center of the distribution. For detailed examples of this see Daníelsson and Goodhart (2002). Let us consider daily S&P 500 index extremes between 1970 and 2009 (as in Figure 9.8) where we first show 1% extreme outcomes and then 0.1% extreme outcomes. It is clear that the time between outcomes becomes more independent as we move into the extremes. There are only two days on which consecutive extremes are observed (towards the end of 2008); both are on the upside.

9.6 SUMMARY

Most statistical methods for risk analysis in this book are focused on relatively frequent small events, such as 1% daily VaR. In such cases, the variance–covariance and historical simulation methods discussed in Chapters 2 and 5 are appropriate.

In some cases our concern relates to more extreme outcomes (e.g., a 0.1% VaR). In such cases different approaches are needed, the most common of which is extreme value theory (EVT). EVT is the statistical theory of the behavior of extreme statistical outcomes and is therefore the appropriate method to use in applications involving extremes.

Because extreme events are by definition uncommon, applications of EVT usually demand larger sample sizes than the other methods discussed in this book, and it is often challenging to identify which observations really are extreme. These issues limit EVT to niche applications.

Several high-quality libraries for EVT estimation exist in R, such as *fExtremes* and *evir*, and most of the analysis in this chapter can be implemented using them. Unfortunately, this richness of implementations does not extend to Matlab.

10
Endogenous risk

All the risk models discussed so far in this book have implicitly assumed that, while market participants are able to forecast risk, their eventual trading decisions do not affect market prices. Such models implicitly assume that financial risk is *exogenous* (i.e., it arises from shocks arriving from outside the financial system). In this view, the change in price of an asset is solely due to reasons outside the control of market participants, such as advances in technology, competitors dropping out, etc. In other words, we assume that the financial institution using the models in practice is a price taker. In reality, this is not so—every trade has a price impact, even if infinitely small.

The notion that all financial risk is exogenous is criticized by Daníelsson and Shin (2003) who propose the term *endogenous risk* for risk from shocks that are generated and amplified *within* the financial system.[1] Endogenous risk emphasizes the importance of interactions between individuals in determining market outcomes. In financial markets, all participants are constantly competing against each other, trying to gain advantage by anticipating each other's moves.

This has long been understood, with an early example provided by John Maynard Keynes (1936), in his discussion of a contest run by a London newspaper where entrants were asked to choose a set of six faces of women they considered the "most beautiful" from 100 photographs. Those who guessed right were rewarded with a prize.

> "It is not a case of choosing those faces which, to the best of one's judgement, are really the prettiest, nor even those which average opinion genuinely thinks the prettiest. We have reached the third degree where we devote our intelligences to anticipating what average opinion expects the average opinion to be. And there are some, I believe, who practice the fourth, fifth and higher degrees."
>
> Keynes, *General Theory of Employment, Interest and Money*, 1936

Financial markets are subject to both exogenous and endogenous risk, but it is the latter that is more damaging because it is behind some of the biggest financial crisis episodes in history, while at the same time being much harder to model. The presence of endogenous risk means that financial risk models are least reliable when needed the most and can lead to the conclusion that it may not be optimal from a financial stability point of view for financial institutions to engage in widespread risk modeling. Financial regulations, such as the Basel Accords, may have the perverse impact of increasing endogenous risk, and hence possibly systemic risk. See Daníelsson et al. (2010b) for more on this issue.

However, endogenous risk is not exclusively confined to financial markets, and we start with an illuminating example from engineering.

---

[1] The endogeneity of risk is formally modeled in Daníelsson et al. (2009).

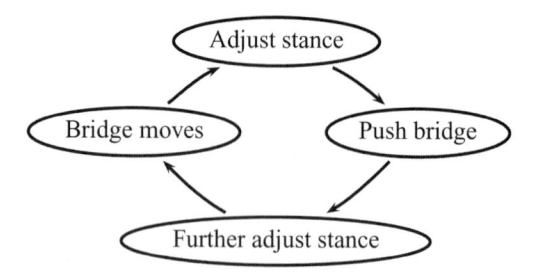

Figure 10.1. Feedback loop of the Millennium Bridge.

10.1 THE MILLENNIUM BRIDGE

On June 10th, 2000, Queen Elizabeth opened the Millennium Bridge—the first new Thames crossing for over a hundred years. Many thousands of people crowded on to the bridge. The structure was designed to cope easily with this kind of weight. But, within moments of the bridge being declared open, it began to wobble violently and amid great embarrassment had to be closed.

The source of the swaying was initially unclear. It is well known that soldiers marching across bridges can cause them to collapse, but if each person's step is an independent event, then the probability of thousands of people ending up walking synchronously is close to zero. It was discovered later that the bridge had been designed to swing gently in the breeze but the engineers had not taken adequate account of how large numbers of people walking across the bridge could exaggerate its movements.

When a bridge moves under your feet, it is a natural reaction to adjust your stance to regain balance. This movement causes everyone to adjust their stance at the same time. Such synchronized movement pushes the bridge, making the bridge swing even more. The increased swinging induces people to adjust their stance even more drastically, and so on. The swinging of the bridge and the synchronized adjustment of pedestrians are mutually reinforcing (as shown in Figure 10.1).

The wobble of a bridge is self-sustaining as a result of people's reactions. It is likely to continue and intensify even though the initial shock, a gust of wind, has long passed. This is an example of a force that is generated and amplified *within* the system. It is an *endogenous* response, very different from a shock that comes from a storm or an earthquake which is *exogenous* to the system.

10.2 IMPLICATIONS FOR FINANCIAL RISK MANAGEMENT

In general, we can surmise that endogenous risk appears whenever there is the conjunction of

(i) individuals reacting to their environment; and
(ii) where individual actions affect their environment.

Financial markets are perhaps the supreme example of such an environment. The danger of a positive feedback loop of actions to outcomes back to actions, amplifying the initial shock, is ever present and well understood among market traders and in the popular financial press. When asset prices fall and traders get closer to their trading limits, they are forced to sell. But this selling pressure sets off further downward pressure on asset prices, which induces a further round of selling. The downward spiral in asset prices here is endogenous.

Most current risk management techniques and regulations, however, are based on the presumption that risk management is a single-person decision problem (i.e., a game against nature). The uncertainty of price movements is assumed to be exogenous and therefore not dependent on the actions of others. A gambling analogy could be made. If the uncertainty facing a trader is indeed exogenous, modeling risk is akin to a gambler facing a spin of a roulette wheel, where the bets placed by him and other gamblers do not affect the outcome of the spin. Whenever an outcome is affected by the actions of others, risk modeling resembles poker more than roulette.

The roulette view of uncertainty relies on the hypothesis that many heterogeneous market participants behave in a random fashion, so their actions in aggregate do not influence the market. Under tranquil market conditions, this view is relatively innocuous. During periods of crises where information and beliefs become much more uniform and people behave in a much more similar way, relying on models built on the assumption of exogeneity is naive. Since many risk management systems are expected to cope with crisis episodes, what happens during tranquil market conditions is largely irrelevant.

However, the main reason the roulette view is useful is that it facilitates quantitative risk modeling by allowing standard statistical techniques to be applied to estimate the probabilities of various outcomes. The models we have seen so far are different ways of refining such estimation procedures. The common ingredient is that financial variables can be represented by a set of equations that are invariant under observation, which implicitly assumes agents do not react to risk measurements. To the extent that the stochastic process governing asset prices depends on what traders do, this view of the world is invalid.

10.2.1 The 2007–2010 crisis

The global financial crisis starting in 2007 was the most severe financial crisis since the Great Depression in the 1930s. It was initially triggered by turmoil in the subprime mortgage markets, where the collapse of housing prices forced banks to write down several hundred billion dollars' worth of loans. At the same time, massive amounts of wealth were wiped off all the major stock markets every day; a typical illustration of the crisis was the 54% fall in the Dow Jones from its peak in 2007 (see Figure 10.2). The crisis quickly spread to the real economy as all major economies suffered recessions.

US house prices had been rising relentlessly prior to 2007, fueled by the low-interest-rate environment in America. This was accompanied by an explosion of securitized products such as collateralized debt obligations and different types of mortgage-backed securities (MBS), many of which were AAA rated. This was primarily achieved by an assumption of low default correlations and extrapolation of the recent past to the future. Rating agencies also worked together with the issuers, allowing models to be manipulated to achieve the desired rating. The popularity of these products ultimately led to a

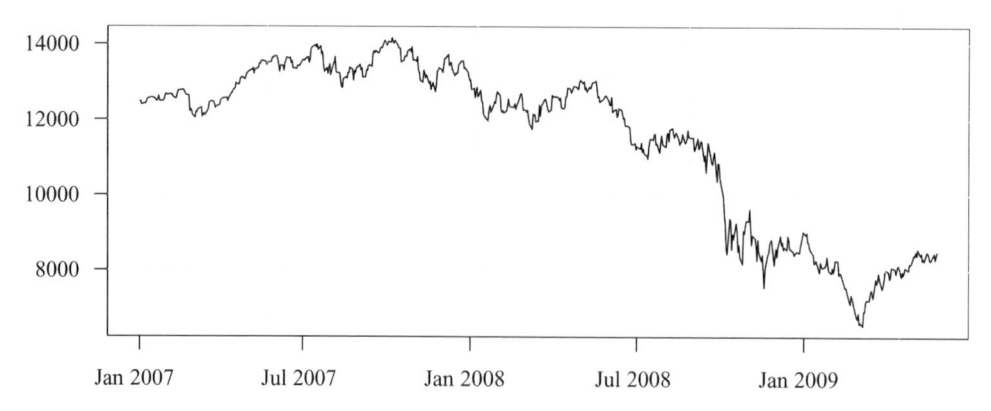

Figure 10.2. Dow Jones 2007–2009.
Data source: Yahoo Finance.

flood of cheap credit and allowed NINJA ("no income, no job or assets") borrowers to become home owners—even if only for a short time.

The increase in subprime mortgage defaults was first noted in February 2007. In the same month, Moody's put 21 US subprime deals on "downgrade review", indicating an imminent downgrade on these bonds. This led to deterioration in the prices of mortgage-related products. There is evidence that holdings of these products were heavily concentrated in the hands of leveraged traders such as hedge funds and investment banks.

When a leveraged trader buys an asset, he can use it as collateral and borrow against its value. However, normally he cannot borrow the entire price. The difference between the security's price and the amount of the loan is called the margin or haircut, and must be financed by the trader's own capital. Margin requirements can be changed on a daily basis depending on market conditions, but an increase in margin requirements can lead to a margin call.

The decline in the price of mortgage-related products led to higher margins being demanded. To meet this requirement for cash, leveraged traders were forced to *deleverage* (i.e., to sell part of their assets). As many market participants faced margin calls at the same time, these sales inevitably depressed prices further. This then set off another round of margin increases, prices fell further and so on.

The situation is depicted in Figure 10.3, showing a feedback loop where market distress feeds on itself. Adrian and Shin (2010) empirically confirm this spiral for investment banks. In this view, it is *endogenous* risk that is doing the harm.

Many of the vehicles that purchased MBSs issued asset-backed commercial paper (ABCP) to fund their purchases. ABCP is a short-term loan that needs to be rolled over regularly. As prices of MBSs and confidence in their credit rating fell, the market for ABCP began to dry up (as shown in Figure 10.4). Figure 10.5 shows the cost of insuring against the default of AAA-rated and AA-rated securities increasing dramatically. The ABX index is based on a basket of 20 credit default swaps referencing assets backed by subprime mortgages of different ratings. The protection buyer pays an upfront fee of (100 − ABX price). The fall in ABX mirrors the rise in both realized and implied default rates on subprime mortgages.

One of the implications of a highly leveraged market going into reversal is that a

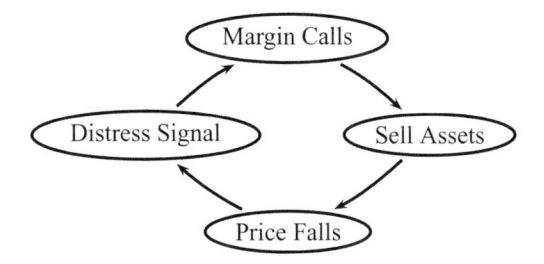

Figure 10.3. Price margin spiral.

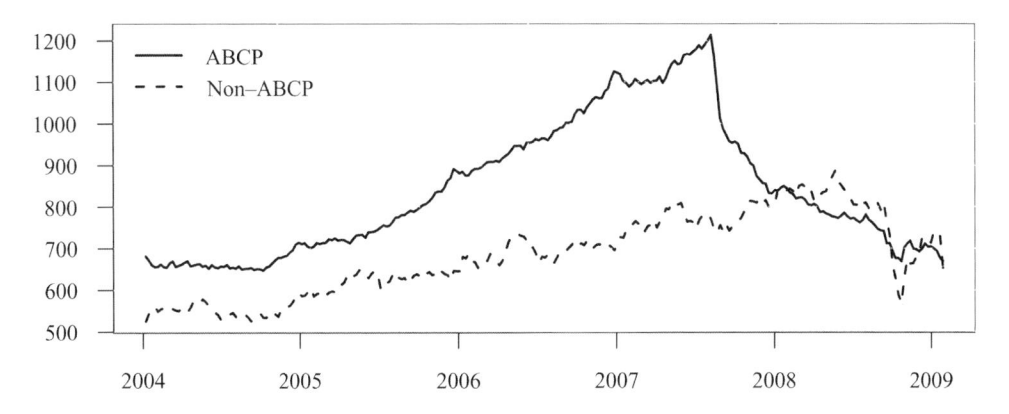

Figure 10.4. Commercial paper volume, US billions.
Data source: Federal Reserve Board.

Figure 10.5. ABX 6-1 prices.
Data source: Thomson Reuters.

moderate fall in asset value is highly unlikely. Either the asset does not fall in value at all or the value falls by a large amount. The logic of mutually reinforcing effects of selling in a falling market dictates this conclusion. In Section 10.3 we study more formally the effect of a leverage ratio constraint on market prices. The leverage ratio is the inverse of the margin or haircut requirement (i.e., if a lender demands a 2% haircut, then the maximum leverage that can be achieved is 50).

10.3 ENDOGENOUS MARKET PRICES

Standard models assume that prices reflect fundamentals, where they are commonly represented as the sum of the present value of future dividends. However, market participants are subject to many constraints, some of which are imposed by outside parties, such as regulators or shareholders. If the same constraints are applied to all market participants, they have the potential to trigger peculiar outcomes (e.g., as in the model below where the demand function is upward sloping).

Let us consider a large bank that has the potential to impact market prices with its trading volume and where it operates with a leverage ratio (L) of 5. While there are several definitions of a leverage ratio, we define it as the ratio of asset values to the value of equity. Initially, the market price of asset P_0 is $10, the bank holds $Q_0 = 100$ units of it and has $D_0 = \$800$ in debt. The value of its assets is $A_0 = Q_0 \times P_0 = \$1{,}000$, and its equity is $E_0 = A_0 - D_0 = 200$. The starting balance sheet is therefore:

Assets	Liabilities
$A_0 = 1{,}000$	$E_0 = 200$
	$D_0 = 800$

The bank meets its leverage constraint since:

$$L = \frac{A_0}{E_0} = 5.$$

At time 1, a shock causes the price of the asset to fall to $P_1 = \$9$, the fall in the value of the asset is matched by a fall in the bank's equity. The balance sheet becomes:

Assets	Liabilities
$A_1 = 900$	$E_1 = 100$
	$D_1 = 800$

and leverage increases from 5 to 9. The bank now exceeds its leverage constraint and needs to reduce its debt. The easiest way is to sell some assets and use the proceeds to pay off the debt. We calculate the units of assets that need to be sold in two cases: first, where the bank is a price taker and, second, where it has significant price impact.

Prices are exogenous

In this case the bank cannot influence market prices no matter how much it chooses to trade. The bank sells just enough assets to keep its leverage ratio at 5. The new debt D_1 is the old debt D_0 less the value of assets sold at the current market price of P_1:

$$D_1 = D_0 - P_1(Q_0 - Q_1).$$

To calculate Q_1:

$$L = \frac{A_1}{A_1 - D_1} = \frac{P_1 Q_1}{P_1 Q_1 - D_1} = \frac{P_1 Q_1}{P_1 Q_1 - D_0 + P_1(Q_0 - Q_1)}$$

therefore $\quad Q_1 = -L \dfrac{D_0 - P_1 Q_0}{P_1}.$ \hfill (10.1)

In our example, the bank now holds $Q_1 = \frac{500}{9}$ units of assets each valued at \$9. By selling $100 - \frac{500}{9}$, the target leverage ratio is reached and the bank needs to do nothing further. Its balance sheet becomes:

Assets	Liabilities
$A_1 = 500$	$E_1 = 100$
	$D_1 = 400$

Prices are endogenous

Let us now suppose the bank exerts a significant price impact. This implies that the market price of the asset will rise if the bank decides to buy and fall if the bank decides to sell. The effect can be captured by a price impact function:

$$\Delta P_2 = \lambda P_1(Q_1 - Q_0)$$

where λ is the price impact factor; ΔP_2 is the change in price $(P_1 - P_2)$; and $P_1(Q_1 - Q_0)$ is the amount the bank wants to sell—in our case \$400. If we let $\lambda = 0.002$, then by selling \$400, prices fall by a further 80 cents to \$8.2, and the effect of this ensures the bank fails to meet its leverage target once again. We can then apply (10.1) again to get the second-order price impact. Another round of selling depresses the market price once more and the bank continues to fail to meet its leverage constraint and will have to continue selling more assets. In Table 10.1 we show the impact of applying (10.1) 10 times (i.e., 10 iterations).

Table 10.1. A downward spiral

Iteration	Q	P	A
1	100.00	10.00	1,000.00
2	55.556	9.000	500.000
⋮	⋮	⋮	⋮
9	25.986	7.721	200.641
10	25.986	7.721	200.636

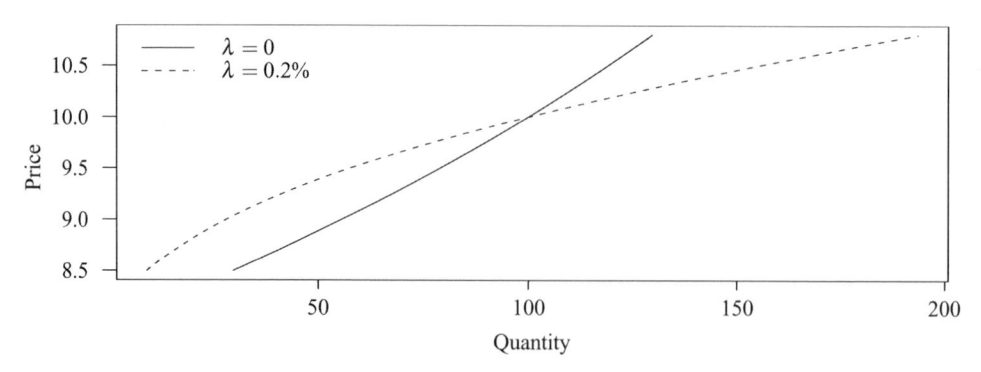

Figure 10.6. Demand functions.

Supply and demand functions

From this example we see that the bank sells when the price falls, and if the initial shock had increased the price of the asset then the bank would be buying more to keep the leverage ratio at 5. In effect, the demand function for the bank is upward sloping—not downward sloping as is usually the case. In Figure 10.6 we show the demand function for both cases (i.e., when the bank exerts a price impact and when it does not). This simple example illustrates that—in the presence of endogenous risk—we often see large rather than moderate changes in asset values as a response to a small shock.

Analogy with VaR

The leverage constraint in this example works in the same way as a VaR constraint. A higher leverage ratio implies a more stringent VaR constraint and vice versa, since the equity of a highly leveraged bank can be easily wiped off by a small negative price shock.

This example suggests that, if all market participants had the same regulatory VaR constraint, all would be forced to react to shocks in the same way and therefore their actions on aggregate would have a significant price impact. By contrast, if each were left to its own devices, different risk appetites would ensure heterogeneity of actions, so prices would be less likely to spiral down.

The capacity of VaR constraints to harmonize the way financial institutions see the world induces them to behave in a similar way and is well documented in the press. This was succinctly noted in the *Economist* (2000):

> "The trouble is that lots of banks have similar investments and similar VaR models. In periods when markets everywhere decline, the models can tell everybody to sell the same things at the same time, making market conditions much worse. In effect, they can, and often do, create a vicious feedback loop."

10.4 DUAL ROLE OF PRICES

Financial innovation has meant that banks and other financial institutions now rely on price-sensitive risk management systems such as VaR. Even accounting has adopted price-sensitive valuations with the proliferation of marking to market.

Prices, as seen above, play two roles. On the one hand, they are a passive reflection of underlying economic fundamentals (an aggregation of all available information), but, on the other hand, they are also an imperative to action. In the leverage ratio example, prices fall as more selling takes place, but the lower prices invoke more selling in the presence of a binding constraint. Some actions induced by price changes are desirable, but often actions in response to binding constraints are not desirable for the whole system even if they are sensible for an individual.

The reliance on prices to allocate resources efficiently can lead to distortion of the very same market prices. Distortion may be so severe that prices cease to convey any fundamentals and, instead, bring about an amplified spiral of actions that can cause great damage.

Financial crises are often accompanied by large price changes, but large price changes by themselves do not constitute a financial crisis. The release of public data such as interest rate decisions is sometimes marked by large price changes at the time of announcement; indeed, this is a sign of a well-functioning market, but the market usually stabilizes quickly after such a move.

The distinguishing feature of crisis episodes is that they seem to gather momentum from endogenous responses of market participants themselves. Perhaps the best example of this is the stock market crash of 1987 and the role played by mechanical trading rules such as delta hedging.

10.4.1 Dynamic trading strategies

October 19, 1987 saw global stock markets drop around 23%, the greatest single-day loss that the Dow Jones Industrial Average (DJIA) had ever suffered in continuous trading up to that point. The fall in the DJIA is shown in Figure 10.7.

The Brady Commission (1988) attributed the magnitude and swiftness of the price decline to practices such as portfolio insurance and dynamic hedging techniques (i.e., the use of automatic trading strategies). These trading techniques have the property that they dictate selling an asset when its price falls below certain threshold values, and buying it when price rises above a threshold. In other words, they dictate a "sell cheap,

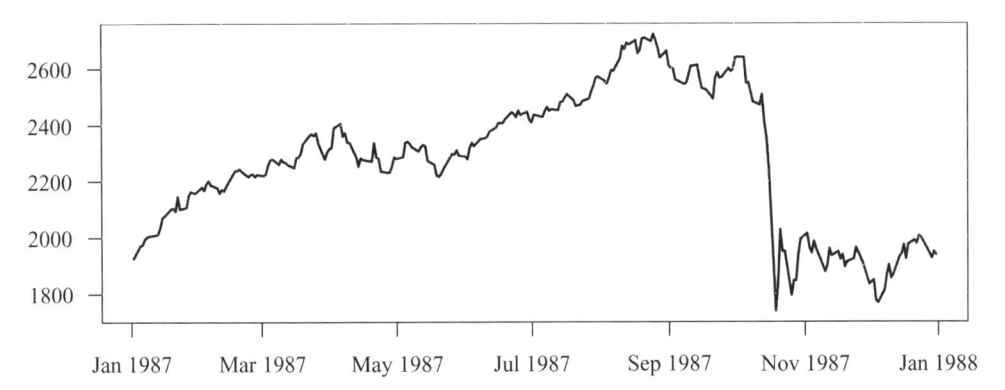

Figure 10.7. 1987 Dow Jones Industrial Average index values.
Data source: finance.yahoo.com.

buy dear" strategy that generates precisely the kind of vicious feedback loop that destabilizes markets.

10.4.2 Delta hedging

Options, which give the holder the right but not the obligation to buy (call) and sell (put) assets at a pre-agreed price (the strike price, X) at a date in the future, are effective hedging instruments. However, traded options exist only for well-established markets, and only for relatively short maturities. For very long-dated options, or for specific assets, *dynamic replication* is the only avenue open to traders if they wish to hedge a large downside exposure, which is equivalent to a short put position.

Dynamic replication is a strategy where we replicate the payoffs of an option by holding a combination of cash and the underlying asset. A simple technical model is illustrated below.

The *delta* (Δ) of a put option is the rate of change of its price, denoted g, with respect to a change in price of the underlying asset, P:

$$\Delta = \frac{\partial g}{\partial P} < 0.$$

Graphically, Δ is the slope of a curve representing the option price and the price of the underlying (as shown in Figure 10.8). Black and Scholes (1973) show that a put can be replicated by holding Δ numbers of the underlying asset. Therefore, a portfolio consisting of:

$$\begin{cases} \Delta & \text{Underlying asset} \\ -1 & \text{Put} \end{cases}$$

is risk free with respect to *small* changes in the underlying price as delta is a linear approximation. This is because the gain or loss from holding the underlying asset (Δ) when the price changes is matched by an exactly offsetting loss or gain from the change

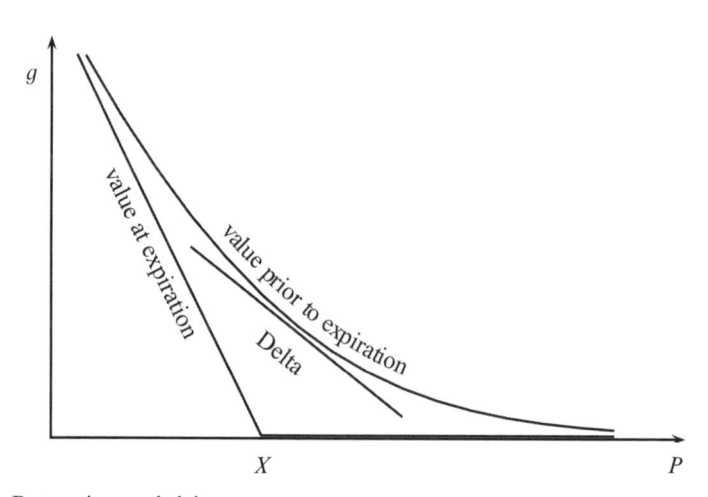

Figure 10.8. Put option and delta.

in price of the put option. An analogous argument can be used to show that the payoff from the put option can be replicated by holding a suitable portfolio of the underlying asset and cash as shown by:

$$\begin{Bmatrix} 1 & \text{Put} \\ 0 & \text{Cash} \end{Bmatrix} = \begin{Bmatrix} \Delta & \text{Underlying asset} \\ -P\Delta + g & \text{Cash} \end{Bmatrix}$$

The portfolio on the right-hand side (the replicating portfolio) is financed by selling short $|\Delta|$ units of the underlying asset at price P and adding the proceeds to the cash balance. Remember that the Δ of a put option is always negative. Now, suppose the price changes to P'. The value of the portfolio at the new price is:

$$\overbrace{\Delta P'}^{\text{Short asset}} + \overbrace{g - P\Delta}^{\text{Cash holding}} = g + \Delta(P' - P)$$

$$\approx g'$$

where g' is the new price of the put option given P'. The trader then forms a new portfolio:

$$\begin{cases} \Delta' & \text{Underlying asset} \\ -P'\Delta' + g' & \text{Cash.} \end{cases}$$

This strategy is illustrated in Figure 10.9. The Δ of the option becomes more negative as the price of the underlying asset falls and less negative as it rises, implying a larger short position in the underlying asset when its price falls and a smaller short position when its price rises. In other words, dynamic replication dictates a "sell cheap, buy dear" strategy similar to the situation with the binding leverage ratio, and it is precisely this feature that contributes to endogenous risk.

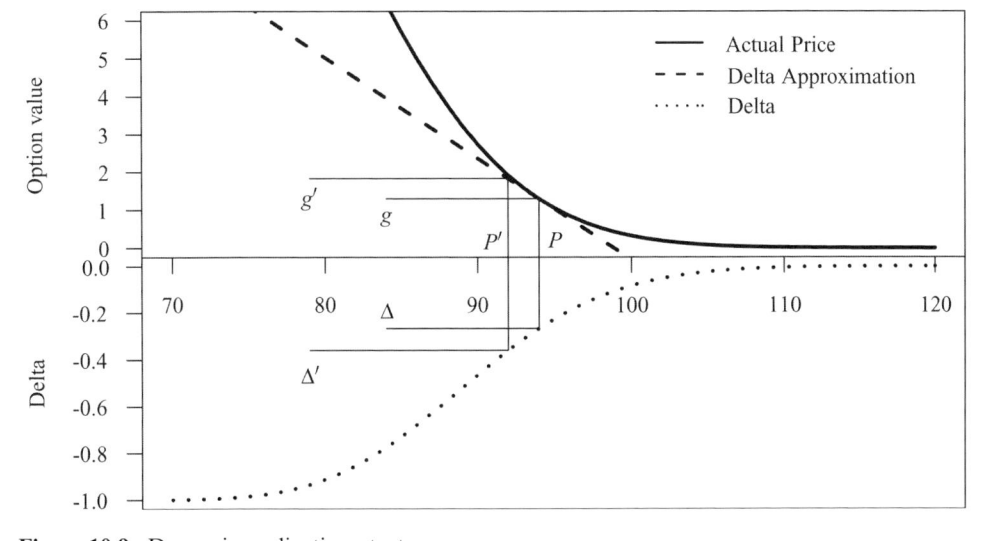

Figure 10.9. Dynamic replication strategy.

10.4.3 Simulation of feedback

We can analyze the impact of dynamic trading strategies by simulating delta hedging. Let us suppose there is a put option with a strike price of $90, the risk-free rate is 10%, annual volatility is 40% and time to maturity is 20 days. The underlying stock is currently trading at $100. All the Black–Scholes assumptions hold.

We start at $t = 1$ by selling Δ stocks short and keeping the proceeds. For each day until expiration, we adjust our stock holdings by any change in Δ. This strategy should cost the same as just buying the put option at $t = 1$. Under Black–Scholes assumptions our delta trading will not impact prices. If, however, a large amount of money in the financial markets is allocated to the strategy, then such trading will have a significant price impact. Suppose that for each $100 traded, prices are affected by $\lambda = 0.2$ times the amount we buy/sell. The results are presented in Figure 10.10.

Figure 10.10 shows that both prices are roughly identical for the first 10 days, but then the market is hit by a seemingly small exogenous shock. However, because of the nature of the dynamic trading strategy, the shock gets amplified and the stock price drops far more than it would in the absence of the significant price impact, causing a market crash.

The mechanism is described in Figure 10.11. When a large enough number of market participants follow this strategy, a downward shock to the price generates sales, which causes the price to fall. But a decline in price entails a fall in the delta of the put which forces traders to sell more. This type of feedback is typical of financial markets.

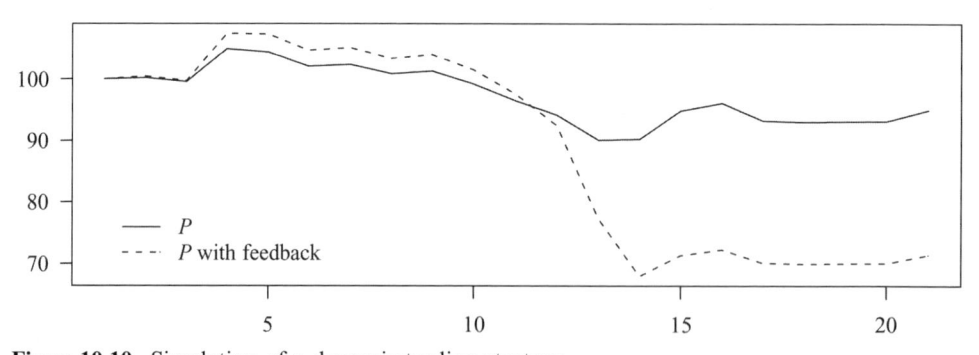

Figure 10.10. Simulation of a dynamic trading strategy.

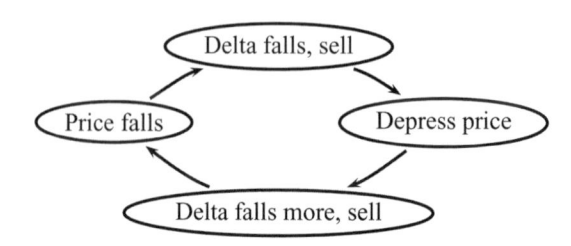

Figure 10.11. Endogenous dynamics of delta hedging.

10.4.4 Endogenous risk and the 1987 crash

The stock market crash of 1987 is a classic example of endogenous risk and the potentially destabilizing feedback effect on market dynamics of concerted-selling pressure arising from mechanical trading rules.

The analysis above suggests that when a large segment of the market are engaged in the same trading strategies, the action-inducing role of prices ensures that the initial shock is amplified, leading to large and rapid declines in prices. Estimates in 1987 indicated that around $100 billion in funds were following formal portfolio insurance programs like the one described above, representing around 3% of the pre-crash market value. However, this is almost certainly an underestimate of the total selling pressure arising from informal hedging techniques such as stop loss orders.

In the period from Wednesday, October 14th to Friday, October 16th, the market declined around 10%. Sales dictated by dynamic hedging models amounted to around $12 billion (either in cash or futures), but actual sales were only around $4 billion. This means that by opening time on Monday morning, there was a substantial amount of pent-up selling pressure. Both the S&P and the Dow Jones fell over 20% on Monday, October 19th. At times, the imbalance between purchases and sales meant that much of the underlying market for stocks did not function. Instead, traders attempted to use the index futures market to hedge their exposures.

The important lesson to emerge from the 1987 stock market crash is that the uncertainty governing stock returns is better described as being *endogenous* rather than *exogenous*.

10.5 SUMMARY

Most models for forecasting risk assume that financial risk is exogenous (i.e., that market participants are affected by the financial system, but do not impact the dynamics of market prices).

When there are diverse opinions in the market and where these diverse opinions are reflected in the diversity of trading strategies and positions, treating risk as being exogenous is appropriate. Endogenous risk is most likely to arise when there is a prevailing consensus concerning the direction of market outcomes, where such unanimity leads to similar positions or trading strategies. In such an environment, uncertainty in the market is generated and modified by the response of individual traders.

Many, if not most, financial crises have endogenous risk at their heart, such as the 1987 crash and many aspects of the 2007–2010 crisis.

In terms of quantitative risk management and stress testing, the margin of error must be chosen with endogeneity in mind. When a bank's portfolio is subjected to a simulated shock, the margin of error should not be based on the assumption of ceteris paribus (i.e., all other market conditions remaining unchanged). If the shock is likely to affect the actions of *other* market participants, the system-wide impact of the shock may be much larger in practice than the initial shock that is being simulated. For the engineers of the Millennium Bridge, it was not enough simply to subject the model of the bridge to strong storms or other outside shocks assuming that other things would remain unchanged.

The financial system has the potential to sustain its own dynamic response, and this potential should be studied carefully.

How should endogenous risk be accounted for in the current framework of risk management? A risk manager needs to be able to make an intelligent distinction between cases where the standard "roulette wheel" view of uncertainty is sufficient and cases where risk endogeneity is important. Common sense and an intuitive understanding of underlying pressures in the market are essential complements to any quantitative risk management tools that merely extrapolate the past.

Appendix A
Financial time series

Financial forecasting—whether of risk or asset prices—depends on methods from time series analysis, often requiring specialized versions of standard time series tools. The objective of this appendix is to provide a foundation to financial time series that is relevant to this book.

Several high-quality textbooks are available for background reading on financial time series analysis. Enders (1995, chs. 2, 4 and 6) contains a general treatment of time series models. A more specialized book is Tsay (2005) which is concerned with financial time series; his chapter 2 covers similar material to this appendix. The R and Matlab codes for many of the topics below are given in Appendices B and C, respectively.

A.1 RANDOM VARIABLES AND PROBABILITY DENSITY FUNCTIONS

A.1.1 Distributions and densities

A random variable (RV) is a function that maps the outcomes of random phenomena to a unique numerical value. For example, suppose the possible outcomes of a discrete RV are $[-2, 0, 1, 3]$ with probabilities $[0.2, 0.1, 0.3, 0.4]$, respectively.

Panel (a) of Figure A.1 shows outcomes and associated probabilities. The function that relates outcomes to their probabilities is called a *probability density function* (PDF); the graph in panel (a) is referred to as the density. A density is usually denoted in lowercase letters, such as $f(\cdot)$. In the example (see previous paragraph), the probability of outcome 1 is 30%, indicated by $f(1) = 0.3$. For a function to be considered a density, it must have nonnegative probabilities that must also sum or integrate to one.

The *cumulative distribution function* (CDF) shows the probability of receiving an outcome or a lower one (i.e., cumulative probabilities). Distribution function is a synonym for CDF. In the example above, we would get $[0.2, 0.3, 0.6, 1.0]$ for the cumulative probabilities—shown in panel (b) of Figure A.1. A distribution is usually denoted in uppercase. Continuing with the example, the probability of receiving an outcome of 1 or less is $0.6 = 0.2 + 0.1 + 0.3 = F(1)$. More generally, we can write:

$$F(x) = \sum_{x_t \leq x} f(x_t)$$

where x_t indicates outcome i; and $f(x_t)$ is the probability of that outcome.

The distribution function represents the area under (or the sum of) the density. In the case of continuous densities, F is the primitive function of f and f the derivative of F,

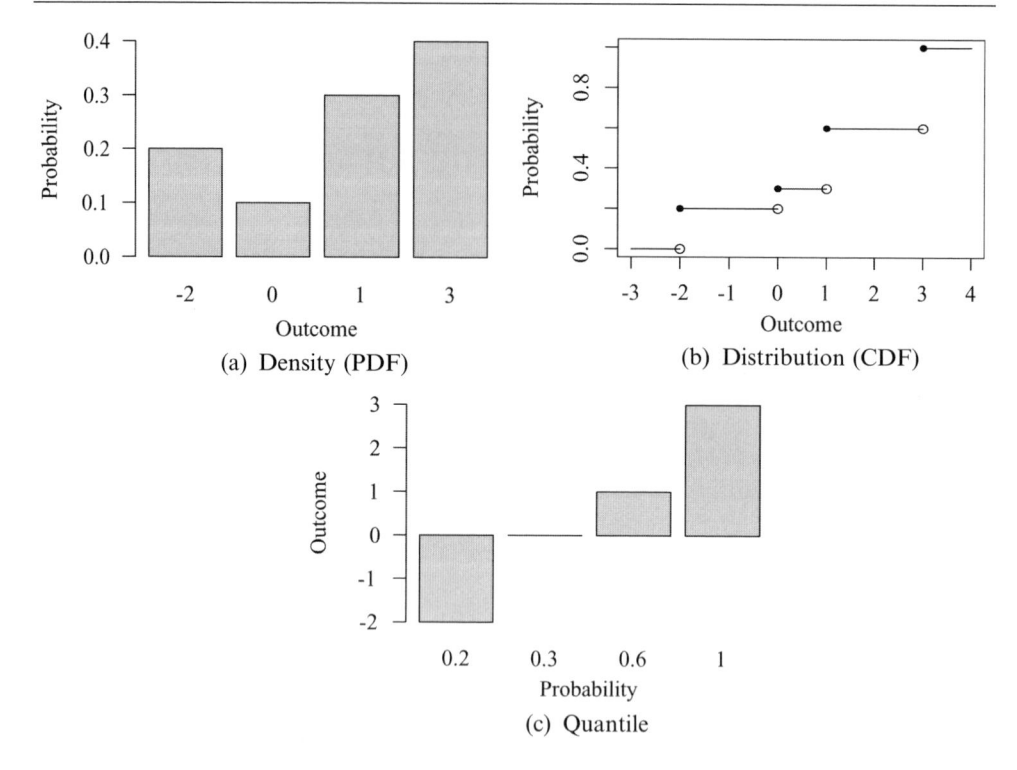

Figure A.1. Discrete distribution.

where they are related as:

$$F(q) = \int_{-\infty}^{q} f(x)dx$$

A.1.2 Quantiles

We often need to identify an outcome associated with a probability by calculating the inverse distribution. Continuing with the example above, we might want to know what outcome has a probability of 0.3 or less. Such an outcome is called a *quantile*, and if the distribution is continuous, the inverse distribution is called a quantile function.

An example of a quantile function is shown in panel (c) in Figure A.1. Another way to refer to a quantile is the term *significance level*, $\gamma(p) = F^{-1}(p)$.

A quantile means the fraction (or percent) of points below a given value. For example, some quantiles of the normal are shown in Table A.1.

A.1.3 The normal distribution

The most common distribution in statistics is the *normal distribution*. The normal distribution is more convenient to work with than most other distributions, and is

Table A.1. Normal outcomes

Probability	Normal predicted outcome (quantile)
1%	−2.33
2%	−2.05
⋮	⋮
50%	0.00
⋮	⋮
98%	2.05
99%	2.33

completely described by the first and second moments; moreover, it is mathematically simple in both univariate and multivariate forms. It also has the convenient property that any linear combination of normal variables is also distributed normally. ϕ is often used as the symbol for the normal density and Φ for the normal distribution.

X is normally distributed if it has the density:

$$\phi(x; \mu, \sigma) = \frac{1}{\sqrt{2\pi}\sigma} \exp\left[-\frac{1}{2}\left(\frac{x-\mu}{\sigma}\right)^2\right]. \tag{A.1}$$

A random variable with the density described above is denoted by:

$$X \sim \mathcal{N}(\mu, \sigma^2).$$

The normal distribution is unimodal, symmetric and centered on μ. The variance, σ^2, governs the spread (or dispersion) of the distribution. We often work with the standard normal distribution which is illustrated in Figure A.2.

Definition A.1 (Standard normal distribution) *Standard normal distribution is the name given to the normal distribution with mean zero and unit variance—that is, a RV X has the distribution $X \sim \mathcal{N}(0, 1)$. It has density $\phi(x) = \frac{1}{\sqrt{2\pi}} e^{-x^2/2}$.*

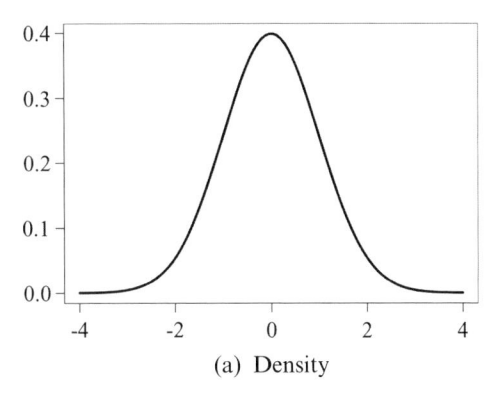

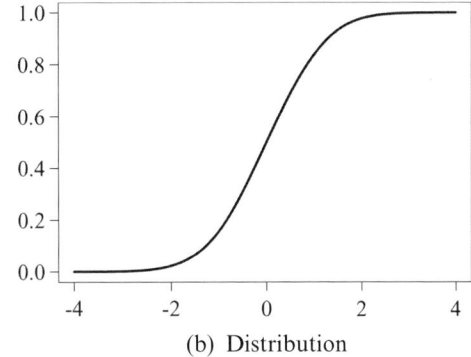

(a) Density

(b) Distribution

Figure A.2. Standard normal distribution.

A.1.4 Joint distributions

Let us suppose we have two RVs X and Y. Their joint distribution function defines the probability that X is less than some x, and Y is less than some y:

$$F_{X,Y}(x,y) = \Pr(X \leq x \text{ and } Y \leq y). \tag{A.2}$$

This definition can be extended to any number of RVs in the same way.

A.1.5 Multivariate normal distribution

In many cases we have to deal with more than one IID normally distributed variable. If we have T realizations of a standard normal $x = (x_1, x_2, \ldots, x_T)'$, the *joint density*, assuming independence, is given by:

$$\phi(x) = \phi(x_1)\phi(x_2)\cdots\phi(x_T)$$

$$= \prod_{t=1}^{T} \phi(x_t)$$

$$= \prod_{t=1}^{T} \frac{1}{\sqrt{2\pi}} \exp\left[-\frac{1}{2}x_t^2\right]$$

$$= (2\pi)^{-\frac{T}{2}} \exp\left[-\frac{1}{2}\sum_{t=1}^{T} x_t^2\right]$$

$$= (2\pi)^{-\frac{T}{2}} \exp\left[-\frac{1}{2}x'x\right].$$

If X has a mean vector $\mu = (\mu_1, \mu_2, \ldots, \mu_T)'$ and covariance matrix $\Sigma = [\sigma_{ij}]$—that is, $X \sim \mathcal{N}(\mu, \Sigma)$—then the density is:

$$\phi(x) = \frac{1}{(2\pi)^{T/2}|\Sigma|^{\frac{1}{2}}} \exp\left[-\frac{1}{2}(x-\mu)'\Sigma^{-1}(x-\mu)\right].$$

If X is multivariate normally distributed, all marginal distributions and conditional distributions must be normally distributed. The bivariate normal distribution is shown in Figure A.3.

A.1.6 Conditional distribution

An important application of the joint distribution is calculation of the *conditional distribution* (i.e., the distribution of RVs, given one of the RVs takes a particular value).

The conditional probability function of an RV X, given Y takes a particular value y, is defined as:

$$f_{X|Y}(x) = \frac{f_{X,Y}(x,y)}{f_Y(y)}.$$

Alternatively, the joint density can be factored as:

$$f_{X,Y}(x,y) = f_X(x) \times f_{Y|X}(y) = f_Y(y) \times f_{X|Y}(x).$$

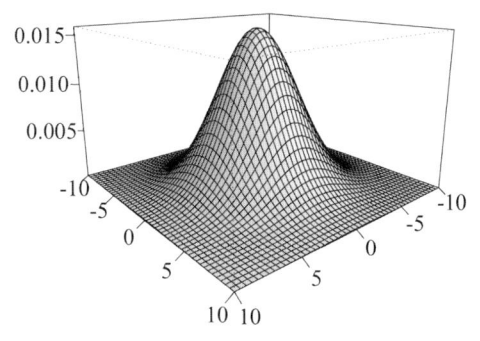

Figure A.3. Three-dimensional plot of the bivariate normal distribution.

A.1.7 Independence

Suppose we have two RVs, X and Y, with joint distribution $F_{X,Y}(x,y)$, where X has marginal distribution $F_X(x)$ and Y has marginal distribution $F_Y(y)$.

Definition A.2 (Independence) X and Y are said to be independent if their joint probability function is the product of their marginal probability functions:

$$F_{X,Y}(x,y) = F_X(x)F_Y(y) \quad \text{for all possible values of } x \text{ and } y.$$

From the definition of conditional probability functions, it follows that if X and Y are independent, the conditional probability function of Y given X is the same as the marginal probability function of Y:

$$F_{Y|X}(y) = F_Y(y).$$

We come across independence and IID frequently throughout the book.

Definition A.3 (IID) *Identically and independently distributed, each RV has the same probability distribution and is independent of every other RV. This implies that every conditional mean, variance and all higher moments are constant.*

A.2 EXPECTATIONS AND VARIANCE

Let us consider a random variable X, for which we have observed a sample $x = \{x_1, \ldots, x_T\}$ of length T. We assume that X has a continuous probability density function f defined on the real line.

The expectation of X, μ, is the expected value or mean of the variable. It is defined by

$$\mu = \mathrm{E}(X) = \int_{-\infty}^{\infty} x f(x) dx \qquad (A.3)$$

and is estimated by the *sample mean*:

$$\hat{\mu} = \bar{x} = \frac{1}{T} \sum_{t=1}^{T} x_t.$$

The variance of X measures the dispersion/spread of the variable around the mean. It is defined as the expectation of $(X - \mu)^2$:

$$\sigma^2 = \mathrm{E}\left[(X - \mu)^2\right] = \int_{-\infty}^{\infty} (x - \mu)^2 f(x) dx. \qquad (A.4)$$

If we assume that μ is known, we compute sample variance by

$$\hat{\sigma}^2 = \frac{1}{T} \sum_{t=1}^{T} (x_t - \mu)^2.$$

In the more realistic case in which μ is unknown we have to use the sample mean and adjust the formula in order to find the unbiased estimator for σ^2:

$$\hat{\sigma}^2 = \frac{1}{T-1} \sum_{t=1}^{T} (x_t - \hat{\mu})^2.$$

The square root of variance is called standard deviation if μ is known and standard error if μ has to be estimated prior to calculating variance. The standard error is sometimes known as *volatility* when referring to financial returns.

The mean and variance are defined for most distributions we encounter in practice, but some distributions such as the Cauchy distribution have an undefined variance and mean.

A.2.1 Properties of expectation and variance

Suppose we have two RVs X and Y and constants a, b, c, then:

$$\mathrm{E}(aX + bY + c) = a\mathrm{E}(X) + b\mathrm{E}(Y) + c.$$

The variance of X is often written as $\mathrm{Var}(X)$ and has the following properties:

$$\mathrm{Var}(X) \geq 0$$

$$\mathrm{Var}(a + bX) = b^2 \mathrm{Var}(X).$$

If X and Y are independent, then:

$$\mathrm{Var}(X + Y) = \mathrm{Var}(X) + \mathrm{Var}(Y).$$

Otherwise

$$\mathrm{Var}(X + Y) = \mathrm{Var}(X) + \mathrm{Var}(Y) + 2\,\mathrm{Cov}(X, Y)$$

where $\mathrm{Cov}(X, Y)$ denotes the covariance of X and Y.

A.2.2 Covariance and independence

Let us consider two random variables X and Y, with T observations $x = \{x_1, \ldots, x_T\}$ and $y = \{y_1, \ldots, y_T\}$.

The covariance of X and Y is defined by:

$$\sigma_{X,Y} = E[(X - \mu_X)(Y - \mu_Y)].$$

If we assume the means μ_X and μ_Y are known, the sample covariance is computed by:

$$\hat{\sigma}_{X,Y} = \frac{1}{T} \sum_{t=1}^{T} (x_t - \mu_X)(y_t - \mu_Y).$$

In the more realistic case where means have to be estimated, we get:

$$\hat{\sigma}_{X,Y} = \frac{1}{T-1} \sum_{t=1}^{T} (x_t - \hat{\mu}_X)(y_t - \hat{\mu}_Y).$$

The magnitude of covariance depends upon the units by which X and Y are measured. A positive covariance indicates that X and Y tend to move in the same direction and vice versa.

Pearson's *correlation coefficient* measures the strength of linear dependence, it is scale independent and defined as:

$$\rho_{X,Y} = \frac{\sigma_{X,Y}}{\sigma_X \sigma_Y}. \tag{A.5}$$

The correlation coefficient can be estimated by:

$$\hat{\rho} = \frac{\hat{\sigma}_{X,Y}}{\hat{\sigma}_X \hat{\sigma}_Y}.$$

ρ is always less than or equal to 1 in magnitude. If ρ is greater than 0 it implies that Y tends to be above average when X is above average, and if ρ is less than 0 then Y tends to be below average when X is above average. If ρ is 0 then there is no *linear relationship* between X and Y.

Since ρ is defined in terms of moments, it only exists for any bivariate probability distribution whose covariance is defined and whose marginal variances are nonzero and bounded.

One should be careful when interpreting the value of ρ. It is a a measure of *linear dependence*, and we can come up with two datasets having the same correlation coefficient that are very differently distributed. This is illustrated in Figure A.4 where four different datasets are plotted, all with the same correlation coefficient of 0.816, but with very different dependence. Moreover, ρ is not invariant to monotonic transformations and, therefore, is not always a good measure of dependence.

A.3 HIGHER ORDER MOMENTS

The mth moment of a random variable X is defined by:

$$E(X^m).$$

Definition A.4 describes the mth *centered* moment of a distribution.

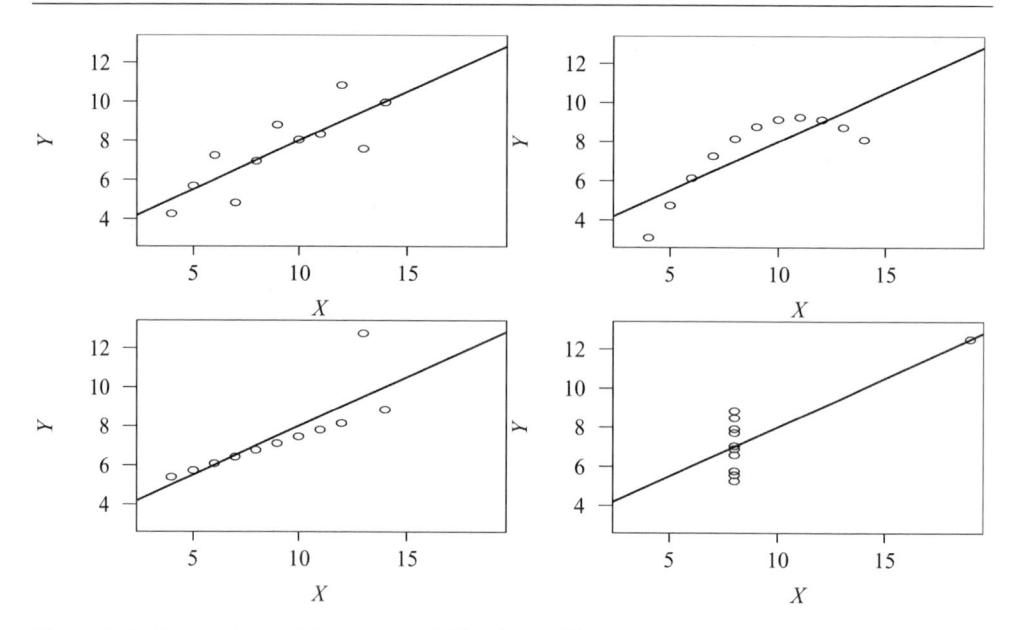

Figure A.4. Cross plots of four sets of bivariate RVs, X and Y, with the same correlation coefficient.

Definition A.4 (Centered moment) *The mth centered moment of an RV is defined by:*

$$E[(X-\mu)^m] = \int_{-\infty}^{\infty} (x-\mu)^m f(x)dx.$$

The first centered moment is another way of referring to the mean, and the *second centered moment* is another way of referring to variance.

A.3.1 Skewness and kurtosis

Skewness (Skew) and *kurtosis* (Kurt) are functions of the third and fourth moments, respectively. Skewness gives information on the asymmetry of a distribution where symmetric distributions have zero skewness. Kurtosis provides information on the "peakedness" of a distribution. If kurtosis is small, this implies the density function is relatively flat near its center. If kurtosis is large, then density is peaked near the center. Skewness and kurtosis are shown in Figure A.5. Definitions A.5 and A.6, respectively, describe them formally.

Definition A.5 (Skewness) *The central third moment of a distribution:*

$$\text{Skew}(X) = \frac{E(X-\mu)^3}{\sigma^3}.$$

Appendix A: Financial time series   205

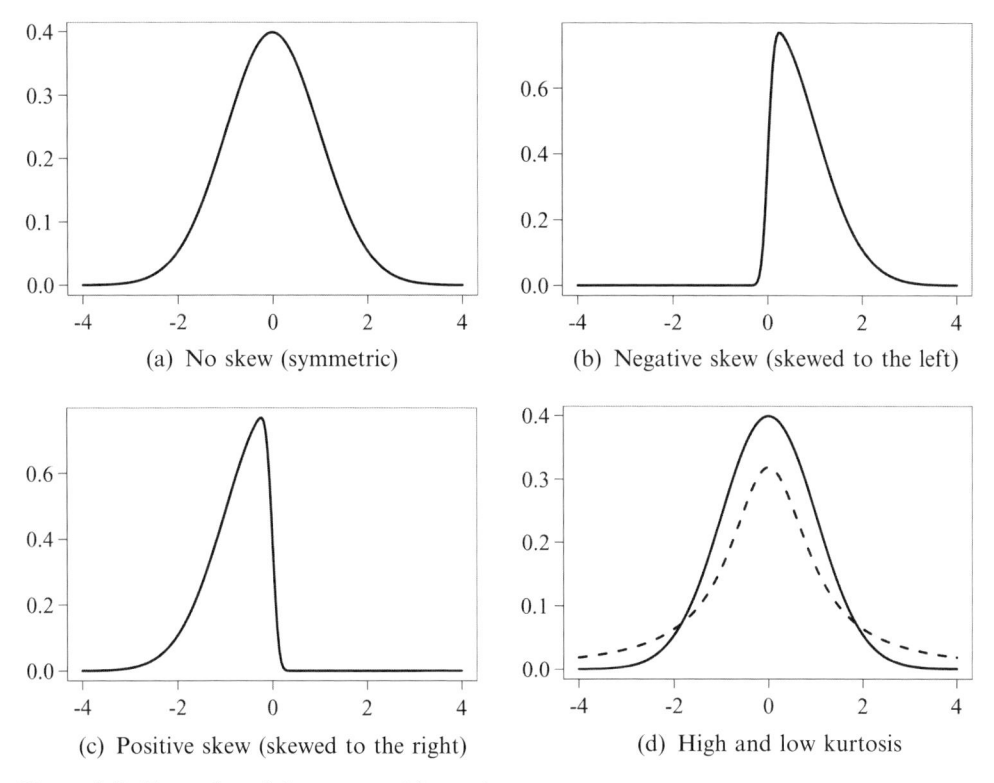

Figure A.5. Examples of skewness and kurtosis.

(a) No skew (symmetric)
(b) Negative skew (skewed to the left)
(c) Positive skew (skewed to the right)
(d) High and low kurtosis

Definition A.6 (Kurtosis) *The central fourth moment of a distribution:*
$$\text{Kurt}(X) = \frac{E(X-\mu)^4}{\sigma^4}.$$

Skewness and kurtosis can be estimated by:

$$\widehat{\text{Skew}}(X) = \frac{1}{(T-1)\hat{\sigma}^3} \sum_{t=1}^{T} (x_t - \bar{x})^3,$$

$$\widehat{\text{Kurt}}(X) = \frac{1}{(T-1)\hat{\sigma}^4} \sum_{t=1}^{T} (x_t - \bar{x})^4.$$

The skewness and kurtosis of the normal distribution are constants that are equal to 0 and 3, respectively. *Excess kurtosis* is kurtosis − 3, so excess kurtosis is 0 for the normal. The concepts of kurtosis and excess kurtosis are often confused.

A.4 EXAMPLES OF DISTRIBUTIONS

Using knowledge of the normal distribution gleaned from above, we can define other distributions that we come across throughout the book.

A.4.1 Chi-squared (χ^2)

Suppose we have $X_1, X_2, \ldots, X_\nu$ RVs where each X is independent and normally distributed with mean 0 and variance 1. Then the variable Z, defined as the sum of squared Xs, follows a chi-squared distribution, (χ^2), with degrees of freedom ν:

$$Z = \sum_{i=1}^{\nu} X_i^2 \sim \chi^2_{(\nu)}.$$

The expectation and variance of Z are given by:

$$\mathrm{E}(Z) = \nu$$
$$\mathrm{Var}(Z) = 2\nu.$$

The chi-squared distribution has support $[0, \infty]$ and its density is given by:

$$f(x; \nu) = \frac{1}{2^{\frac{\nu}{2}} \Gamma\left(\frac{\nu}{2}\right)} x^{\frac{\nu}{2}-1} \exp^{-\frac{x}{2}}$$

where Γ denotes the Gamma function, defined as:

$$\Gamma(x) = \int_0^\infty e^{-t} t^{x-1} dt$$

Panel (a) of Figure A.6 shows the chi-squared distribution for several values of ν.

A.4.2 Student-t

Another distribution which is important in practice is the Student-t. If we have a standard normal RV X and a $\chi^2_{(\nu)}$ RV Z, which are independent of each other, then the variable U defined below has a Student-t distribution with ν degrees of freedom:

$$U = \frac{X}{\sqrt{\frac{Z}{\nu}}} \sim t_{(\nu)}.$$

The expectation and variance of U are given by:

$$\mathrm{E}(U) = \begin{cases} 0 & \text{if } \nu > 1 \\ \text{undefined} & \text{otherwise,} \end{cases}$$

$$\mathrm{Var}(U) = \begin{cases} \dfrac{\nu}{\nu - 2} & \text{for } \nu > 2 \\ \infty & \text{for } \nu = 2 \\ \text{undefined} & \text{otherwise.} \end{cases}$$

Appendix A: Financial time series 207

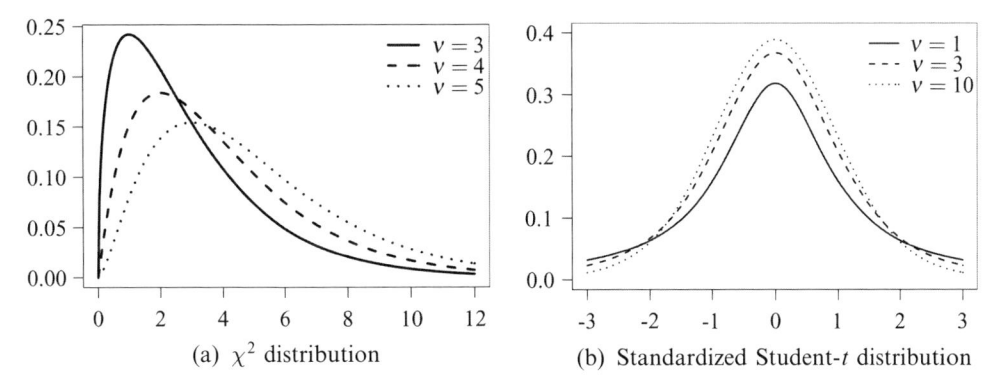

Figure A.6. Distributions related to the normal.

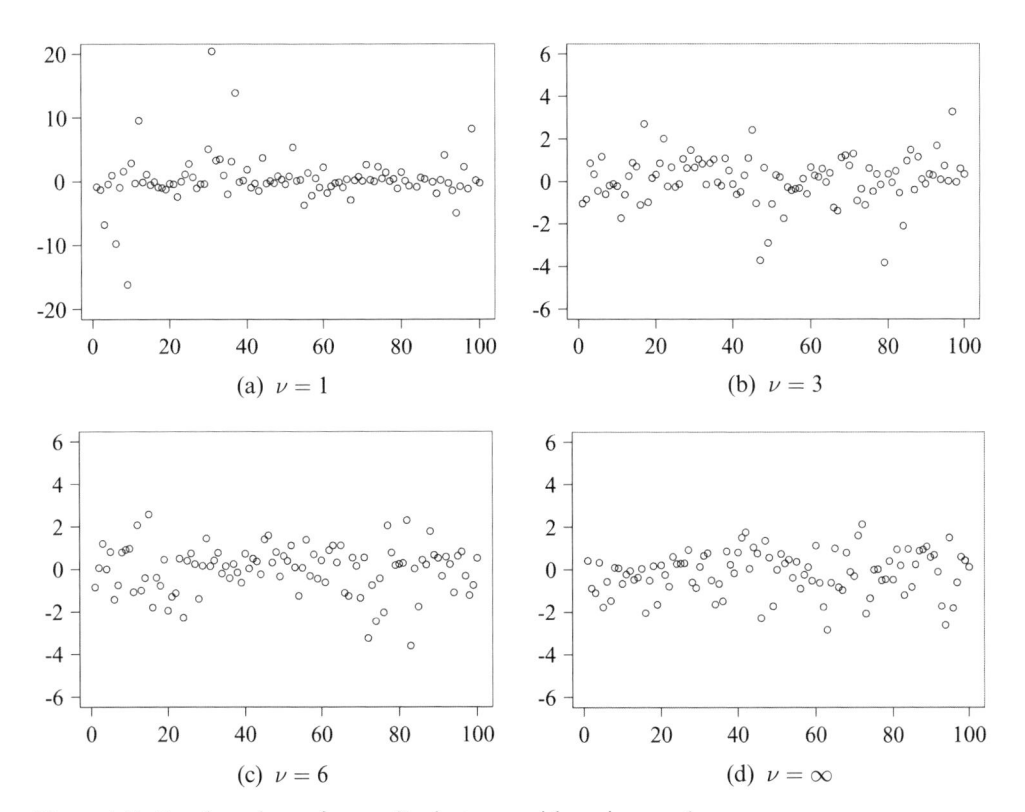

Figure A.7. Random draws from a Student-$t_{(\nu)}$, with variance = 1.

Figure A.6 shows some densities for the $\chi^2_{(\nu)}$ and the Student-t while Figure A.7 shows some random numbers from the Student-t. Note that fewer extreme observations are obtained as the degrees of freedom increase. As the degrees of freedom approach infinity, the Student-t distribution tends to the normal distribution.

The Student-t distribution has support $[-\infty, \infty]$ and its density is:

$$f(x; \nu) = \frac{\Gamma\left(\frac{\nu+1}{2}\right)}{((\nu-2)\pi)^{\frac{1}{2}}\Gamma\left(\frac{\nu}{2}\right)} \left(1 + \frac{x^2}{\nu-1}\right)^{-\frac{\nu+1}{2}}, \quad \nu > 2.$$

A.4.3 Bernoulli and binomial distributions

We encounter the Bernoulli distribution and binomial distribution when modeling the sequence of VaR violations—the "hit sequence"—used in backtesting. Unlike previous distributions we have discussed, both are discrete. The Bernoulli distribution applies to an RV, X, which can only take one of two possible values, for simplicity labeled 0 and 1. Outcome 1 occurs with probability p and outcome 0 with probability $1 - p$. Therefore, the density of the Bernoulli distribution is given by:

$$f(x) = p^x(1-p)^x \quad \text{for } x \in \{0, 1\}.$$

The expected value and variance of X is:

$$\text{E}(X) = p$$
$$\text{Var}(X) = p(1-p).$$

The parameter p can be estimated by:

$$\hat{p} = \frac{v_1}{T}$$

where v_1 is the number of "ones" obtained in the sample.

If we have a sequence of independent RVs, $X_1, X_2, \ldots, X_T$, each of which is Bernoulli distributed with parameter p, then the sum of the sequence, Z, is:

$$Z = \sum_{t=1}^{T} X_t \sim \text{Binomial}(T, p).$$

The binomial distribution models the number of "ones" in a sequence of Bernoulli trials. For example, if we roll a fair die 10 times, the number of sixes we would get is distributed binomially with $T = 10$ and $p = \frac{1}{6}$.

The density of the binomial distribution is given by:

$$f(t) = \binom{T}{t} p^t (1-p)^{T-t},$$

for $t = 1, \ldots, T$. The expected value and variance of Z is given by:

$$\text{E}(Z) = Tp$$
$$\text{Var}(Z) = Tp(1-p).$$

A.5 BASIC TIME SERIES CONCEPTS

It is useful to define a few concepts and operators that form the foundations of time series analysis. Suppose we have a sequence of IID RVs, $\{X_t\}$, with mean μ and variance σ^2. The *ith lag* of X_t is indicated by X_{t-i} and the *jth lead* by X_{t+j}.

A.5.1 Autocovariances and autocorrelations

The autocovariance, $\varsigma_{t,i}$, is the covariance between different observations of the same variable, i observations apart:

$$\varsigma_{t,i} = E[(X_t - \mu)(X_{t-i} - \mu)]. \tag{A.6}$$

Analogous to the definition of the correlation coefficient between two variables, the *ith autocorrelation* is defined as:

$$\rho_{t,i} = \frac{\varsigma_{t,i}}{\varsigma_0}$$

where ς_0 is the variance of X. If X is covariance stationary, the autocorrelation does not depend on t and we can simply write it as ρ.

The autocorrelation function (ACF) is a common method of exploring predictability in statistical data. It measures how returns on one day are correlated with returns on previous days. If the ACF is statistically significant, we have strong evidence for predictability.

A.5.2 Stationarity

A stationary process is one where the probability laws that govern the behavior of the process do not change over time. The statistical properties of a stationary process are identical wherever we look at the data.

In other words, the joint probability distribution function of $\{x_{t-i}, \ldots, x_t, \ldots, x_{t+i}\}$ is independent of t for all i. This implies, of course, that the mean and variance are fixed throughout time if the variance is bounded:

$$E(X_t) = \mu, \quad \forall t = 1, \ldots, T$$
$$\text{Var}(X_t) = \sigma^2, \quad \forall t = 1, \ldots, T.$$

Similarly, autocovariances and autocorrelations are given by:

$$\rho_i = \frac{\text{Cov}(X_{t-i}, X_t)}{\sqrt{\text{Var}(X_t)\text{Var}(X_{t-i})}} = \frac{\varsigma_i}{\varsigma_0}$$

and are only dependent on i—not t.

If we only assume that the first two moments are fixed, the process is said to be weakly stationary. A stochastic process is said to be covariance stationary if neither its mean nor autocovariances depend on time.

Definition A.7 (Covariance stationary) *A sequence of RVs, X_t, are covariance stationary if:*

$$E(X_t) = \mu < \infty, \quad \forall t$$
$$\text{Var}(X_t) = \sigma^2 < \infty, \quad \forall t$$
$$\text{Cov}(X_t, X_{t-i}) = \varsigma_i < \infty, \quad \forall t, i.$$

A.5.3 White noise

An important example of a stationary process is white noise, which is described in Definition A.8.

Definition A.8 (White noise) *A sequence of RVs, X_t, that have zero mean, constant variance and zero autocovariance at all lags, that is:*

$$E(X_t) = 0$$

$$\text{Var}(X_t) = \sigma^2$$

$$\text{Cov}(X_t, X_s) = 0 \quad \forall t \neq s.$$

If $X \sim \mathcal{N}(0, \sigma^2)$, then the process is known as Gaussian white noise. Moreover, if a variable is white noise, its autocorrelations, ρ_i, are asymptotically independent and follow $\rho_i \sim \mathcal{N}(0, T^{-1})$.

A.6 SIMPLE TIME SERIES MODELS

A common way to model predictability is by making use of the *ARMA family* of models. These models are relevant to stationary time series and are some of the most frequently applied models in financial time series analysis.

A.6.1 The moving average model

A first-order moving average MA(1) model is constructed as:

$$X_t = \mu + \epsilon_t + \alpha \epsilon_{t-1}$$

where the shocks ϵ_t are IID. More generally, the MA(L_1) model is:

$$X_t = \mu + \epsilon_t + \alpha_1 \epsilon_{t-1} + \cdots + \alpha_{L_1} \epsilon_{t-L_1}.$$

If the noise is $\epsilon_t \sim \mathcal{N}(0, \sigma^2)$ for all $t = 1, \ldots, T$, it is easy to show for the MA(1) that:

$$E(X_t) = \mu$$

$$\text{Var}(X_t) = (1 + \alpha^2)\sigma^2$$

$$\varsigma_1 = \alpha \sigma^2$$

$$\varsigma_k = 0, \quad k \geq 2.$$

This property is shown in Figure A.8 where we simulate a MA(1) process where $\alpha = 0.8$. As expected, we find no significant autocorrelation after lag 1. Moreover, MA(L_1) models are always stationary.

(a) Simulated MA(1) process: $\alpha = 0.8$

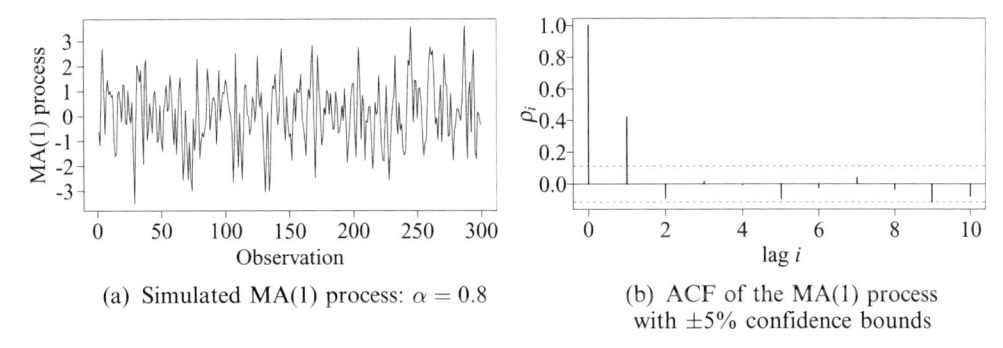

(b) ACF of the MA(1) process with $\pm 5\%$ confidence bounds

Figure A.8. Simulated MA(1) process and its ACF.

A.6.2 The autoregressive model

A first-order autoregressive AR(1) process is generated by:

$$X_t = \mu + \beta X_{t-1} + \epsilon_t$$

where the shocks ϵ_t are IID. In general, the AR(L_2) model is given by:

$$X_t = \mu + \beta_1 X_{t-1} + \beta_2 X_{t-2} + \cdots + \beta_{L_2} X_{t-L_2} + \epsilon_t.$$

The AR(1) model has the following properties, when $\epsilon_t \sim \mathcal{N}(0, \sigma^2)$:

$$\text{Var}(X_t) = \frac{\sigma^2}{1 - \beta^2}$$

$$\varsigma_i = \beta^i \frac{\sigma^2}{1 - \beta^2}$$

$$\rho_i = \beta^i.$$

Clearly, for variance to be finite we must have $|\beta| < 1$; this is the condition for stationarity in the AR(1) model which also ensures that autocorrelations of a stationary AR(1) process decline geometrically. An example of an AR(1) process and its ACF is shown in Figure A.9.

(a) Simulated AR(1) process: $\beta = 0.8$

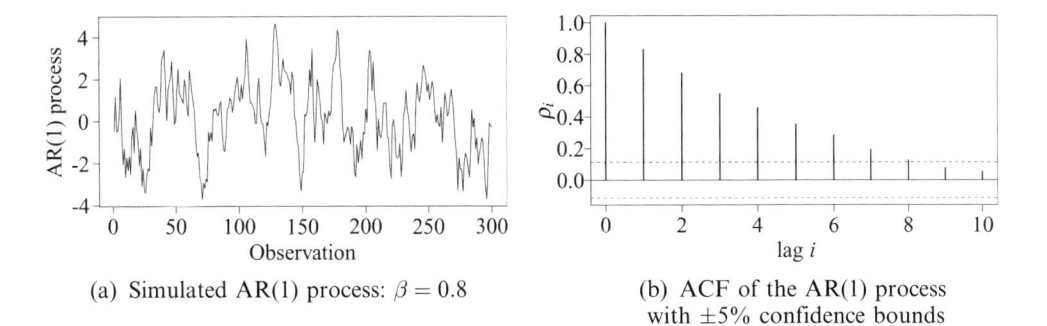

(b) ACF of the AR(1) process with $\pm 5\%$ confidence bounds

Figure A.9. Simulated AR(1) process and its ACF.

A.6.3 ARMA model

Putting the moving average and autoregressive models together yields the ARMA (autoregressive moving average) model. The ARMA(1,1) model is written as:

$$X_t = \mu + \beta X_{t-1} + \epsilon_t + \alpha \epsilon_{t-1}.$$

In general, the ARMA(L_2, L_1) model is:

$$X_t = \mu + \beta_1 X_{t-1} + \cdots + \beta_{L_2} X_{t-L_2} + \epsilon_t + \alpha_1 \epsilon_{t-1} + \cdots + \alpha_{L_1} \epsilon_{t-L_1}.$$

The condition for an ARMA series to be stationary is the same as for the AR series; the ACF of an ARMA(1,1) model behaves in a similar way to the AR(1) model.

A.6.4 Random walk

The random walk is a special case of the AR(1) model and can be obtained when $\beta = 1$ and $\mu = 0$, so:

$$X_t = X_{t-1} + \epsilon_t.$$

The random walk suggests that the optimal forecast of the level at $t + 1$ is given by the observed level at t.

When $\beta = 1$ the situation is quite different than when $\beta < 1$, since X_t retains the entire history of the process in the former case while in the latter case history is progressively downweighted. This means that over time the random walk does not settle down around some long-term mean but, instead, can take any value. The random walk model is a common model for prices of financial assets.

The random walk can be rewritten in terms of lagged disturbances to give:

$$X_t = X_0 + \sum_{i=1}^{t} \epsilon_i \qquad (A.7)$$

where X_0 is the starting value of the process. From (A.7), $\text{Var}(X_t) = \sigma^2 t$ and, hence, the process is nonstationary. If the process is infinitely long, any outcome is equally likely. This is sometimes called a unit root process.

Figure A.10 shows 1,000 realizations from both a random walk model and a stationary AR(1) model. The same random shocks were used in both cases. Both figures have the same scale.

A.7 STATISTICAL HYPOTHESIS TESTING

Statistical testing is a method for making decisions using observed data. If something is said to be statistically significant it is unlikely to have happened by chance. We often use the phrase significance testing to refer to statistical testing.

Generally, a test produces a test statistic with an assumed distribution, often the normal, chi-squared or Student-t. Many test statistics only have this distribution asymptotically, perhaps relying on a central limit theorem. In most cases, we compare the significance of a test statistic by its p-value.

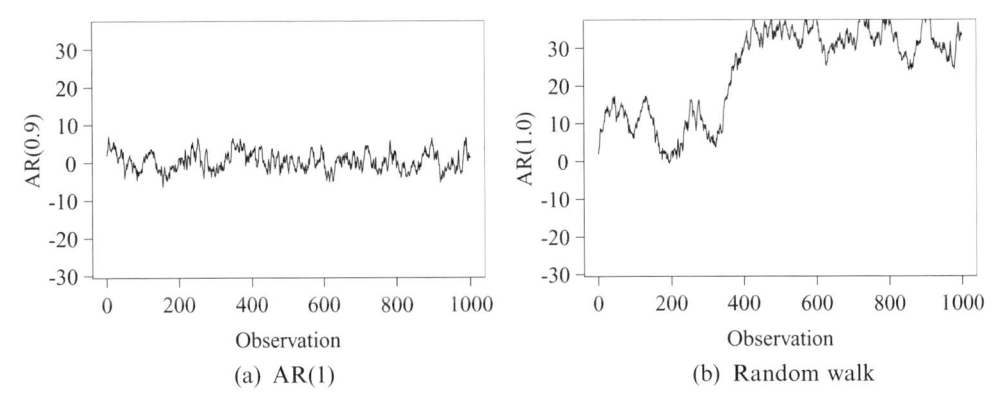

Figure A.10. Simulation of an AR(1) with $\beta = 0.9$ and a random walk process.

A.7.1 Central limit theorem

A fundamental result in probability is the central limit theorem (CLT) which states that the mean of a sufficiently large number of IID random variables will be approximately normally distributed.

Suppose we have a sequence of independent and identically distributed random variables $X_1, \ldots, X_T$, with finite expectation μ and variance σ^2. For any T consider the mean of the first T terms of the sequence

$$\bar{X}_T = \frac{X_1 + \cdots + X_T}{T}.$$

Then, the sequence $(\bar{X}_T - \mu)/(\sigma/\sqrt{T})$ converges in distribution to the standard normal distribution. That is,

$$\lim_{T \to \infty} \Pr\left\{ \frac{\bar{X}_T - \mu}{\sigma/\sqrt{T}} \right\} = \Phi(x)$$

for all $x \in (-\infty, \infty)$.

This result is particularly useful in determining the distribution of estimators. It does depend on the sample being sufficiently large and, for many finite samples, only holds approximately, with the approximation error increasing as the sample size decreases.

The central limit theorem only applies to the sum or mean of observations, but in risk modeling the mean is usually of little interest and, for any risk measures such as VaR or volatility, the CLT no longer applies and the resulting distribution is not necessarily the normal.

A.7.2 p-values

The *p*-value is the probability of obtaining a test statistic at least as extreme as the one observed, assuming that the null hypothesis is true. The lower the *p*-value, the less likely it is that the null hypothesis is true and, consequently, the less *significant* the result is. It is common to reject the null if the *p*-value is less than 0.05 or 0.01.

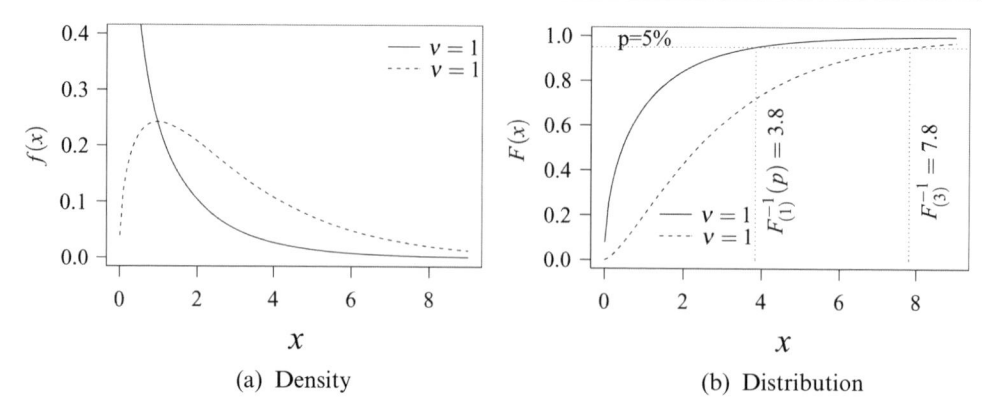

Figure A.11. Chi-squared distribution with degrees of freedom 1 and 3, with the 5% probability and corresponding quantiles indicated.

For example, we see many cases of a χ^2-distributed test statistic in this book. Figure A.11 shows the density and distribution for a $\chi^2_{(1)}$ and $\chi^2_{(3)}$, identifying both the 5% probability and quantile. Taking the $\chi^2_{(1)}$ as an example, we reject at the 5% level if the test statistic exceeds 3.8. The *p*-value is the probability associated with the test statistic.

It is easy to calculate the *p*-value in R and Matlab. Let us suppose the test statistic is from a $\chi^2_{(1)}$ and has a value of 5. We can then calculate the *p*-value as 2.5% in R with 1-pchisq(5,1) and 1-chi2cdf(5,1) in Matlab.

A.7.3 Type 1 and type 2 errors and the power of the test

Type 1 error is the error of rejecting a true null hypothesis, while type 2 error is the error of failing to reject a null hypothesis when it is in fact not true.

The power of a test is the probability that the test will reject a false null hypothesis (i.e., not making a type 2 error). As power increases, the chance of a type 2 error decreases. Power analysis is often used to calculate the minimum sample size required to accept the outcome of a statistical test with a particular level of confidence.

A.7.4 Testing for normality

We frequently need to test whether a particular sample corresponds to a particular distribution, perhaps the normal distribution. The two most common tests for distributions are the Jarque–Bera (JB) test and the Kolmogorov–Smirnov (KS) test. The former applies only to the normal distribution, while the latter test can be applied to almost any distribution.

If a dataset is normally distributed, then skewness and excess kurtosis are equal to zero. In particular, they have the following distributions:

$$\text{Skewness} \sim \mathcal{N}\left(0, \frac{6}{T}\right), \quad \text{Kurtosis} \sim \mathcal{N}\left(3, \frac{24}{T}\right).$$

We can use this result to form the JB test for normality:

$$\frac{T}{6}\text{Skewness}^2 + \frac{T}{24}(\text{Kurtosis} - 3)^2 \sim \chi^2(2).$$

The other common test for normality is the KS test. This tries to determine if two datasets differ significantly by comparing sample data with an underlying distribution such as the normal.

The KS test has the advantage of making no assumptions about the distribution of data. Technically speaking, it is nonparametric and distribution free. More generally, the KS test can also be used to test against other distributions and samples.

A.7.5 Graphical methods: QQ plots

QQ plots are used to assess whether a dataset has a particular distribution or whether two datasets have the same distribution. The QQ plot compares the quantiles of a sample dataset against the quantiles of a reference distribution for a single dataset.

To make a normal QQ plot, we take the lowest observation in a data sample x (i.e., $x_{(1)}$). If we sort the vector x from the smallest to largest observation, then the smallest observation is indicated by $x_{(1)}$, etc. such that $x_{(1)} \leq x_{(2)} \leq \cdots \leq x_{(T)}$.

The empirical cumulative probability of an observation is $1/T$. On a graph, draw one point at coordinates $(F^{-1}(1/T), x_1)$ and a second point at $(F^{-1}(2/T), x_{(2)})$, and so on. Now superimpose on this a line with the following coordinates, $(F^{-1}(t/T), F^{-1}(t/T))$, $t = 1, \ldots, T$. This is a QQ plot. Examples of QQ plots are given in Figure 1.8.

An S-shaped QQ plot implies that one distribution has longer tails than the other because the value for a given quantile is more extreme. A U-shaped QQ plot means that one distribution is skewed relative to the other. There are no restrictions as to the choice of reference distribution in a QQ plot.

A.7.6 Testing for autocorrelation

If we have the following model for X:

$$X_t = \mu + \sum_{i=1}^{N} \beta_i X_{t-i} + \epsilon_t$$

where μ is some mean; and ϵ_t is a Gaussian white noise process, then it can be shown that:

$$\hat{\beta}_i \approx \mathcal{N}(0, T^{-1}).$$

This result is used to construct autocorrelation tests. Given the null hypothesis $H_0: \beta_i = 0$, a standard normal test statistic, Z, could be derived:

$$Z = \sqrt{T}\hat{\beta}_i \sim \mathcal{N}(0, 1).$$

It should be emphasized that this result only holds asymptotically. In finite samples, $\hat{\beta}_i$ is negatively biased as deviations from the sample mean must sum to zero by construction; hence, positive deviations must be followed by negative deviations on average. The bias is of the order of $1/T$; therefore, this effect can be significant for small sample sizes.

We can use these results to derive a common test for autocorrelations: the Ljung–Box (LB) test. The LB test is based on the autocorrelation plot and tests overall randomness based on a number of lags, instead of testing randomness at each lag separately.

Let us refer to the LB test statistic by J_N, where N is the number of lags. It is defined by:

$$J_N = N \sum_{i=1}^{N} \hat{\beta}_i^2 \sim \chi^2_{(N)}.$$

This test is designed to detect departures from zero correlations in either direction and at all lags; therefore, it has considerable power against a broad range of alternative hypotheses. However, selection of the number of autocorrelations N merits careful thought.

A.7.7 Engle LM test for volatility clusters

Engle (1982) proposed a test for volatility clusters in an ARCH model, where the null hypothesis is that the conditional volatilities are constant. Starting with the distribution of returns:

$$Y_t = \sigma_t Z_t, \quad Z_t \sim \mathcal{N}(0, 1).$$

The test proposed by Engle is a Lagrange multiplier (LM) test known as the ARCH LM test. Let us regress the squared returns of Y_t^2 on N lags of itself:

$$Y_t^2 = \alpha_0 + \alpha_1 Y_{t-1}^2 + \cdots + \alpha_N Y_{t-N}^2 + \epsilon_t \tag{A.9}$$

then under null hypothesis there is no predictability in volatility:

$$H_0 : \alpha_1 = \alpha_2 = \cdots = \alpha_N = 0$$

and the test statistic is:

$$J_0 = TR^2 \sim \chi^2_N$$

where R^2 is the estimate of the fit of (A.9). The larger the volatility clusters, the more of the residuals are picked up by the model, and hence the larger the J_0. This test has the advantage that robust standard errors can be used to test the above null hypothesis, whereas the Ljung–Box test is based on the assumption that the process is identically and independently distributed (IID), which is generally not realistic.

Appendix B
An introduction to R

R is a freely available popular language for statistical and mathematical analysis (RDCT, 2009) and can be downloaded from the R Project for Statistical Computing at http://www.r-project.org/. It is a descendant of an earlier language called SPlus, still available commercially. R has become the language of choice for many econometricians and statisticians, not only because it is free, but more importantly because of the availability of many high-quality libraries for specialized calculations.

R is a language that allows the user to write programs tailored to specific needs and has many functions for statistical analysis and excellent graphing capabilities. Indeed, most of the plots and numerical output in this book have been produced using R.

It comes with a series of default packages. A package is just a collection of functions, often used for particular tasks; there are hundreds of free user-contributed packages that are available on the R website, many of a very high quality. To install a package (e.g., copulas), use the command `install.package(copulas)` or use the GUI. Packages only need to be installed once. To load a package, type `library(copulas)` or use the GUI. Given the number of packages on offer, many with overlapping functionality, there is sometimes no easy way to determine which package is the best; we should experiment with different packages or alternatively check online for other users' experiences.

There are a large number of books written about R. Dalgaard (2002) is an elementary-level introduction to R while Crawley (2007) is a comprehensive book dealing with a wide variety of statistical methods. Murrell (2006) is for those who want to know more about R's graphing facilities, and Adler (2010) gives a good up-to-date overview. Plenty of guides are also freely available online.

R has a comprehensive set of documentation built in. To learn about the `plot` function, for example, type `?plot` or `help(plot)` and the relevant help file will appear. In the following, we focus on those R commands that are the most relevant for this book.

B.1 INPUTTING DATA

R stores variables, data, functions and results as *objects*, then performs operations on these objects. To create a variable (an object in R terminology) we can use Listing B.1.

Listing B.1. Variables

```
x = 10      # assigns 10 to x
x           # prints contents on x on the screen
10          # the output
```

The character # is used to add comments and R ignores what comes after it.

In R there are several ways of inputting data. For portfolios it is important that data are input as a vector or matrix with the correct dimensions. For small sample sizes, we can use the concatenate, c(), function. The dim() function returns the dimension of an object if it is a vector or a matrix, and NULL otherwise.

Listing B.2. Vectors

```
y = c(1,3,5,7,9)
y
1 3 5 7 9
y[3]
5
dim(y)
NULL        # since it's not a matrix
length(y)
[1] 5
```

If we want to create a matrix, we need to use the matrix() function. Inputs are data as well as the number of rows and columns.

Listing B.3. Matrices

```
y = matrix(nrow = 2, ncol = 3)   # defining a matrix with 2 rows and 3
                                   columns
y                                 # nothing has been assigned
      [,1]  [,2]  [,3]
[1,]  NA    NA    NA
[2,]  NA    NA    NA
dim(y)
2 3
y = matrix(c(1,2,3),3,1)          # create a column matrix with elements
                                    1,2,3
```

If we need to create a sequence of numbers, the seq() function is useful.

Listing B.4. Sequences

```
seq(1:10)
[1]  1   2   3   4   5   6   7   8   9   10
seq(from = 1, to = 10, by = 2)
[1]  1   3   5   7   9
seq(from = 1, to = 10, length = 5)
[1]  1.00   3.25   5.50   7.75   10.00
```

Data, saved as a tab-delimited text file or a comma-separated value (CSV) file, can be imported directly into R as a dataframe by using the functions in Listing B.5.

Listing B.5. Import CSV data

```
mydata = read.table("data.txt")
mydata = read.csv("data.csv")
```

The optional argument header=TRUE tells R that the first row of the file contains the variable names, and the optional sep argument specifies the field separator character. The default for read.table is "white space" (i.e., one or more spaces, tabs, new lines or carriage returns). For a .csv the default is sep=",".

Alternatively, we can use the scan() function, which also imports data as a matrix.

Listing B.6. Import data with scan and matrix

```
mydata = matrix(scan(file = "data.dat"), byrow = TRUE, ncol = 3)
```

Finally, we can download prices from a website like finance.yahoo.com and use the function get.hist.quote() from the tseries library. We then convert the prices into returns and plot the returns. By default, get.hist.quote() returns a four-column matrix with open and closing prices, as well as the price high and low. To get adjusted closing prices we need to include quote="AdjClose" in the get.hist.quote() statement. Note that prices and returns are represented as a time series object, and we may need to convert them into regular matrices by coredata().

Listing B.7. Download S&P 500 data in R

```
library("tseries")          # load the tseries library
price = get.hist.quote(instrument = "^gspc", start = "2000-01-01",
   quote="AdjClose")        # download the prices, from January 1, 2000
                            #   until today
y = diff(log(price))        # convert the prices into returns
y = coredata(y)
plot(y)                     # plot the returns
```

B.2 SIMPLE OPERATIONS

There are three main types of operators in R (summarized in Table B.1).

The functions in R for manipulating data are too numerous to be listed, but we present some of them in Listing B.8.

Table B.1. Basic operators in R

Arithmetic		Comparison		Logical	
+	Addition	<	Lesser than	! x	Logical NOT
-	Subtraction	>	Greater than	x & y	Logical AND
*	Multiplication	<=	Lesser or equal	x | y	Logical OR
/	Division	>=	Greater or equal	x || y	Identical
^	Power	==	Exactly equal		
%%	Modulo	!=	Different		

Listing B.8. Basic data manipulation

```
sum(y)       # sum of elements of y
prod(y)      # product of elements of y
max(y)       # maximum
min(y)       # minimum
range(y)     # return minimum and maximum
length(y)    # number of elements of y
mean(y)      # arithmetic mean
median(y)    # median
var(y)       # variance
cov(y)       # covariance matrix
cor(y)       # correlation matrix
sort(y)      # sort y in increasing or decreasing order
log(y)       # natural logarithm
na.omit(y)   # omit missing data NA
unique(y)    # remove duplicate elements of y
```

To calculate skewness and kurtosis, we first need to load the package *moments* (see Listing B.9).

Listing B.9. Higher moments

```
mean(y)
var(y)
sd(y)       # standard error
library(moments)
skewness(y)
kurtosis(y)
```

B.2.1 Matrix computation

When dealing with portfolios, we often need matrices. R has special facilities for matrix calculations. To perform matrix multiplications, we need to enclose the * between %

symbols and to ensure matrix dimensions match up by using the t() function to transpose a matrix if necessary (see Listing B.10).

Listing B.10. Matrix multiplication

```
z = matrix(c(1,2,3,4),2,2)      # 2 by 2 matrix
x = matrix(c(1,2),1,2)          # 1 by 2 row matrix
z %*% x
Error in z %*% x : non-conformable arguments
                                # dimensions of the matrices do not
                                    match
z %*% t(x)
     [,1]
[1,]   7
[2,]  10
```

Other useful functions include rbind() and cbind(), which bind matrices along rows or columns, respectively. The function diag() can be used to extract or modify the diagonal of a matrix or to build a diagonal matrix. solve() computes the inverse of a matrix and eigen() returns both eigenvalues and eigenvectors.

Listing B.11. Matrix manipulation

```
m1 = matrix(c(1,2,3,4),2,2)
m2 = matrix(1,nrow = 2,ncol = 2)
rbind(m1,m2)
        [,1]        [,2]
[1,]      1           3
[2,]      2           4
[3,]      1           1
[4,]      1           1
cbind(m1,m2)
        [,1]        [,2]        [,3]        [,4]
[1,]      1           3           1           1
[2,]      2           4           1           1
diag(m1)
[1]       1           4
diag(2)
        [,1]        [,2]
[1,]      1           0
[2,]      0           1
solve(m1)
        [,1]        [,2]
[1,]     -2         1.5
[2,]      1        -0.5
```

```
eigen(m1)
$values
[1]              5.3722813    -0.3722813
$vectors
                 [,1]         [,2]
[1,]             -0.5657675   -0.9093767
[2,]             -0.8245648    0.4159736
```

B.3 DISTRIBUTIONS

An abundance of distributions are already programmed into R, albeit we may need to load different packages to access some multivariate distributions. For each distribution, there are usually four functions. We can generate random numbers from that distribution, obtain the density and probability function for given quantiles, and get the quantile for given probabilities. The four functions are demonstrated in Listing B.12 for the normal distribution.

Listing B.12. Distribution functions

```
q = seq(from = -3, to = -3, length = 300)      # specify a set of
                                                 quantiles
p = seq(from = 0.01, to = 0.99, length = 300)  # specify a set of
                                                 probabilities
rnorm(100, mean = 0, sd = 1)                   # generate 100 random
                                                 numbers from the
                                                 standard normal
pnorm(q, mean = 0, sd = 1)                     # obtain the CDF for
                                                 given quantiles
dnorm(q, mean = 0, sd = 1)                     # obtain the PDF for
                                                 given quantiles
qnorm(p, mean = 0, sd = 1)                     # obtain the quantile
                                                 values for given
                                                 probabilities
```

We demonstrate in Listing B.13 the random data generation functions for other common distributions that do not require additional packages. Replace the letter r with d, p or q to get the counterpart functions.

Listing B.13. Common distributions

```
S=10                                           # number of simulations
df=3                                           # degees of freedom
rt(S,df)                                       # Student-t
rlnorm(S)                                      # log-normal
```

```
runif(S,min=0,max=1)                  # uniform
rchisq(S,df)                          # chi-squared
rbinom(S,size=4,prob=0.1)             # binomial
rpois(S,lambda=0.1)                   # Poisson
rexp(S,rate=1)                        # exponential
rgamma(S,shape=2,scale=1)             # gamma
rweibull(S,shape=2,scale=1)           # Weibull
rcauchy(S,location=0,scale=1)         # Cauchy
```

For multivariate distributions and some others, we need to download external packages. Sometimes, there are more than one package that offer the same function, and we present in Listing B.14 the ones that have been used in this book.

Listing B.14. Other distributions

```
library(MASS)
mu = c(1,1)                                   # mean
Sigma = matrix(c(1, 0.5, 0.5, 2),ncol=2)      # covariance matrix
mvrnorm(S,mu,Sigma)                           # multivariate normal
library(mvtnorm)
rmvt(S,Sigma,df)                              # multivariate Student-t

library(Rlab)
rbern(S, prob=0.4)                            # Bernoulli
library(evir)
rgev(S, xi=1, mu=0, sigma=1)                  # generalized extreme value
rgpd(S, xi=2, mu=0, beta=1)                   # generalized Pareto
                                                distribution
```

Section 5.3.3 shows how we can use maximum likelihood to estimate the parameters of the Student-t, and similar functions can also be used to estimate the parameters of most common distributions.

B.3.1 Normality tests

To test for normality we can, for example, use the Jarque–Bera test or draw a QQ plot with the normal as the reference distribution. The Jarque–Bera test returns the test statistic, the p-value and the alternative hypothesis.

Listing B.15. Testing for normality

```
library(moments)
jarque.bera.test(y)
   Jarque-Bera Normality Test
data: y
```

```
JB = 339444.9, p-value < 2.2e-16

library(car)
qq.plot(y, distribution = "norm",mean = 0,sd = 1)    # normal QQ
qq.plot(y, distribution = "t",df = 3)                 # Student-t3 QQ
                                                        plot
```

Different software or even different subroutines within the same software package may present a QQ plot in different ways. For example, the normal distribution may be on the *x*-axis or the *y*-axis, it may be standardized or have the same variance as the data. While sometimes confusing, this is not a serious concern.

B.4 TIME SERIES

With time series data, we are often interested in the autocorrelation and partial autocorrelation of the data. We can also easily implement the Box–Ljung test, which returns the value of the statistic, degrees of freedom and the *p*-value of the test.

Listing B.16. ACF

```
library(stats)
acf(y, lag.max = 20, plot = TRUE)           # plot the ACF up to 20 lags
acf(y, lag.max = 20, type = "partial", plot = TRUE)
                                            # plot the partial ACF up
                                              to 20 lags
pacf(y, lag.max = 20, plot = TRUE)          # another way to calculate
                                              the PACF
Box.test(y,lag = 20,type = "Ljung-Box")     # Box-Ljung test

X-squared = 142.3885, df = 20, p-value < 2.2e-16
```

After conducting exploratory data analysis, we might want to fit an AR, MA or ARMA model to the data. R has a built-in function `arima()` that can help. Estimated parameters along with their standard errors are returned.

Listing B.17. ARMA models

```
arima(y, order = c(1, 0, 0),include.mean = TRUE)
                         # fits an AR(1) with a mean term
arima(y, order = c(0, 0, 1),include.mean = FALSE)
                         # fits a MA(1) without a mean term
arima(y, order = c(1, 0, 1),include.mean = TRUE)
                         # fits an ARMA(1,1), output shown
```

```
Call:
arima(x = y, order = c(1, 0, 1), include.mean = TRUE)

Coefficients:
          ar1          ma1         intercept
        -0.4580       0.5002        2e-04
s.e.     0.0775       0.0754        1e-04

sigma^2 estimated as 0.0001349: log-likelihood = 64926.08,
   aic = -129844.2
```

It is also possible to simulate data from a time series model by using the function arima.sim().

Listing B.18. Simulate ARMA

```
x = arima.sim(list(order = c(1,0,0),ar = 0.8),n = 10)
           # simulate 10 data points from an AR(1) with parameter 0.8
Time Series:
Start = 1
End = 10
Frequency = 1
[1]   -0.3457084    1.6319438   -1.1513445   -1.2760566    0.1160679
       0.5026084    1.4810065    0.8608933   -0.3298654    1.3049195

x1 = arima.sim(list(order = c(2,0,2), ar = c(0.9, -0.5),
  ma = c(-0.2, 0.2)),n = 300)
           # simulate 300 data values from an ARMA(2,2) model
```

B.5 WRITING FUNCTIONS IN R

One advantage R has over many other software packages is its flexibility to program specialized functions. Typically, a function is useful when we want to repeat the same task(s) many times. The input that a function takes are known as *arguments*. The syntax for writing a function is: function(arg1,arg2..){body}.

It is best demonstrated by an example. We write a simple function for calculating excess kurtosis in Listing B.19.

Listing B.19. A simple function

```
mykurtosis = function(x) {
   m4 = mean((x - mean(x))^4)
   kurt = m4/(sd(x)^4)-3
   kurt
```

```
}
mykurtosis(y)
[1]    7.40799
```

This simple function only takes one argument *x* which is a vector of observations. It is generally good practice to write each statement in the body on a separate line, which makes for easier editing. We can also assign default values to arguments in a function such that the function will calculate using the default value if an argument has no value.

Listing B.20. Programming kurtosis

```
mykurtosis1 = function(x,excess=3) {
   m4 = mean((x - mean(x))^4)
   kurt = m4/(sd(x)^4)-excess
   kurt
}
mykurtosis1(y)
[1]    7.40799
mykurtosis1(y,0)
[1]   10.40799
```

The excess argument here takes on a default value of 3. Executing this function without specifying the excess produces the same output as before. Default values can be numeric or consist of a character string such as "norm", in which case quotation marks are required or there needs to be a logical value such as TRUE or FALSE. The order in which we input the arguments is not important if the names of the arguments are used.

Note that customized functions must be loaded into R's memory to be executed. One can either type the functions directly into R or save them as a text file with the extension .r and use the command source() to run it. We can either use the built-in editor in R or any other text editor.

B.5.1 Loops and repeats

Although it is good programming practice to avoid loops wherever possible, from time to time it will be unavoidable to repeat some procedures. The main idea in loops is that we assign an index, perhaps *i*, to take on a sequence of values; a set of commands are executed with each different value of *i*. A simple for loop is shown in Listing B.21.

Listing B.21. A for loop

```
x = rnorm(5)                  # generate 5 random numbers
z = numeric(length(x))        # create vector the same length as x
for (i in 1:length(x)){
   z[i] = x[i] + 0.5
}
```

Each element in vector y is the sum of the corresponding element in vector x and 0.5. The loop runs until i reaches five. As with functions, several instructions can be executed if they are placed within curly brackets.

It is common to see if statements such as:

if (some condition is met) do something

The statement if...else.. allows us to further specify commands to be executed whenever the condition in if is not met. This is illustrated in Listing B.22.

Listing B.22. An if-else loop

```
a = 10
if (a %% 3 == 0) {
   print("a is a multiple of 3")
}
else {
   print("a is not a multiple of 3")
}
```

Another statement used in loops is while, the syntax is similar to if but the index value needs to change inside the loop.

Listing B.23. A while loop

```
a = 1
n = 1
while (a < 100) {
   a = a * n
   n = n + 1
}
```

However, some loops can be easily avoided by using logical subscripts. We present an example in Listing B.24 where we want to replace all the negative values in a vector by zero.

Listing B.24. Loop avoidance

```
x = rnorm(5)                                    # using a loop
for (i in 1:length(x)) if (x[i] < 0) x[i] = 0   # avoiding a loop
x[x < 0] = 0
```

There are other functions—such as apply, sapply, lapply—that provide ways to avoid using loops.

B.6 MAXIMUM LIKELIHOOD ESTIMATION

R is well suited for programming likelihood functions. There are two steps involved in the estimation process. First, we write the log-likelihood function for general terms and, then, we optimize the log-likelihood function, given a particular dataset. It is more common to minimize the negative of the log-likelihood value, and this yields the same answer as maximizing the log-likelihood. There are several different commands for optimization, we focus on nlm() here. Others include optim(), constrOptim(), etc. To illustrate how optimization works, we first program the normal log-likelihood function and then estimate the mean and variance of simulated data using ML.

Listing B.25. Normal likelihood function

```
norm_loglik = function(theta,x){
  n = length(x)
  mu = theta[1]
  sigma2 = theta[2]^2
  loglike = -0.5 * n * log(sigma2) - 0.5 * (sum((x - mu)^2/sigma2))
  return(-loglike)
}
```

In Listing B.25 theta is a vector containing the mean and the standard deviation. We set the sample size, specify the log-likelihood function and ensure R returns the negative of this function. In Listing B.26 we simulate IID data from a normal distribution with mean 3 and standard deviation 2. The nlm() function requires us to specify the starting values for optimization; we set them equal to the median and half the interquartile range of the data. By setting hessian=TRUE, R will return the hessian matrix evaluated at the optimum, and hence we can obtain the information matrix. iterlim allows us to set the maximum number of iterations to be performed before the program is terminated.

Listing B.26. Maximum likelihood example

```
x = rnorm(100,mean = 3,sd = 2)
theta.start = c(median(x),IQR(x)/2)      # starting values
out = nlm(norm_loglik,theta.start,x=x,hessian=TRUE,iterlim=100)
out
$minimum                                 # log-likelihood value at
                                              optimum
[1]    115.8623

$estimate                                # MLE estimates
[1]    3.130798        -1.932131

$gradient                                # gradient at optimum
[1]    -2.414775e-06    9.414420e-07
```

```
$hessian
          [,1]                  [,2]
[1,]    26.787168484        0.004294851
[2,]     0.004294851       53.588122739


$code
[1]    1


$iterations                             # no. of iterations to
                                                convergence
[1]    16


solve(out$hessian)                      # information matrix

          [,1]                  [,2]
[1,]    3.733131e-02       -2.991939e-06
[2,]   -2.991939e-06        1.866085e-02
```

B.7 GRAPHICS

R has versatile graphical facilities, where it is possible to make a wide variety of statistical graphs and build entirely new types of graph. For an overview of what R can do, we can visit the R graph gallery at http://addictedtor.free.fr/graphiques/, where the source code for each graph is available to download. All the graphs in this book were produced with R in eps format.

One of the most frequently used plotting functions in R is the plot() function; it can produce line graphs, scatterplots, etc. There are many graphical parameters such as color, style, headings and axes, as well as other formats that we can either customize inside the plot() command or by using the par() function. If data are arranged in a matrix, the matplot() function may be useful. Histograms and bar charts can be produced with the commands hist() and barplot(), respectively.

There are three basic functions that can handle plots of three variables. The image(x,y,z...) plot draws a grid of rectangles using different colors to represent the value of z, the contour(x,y,z..) function draws contour lines to represent different values of z and finally the persp(x,y,z..) plots 3D surfaces. The copula plots in Figure 1.12 were produced using these functions.

It is easy to control the size of graphs and store them in a format of choice. For example, the commands given in Listing B.27 will produce an encapsulated postscript file of a figure that is 5 inches high and 5 inches wide, which can be included in another document. Other supported devices include pdf(), png(), jpeg(), tiff(), bitmap().

Listing B.27. Save plot in R

```
postscript("file.eps", horizontal=FALSE, onefile=FALSE, height=5,
    width=5, pointsize = 10, useKerning = FALSE)
plot(y,type = 'l')
dev.off()
```

Appendix C
An introduction to Matlab

Matlab is a powerful software and language for technical computing, it is a state-of-the-art software for matrix computation—indeed, the name Matlab stands for matrix laboratory. It is a popular tool in mathematics, statistics, engineering, finance and economics.

Matlab comes with a comprehensive family of *toolboxes*, which are collections of functions that aim to solve particular problems. However, Matlab does not have good econometric functions built in. Fortunately, a library of Matlab econometric functions is available called the *Econometrics Toolbox for Matlab*. It is available from http://www.spatial-econometrics.com/ and was developed by James P. LeSage (JPL). Both the manual and source code is available on JPL's website and we use functions from this toolbox throughout this book. Other useful free toolboxes for Matlab are the *UCSD GARCH Toolbox* and the *Oxford MFE Toolbox*; the latter was developed by Kevin Sheppard and is available from http://www.kevinsheppard.com

Matlab has an extensive set of both online and printed documentation. To obtain more information about a function (e.g., plot), we can type doc plot or help plot in the command window. There are also plenty of books on Matlab. Hanselman and Littlefield (2001) is a good introductory guide as is Hahn and Valentine (2007). For specific applications to finance and risk measurement, Dowd (2002) is written for students. Comprehensive help, including demos and videos, are also available online at http://www.mathworks.com/access/helpdesk/help/helpdesk.html

C.1 INPUTTING DATA

Matlab stores information as *Matlab variables*. If we can't recall the name of a variable, the who command prints a list of available variables; if we end an input with a semicolon the output is suppressed; and the character % is used to denote comments.

Listing C.1. Variables

```
x = 10;
y = 5;
z = x + y;
who
Your variables are:
ans     x     y     z
```

Creating an array or matrix is simple. Commas or spaces are used to separate elements in a particular row and semicolons are used to separate individual rows. We can also create a row vector by using a colon. The command `size()` returns the dimension of the matrix.

Listing C.2. Arrays

```
a = 1:5
a =
    1    2    3    4    5
b = [1,2,3,4;5,6,7,8]
b =
    1    2    3    4
    5    6    7    8
size(b)
ans =
    2    4
```

For sequences of data, we can either use two colons or the `linspace()` command. `logspace()` generates logarithmically spaced vectors:

x = first:increment:last
linspace(first_value, last_value, number_of_values)

Listing C.3. Sequences

```
x = 0:2:10
x =
    0    2    4    6    8    10
x = linspace(0, 10, 6)
x =
    0    2    4    6    8    10
x = logspace(0,2,4)
x =
    1.0000    4.6416    21.5443    100.0000
```

Data files saved on a hard drive can be imported using the `load()` command.

Listing C.4. Load files

```
sp = load('sp.dat');     % loads file sp.dat into variable sp
```

Table C.1. Basic operators in Matlab

Arithmetic		Comparison		Logical	
+	Addition	<	Lesser than	~	Logical NOT
-	Subtraction	>	Greater than	&	Logical AND
*	Multiplication	<=	Lesser or equal	|	Logical OR
/ or \	Division	>=	Greater or equal	xor	Exclusive OR
^	Power	==	Equal to		
rem	Modulo	~=	Not equal to		

We can download prices from a website like finance.yahoo.com. We can do this by using the GUI function, FTSTool, from the financial and data feed toolboxes. However, it may be easier to use the Matlab function urlread() which can directly read web pages, such as finance.yahoo.com. Several free user-contributed functions are available to ease the process, such as hist_stock_data().[1] When a website like finance.yahoo.com returns the data they are sorted from the newest date to the oldest date, so that the first observation is the newest. If we want it sorted from the oldest to newest, we will have to do it manually by using a sequence like end:-1:1. Of course, it would be more expedient just to modify the hist_stock_data() function.

Listing C.5. Download S&P 500 data in Matlab

```
price = hist_stock_data('01012000','31122000','^gspc');
                                % download the prices,
                                  from January 1, 2000
                                  until December 31, 2009
y = diff(log(price.Close(end:-1:1)))   % convert the prices into
                                         returns
plot(y)                         % plot the returns
```

Section 1.2.2 shows how we can download financial data directly into Matlab.

C.2 SIMPLE OPERATIONS

We present some frequently used Matlab commands in Table C.1—most are similar to their R counterparts.

Note that "=" and "==" are two different things: "==" compares two variables and returns ones where they are equal and zeros where they are not; "=", on the other hand, is used to assign the output of an operation to a variable. The basic functions to calculate sample statistics are given in Listing C.6.

---
[1] This function can be obtained directly from the webpage of the Matlab vendor http://www.mathworks.com/matlabcentral/fileexchange/18458-historical-stock-data-downloader.

Listing C.6. Basic data analysis

```
% y has already been loaded
length(y)           % number of elements in y
sum(y)              % sum of elements
prod(y)             % product of elements
range(y)            % difference between maximum and minimum
mean(y)             % mean
median(y)           % medium
var(y)              % variance
std(y)              % standard error
sqrt(var(y))        % another way to get the s.e.
corrcoef(y)         % correlation coefficients
skewness(y)         % get the skewness
kurtosis(y)         % get the kurtosis (NOT excess)
quantile(y,0.01)    % returns the quantiles at p
min(y)              % minimum value
max(y)              % maximum value
sort(y)             % sort in ascending or descending order
abs(y)              % absolute value
diff(y)             % differences between elements
```

C.2.1 Matrix algebra

Matlab was originally developed to provide an easy-to-use interface to work with numerical linear algebra computations and offers a range of valuable matrix algebra functions. Note that matrix algebra is defined only for 2D arrays—not for higher dimensional arrays.

Matrix addition and subtraction is straightforward. We need to be a bit more careful with multiplication and division. The commands .* and ./ are used for element-by-element multiplication and division and not matrix multiplication. Listing C.7 illustrates matrix calculations.

Listing C.7. Matrix calculations

```
A = [2,4;7,3]
B = [3,2;1,4]
A .* B
ans =
     6     8
     7    12
A * B
ans =
    10    20
    24    26
```

```
C = [1,2]
A * C
??? Error using ==> mtimes
Inner matrix dimensions must agree.
A * C'         % ' acts as a transpose operator
ans =
    10
    13
diag(C)        % place elements on the main diagonal
ans =
    1    0
    0    2
eye(3)         % produces identity matrices
ans =
    1    0    0
    0    1    0
    0    0    1
```

We give a brief description of a selection of matrix functions that are useful for solving linear algebra problems in Listing C.8.

Listing C.8. Useful matrix functions

```
M = [1 2;3 6]       % enter matrix
rank(M)             % matrix rank
inv(M)              % matrix inverse
det(M)              % determinant
eig(M)              % vector of eigenvalues
[V,D] = eig(M)      % returns eigenvectors and eigenvalues
sqrtm(M)            % matrix square root
trace(M)            % sum of diagonal elements
null(M)             % null space
poly(M)             % characteristic polynomial
chol(M)             % Cholesky Factorization
```

C.3 DISTRIBUTIONS

The statistics toolbox in Matlab supports a wide range of distributions. There are three useful distribution GUIs in the toolbox: disttool leads to a GUI that allows us to see the influence of parameter changes on the shapes of PDFs and CDFs; dfittool is an interactive way of fitting a probability distribution to our data; and randtool generates random samples from specified probability distributions and displays the samples as histograms. We type these on the command line to access the GUI.

For each supported distribution, there are seven available functions, but we are primarily interested in five: the PDF and CDF functions end in pdf and cdf, respectively; the quantile functions end in `inv`; random numbers end in `rnd`; and negative log-likelihood functions end in `like`. We illustrate the functions for the normal distribution in Listing C.9.

Listing C.9. Distribution functions

```
q = 0                        % specify quantiles
p = 0.5                      % specify probabilities
mu = 1                       % mean
sigma = 2                    % standard deviation
normpdf(q,mu,sigma)          % return density at q
normcdf(q,mu,sigma)          % return cumulative prob at q
norminv(p,mu,sigma)          % return quantile at p
normrnd(mu,sigma,10,2)       % return m by n matrix
normfit(x)                   % return estimated parameters
```

We give the random data generation function for other common continuous and discrete distributions in Listing C.10.

Listing C.10. Common distributions

```
trnd(df)                     % Student-t
chi2rnd(df)                  % chi-squared
unifrnd(A,B)                 % continuous uniform
lognrnd(mu,sigma)            % log normal
exprnd(mu)                   % exponential
gevrnd(K,sigma,mu)           % generalized extreme value
gprnd(K,sigma,theta)         % generalized Pareto
binornd(N,P)                 % binomial
poissrnd(lambda)             % Poisson
```

It is also easy to work with multivariate distributions (Listing C.11). The statistics toolbox supports multivariate normal and Student-t as well as the main three bivariate Archimedean copula families: Clayton, Frank and Gumbel (there are others).

Listing C.11. Multivariate distributions

```
mvnrnd(mu,sigma)    % normal
mvtrnd(C,df)        % Student-t, C is correlation matrix
                    % the lines below generate random numbers from
                        different copulas, rho is correlation matrix, NU
                        is degrees of freedom, N random vectors returned
copularnd('Gaussian',rho,N)
copularnd('t',rho,NU,N)
copularnd('Clayton',alpha,N)
```

C.3.1 Normality tests

There are several hypothesis tests in the statistics toolbox. To test if data conform to normality, we can make use of either a Jarque–Bera test or a Kolmogorov–Smirnov test. The command `jbtest()` using a Jarque–Bera test of the null hypothesis checks whether the data sample comes from a normal distribution with unknown mean and variance or not.

The command `kstest()` uses a Kolmogorov–Smirnov test to compare sample data with a standard normal distribution—the default distribution. There is an option to specify the distribution. Default significance in both tests is 5%. Alternatively, a QQ plot—a simple graphical tool—can be used to compare sample quantiles against theoretical quantiles from the normal distribution or another set of sample quantiles.

Listing C.12. Testing for normality

```
% y is the data
alpha = 0.01
[h,p,jbstat,critval] = jbtest(y,alpha)
                        % alpha is significance level of test
h                       % returns 1 if the null is rejected and 0 if not
p                       % returns the p-value
jbstat = 20.0648        % returns the test statistic
critval = 11.5875       % returns critical value of test, if
                          jbstat > critval, null is rejected

[h,p,ksstat,critval] = kstest(y,[],alpha)
                        % [] is the option to specify a distribution
h = 1
p = 0
ksstat = 0.4814
critval = 0.1020

qqplot(y)               % QQ plot of x against a normal distribution.
qqplot(x,y)             % QQ plot of two samples, where vector x must be
                          present
```

C.4 TIME SERIES

To analyze the autocorrelation and partial autocorrelation of the data, we can use the commands `sacf` and `spacf()` from the *UCSD GARCH* toolbox: they plot the sample (partial) autocorrelations and standard deviation using either heteroskedasticity-robust standard errors or classic (homoskedastic) standard errors. The command `sacf(data,lags,robust,graph)` has four input arguments: `data` is self-explanatory; `lags` indicates the number of autocorrelations to compute; `robust` is an optional logical argument which defaults to using robust standard errors; and `graph` can be set equal to zero if we do not want a graph plotted. The syntax of the sample partial autocorrelation function `spacf()` is similar. The Box–Ljung test `ljungbox(data,lags)` is also supported by the toolbox.

To estimate an AR, MA or ARMA process, we can make use of the command `armaxfilter()`, which has many input and output arguments. We need to study the help file carefully. One of the optional input arguments, `startingvals`, allows the user to specify starting values. Simulation of these models is enabled by the function `armaxsimulate(T,ar,ma,const,ARparams,MAparams)`

C.5 BASIC PROGRAMMING AND M-FILES

In order to create our own function in Matlab, it has to be in a separate M-file. An M-file is a text file with a .m extension. There are two types of M-files: a script M-file and a function M-file.

A script M-file is just a collection of Matlab statements that are executed by running the script, instead of being typed directly into the command window. This is done by typing the file name (i.e., the part before the .m) in the command window. An example is given in Listing C.13.

Listing C.13. A script M-file

```
a = randn(10);
b = a * 5 + 2;
plot(b)
```

We save this as "myscript.m" in the *current directory*. This script is run if `myscript` is typed in the command window. If we wish to edit, or add a statement to, the script, we simply type `edit myscript` in the command window and Matlab will open the text editor.

A function M-file is similar to a script M-file in that it also has a .m extension and is an external text file created using a text editor. We illustrate this in Listing C.14 by writing a simple function to calculate kurtosis.

Listing C.14. A function M-file

```
function k = mykurtosis(x)
% PURPOSE: simple function to calculate kurtosis
% RETURNS: excess kurtosis of input data
   m4 = mean((x - mean(x)).^4);
   k = m4/std(x)^4 - 3
end
```

A function M-file's name needs to match that of the function created. In Listing C.14 this should be saved as "mykurtosis.m". The first line of a function M-file defines it as a function, specifies the function name and defines the input and output variables. The following comments are displayed if the user calls `help mykurtosis` or `doc` mykurtosis. We then program the function. Note that no end command is needed here, the function terminates after the last statement is executed. If the M-file has more than one function, an end is needed after each one.

To call this function, we need to ensure that the directory in which this M-file is saved is in Matlab's search path.[2] Listing C.15 shows what we then need to type in the command window.

Listing C.15. Calling a function M-file

```
mykurtosis(y)
k = 1.3502
```

The function can be called within a script M-file. We can modify the kurtosis function by adding more input and output arguments. The number of input and output arguments used in a function can be determined by the functions nargin and nargout. Listing C.16 illustrates the use of nargin, which is also used to assign default values to input arguments.

Listing C.16. Kurtosis function

```
function k = mykurtosis1(x,a)
                % PURPOSE: simple function to calculate kurtosis
                % RETURNS: default: excess kurtosis
    if nargin == 1
       a = 3;
    end
    m4 = mean((x - mean(x)).^4);
    k = m4/std(x)^4 - a
```

If the user only specifies the data x, the default value of the a argument is set to three. Notice that, unlike R, the order in which we input the function arguments is important.

C.5.1 Loops

Matlab can easily handle programming tasks such as loops and conditional statements. We start with the for loop where we assign an index i to take on a sequence of values; the same set of commands are executed for each unique value of i. An example is given in Listing C.17.

---
[2] We can check this out by clicking on "file" and then "set path".

Listing C.17. A `for` loop

```
x = randn(1,5);
z = NaN(1,5);      % allocate output vector
for i=1:5
   z(i) = x(i) + 0.5;
end
```

At each iteration, `i` is assigned to the next column of row vectors `x` and `y`. After `i=5`, the `for` loop terminates. To minimize the amount of memory allocation, we should preassign an empty vector to hold the result of each iteration. Note that the `for` loop cannot be terminated between `for` and `end` by assigning the index `i` to be 5, but we could use `break`.

Each `i` denotes a different *column*, `x` or `z`, which needs to be created with the right dimensions. It is of course possible to have nested `for` loops (i.e., a loop within a loop), in which case two `end` commands are required to terminate the loops.

The most frequently used loops involve the `if` statement, which executes a set of commands when a particular condition is satisfied. Adding an `else` argument enables the decision-making process to be more sophisticated. We provide an example in Listing C.18 in which statements are used to decide whether 3 is a factor of a given number.

Listing C.18. An `if-else` loop

```
a = 10;
if (rem(a,3)) == 0
   disp('a is a multiple of 3')
else
   disp('a is not a multiple of 3')
end
```

When there are three or more alternatives, we can use the command `elseif (condition)` followed by the procedures to be carried out if the condition is true. For each `if`, an `end` is required to terminate the loop. The `if..else..end` loop can be embedded within `for` and `while` loops. It is good practice to use indents when programming complex loops to make sure we break out of each loop at the appropriate time.

A `while` loop executes a set of commands when some condition is fulfilled. An example is provided in Listing C.19. A feature of the `while` loop is that the index variable changes inside the loop.

Listing C.19. A `while` loop

```
a = 1;
n = 1;
while a < 100
   a = a * n;
   n = n + 1;
end
```

If the condition after the `while` command is an array rather than a scalar, then all elements of the array need to be true for the loop to continue. If you wish the loop to continue when any element is true, use the function `any`—that is, `while any(a < 100)` where a is an array.

A `switch case` loop evaluates a set of statements based on the value of a variable. Listing C.20 demonstrates a simple example of the use of `switch case`.

Listing C.20. A `switch case` loop

```
x = 30;
units='kg';
switch units
   case{'kilograms','kg'}
      y = x * 1000;
   case{'grams','g'}
      y = x;
   case{'ounce','oz'}
      y = x * 28.35;
   case{'pounds','lb'}
      y = x * 453.6;
   otherwise
      disp(['Unknown Units:' units])
      y = NaN;
end
```

This implementation allows evaluation of at most one set of commands. If the first `case` statement is satisfied, then the commands following it are executed and the remaining statements skipped. If the first comparison is not satisfied, then and only then will the second case be considered, and so on.

Generally, loops are slow and not examples of efficient programming. They should be avoided if possible and whenever there is an equivalent approach—usually involving matrices that are orders of magnitude faster. The difference in the two approaches is highlighted in Listing C.21. We want to calculate $\sum_{i=1}^{1000} a_i b_i$.

Listing C.21. Loop avoidance

```
a = 1:1000
b = 1000 - a
% using loops we have:
ssum = 0;
for i = 1:1000
    ssum = ssum + a(i) * b(i);
end
% using matrices:
ssum = a * b'
```

C.6 MAXIMUM LIKELIHOOD

In maximum likelihood (ML) estimation, we need to write the likelihood function. To illustrate how Matlab can be used to do this, we maximize the likelihood function for IID normal observations. In this case only the mean and variance need to be estimated. We first simulate data from a normal distribution and then ask Matlab to maximize the likelihood function.

Listing C.22. Maximum likelihood estimation

```
randn('seed',1);              % set the seed so we always get same RNs
N = 100;                      % number of observations
x = randn(N,1) * 2+3;         % mean 3, sd 2
theta0 = [-2, 5];             % starting values
global x;                     % share x with likfunc
[theta, likelihood_value] = fminunc(@likfunc, theta0)
theta = 2.8082 1.9366
likelihood_value = 116.0928
```

The function `fminunc` ascertains the minimum of an unconstrained function from starting values. Various outputs are possible including the Hessian, the number of iterations required for convergence, etc. We can set the maximum number of iterations using the `MaxIter` option. The likelihood function is specified in a separate M-file.

Listing C.23. Normal log-likelihood

```
function loglik = likfunc(theta)
% Normal log-likelihood function
    global x;
    T = length(x);
    mu = theta(1);
```

```
sigma2 = theta(2)^2;

loglik = 0.5 * T * log(sigma2);
loglik = loglik + 0.5 * (sum((x-mu).^2 / sigma2));
```

Note the `global` statements; they allow us to share a variable between the two parts of the code. The use of `global` is not very good programming practice; it would be better to pass x as an optional parameter, which is straightforward to do.

C.7 GRAPHICS

Matlab provides many high-level graphing functions. These include line plots, bar and histogram graphs, contour plots, surface plots and animation. The user can exert control over the general appearance of the graphs such as color, labeling, axis formats, etc. We can develop our own graphics functions using Handle Graphics, Matlab's object-orientated graphics system.

The common function for plotting bivariate data is the `plot()` function which can produce different types of line plots. We can make use of the help file for the wide range of optional arguments. Aside from `plot()`, `hist()` plots a histogram, `bar()` a bar chart, `pie()` a pie chart and `scatter()` produces a scatterplot. To add new plots to an existing plot, we can use the `hold on` command and enter `hold off` to declare the plot complete. Commands like `title`, `xlabel`, `ylabel`, `legend`, `text`—which work on all graphics—allow the user to customize graphs.

The main function to make 3D graphics is the `plot3()`—other functions include `mesh()`, `surf()`, `contour` and `contour3`. We can adjust many settings on 3D plots such as size, perspective, shading, etc.

Matlab graphics are usually displayed in a separate figure window, which has a menu bar at the top. It is possible to save the current figure in one of many formats. Click on `File` then `Save As` and then choose a directory, file name and file type for the graphic. From the command window, the function `print()` is responsible for all printing and exporting. Supported devices/formats include bmp, jpeg, eps and tiff.

Appendix D
Maximum likelihood

Perhaps the most common statistical model we encounter is the classical linear regression model, where dependent and explanatory variables have a linear relationship. The parameters of this model can be easily estimated by ordinary least squares. However, this technique is not suitable for *nonlinear* models like the GARCH family of models where the relationship between volatility and returns is nonlinear.

There are many techniques available for estimating nonlinear models (e.g., the generalized method of moments), but the most common method is maximum likelihood (ML). The main idea behind ML—given we observe a sample of data and have a distribution model in mind—relates to its ability to ascertain the most likely parameter values that could generate the observed data? In other words, ML estimation (MLE) finds the parameters that maximize the probability (or likelihood) of observing the sample data.

For example, suppose we have the following small sample of data which we believe to have been generated by a normal distribution:

$$\{0.83,\ 1.06,\ 1.13,\ 0.92,\ 1.12,\ 1.10,\ 0.95,\ 1.01,\ 0.99,\ 1.03\}$$

The normal distribution only has two parameters: mean and variance. By looking at this sample, it is highly unlikely that the mean could be 100 or 1,000; however, we can make a reasonable guess that the mean must be close to one. Similarly, standard deviation cannot be 10 or 100, but is somewhere around 0.1. In arriving at these conclusions, we have used maximum likelihood.

The ML approach can be succinctly summarized according to "the likelihood principle" as:

"All information about parameters θ that can be obtained from a sample is contained in the likelihood function of θ for a given dataset."

D.1 LIKELIHOOD FUNCTIONS

Suppose we have an IID random variable (RV) following a parametric distribution with density $f(\cdot)$ which has a vector of parameters θ. We then draw a sample $x = \{x_1, x_2, \ldots, x_T\}$ from this RV:

$$f(x) = f(x_1)\ldots f(x_T). \tag{D.1}$$

The joint PDF reveals the probability of outcomes given the parameters. However, our problem is exactly the opposite: we want to determine the parameters given the outcomes or data. For this purpose, we introduce the term *likelihood function*, $\mathcal{L}(\theta; x)$, defined as:

$$\mathcal{L}(\theta; x) = \prod_{t=1}^{T} f(x_t; \theta).$$

This is mathematically identical to (D.1) but the name of the function is different because our interest is in the parameters which in this case are variables, conditional on the observations. Estimators of the parameters, $\hat{\theta}$, are then obtained by maximizing the likelihood function with respect to the parameters. In practice, it is more convenient to work with the logarithm of the likelihood function (a sum rather than a product but still monotonically increasing); this, of course, does not change the answer. ML estimates are therefore defined as:

$$\hat{\theta}_{ML} = \arg\max_{\theta} \mathcal{L}(\theta; x)$$

$$= \arg\max_{\theta} \log\mathcal{L}(\theta; x).$$

D.1.1 Normal likelihood functions

The normal distribution has been used extensively in this book. A simple derivation of its log-likelihood function is:

$$X \sim \mathcal{N}(\mu, \sigma^2)$$

$$f(x; \mu, \sigma) = \frac{1}{\sqrt{2\pi\sigma^2}} \exp\left[-\frac{1}{2}\frac{(x-\mu)^2}{\sigma^2}\right].$$

For a sample of T IID observations:

$$\mathcal{L}(\mu, \sigma; x) = \prod_{t=1}^{T} f(x_t; \mu, \sigma)$$

$$= \prod_{t=1}^{T} \frac{1}{\sqrt{2\pi\sigma^2}} \exp\left[-\frac{1}{2}\frac{(x_t-\mu)^2}{\sigma^2}\right].$$

Taking logarithm we get:

$$\log\mathcal{L}(\mu, \sigma; x) = \sum_{t=1}^{T}\left(\log\frac{1}{\sqrt{2\pi\sigma^2}} - \frac{1}{2}\frac{(x_t-\mu)^2}{\sigma^2}\right)$$

$$= \sum_{t=1}^{T}\left(-\frac{\log(2\pi)}{2} - \frac{1}{2}\log\sigma^2 - \frac{1}{2}\frac{(x_t-\mu)^2}{\sigma^2}\right)$$

$$= -\frac{T\log(2\pi)}{2} - \frac{T}{2}\log\sigma^2 - \frac{1}{2}\sum_{t=1}^{T}\left(\frac{(x_t-\mu)^2}{\sigma^2}\right).$$

We can ignore constant values because they have no effect on the solution, therefore the log-likelihood function can be shortened to:

$$\log\mathcal{L}(\mu, \sigma; x) = -\frac{T}{2}\log\sigma^2 - \frac{1}{2}\sum_{t=1}^{T}\frac{(x_t - \mu)^2}{\sigma^2}.$$

This maximization problem can be solved analytically by differentiating the log-likelihood function with respect to μ and σ. Setting the log-likelihood function equal to zero gives the estimators:

$$\hat{\mu}_{ML} = \frac{1}{T}\sum_{t=1}^{T}x_t$$

$$\hat{\sigma}^2_{ML} = \frac{1}{T}\sum_{t=1}^{T}(x_t - \hat{\mu}_{ML})^2.$$

The latter is biased since there is no adjustment to the degrees of freedom, but it is asymptotically not biased. We can verify the solution by computing the Hessian matrix and see whether it is negative definite.

In this case, we only need to calculate the sample mean and variance and there is no need to resort to maximum likelihood.

Generally, we have more complicated likelihood functions and cannot use such analytical solutions. In these cases, we have to resort to computer algorithms to numerically maximize the likelihood function.

D.2 OPTIMIZERS

In software packages such as R and Matlab the negative likelihood function is minimized by using an algorithm called an *optimizer*. An algorithm is a set of instructions or steps that lead to the solution of a problem and is iterative in nature. In most cases, we have to specify *starting values* θ_0 and the algorithm calculates an improved value θ_1. This process is repeated through a sequence of points $\theta_0, \theta_1, \ldots, \theta_n$ until an optimal point θ^* is approached. Each step is an iteration. To demonstrate optimization in Matlab, type bandem in the command line to see how different numerical algorithms solve the problem.

Most optimizers work by minimizing a function; hence we need to minimize the negative log-likelihood.

A well-known algorithm is the *Newton–Raphson* method, based on finding zeros of functions; it can be used as an optimization method by applying it to the derivative of the function. The Newton–Raphson is based on the Taylor expansion up to degree 2 of the likelihood function.

After the first minimum of the quadratic approximation is found, the process is repeated. Hence we re-apply the quadratic approximation around the minimum of the initial quadratic approximation and find a new minimum. This is carried out until the values converge to the minimum of the objective function. The reason quadratic models are popular is they are one of the simplest smooth functions with well-defined first and second derivatives and, usually, a rapid rate of convergence.

D.3 ISSUES IN ML ESTIMATION

We obtain parameter estimates with maximum likelihood by numerically maximizing the likelihood function. This is sometimes called hill climbing.

Issues arise when using iterative algorithms. It is not always true that an algorithm will generate a sequence that will *converge* to a solution, particularly if the starting value is far from the solution point. Even if it is known that an algorithm will converge to the solution, the problem cannot be regarded as solved as it may require an enormous amount of time before convergence is achieved.

Furthermore, some likelihood functions are not well behaved and can have more than one peak. This happens frequently for multivariate models. The algorithm may not be successful in finding the solution or finding a local maxima. Unfortunately, there is no overall solution to this problem, but the impact can be minimized by trying various *random* starting values. One disadvantage of MLE is that parameter estimates can be very sensitive to the choice of starting values.

MLE can become unstable when there are a large number of parameters, such as happens in many multivariate volatility models, or the algorithm may terminate with an unpleasant error message when the user specifies an insufficient number of iterations. In this instance, we might increase the number of allowed iterations. In R we could look at the `iterlim` setting. In Matlab we could search for help on `optimset`, especially the `MaxFunEvals` and `MaxIter` functions (see Sections 2.4.4 and 3.6.1 for some of the issues that arise in the context of volatility models).

Let us consider the simple example shown in Figure D.1(a). In this case we wish to

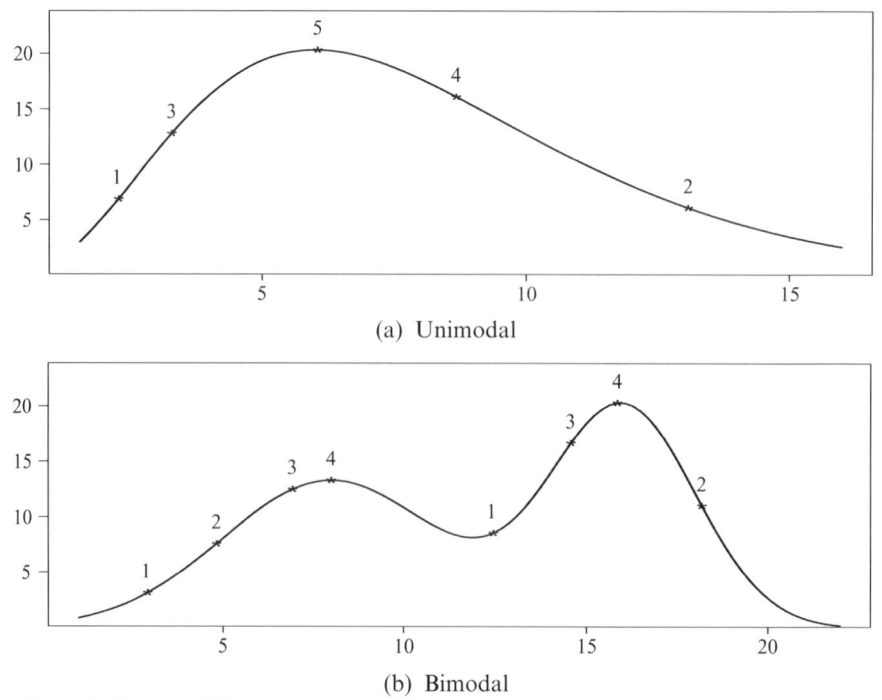

(a) Unimodal

(b) Bimodal

Figure D.1. Paths up a hill.

maximize some function. We have to start somewhere: so we choose 2 and get a function value of 6. Since the first derivative is positive, we deduce the solution is to the right: so the algorithm tries another point, at 13, and finds a higher value of 7. It then tries 3, 9 and, finally, 6 to yield the correct answer. At that point the derivative is zero. It is straightforward in this case to find the maxima as the function was unimodal and one dimensional.

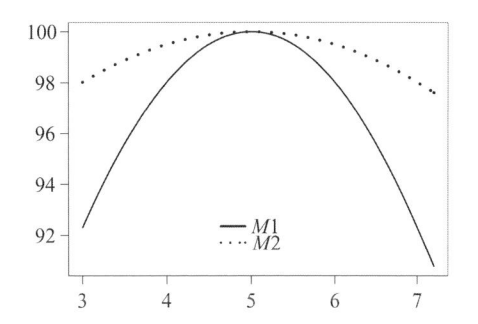

Figure D.2. Log-likelihood for models $M1$ and $M2$.

What if the function looks like Figure D.1(b)? The likelihood function here is bimodal (i.e., it has two maxima: one local at around 8 and one global at around 16). If we naively start searching for the maxima at low values of θ, and stop at the first maxima we find, we will miss the best solution. This is often a big problem in MLE. The reason is that most computer hill-climbing algorithms can only find the next maxima.

D.4 INFORMATION MATRIX

The first-order condition of MLE is that the first derivative of the likelihood function must be zero at the maxima. By intuitively looking at Figure D.2—given the shapes of two likelihood functions, $M1$ and $M2$—there seems to be more uncertainty about the solution for $M2$ than there is for $M1$, and we would expect the standard error of the parameter estimate for $M2$ to be higher. Mathematically, this manifests itself in the *second* derivative of the likelihood function at the maxima, which must be negative because the likelihood function is downward sloping in all directions. The flatter the likelihood function is at the top, the closer the second derivative is to zero. Ultimately, this means that we can use second derivatives to measure the standard errors of parameter estimates.

The matrix of second derivatives is called the *Hessian matrix*. The negative expectation of the Hessian matrix is named the *information matrix*.

Definition D.1 (Information matrix)

$$I(\theta) = -\mathrm{E}\left[\frac{\partial^2 \log \mathcal{L}(\theta|X)}{\partial \theta\, \partial \theta'}\right]. \tag{D.2}$$

The Cramér–Rao lower bound gives the maximum sampling precision:

$$\mathrm{Var}\left[\hat{\theta}\right] \geq I(\theta)^{-1}.$$

In maximum likelihood analysis we usually estimate the covariance matrix of parameters by the negative inverse of the Hessian matrix.

D.5 PROPERTIES OF MAXIMUM LIKELIHOOD ESTIMATORS

Maximum likelihood estimators are attractive because of their asymptotic properties. Under mild regularity conditions, we can establish four main results. We denote the ML estimator by $\hat{\theta}_{ML}$—which could be a vector or scalar—and the true parameter by θ.

Consistency $\hat{\theta}_{ML}$ is consistent if it converges in *probability* to θ. As the sample size, T, tends to infinity, the distribution of the estimator becomes increasingly concentrated around the true parameter value. This is expressed as:

$$\plim_{T \to \infty} \hat{\theta}_{ML} = \theta.$$

Asymptotic normality As T tends to infinity, the distribution of $\hat{\theta}_{ML}$ approaches a normal distribution with mean θ and variance $I(\theta)^{-1}$:

$$\hat{\theta}_{ML} \stackrel{a}{\sim} \mathcal{N}(\theta, I(\theta)^{-1}).$$

Asymptotic efficiency An estimator is efficient if it is unbiased and achieves minimum variance for all parameters. $\hat{\theta}_{ML}$ attains the Cramér–Rao lower bound for consistent estimators.

Invariance The MLE is invariant with respect to certain data transformations.

A simple example illustrates some of these properties. A sample of 100 data points is simulated from a Poisson distribution with hazard rate 2. The ML estimate for the hazard rate is 2.02 using the simulated sample data. A plot of log-likelihood vs. parameter values is shown in Figure D.3. At 2.02 the log-likelihood function is at a maximum. The distribution of estimates, resembling the normal with mean 2, is shown in Figure D.3(b)—calculated by generating 5,000 samples of size 100. The consistency of the estimator is demonstrated by Figure D.3(c): as the sample size is increased from 100 to 5,000, the variance of estimates decreases and the distribution[1] of estimates becomes increasingly concentrated around the true parameter value of 2.

D.6 OPTIMAL TESTING PROCEDURES

We discussed testing in Section A.7, where we considered the significance of a test statistic. Often, these test statistics come from a likelihood-based test, such as the likelihood ratio tests discussed in Section D.6.1. In these cases, we have some model and want to test whether a restricted version of that model is statistically significant. We have seen many examples of such tests throughout this book (e.g., the comparison of volatility models in Section 2.5.1 and the significance of backtests in Section 8.3).

Having obtained parameter estimates, we often would like to check whether they are significantly different from some value since there may be other restrictions we wish to impose. We discuss here the three most commonly used hypothesis testing procedures,

---
[1] This figure plots the frequency polygon.

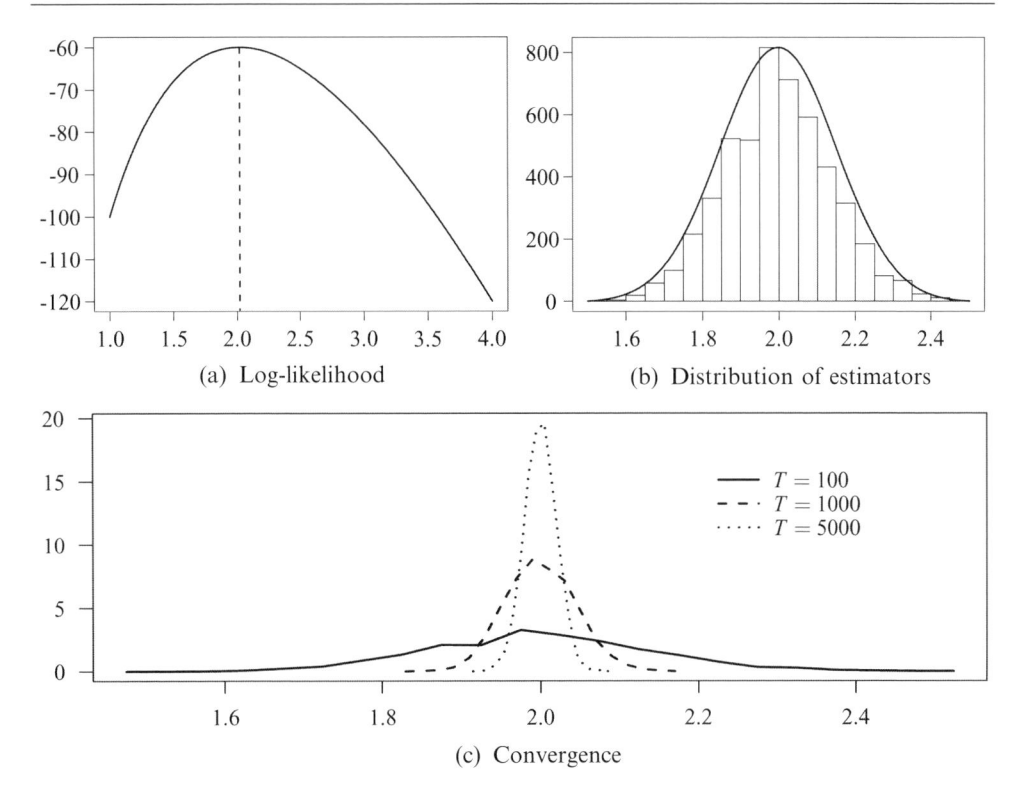

Figure D.3. Example from a Poisson distribution.

the likelihood ratio (LR), Wald (W) and Lagrange multiplier (LM) tests. All three approaches fall within the ML framework. These three tests are asymptotically equivalent and equally powerful.

In all cases, we start with a model called the "unrestricted model", indicated by U, and then form a restricted version of that model, indicated by R. Note that the restricted model must be nested within the unrestricted model.

D.6.1 Likelihood ratio test

We estimate the U model and note its maximized log-likelihood value $\mathcal{L}_U$. We then obtain estimates for the R model and likewise note $\mathcal{L}_R$. It is important to keep in mind that $\mathcal{L}_R$ can never be larger than $\mathcal{L}_U$. If the null hypothesis or restriction is true, then the distance between $\mathcal{L}_R$ and $\mathcal{L}_U$ should not be too large.

The LR test statistic is given by:

$$\text{LR} = 2\Big(\mathcal{L}_U(\hat{\theta}_U) - \mathcal{L}_R(\hat{\theta}_R)\Big) \sim \chi^2_{(r)}$$

where r is the number of restrictions. Figure D.4 illustrates the LR test, where the impact of the restriction in this case is to shift the likelihood function left and downwards.

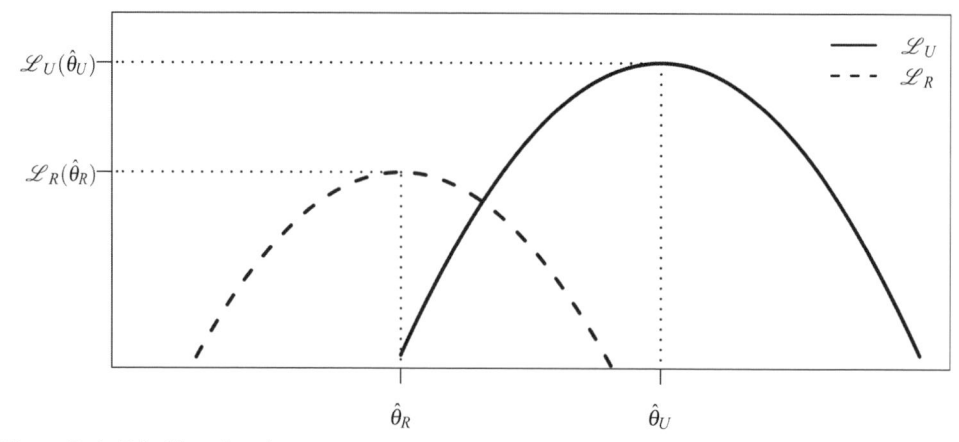

Figure D.4. Likelihood ratio test.

This test is in general easy to construct. A disadvantage of the LR test is that we have to estimate both the restricted and unrestricted model. However, given the computing power available, this issue is irrelevant in most applications.

D.6.2 Lagrange multiplier test

The Lagrange multiplier test is based solely on the R model. We maximize the (unrestricted) likelihood function with respect to the parameters and subject it to a set of restrictions defining the Lagrangian function. If the null hypothesis is true, imposing the restriction will not lead to a significant difference in the maximized value of the likelihood function, implying that the value of the Lagrange multiplier λ will be small. The closer the true model is to the restricted model, the lower λ is. The LM test's de facto null hypothesis is $H_0 : \lambda = 0$. We can formulate the test in a simpler way, however. The gradient or the first derivative of the unrestricted likelihood function evaluated at $\hat{\theta}_R$ should be approximately zero if H_0 is true. This is illustrated in Figure D.5.

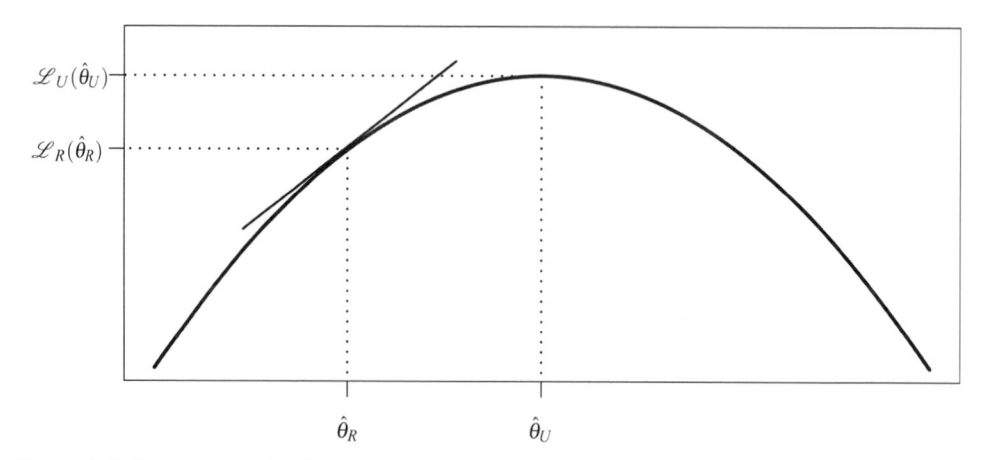

Figure D.5. Lagrange multiplier test.

The LM test statistic is given by:

$$\text{LM} = \left(\frac{\partial \mathcal{L}_U(\hat{\theta}_R)}{\partial \hat{\theta}_R}\right)' [I(\hat{\theta}_R)]^{-1} \left(\frac{\partial \mathcal{L}_U(\hat{\theta}_R)}{\partial \hat{\theta}_R}\right) \sim \chi^2_{(r)}.$$

D.6.3 Wald test (W)

A common test often implemented in econometric packages is the Wald test. In this approach we estimate the parameters involved in the null hypothesis using the U model. We then apply the restrictions and check statistically how badly they are violated. If the restrictions are valid, then $\hat{\theta}_U$ should approximately satisfy them. The Wald test only requires us to estimate the U model. Mathematically, we also have to correct for sampling variability—intuitively, this is curvature of the likelihood function at $\hat{\theta}_U$.

Note we would normally use the information matrix to estimate $\text{Var}(\hat{\theta}_U)$. There are two weaknesses of the Wald test: as a pure significance test it does not take into account alternative hypotheses, therefore its power may be limited in some circumstances; and it is sensitive to the formulation of restrictions. However, the Wald test relies on weaker distributional assumptions than the LR and LM tests.

The choice of test is primarily a matter of convenience. In many cases it is much easier to calculate the restricted estimator than the unrestricted estimator—as a result some implementations have preferred the LM approach in the past, but this is much less of an issue now.

Bibliography

Adler, J. (2010), *R in a Nutshell*, O'Reilly.
Adrian, T. and Shin, H.S. (2010), "Liquidity and leverage," *Journal of Financial Intermediation*, **19**(3), 418–437.
Alexander, C. (2001), *Market Models: A Guide to Financial Data Analysis*, John Wiley & Sons Ltd.
Alexander, C. and Chibumba, A. (1994), "Multivariate orthogonal factor GARCH," University of Sussex discussion paper in mathematics.
Ang, A. and Chen, J.S. (2002), "Asymmetric correlations of equity portfolios," *Journal of Financial Economics*, **63**(3), 443–494.
Ang, A., Chen, J. and Xing, Y. (2001), "Downside risk and expected returns," Columbia Business School working paper.
Artzner, P., Delbaen, F., Eber, J. and Heath, D. (1999), "Coherent measures of risk," *Mathematical Finance*, **9**(3), 203–228.
Balkema, A.A. and de Haan, L. (1974), "Residual life time at great age," *Annals of Probability*, **2**, 794–804.
Basel Committee (1996), *Amendment to the Capital Accord to Incorporate Market Risks*, Basel Committee on Banking Supervision. Available at http://www.bis.org/publ/bcbs24.pdf
Bauwens, L., Laurent, S. and Rombouts, J.V. (2006), "Mulivariate GARCH models: A survey," *Journal of Applied Econometrics*, **21**, 79–109.
Berkowitz, J. (2000), "A coherent framework for stress testing," *Journal of Risk*, **2**, 5–15.
Black, F. and Scholes, M. (1973), "The valuation of option contracts and a test of market efficiency," *Journal of Political Economy*, **27**, 399–418.
Bollerslev, T. (1986), "Generalized autoregressive conditional heteroskedasticity," *Journal of Econometrics*, **51**, 307–327.
Bollerslev, T. (1990), "Modelling the coherence in short-run nominal exchange rates: A multivariate generalized ARCH approach," *Review of Economics and Statistics*, **72**, 498–505.
Bollerslev, T. and Wooldridge, J. (1992), "Quasi-maximum likelihood estimation and inference in dynamic models with time-varying covariances," *Econometric Reviews*, **11**, 143–172.
Brady Commission (1988), *Report of the Pesidential Task Force on Market Mechanisms*, technical report, Government Printing Office, Washington, D.C.
Campbell, S.D. (2005), *A Review of Backtesting and Backtesting Procedures*, Technical Report 2005-21, Federal Reserve staff working paper in the Finance and Economics Discussion Series.
CGFS (2000), *Stress Testing by Large Financial Institutions: Current Practice and Aggregation Issues*, CGFS Publications 14, Committee on the Global Financial System, Bank for International Settlements.
Cheng, N.Y.-P., Wang, J.-N. and Yeh, J.-H. (2010), "How accurate is the square-root-of-time rule at scaling tail risk: A global study," working paper.
Christoffersen, P.F. (1998), "Evaluating interval forecasts," *International Economic Review*, **39**, 841–862.
Clark, P. (1973), "A subordinated stochastic process model with finite variance for speculative prices," *Econometrica*, **41**, 135–155.

Crawley, M. (2007), *The R Book*, John Wiley & Sons Ltd.
Dalgaard, P. (2002), *Introductory Statistics with R*, Springer-Verlag.
Daníelsson, J. (1994), "Stochastic volatility in asset prices: Estimation with simulated maximum likelihood," *Journal of Econometrics*, **61**, 375–400.
Daníelsson, J. (2002), "The emperor has no clothes: Limits to risk modelling," *Journal of Banking and Finance*, **26**(7), 1273–1296. Available at http://www.RiskResearch.org
Daníelsson, J. and de Vries, C.G. (1997), "Tail index and quantile estimation with very high frequency data," *Journal of Empirical Finance*, **4**, 241–257.
Daníelsson, J. and de Vries, C.G. (2000), "Value at risk and extreme returns," London School of Economics, Financial Markets Group Discussion Paper No. 273. Available at http://www.Risk Research.org
Daníelsson, J. and de Vries, C.G. (2003), "Where do extremes matter?" Available at http://www.Risk Research.org
Daníelsson, J. and Goodhart, C. (2002), "The inter-temporal nature of risk," in: M. Balling, F. Lierman and A. Mullineux (Eds.), *Technology and Finance*, Routledge International Studies in Money and Banking No. 17, Ch. 2, pp. 18–40, Routledge.
Daníelsson, J. and Morimoto, Y. (2000), "Forecasting extreme financial risk: A critical analysis of practical methods for the Japanese market," *Monetary and Economic Studies, Bank of Japan*, **18**(2), 25–48.
Daníelsson, J. and Shin, H.S. (2003), "Endogenous risk," *Modern Risk Management: A History*, Risk Books. Available at http://www.RiskResearch.org
Daníelsson, J. and Zigrand, J.-P. (2006), "On time-scaling of risk and the square-root-of-time rule," *Journal of Banking and Finance*, **30**, 2701–2713.
Daníelsson, J., Hartmann, P. and de Vries, C.G.. (1998), "The cost of conservatism: Extreme returns, value-at-risk, and the Basel multiplication factor," *Risk*, January. Available at http://www.RiskResearch.org
Daníelsson, J., de Haan, L., Peng, L. and de Vries, C. (2001), "Using a bootstrap method to choose the sample fraction in tail index estimation," *Journal of Multivariate Analysis*, **76**.
Daníelsson, J., Shin, H.S. and Zigrand, J.-P. (2009), "Risk appetite and endogenous risk." Available at http://www.RiskResearch.org
Daníelsson, J., Jorgensen, B.N., Mandira, S., Samorodnitsky, G. and de Vries, C.G. (2010a), "Fat tails, VaR and subadditivity." Available at http://www.RiskResearch.org
Daníelsson, J., Shin, H.S. and Zigrand, J.-P. (2010b), "Endogenous and systemic risk." Available at http://www.RiskResearch.org
Davison, A.C. and Smith, R.L. (1990), "Models for exceedances over high thresholds," *Journal of the Royal Statistical Society, Ser. B.*, **52**(3), 393–442.
de Haan, L., Resnick, S., Rootzén, H. and de Vries, C.G. (1989), "Extremal behavior of solutions to a stochastic difference equation with application to ARCH processes," *Stochastic Processes and Their Applications*, **32**, 213–224.
de Vries, C.G. (1998), "Second order diversification effects." Available at www.few.eur.nl/few/people/cde/workingpapers/workingpapers.htm
Ding, Z. (1994), "Time series analysis of speculative returns," PhD dissertation, University of California.
Ding, Z., Granger, C.W.J. and Engle, R.F. (1993), "A long memory property of stock market returns and a new model," *Journal of Empirical Finance*, **1**, 83–106.
Dowd, K. (2002), *An Introduction to Market Risk Measurement*, John Wiley & Sons Ltd.
The Economist (2000), "Is the end in sight?", October 12 edition.
Embrechts, P., Kuppelberg, C. and Mikosch, T. (1997), *Modelling Extremal Events for Insurance and Finance: Applications of Mathematics*. Springer-Verlag.
Enders, W. (1995), *Applied Econometric Time Series*. John Wiley & Sons Ltd.

Engle, R.F. (1982), "Autoregressive conditional heteroskedasticity with estimates of the variance of United Kingdom inflation," *Econometrica*, **50**, 987–1007.

Engle, R. (2002), "Dynamic conditional correlation: A simple class of multivariate generalized autoregressive conditional heteroskedasticity models," *Journal of Business and Economic Statistics*, **20**(3), 339–350.

Engle, R. and Kroner, K. (1995), "Multivariate simultaneous generalized ARCH," *Econometric Theory*, **11**(1), 122–150.

Engle, R., Lilien, D.M. and Robins, R.P. (1987), "Estimating time varying risk premia in structure: The ARCH-M model," *Econometrica*, **58**, 525–542.

Fama, E. (1963), "Mandelbrot and the stable partition hypothesis," *Journal of Business*, **36**(4), 420–429.

Fama, E. (1965), "The behavior of stock-market prices," *Journal of Business*, **38**(1), 34–105.

Feller, W. (1971), *An Introduction to Probability Theory and Its Applications*, Vol. 2, Second Edition. John Wiley & Sons, Inc.

The Financial Times (2007), "Goldman pays the price of being big," August 13 edition.

Fisher, R.A. (1925), *Statistical Methods for Research Workers*, Oliver & Boyd, London.

Fisher, R.A. and Tippett, L.H. (1928), "Limiing forms of the frequency distribution of the largest or smallest member of a sample," *Proceedings of the Cambridge Philosophical Society*, **12**, 180–190.

Francq, C. and Zakoian, J.-M. (2010), *GARCH Models: Structure, Statistical Inference and Financial Applications*, John Wiley & Sons Ltd.

Glosten, L.R., Jagannathan, R. and Runkle, D. (1993), "Relationship between the expected value and the volatility of the nominal excess return on stocks," *Journal of Finance*, **48**, 1779–1802.

Gnedenko, B.V. (1943), "Sur la distribution limite du terme maximum d'une série aléatoire," *Ann. of Math.*, **44**, 423–453.

Greenspan, A. (1997), Discussion at *Symposium on Maintaining Financial Stability in a Global Economy*. The Federal Reserve Bank of Kansas.

Hahn, B. and Valentine, D. (2007), *Essential Matlab for Engineers and Scientists*, Newnes.

Hanselman, D. and Littlefield, B. (2001), *Mastering Matlab 6*, Prentice Hall.

Hansen, P.R. and Lunde, A. (2005), "A forecast comparison of volatility models: Does anything beat a GARCH(1,1)?" *Journal of Applied Econometrics*, **20**, 873–889.

Hill, B.M. (1975), "A simple general approach to inference about the tail of a distribution," *Ann. Statist.*, **35**, 1163–1173.

Jansen, D. and de Vries, C.G. (1991), "On the frequency of large stock returns: Putting booms and busts into perspective," *Review of Economics and Statistics*, **73**, 18–24.

J.P. Morgan (1993), *RiskMetrics Technical Manual*.

Keynes, J.M. (1936), *The General Theory of Employment, Interest and Money*, Macmillan.

Koedijk, K.G., Schafgans, M. and de Vries, C.G. (1990), "The tail index of exchange rate returns," *Journal of International Economics*, **29**, 93–108.

Laurent, S. (2009), *G@RCH 6: Estimating and Forecasting GARCH Models*, Timberlake Consultants Ltd.

Li, D.X. (2000), "On default correlation: A copula function approach," *Journal of Fixed Income*, **9**, 43–54.

Longin, F. and Solnik, B. (2001), "Extreme correlation of international equity markets," *Journal of Finance*, **56**(2), 649–676.

Lopez, J.A. (1998), "Methods for evaluating VaR estimates," *Economic Policy Review*, **4**(3),

Lopez, J.A. (1999), "Regulatory evaluation of value-at-risk models," *Journal of Risk*, **1**, 37–64.

Mandelbrot, B.B. (1963), "The variation of certain speculative prices," *Journal of Business*, **36**, 392–417.

McNeil, A.J., Frey, R. and Embrechts, P. (2005), *Quantitative Risk Management: Concepts, Techniques, and Tools*. Princeton University Press.

Murrell, P. (2006), *R Graphics*. Chapman & Hall.
Nelsen, R.B. (1999), *An Introduction to Copulas*, Springer-Verlag.
Nelson, D.B. (1991), "Conditional heteroskedasticity in asset pricing: A new approach," *Econometrica*, **59**, 347–370.
Patton, A. (2002), "On the out-of-sample importance of skewness and asymmetric dependence for asset allocation," University of California San Diego working paper.
Patton, A. (2009), "Copula-based models for financial time series," in: T. Andersen, R. Davis, J.-P. Kreiss and T. Mikosch (Eds.), *Handbook of Financial Time Series*, Springer-Verlag.
Pickands, J. (1975), "Statistical inference using extreme order statistics," *Annals of Statistics*, **3**, 119–131.
RDCT (2009), *R: A Language and Environment for Statistical Computing*. R Development Core Team, R Foundation for Statistical Computing.
Schwert, G.W. (1989), "Why does stock market volatility change over time," *Journal of Finance*, **44**, 1115–1153.
Sklar, A. (1959), "Fonctions de répartition à *n* dimensions et leurs marges," *Publ. Inst. Statis. Univ. Paris*, **8**, 229–231.
Tauchen, G.E. and Pitts, M. (1983), "The price variability–volume relationship on speculative markets," *Econometrica*, **51**, 485–505.
Taylor, S.J. (1986), *Modelling Financial Time Series*. John Wiley & Sons Ltd.
Tsay, R.S. (2005), *Analysis of Financial Times Series*. John Wiley & Sons Inc., Hoboken.
Tse, Y.K. and Tsui, A.K.C. (2002), "A multivariate GARCH model with time-varying correlations," *Journal of Business and Economic Statistics*, **20**, 351–362.
The Wall Street Journal (2007), "One 'quant' sees shakeout for the ages: '10,000 years'," August 11 edition.

Index

ABCP see asset-backed commercial paper
ABX index 186–8
ACF see autocorrelation ...
AdjClose 7–9, 23–4, 94–5, 147–8, 219
AIG 152
algorithms, definition 247
analytical VaR 111–20, 132–3, 142
aparch() 53
APARCH models 44, 46, 52–4, 56
  see also GARCH ...
  application 52–3
  critique 52, 56
  definition 52–4
  goodness-of-fit measures 46
  LR 52–3
  Matlab 53–4
  R 53–4
ARCH 35–8, 41, 42–51, 180–1, 216
  see also GARCH ...; Lagrange multiplier test
  application 46–51, 180–1
  ARCH-M model 41
  critique 38
  definition 35, 36–8, 42, 216
  EVT 180–1
  fat tails 36–8, 180–1
  LR 44–51
  Matlab 48–51
  parameter restrictions 37–8, 43–4
  R 48–51
  unconditional volatility 36
  usefulness assessment 38
ARCH-M model, definition 41
arima() 224–5
arima.sim() 225
arithmetic returns see simple returns
ARMA see autoregressive moving average models
armaxfilter() 238
arrays, Matlab concepts 232–3, 234–5
AR see autoregressive models
Asian crisis in 1997 5–6, 11, 164
asset allocations 57–71

asset-backed commercial paper (ABCP) 186–8
asymmetric power GARCH see APARCH models
asymptotic properties, MLE 154–60, 247–53
at-the-money options 116–20, 139–40
autocorrelation 6–9, 12–14, 29, 38, 48–52, 209–12, 215–16, 224–5, 237–8
  see also autoregressive models; correlation ...; Ljung–Box test; predictability
  definition 209–10
  Matlab concepts 9, 13–14, 237–8
  R concepts 8–9, 13–14, 224–5
  S&P 500 summary return statistics from 1928 to 2009 6–9, 12–14, 38
  test statistics 215–16
  volatility clusters 12–14
autocovariance
  see also covariance
  definition 209–10
autoregressive models (ARs)
  see also autocorrelation
  definition 211–12
autoregressive moving average models (ARMA) 210, 212, 224–5, 238
  definition 212
  Matlab concepts 238
  R concepts 224–5

backtesting 38, 44, 76, 89, 91, 93, 98, 143–66, 208
  assumptions 146, 162–3
  Basel Accords 146, 155
  Bernoulli coverage test 153–60
  critique 143, 146, 162–3, 166
  data mining 163
  definition 143–6
  ES 89, 91, 143, 160–2
  "frozen" portfolios 146
  "hit sequence" 153–60, 208
  independence test 153, 155–60
  loss-function-based backtests 159–60
  Matlab 148–53

Index

backtesting (cont.)
  problems 162–3, 166
  R 147–53
  S&P 500 sample returns from 1994 to 2009 147–53, 157–9
  significance tests 153–60
  structural breaks in the data 162–3
  VaR 76, 89, 91, 98, 143–66
  violations 143–66, 208
banks 20, 22–4, 143, 146–7, 165, 183–4, 186, 188–90
bar() 129
bar charts 128–9, 229–30, 243
barplot() 128–9
Basel Accords 33, 90, 146–7, 155, 178, 183–4
bear markets 9, 21–9
Bear Stearns (BS) 22–3
"beauty" contests 183
BEKK 69–71
  see also MVGARCH B
Bernoulli distributions 153–60, 208, 223
bern_test() 155, 158
bimodal likelihood function 248–9
binomial distributions 208, 223, 236–7
bivariate normal distributions 21–2, 24–8, 200–1, 203, 243
  definition 200–1
  exceedance correlations 24
Black–Scholes options pricing model 5, 20–1, 54, 115–20, 125, 129–42, 192–4
  assumptions 116, 129
  definition 115–16
  Matlab 117–19, 129–32, 135–6, 139–40
  R 117–19, 129–32, 135–6, 139–40
block maxima EVT approach 172
bonds 73, 84, 88–9, 110, 111–20, 121–42, 164–5
  convexity 112–13
  crash of April 1994 164
  credit rating agencies 28, 164–5, 185–8
  definition 112
  duration-normal VaR 112–15
  interest rates 111–15, 125–9
  Matlab 112, 125–6
  Monte Carlo simulations 121, 124–9, 142
  portfolios 115, 124–9, 142, 164–5
  prices 111, 112–15, 121, 124–9, 142 R 112, 125–6 VaR 111–20
bounded moments 18–21
Box–Muller random number method 124
Brady Commission 191–2

Brownian motion 5, 129
  see also derivatives
  bs() 117–19, 129–32, 135–6, 139–40
bull markets 9, 21–9
burn time 60–2

c() 218
calendar time, definition 133, 144–5
call options
  concepts 115–42, 192–6
  definition 115, 192
capital adequacy requirements 143, 146–7, 165, 183–4
cash flows, bonds 111–20, 125–9
cat() 158
Cauchy distributions 202, 223
cbind() 23, 59, 67, 94, 221–2
CCC 63–5, 70–1
CDFs see cumulative distribution functions
CDOs see collateralized debt obligations
CDSs see credit default swaps
centered moment of a distribution, definition 18–21, 203–4
central limit theorem (CLT)
  see also scaling laws
  definitions 89–90, 212–13
chi-squared (χ^2) distributions 120, 206–7, 212, 214, 223, 236–7
  definition 206–7
  test statistics 214
chi2cdf() 158, 214
Clayton copula 28–9, 236
CLT see central limit theorem
coherent risk measures 80, 81–4
  see also expected shortfall
collateralized debt obligations (CDOs) 25, 185–6
comments, R 217–18, Matlab 231
conditional correlations
  see also CCC; DCC
  concepts 63–71
conditional distributions, concepts 93, 200–1
conditional means, concepts 41
conditional probability functions, definition 173–4, 200–1
conditional volatility 1, 11–29, 32, 34, 35–51, 57–71, 98–110, 148–53
  see also GARCH . . .
  definition 11
consistency property, MLE 250
Consumer Price Index (CPI) 5–6
contagion 57
continuous time, concepts 55–6, 129–42

Index   261

continuously compounded returns 1, 3–29, 100–1
  see also returns
  definition 3–5, 100
  VaR 100–1
convergence 18–20, 248–51
convexity 111–20
convolution 176–82
copulas 25–9, 169, 217, 229, 236–7
  see also Clayton …; default risks; Frank …; Gumbel …; marginal returns
  application illustration 27–9
  challenges 28
  critique 28
  definition 25–7, 236
  Gaussian copula 25–9
  nonlinear dependence 25–9
  Student-*t* distributions 26–8
  theory 25–7
  types 28–9, 236
coredata() 7–9, 94, 147–8, 219
correlation coefficient 1–29, 57–71, 137–42, 166, 203–4, 220, 234
  see also autocorrelation; nonlinear dependence; Pearson …
  definition 203
  exceedance correlations 23–4
correlation matrix 57–71
cov() 60, 108
covariance 31, 37–9, 44, 57–71, 93–110, 137–42, 166, 200, 209–10, 220, 249
  see also autocovariance; multivariate volatility models; variance
  definition 202–3
  independence 202–3
  matrix 57–71, 93–110, 137–42, 166
  stationary 37–9, 44, 69, 209–10
CPI *see* Consumer Price Index
Cramér–Rao lower bound 173, 249, 250
credit default swaps (CDSs) 167–8, 186–8
credit rating agencies 28, 164–5, 185–8
credit risk, capital requirements 146–7, 165
crisis periods, nonlinear dependence 21–9
csv() 219
cumulative distribution functions (CDFs)
  concepts 176–9, 197–201, 215, 222–3, 235–7
  definition 197–8

data mining, backtesting problems 163
DCC 63–7, 70–1
de-meaned returns 35–41, 51–2
decay factors, EWMA 31–56

decision making, risk management 75, 196
default risks 28, 185–7
  see also copulas
degrees of freedom 1–29, 40–1, 44–5, 102–3, 169–70, 206–8, 222–3, 224–5, 247
deleverage, definition 186
delta 111, 116–20, 192–6
  see also gamma
  definition 116–17
  hedging strategies 192–6
  Matlab 117–19
  R 117–19
delta-normal VaR 119–20
densities
  concepts 76–85, 86–91, 103–4, 131–2, 197–201
  definition 197–8
density plots, options 131–2
derivatives 2, 5, 12, 20–1, 31–56, 73–5, 78–9, 80–1, 111, 115–20, 121–42, 164, 167, 192–6
  see also futures; options; swaps
  the "Greeks" 78–9, 111, 115–20, 192–3
  stochastic volatility models 56
diag() 65, 221–2, 235
diff() 7–9, 23–4, 50, 59, 94, 147–8, 219, 233, 234
dim() 218
discounted cash flows, bonds 112–15, 125–9
discrete distributions 208, 236–7
  see also Bernoulli …; binomial …
Disney 24, 26, 27–8
distribution-free risk measures 73–5, 90–1
  see also risk measures
distributions 168–70, 197–216, 222–4, 235–7
  see also Bernoulli …; binomial …; Cauchy …; chi-squared …; cumulative …; exponential …; Fréchet …; Gamma …; Gumbel …; joint …; normal …; Pareto …; Student-*t* …; Weibull …
  EVT 168–70
  Matlab concepts 235–7
  R concepts 222–4
distributions of financial returns, measurement difficulties 73–5
diversification 81–4
dividend yields 5–6
DJIA *see* Dow Jones Industrial Average
dnorm() 87, 104, 118–19, 128–9, 131–2, 222–3

Dow Jones Industrial Average (DJIA) 2, 185–6, 191–2, 195
duration 111–20
  see also yield curves
duration-normal VaR, bonds 112–15
dynamic replication strategies 192–6
dynamic trading strategies, endogenous risk 191–6

the Economist 190
efficient estimators, definition 250
EGARCH
  see also GARCH ...
  definition 51–2
eigenvalues 222, 235
eigenvectors 222, 235
electricity prices 84
elseif statements, Matlab concepts 240–1
empirical identification of stylized facts of financial returns 9–29
encapsulated postscript files 229–30
endogenous risk 165, 183–96
  Basel Accords 183
  definition 165, 183–4, 195
  delta hedging strategies 192–6
  dynamic trading strategies 191–6
  financial crises 185–8, 191–6
  gambling analogies 185, 196
  global financial crisis from 2007 185–8, 191, 195–6
  implications for risk management 184–8
  the Millennium Bridge 184, 195–6
  stock market crash of 1987 191–6
  VaR 190
Engle LM test see Lagrange multiplier test
ergodicity 3
  see also returns
ERM crisis 164
ES see expected shortfall
estimation window 31–56, 106–8, 144–66
European options 54, 115–16, 125, 129–42
Evir R library 182
EVT see extreme value theory
EWMA 32–5, 43, 45–6, 56, 59–62, 65–7, 70–1, 93, 106–8, 146–7, 148–53, 158–62
  see also RiskMetrics
  applications 34–5, 59–62, 65–7, 93, 106–8, 146–7, 148–53, 158–62
  backtesting 146–7, 148–53, 158–62
  Basel Accords 33
  critique 34–5, 56, 60–2, 67, 70, 150–3
  decay factors 31–56

definition 32–3, 59–60
derivation 33–4, 59–60
GARCH comparisons 34–5, 43, 150–3
LR 45–6
Matlab 60, 67, 107–8, 148–53
multivariate volatility models 59–62, 65–7, 70–1, 107–8
R 60, 67, 107–8, 148–53
unconditional volatility 35, 43, 60–2
VaR 107–8, 146–7, 148–53, 158–62
exceedance correlations, nonlinear dependence 23–4
excess kurtosis 16, 36–7, 170–1
  see also kurtosis ...
excess returns
  see also returns
  definition 4–5
exogenous risk 183, 188–9, 195
exotic options 139–40
exp() 117–19, 131, 134, 137–9
expected returns, concepts 104–5
expected shortfall (ES) 73, 85–90, 93–110, 143, 160–2, 166
  see also coherent risk measures; risk measures
  application 93–110, 143, 160–2, 166
  backtesting difficulties 89, 91, 143, 160–2
  critique 88–9
  definition 85–9
  HS 97–8, 160–2
  Matlab 87–8, 97–8, 104, 161–2
  normality issues 103–4 R 87–8, 97–8, 104, 161–2
expected values 201–3, 206–10
  see also sample means
exponential distributions 32–5, 223, 236–7
  see also EWMA
extremal index 168, 179–82
extreme value theory (EVT) 16–21, 37, 167–82, 236–7
  see also fat tails
  application 172–82
  asset returns 170–1
  convolution 176–82
  critique 168
  definition 167–70, 181–2
  distributions 168–70
  extremal index 168, 179–82
  implementation approaches 172–6
  libraries 182
  Matlab 182
  POT 172–82
  R 182

reading recommendations 167
risk analysis 173–82
S&P 500 sample returns from 1970 to 2009 175–81
threshold considerations 174–5
time dependence 179–82
types of tails 168–9
extreme values 16–21, 37, 163–6, 167–82, 236–7
eye() 235
eyeball method, EVT thresholds 174–5

fat tails 1, 9–29, 36–8, 48–51, 83–9, 102–3, 150–3, 167–82, 204–5, 215
see also extreme value ... ; kurtosis ... ; Pareto distributions; Student-*t* distributions; stylized facts of financial returns
ARCH 36–8, 180–1
definition 9, 14, 16–21, 167–9, 170–1
graphical detection methods 16, 17–21, 48–51, 150–3
implications in finance 20–1, 167–82
low volatility levels 11
nonnormality issues 14–16
QQ plots graphical detection method 17–18, 48–51
sequential moments graphical detection method 18–21
statistical tests 16–21, 170–1
super-fat tails 83–4
tail index measures 18–21, 37–8, 167–82
feedback effects 165, 184–96
fExtremes R library 182
finance.yahoo.com 1, 7, 219, 233
financial crisis from 2007 5, 10–11, 20–1, 28, 98, 152–3, 164, 168, 185–8, 191, 195–6
financial innovations 190–6
financial markets 1–29, 183–96
endogenous risk 165, 183–96
stylized facts of financial returns 9–29
financial time series 1–29, 94, 197–216
Financial Times 20
find() 131, 158, 162
first centered moment of a distribution
see also means
definition 16, 203–4
fit.st() 102–3
fminunc() 242
for loops 60, 106–8, 127–9, 148–53, 156–8, 161–2, 226–8, 239–42
foreign exchange risks, concepts 79, 84, 142, 164

fourth centered moment of a distribution see kurtosis ...
Frank copula 236
Fréchet distributions 169–71, 172–3
"frozen" portfolios, backtesting 146
FTSE 2, 21
FTSTool 8, 233
function() 118–19, 155–7
functions 225–7, 238–42
see also arguments; M-files
futures 80–1, 131–2

gambling analogies, endogenous risk 185, 196
gamma 111, 116–20
see also delta
Gamma distributions 223
Gamma function 206
GARCH family of models 32, 34–56, 62–3, 93, 108–10, 146, 148–53, 158–9, 167–8, 171, 174, 180–1, 245
see also conditional volatility; variance; volatility models
APARCH models 44, 46, 52–4, 56
application 46–51, 93, 108–10, 146, 148–53, 158–9, 167–8, 174, 180–1
backtesting 146, 148–53, 158–9
BEKK 69–71
CCC 63–5, 70–1
critique 34–5, 55–6, 150–3
DCC 63–7, 70–1
definitions 35–6, 38–41
EGARCH 51–2
EVT 167–8, 171, 174, 180–1
EWMA comparisons 34–5, 43, 65–7, 150–3
extensions 51–4, 67–71
GJR-GARCH 51–2, 53–4
graphical analysis 48–51
likelihood functions 42–4, 46–51, 52–3, 56, 69–71
LR 44–51, 52–4
Matlab 48–51, 53–4, 65, 108–10, 148–53
"memory" measures 39–41
MLE 41–4, 56, 69–71
multiperiod volatility 39–40
multivariate volatility models 44, 62–3, 65–71
MVGARCH 67–71
normal GARCH 40–1, 56
OGARCH 62–3, 65–7, 70–1
parameter restrictions 38–9, 43–4

GARCH family of models (*cont.*)
  power GARCH models 52 R 48–51, 53–4, 65, 108–10, 148–53
  skew *t*-GARCH model 41, 42–4, 46–51, 52–3
  stochastic volatility model comparisons 55–6
  t-GARCH model 40–1, 46–51, 109, 152
  unconditional volatility 38–9, 43, 152–3
  VaR 108–10, 146, 148–53, 158–9, 167, 174
garchfit()
  Matlab concepts 48–51, 53–4, 65, 109, 150–3
  R concepts 48–51, 53–4, 65, 109, 149–50
garchset() 50–1, 109, 148–53
Gaussian copula 25–9
Gaussian white noise 210, 215
  see also white noise
GDP 6
generalized extreme values (GEVs) 169–70, 172–4, 236–7
generalized method of moments 245
generalized Pareto distribution (GPD), POT concepts 172–4
GEO fund 20
geometric Brownian motion, definition 129
get.hist.quote(), R concepts 7–8, 23, 50, 59, 94, 147–8, 219
GEVs *see* generalized extreme values
GJR-GARCH 51–2, 53–4
  see also GARCH ...
global financial crisis from 2007 5, 10–11, 20–1, 28, 98, 152–3, 164, 168, 185–8, 191, 195–6
  causes 185–8, 191, 195–6
  CDOs 185–6
  margins 168, 186–7
  NINJA borrowers 186
  subprime mortgage markets 185–8
Global Financial Data 5, 7
gogarch() 63
Goldman Sachs (GS) 20, 22–3
goodness-of-fit measures 45–51
GPD *see* generalized Pareto distribution
graphical detection methods for fat tails 16, 17–21, 48–51, 150–3
  see also QQ plots; sequential moments ...
graphics
  GARCH family of models 48–51, 150–3
  Matlab concepts 243
  R concepts 229–30
Great Depression in the 1930s 5–6, 7, 10–11, 185

the "Greeks" 78–9, 111, 115–20, 192–3
  see also delta; gamma
Greenspan, Alan 20
Gumbel distributions 169–70, 172–3, 236

haircut 186–8
half-life of a shock, definition 39–40
Handle Graphics Matlab system 243
hazard rates 250
hedge funds 186, 191–2
help() 217, 238–9
Hessian matrix 228–9, 242–3, 247, 249
  see also information matrix
heteroskedasticity 237–8
high peaks 6–9, 204–5, 214–15
  see also kurtosis ...
higher moments 201, 203–5, 220
hill climbing, MLE 248–9
Hill estimator method, POT concepts 172, 173–82
hist() 128–9, 131–2
histfit() 129, 132
histograms 14–15, 229–30, 235–7, 243
historical simulations (HS) 11–12, 73, 93–8, 109–10, 142, 146, 149–53, 158–62, 167, 174, 181, 210–12
  see also nonparametric estimation methods; simulations
  backtesting 146, 149–53, 158–62
  definition 93, 95–8
  Matlab 95–7, 149–53
  multivariate HS 96–7 R 95–7, 149–53
  univariate HS 95–6
  window sizes 97–8, 146, 149–53
hist_stock_data(), Matlab concepts 23, 50, 59, 94–5, 148, 233
"hit sequence", VaR violations 153–60, 208
holding periods, VaR 76–85, 89–91, 146, 178–9
HS *see* historical simulations

IBM 24, 26, 27–8, 57–81, 93–110
if ... else ... statements 227–8, 240–1
IID 1–29, 35–41, 45–6, 90, 105, 106–10, 116–20, 124, 133, 169–70, 179–80, 200–1, 208–13, 216, 242–3, 245–53
implied volatility models 32, 54–6
in-the-money options 116–20
independence test, backtesting 153, 155–60
ind_test() 156–7
inflation 5
information matrix 228–9, 242–3, 249
  see also Hessian matrix

insurance 82, 186–8
integrate() 104
interest rate risks, concepts 79, 142
interest rates 79, 111–20, 125–9, 133–42, 185–6, 191–2
Internet bubble 5, 29
invariance property, MLE 250
inverse normal distributions, concepts 25, 123–4
investment banks 20, 22–4, 186
Ito's lemma, concepts 112–13

Jarque–Bera distribution test (JB) 6–9, 16–17, 47–51, 214–15, 223–4, 237
 see also *p*-value ...
jbtest() 237
joint density 26–9, 42–4, 159, 200, 245–6
 see also multivariate normal distributions
joint distributions 25–9, 200, 209–10, 245–6
 see also copulas
J.P. Morgan 33, 34–5
 see also RiskMetrics
JPL Matlab toolbox 9, 231
jumps 73–4

Keynes, John Maynard 183
Kolmogorov–Smirnov distribution test (KS) 16–17, 74, 214–15, 237
KS *see* Kolmogorov–Smirnov distribution test (KS)
kstest() 17, 237
ks.test() 17
kurtosis 6–9, 16–21, 36–8, 170–82, 204–5, 214–15, 220, 225–6, 234, 238–9
 see also fat tails
 definition 16, 170–1, 204–5
 estimation formula 170–1, 205
 excess kurtosis 16, 36–7, 170–1
 Matlab concepts 9, 238–9
 R concepts 8–9, 220, 225–7
 S&P 500 summary return statistics from 1928 to 2009 6–9

Lagrange multiplier test (LM) 12, 13–14, 35–6, 216, 251, 252–3
 see also ARCH; volatility clusters
lags, volatility models 31–56
lambda 60, 148–53
latent variables 31–56, 75
LB *see* Ljung–Box test
LCGs *see* linear congruental generators
legend() 67
Lehmans 21, 152

LeSage, James P. (JPL) 231
leverage effect, concepts 51–2, 56, 186–96
leverage ratios, concepts 188–96
library(), R concepts 7–9, 13–14, 17, 48–51, 59, 63, 94, 102–3, 109, 137, 147–8, 217, 220, 223–4
likelihood functions 37–8, 41–4, 46–51, 64, 69–71, 153–60, 223, 228–9, 242–3, 245–53
 see also maximum ...; optimizers
 APARCH models 52–3
 ARCH 42–4, 46–51
 definition 245–7
 estimation issues 43–4
 GARCH 42–4, 46–51, 52–3, 56, 69–71
 Matlab concepts 242–3
 R concepts 228–9
 stochastic volatility models 56
likelihood ratio tests (LR) 44–6, 52–3, 154–60, 250–2
linear algebra computations, Matlab concepts 234–5
linear congruental generators (LCGs) 122–3, 140
 see also random number generators
linear dependence
 see also correlation ...
 concepts 9, 21–2, 203
linear regression methods 41
 see also ordinary least squares
linear relationships, definition 203
linspace() 232–3
liquidity issues, portfolios 78–9
list() 117–19
Ljung–Box test (LB) 6–9, 13–14, 47–51, 216, 224–5, 238
 see also autocorrelation; *p*-value ...
LM *see* Lagrange multiplier test
load() 232–3
log-likelihood function 42–4, 46–51, 56, 64, 172–3, 228–9, 236, 242–3, 246–9, 250–1
log-normal distributions 130–2, 133–42, 173, 222–3, 236–7
logarithm of the likelihood function 246
logarithmic returns *see* continuously compounded returns
logspace() 232–3
loops and repeats
 inefficiencies 241
 Matlab concepts 60, 106–8, 127–9, 148–53, 156–8, 161–2, 239–42

266 Index

loops and repeats (*cont.*)
  R concepts 60, 106–8, 127–9, 148–53, 156–8, 161–2, 226–8
loss-function-based backtests 159–60
low peaks 204–5
  see also kurtosis . . .
LR *see* likelihood ratio tests
LTCM 164

M-files, Matlab concepts 238–42
manipulation issues, VaR 80, 84–5
marginal distributions, definition 26–8, 200–1
margins, global financial crisis from 2007 168, 186–7
market efficiencies 13–14
market risks 105, 146–7, 165
marking-to-market valuations 190–1
MAs *see* moving average models
MASS R library 137
Matlab 1, 7–29, 31, 46–56, 58–71, 87–8, 95–8, 104, 106–8, 112, 117–19, 125–6, 127–32, 135–6, 139–40, 148–53, 156–8, 161–2, 197, 214, 231–43, 247, 248
  APARCH models 53–4
  ARCH 48–51
  ARMA 238
  autocorrelation 9, 13–14, 237–8
  backtesting 148–53
  basic operations 7–9, 233
  basic programming 238–42
  Bernoulli coverage test 155, 158
  Black–Scholes options pricing model 117–19, 129–32, 135–6, 139–40
  bond prices 112, 125–6
  CCC 65
  DCC 65, 67
  definition 231
  delta 117–19
  distributions 235–7
  econometrics 231
  ES 87–8, 97–8, 104, 161–2
  EVT 182
  EWMA 60, 67, 107–8, 148–53
  financial time series 7–9, 197
  gamma 117–19
  GARCH family of models 48–51, 53–4, 65, 108–10, 148–53
  graphics 243
  Hill estimator method 175–6
  HS 95–7, 149–53
  independence coverage test 156–8
  information sources 231

inputting data 7–9, 23, 48–51, 58–9, 94–5, 147–8, 231–3
introductory background 231–43
kurtosis (peakedness of a distribution) 9, 238–9
likelihood functions 242–3
linear algebra computations 234–5
loops and repeats 60, 106–8, 127–9, 148–53, 156–8, 161–2, 239–42
JPL toolbox 9, 231
M-files 238–42
MAs 106–8, 149–53
matrix computations 60–2, 234–5
MFE toolbox 9, 43, 53, 152, 231
MLE 242–3
Monte Carlo simulations 130–2, 133–9
multivariate volatility models 58–71, 108
normality testing 237
OGARCH 62–3, 67
optimizers 247, 248
p-value test statistic 214
reading recommendations 231
RNGs 123–4
S&P 500 index 7–9, 46–56, 233
simple operations 7–9, 233–5
Student-*t* VaR 102–3
time series 7–9, 237–8
toolboxes Matlab 8–9, 17, 48–51, 53–4, 62–3, 152–3, 231–43
univariate volatility models 46–56, 107–8
UCSD GARCH Matlab toolbox 53–4, 62–3, 231, 237–8
VaR 87–8, 101–3, 106–8, 133–9, 147–53
yield curves 126–9
matplot() 67, 127–9
matrix(), R concepts 97, 127–9, 137–9, 161–2, 218–19, 220–3
matrix algebra, Matlab concepts 234–5
matrix computations 60–2, 218–19, 220–2, 234–5
max() 6–9, 131–2
MaxFunEvals 248
maximum domain of attraction (MDA) 170–3
maximum likelihood (ML)
  see also ML estimation; nonlinear models; Student-*t* distributions
  concepts 41–4, 56, 64, 69–71, 153–60, 223, 228–9, 242–3, 245–53
  definition 245–6
MaxIter 248
MBSs *see* mortgage-backed securities
mean squared error (MSE) 174–5

mean-variance analysis, concepts 73–5
mean 6–9, 13–14, 32, 35–41, 58–71, 73–6, 93–110, 128–9, 131–2, 161–2, 175–6, 199–201, 204–10, 213, 220, 226, 234, 236–7, 238–9, 242–3, 245–53
  ARCH-M model 41
  risk models 73–6, 213
  S&P 500 summary return statistics from 1928 to 2009 6–9, 13–14
median 234
"memory" measures, GARCH family of models 39–41
Mersenne twister 123–4
Mexican peso devaluation in December 1994 163–4
MFE Matlab toolbox 9, 43, 53, 152-3, 231
Microsoft 22–3, 58–71, 93–110
the Millennium Bridge 184, 195–6
min, S&P 500 summary return statistics from 1928 to 2009 6–9
ML *see* maximum likelihood
ML estimation (MLE) 41–3, 56, 64, 69–71, 102–3, 228–9, 242–3, 245–53
  definition 228–9, 245–6
  GARCH 41–4, 56, 69–71
  Hessian matrix 228–9, 242–3, 247, 249
  hill climbing 248–9
  issues 248–9
  Matlab concepts 242–3
  properties 250
  R concepts 228–9
  volatility models 41–4
mle() 102–3
MLE
  see also ML estimation
modified duration 111–20
money markets 129–42
monotonic transformations 203
monotonicity axiom of coherent risk measures 81–2, 203, 246
Monte Carlo simulations 110, 111, 115, 120, 121–42, 164
  bonds' pricing methods 121, 124–9, 142
  critique 121
  definition 121
  issues to be addressed 140–2
  Matlab 130–2, 133–9
  number of simulations 140–2
  options' pricing methods 121, 124–5, 129–42
  portfolio VaR 137–42, 164
  R 130–2, 133–9
  RNG quality issues 140–2

  uses 121–2, 124–42
  VaR 110, 111, 115, 120, 121, 132–42
Morgan Stanley (MS) 22–3
mortgage-backed securities (MBSs) 185–6
moving average models (MAs) 32–5, 38, 93, 106–8, 149–53, 158–9, 180, 210–12, 224–5, 238
  see also EWMA; stationarity
  critique 33, 149–53
  definition 32–3, 210–11
  Matlab 106–8, 149–53
  R 106–8, 149–53
  VaR 106–8, 149–53, 158–9
MSE *see* mean squared error
mth centered moment of a distribution, definition 18–21, 203–4
multigarch() 53–4
multiperiod volatility, GARCH family of models 39–40
multivariate HS 96–7
multivariate normal distributions 9–29, 101–2, 199–200, 203, 223, 236–7
  see also nonlinear dependence
multivariate volatility models 1, 9–29, 31, 56, 57–71, 93, 100–1, 107–10, 137–42, 199–200, 203, 223, 236–7, 248
  see also BEKK; CCC; DCC; EWMA; GARCH ...; MVGARCH; OGARCH; volatility models
  application 58–71, 107–10
  complexities 57–8
  definition 31, 57–8
  estimation comparisons 65–7
  extensions of GARCH 67–71
  GARCH family of models 44, 62–3, 65–71, 93
  Matlab 58–71, 108
  nonlinear dependence 25
  positive semi-definiteness 58–71
  R 58–71, 108
mutual funds 2
MVGARCH 67–71
  see also BEKK; GARCH ...
mvrnorm() 137–9

NaN (not a number) 43–4, 51, 61, 69, 129, 148–53, 161–2
nargin/nargout 239
New York Stock Exchange (NYSE) 1–29
Newton–Raphson method
  see also Taylor expansion
  definition 247
Nikkei 225 index 2

NINJA borrowers 186
NLD *see* nonlinear dependence
nlm() 228–9
nonlinear dependence (NLD) 1, 9, 21–9, 95–8
  see also correlation ...; multivariate ...; stylized facts of financial returns
  copulas 25–9
  crisis periods 21–4, 29
  definition 9, 21–8
  exceedance correlations 23–4
  models 25–9
  multivariate volatility models 25
  sample evidence 21, 22–3
nonlinear models 245–53
  see also maximum likelihood
nonnormality issues 14–29, 31–56
  see also fat tails
nonparametric estimation methods 93–8, 109–10, 149–53
  see also historical simulations
nonuniform RNGs 123–4
normal distributions 1–29, 42–4, 46–51, 56, 64, 73–6, 79, 87–91, 93, 98–9, 101–2, 103–4, 171, 172–3, 176, 198–216, 222–4, 228–9, 236–7, 242–3, 246–53
  see also multivariate ...; standard ...
  assumptions 1, 16–29, 75–6, 79, 91, 93, 98–9, 101–2
  definition 16–21, 25, 198–9
normal GARCH 40–4, 56
  see also GARCH ...
normal likelihood functions 228–9, 246–7
normality testing 6–9, 14–15, 16–21, 47–51, 74–5, 79, 214–15, 223–4, 237
  see also fat tails; Jarque–Bera ...; Kolmogorov–Smirnov ...
  critique 20
  definition 214–15, 223–4, 237
  Matlab concepts 237
  R concepts 223–4
  S&P 500 summary return statistics from 1928 to 2009 6–9
normcdf() 118–19, 124
norminv() 87, 101–2, 104, 106–9, 161–2
normpdf() 87, 104, 118–19, 161–2
numerical methods 121–42
  see also Monte Carlo simulations
NYSE *see* New York Stock Exchange

objects, R concepts 7–9, 217–30
OGARCH 62–3, 65–7, 70–1
  see also GARCH ...

critique 70–1
definition 62–3
Matlab 62–3, 67
R 62–3, 67
oil price returns 19
operational risk, capital requirements 146–7
optimizers 43–4, 228–9, 247–8
  see also likelihood functions
options 5, 12, 20–1, 54, 73, 80–1, 84–5, 110, 111–20, 121, 124–5, 129–42, 192–6
  see also American ...; call ...; derivatives; European ...; put ...
  Black–Scholes options pricing model 5, 20–1, 54, 115–20, 125, 129–42, 192–4
  definition 115–16, 192–3
  delta 111, 116–20, 192–6
  delta-normal VaR 119–20
  density plots 131–2
  exotic options 139–40
  gamma 111, 116–20
  the "Greeks" 78–9, 111, 115–20, 192–3
  Monte Carlo simulations 121, 124–5, 129–42
  portfolio VaR 139–42
  types 115
  VaR 111, 119–20, 133–42
ordinary least squares 41, 245
out-of-sample forecast comparisons, volatility models 44–6
out-of-the-money options 116–20
outstanding shares, value-weighted indices 2–9
Ox language 69
Oxford MFE toolbox 9, 152–3, 231

p-value test statistic 6–9, 13–14, 153–60, 212–14, 224–5, 237
  see also Jarque–Bera ...; Ljung–Box ...
pacf() 224–5
packages, R concepts 217, 223
parameters 37–9, 43–4, 57–71, 245–53
  ARCH restrictions 37–8, 43–4
  GARCH restrictions 38–9, 43–4
  ML 43–4, 245–53
parametric estimation methods 93–4, 98–110, 172–4
  see also variance–covariance method
Pareto distributions 169–70, 171, 172–4, 223, 236–7
PCA *see* principal components analysis
pchisq() 158, 214
PDFs *see* probability density functions

peaks over threshold approach (POT) to EVT, concepts 172–82
Pearson's correlation coefficient
see also correlation coefficient
definition 203
pie charts 243
plot() 7–9, 13–14, 50–1, 67, 123–4, 217, 219, 224, 229–30, 231, 233, 237–8, 243
pnorm() 117–19, 123–4, 222–3
points, stock market indices 1–9
Poisson distributions 223, 236–7, 250–1
poker 185
portfolio VaR, Monte Carlo simulations 137–42, 164
portfolios 1, 12–29, 41, 57–71, 73–91, 93–110, 121–42, 192–6
see also expected shortfall; multivariate volatility models; Value at Risk
backtesting 143–66
bonds 42, 115, 124–9, 164–5
conditional means 41
dynamic replication strategies 192–6
liquidity issues 78–9
options 139–42
positive feedback loops 184–96
positive homogeneity axiom of coherent risk measures, concepts 82
positive semi-definiteness, multivariate volatility models 58–71
postscript files 229–30
POT *see* peaks over threshold approach ...
power GARCH models, definition 52
power of the test
see also type-1/2
errors definition 214
predictability 12–14, 210–16
see also autocorrelation; time series
price-weighted indices 2–9
prices 1–29, 98, 152–3, 164, 168, 183–96
see also returns; stock market indices
definitions 2–9
dual roles 190–6
endogenous risk 183–96
exogenous risk 188–9, 195
financial crises 185–8, 191–6
global financial crisis from 2007 5, 10–11, 20–1, 28, 98, 152–3, 164, 168, 185–8, 195–6
marking-to-market valuations 190–1
statistical analysis techniques 1–29
stock market crash of 1987 7, 10–11, 14, 21, 164, 191–6

principal components analysis (PCA) 62–3, 71, 129
print 243
probabilities, VaR 33, 54–5, 73, 76–91, 208, 213
probability density functions (PDFs) 76–85, 86–91, 197–216, 222–3, 229–30, 235–7
probability integral transformation 25–9
see also copulas
profit and loss 73–91, 93–110, 133–42, 160
pseudo random number generators 121–4
put options 84–5, 115–20, 136–42, 192–6
definition 115, 192
VaR manipulations 84–5

QML *see* quasi-maximum likelihood
qnorm() 87, 101–2, 104, 107–8, 149–50, 161–2, 222–3
QQ plots 17–21, 48–51, 215, 223–4, 237
see also quantiles
QRMlib 102–3
qt() 102–3
quad() 104
quadratic approximations, concepts 247
quantile function, definition 198
quantiles 17–21, 28–9, 76–7, 80–5, 93–110, 142, 173–4, 198–201, 215, 222–3, 234, 236
see also QQ plots; Value at Risk
quantitative trading 31
quasi-maximum likelihood (QML), definition 41

R 1, 7–29, 31, 46–56, 58–71, 87–8, 97–8, 104, 117–19, 129–32, 135–6, 139–40, 155, 158, 161–2, 214, 217–30, 247
ACF 224–5
APARCH models 53–4
ARCH 48–51
ARMA 224–5
autocorrelation 8–9, 13–14, 224–5
backtesting 147–53
Bernoulli coverage test 155, 158
Black–Scholes options pricing model 117–19, 129–32, 135–6, 139–40
bond prices 112, 125–6
CCC 65
comments 217–18
data manipulation functions 7–9, 219–20
DCC 65, 67
definition 217
delta 117–19
distributions 222–4

R (cont.)
    ES 87–8, 97–8, 104, 161–2
    EVT 182
    EWMA 60, 67, 107–8, 148–53
    financial time series 7–9, 197
    gamma 117–19
    GARCH family of models 48–51, 53–4, 65, 108–10, 148–53
    graphics 229–30
    higher moments 220
    Hill estimator method 175–6
    HS 95–7, 149–53
    independence coverage test 156–8
    information sources 217
    inputting data 7–9, 23, 48–51, 58–9, 94–5, 147–8, 217–19
    introductory background 217–30
    kurtosis 8–9, 225–7
    libraries 217
    likelihood functions 228–9
    loops and repeats 60, 106–8, 127–9, 148–53, 156–8, 161–2, 226–8
    MAs 106–8, 149–53
    matrix computations 60–2, 218–19, 220–2
    MLE 228–9
    Monte Carlo simulations 130–2, 133–9
        multivariate volatility models 58–71, 108
    normality testing 223–4
    OGARCH 62–3, 67
    operations 7–9, 219–22
    optimizers 228–9, 247
    p-value test statistic 214
    packages 217, 223
    reading recommendations 217
    RNGs 123–4
    S&P 500 index 7–9, 46–56
    simple operations 7–9, 219–22
    Student-*t* VaR 102–3
    time series 7–9, 224–5
    univariate volatility models 46–56, 107–8
    VaR 87–8, 101–3, 106–8, 133–9, 147–53
    writing functions 225–7
    yield curves 126–9
rand() 124
randn() 124, 127–9, 131–2, 134, 238–40, 242–3
random number generators (RNGs) 121–4, 140–2
    see also Monte Carlo simulations
    definition 122–3
    issues to be addressed 140–2
    linear congruental generators 122–3
    Matlab 123–4
    nonuniform
    RNGs 123–4
    R 123–4
random numbers 121–42, 222–3, 226–7, 236
    see also Monte Carlo simulations
    definition 121–2
random shocks 35–41, 55–6, 57–71, 163–6, 167–82
random variables (RVs) 25–9, 197–201, 245–53
random walks 129–42, 212–13
rbind() 221–2
realized volatility models 32, 54, 55–6
regular variation, definition 170–1
repmat() 127–9, 138–9
reshape() 63, 65
residuals 31–56
return() 118–19, 155–8
returns 1–29, 57–71, 73–91, 99–110, 132–42, 143–66, 170–1, 202, 219, 245–53
    see also continuously compounded ...; ergodicity; excess ...; prices; S&P ...; simple ...; stationarity
    definitions 2–5
    EVT 170–1
    expected returns 104–5
    leverage effect 51–2, 56
    statistical analysis techniques 1–29
    stylized facts of financial returns 9–29, 45
    types 2–5
risk
    see also credit ...; endogenous ...; foreign exchange ...; interest rate ...; market ...
    attitudes 73–5
    aversion 24, 73–5
    default risks 28, 185–7
    definitions 73–5
    endogenous risk 183-196
    exogenous risk 183, 195
    neutrality concepts 125
    profiles 76
    transformation concepts 111–20, 121–42
    types 79, 146–7, 183–96
risk management 12, 20–1, 57, 78–9, 89–90, 143, 163–6, 167–82, 184–96
    see also extreme value theory; stress testing
    decision making 75, 196
    endogenous risk 184–96
    fat tail implications 20–1, 167–82
    holding periods 89–90, 146, 178–9
    scaling laws 89–90
    VaR 78–9

risk measurement, definition 75
risk measures 6–7, 9–14, 73–91, 93–110,
    111–20, 121–42, 143–66, 213
  see also expected shortfall; Value at Risk;
    volatility
  backtesting 38, 44, 76, 89, 91, 93, 98,
    143–66, 208
  CLT 213
  coherent risk measures 80, 81–4
  critique 11, 73–5, 90–1, 149–53
  decision making 75, 196
  definitions 73–5
  difficulties 73–5, 78, 90–1
  EVT 173–82
  implementation 93–110, 111–20, 121–42,
    143–66
  nonparametric estimation methods 93–8,
    109–10, 149–53
  parametric estimation methods 93–4,
    98–110, 172–4
  quality of forecasts 143–66
  scenario analysis 165–6
  stress testing 143, 163–6
  types 73–91, 149–53
  underestimates 20–1, 76, 143–66
risk models 6–7, 9–14, 20, 29, 31, 33,
    73–91, 143–66, 184–96, 213
  definition 20, 75
  means 73–6, 213
  quality of forecasts 143–66
  stress testing 143, 163–6
risk-free rates 4–5, 13–14, 115–20, 129–42
RiskMetrics 32, 33–4
  see also EWMA
RNGs see random number generators
rnorm() 124, 127–9, 131, 134, 222–3, 226–9
roulette view of uncertainty 185, 196
rt() 124
runif() 124
RVs see random variables

S&P 500 index 1–29, 31–56, 93–110,
    147–53, 157–9, 175–81, 195, 233
  log scale from 1791 to 2009 5–6
  nonnormality issues 14–15
  sample returns from 1970 to 2009 175–81
  sample returns from 1994 to 2009 147–53,
    157–9
  summary return statistics from 1928 to 2009
    6–9, 10–11, 12–14
sacf() 9, 14, 237–8

sample means
  see also expected values
  definition 202
scaling laws
  see also central limit theorem
  definition 89–90
scan() 219
scatterplots 25–8, 243
scenario analysis 163–6
  see also stress testing
sd() 101–2, 106–8, 128–9, 131–2, 149–50
second centered moment of a distribution
  see also variance
  definition 16, 204
securitization 185–6
seeds, concepts 123–42
sensitivities 78–9, 111, 115–20, 192–6
  see also "Greeks"
seq() 123–4, 128–9, 131–2, 218–19, 222
sequential moments graphical detection
    method, fat tails 18–21
set.seed() 124, 127–9, 131, 134, 137
shape parameter, definition 169
Sheppard, Kevin 231
shocks 35–41, 55–6, 57–71, 163–6, 167–82
  see also scenario analysis
significance levels see quantile . . .
significance testing 212–16, 250–3
  see also statistical hypothesis testing
simple returns 3–9, 99–100
  see also returns
simulations 11–12, 73, 93–8, 121–42, 164–5,
    194–5, 210–12
  see also Monte Carlo simulations
  dynamic trading strategies 194–5
  stress testing 164–5
  volatility clusters 11–12
size() 232–3
skew t-GARCH model 41, 42–4, 46–51,
    52–3
  see also GARCH . . .
skewness 1–29, 41, 51–2, 168–9, 204–5,
    214–15, 220, 230, 234
  see also fat tails
  definition 16, 204–5
  estimation formula 205
  S&P 500 summary return statistics from
    1928 to 2009 6–9
  skew t-GARCH model 41, 42–4, 46–51,
    52–3
Sklar's theorem 27
solve() 221–2
sort() 95–7, 134–9, 149–50, 161–2, 175–6

source() 118–19, 226
spacf() 237–8
SPlus 217
   see also R
sqrt() 60, 63, 65, 101–2, 107–9, 117–19, 134–6, 149–50, 161–2
square-root-of-time scaling 90, 178–9
squared returns 6–7, 12–14, 46–52, 60, 63, 65, 101–2, 107–9, 117–19, 134–6, 149–50, 161–2
   see also volatility S&P 500
   summary return statistics from 1928 to 2009 6–7, 12–14
   uses 13–14, 46–52
stagflation of the 1970s 5–6
standard deviation 6–11, 101–2, 106–8, 115–20, 126, 128–9, 131–2, 147, 149–50, 199–205, 220, 234, 236–7, 238–9, 245–53
   see also volatility
   definition 9–11, 202
   S&P 500 summary return statistics from 1928 to 2009 6–9, 10–11
standard error 11, 32–5, 56, 202, 220, 234, 237–8
standard normal distributions
   see also normal distributions
   definition 199–200
stationarity 3, 37–8, 209–10
   see also moving average models; returns; white noise
statistical analysis techniques, prices and returns 1–29
statistical hypothesis testing 16–21, 46–51, 153–60, 212–16, 223–4, 237, 250–3
   see also Lagrange multiplier ...; likelihood ratio ...; normality ...; p-value ...; QQ plots; significance ...; type-1/2 errors; Wald ...
statistical tests for fat tails 16–21, 170–1
std() 106–8, 150
stochastic volatility models (SV) 32, 54, 55–6, 181–2, 185
stock market crash of 1987 7, 10–11, 14, 21, 164, 191–6
stock market indices 1–29, 31–56
   see also Dow Jones ...; FTSE; Nikkei ...; price-weighted ...; S&P ...; value-weighted ...
   types 2
stress testing 143, 163–6, 167–8
   see also extreme value ...; risk management; scenario analysis

strike prices, options 115–20, 136–42
structured credit products 25
Student-*t* distributions 1–29, 35–6, 40–4, 46–51, 52–3, 73–5, 93, 98, 102–3, 152, 168–71, 206–7, 212, 222–4, 236–7
   see also fat tails; maximum likelihood
   copulas 26–8
   definition 206–7
   exceedance correlations 24
   Matlab 102–3
   R 102–3
   t-GARCH model 40–1, 46–51
   VaR 102–3
stylized facts of financial returns 9–29, 45
   see also fat tails; nonlinear dependence; volatility clusters
subadditivity axiom of coherent risk measures 81–91
   definition 81–3
   volatility 82–3
subprime CDOs 25, 185–6
subprime mortgage markets 185–8
   see also global financial crisis from 2007
sum() 125–6, 128–9, 155–8
super-fat tails 83–4
supply/demand functions, banks 190
swaps 164, 167
switch case loops, Matlab concepts 241–2
systemic risk 183–96
   see also risk

t-GARCH model 40–1, 46–51, 109, 152
   see also GARCH ...; Student ...
tail() 94–5
tail index measures 18–21, 37–8, 167–82
   see also extreme value theory
tail VaR see expected shortfall
tarch() 152
Taylor expansion 171, 247
   see also Newton–Raphson method
testing window
   concepts 143–66
   definition 144
third centered moment of a distribution see skewness ...
threshold values 168–82
time aggregation 105, 176–82
time dependence, EVT 179–82
time series 1–29, 94–5, 147–53, 157–9, 197–216, 224–5, 237–8
   basic concepts 208–10, 224–5
   financial time series 7–9, 94, 197–216
   Matlab concepts 7–9, 237–8

R concepts 7–9, 224–5
reading recommendations 197
simple models 210–12
time series objects, definition 94
time to maturity 111–20
time-dependency 11–12, 106–10
tinv() 103
toolboxes, Matlab 8–9, 17, 48–51, 53–4, 62–3, 152–3, 231–43
TOPIX 2
trading time, definition 133
transaction costs 13–14
translation invariance axiom of coherent risk measures 82
trnd() 124
tseries R library 7–8, 94–5, 219
type-1/2 errors, definition 154–5, 214

UCSD GARCH Matlab toolbox 53–4, 62–3, 231, 237–8
unconditional coverage test, backtesting 153–60
unconditional volatility 1, 11–29, 35, 36, 38–9, 43, 60–2, 152–3, 180–1
  ARCH 36
  definition 11, 35
  EWMA model 35, 43, 60–2
  GARCH family of models 38–9, 43, 152–3
underestimates, risk measures 20–1, 76, 143–66
underforecast risk, violation ratios 146–66
underlying assets 111, 115–20, 121–42, 192–6
  see also options
unimodal likelihood function, concepts 248–9
univariate HS 95–6
univariate volatility models 1–29, 31–56, 57–8, 69, 94, 101–2, 107–10, 199
  see also APARCH; ARCH; EWMA; GARCH . . .; implied . . .; realized . . .; stochastic . . .; volatility models
  application 34–5, 46–53, 69, 107–10
  definition 31
  Matlab 46–56, 107–8
  R 46–56, 107–8
urlread() 233
US 5–6, 185–8

Value-at-Risk (VaR) 33, 54–5, 73, 76–91, 93–110, 111–20, 121, 132–42, 143–66, 167, 173–82, 190, 208, 213
  see also expected shortfall; risk measures

application 80–5, 93–110, 111–20, 132–42, 143–66, 173–82
backtesting 76, 89, 91, 98, 143–66
bonds 111–20
calculation steps 78, 91
CLT 213
coherent risk measures 80, 81–4
continuously compounded returns 100–1
convexity 114–15
critique 76, 78–9, 80–5, 88–9, 91, 152–3
definition 76–80, 99–100
delta-normal VaR 119–20
duration-normal VaR 112–15
endogenous risk 190
EVT 173–82
EWMA 107–8, 146–7, 148–53, 158–62
expected returns 104–5
GARCH family of models 108–10, 146, 148–53, 158–9, 167, 174
holding periods 76–85, 89–91, 146, 178–9
HS 93–8, 149–53, 158–62
implementation 93–110, 111–20, 121, 132–42, 143–66, 173–82
interpretation and analysis 78–9, 150–3
manipulation issues 80, 84–5
MAs 106–8, 149–53
Matlab 87–8, 101–3, 106–8, 133–9, 147–53
Monte Carlo simulations 110, 111, 115, 120, 121, 132–42
multivariate implementation framework 100–2
normality issues 79, 91, 93, 98–9, 101–2
options 111, 119–20, 133–42
paradox 80
popularity 76–7, 88–9, 91
portfolio VaR 137–42, 164
positive/negative numbers 77–8, 79–80
quantile limitations 80–1, 84–5
R 87–8, 101–3, 106–8, 133–9, 147–53
simple returns 99–100
square-root-of-time scaling 90, 178–9
stress testing 165–6
Student-t distributions 102–3
subadditivity axiom 83–91
time aggregation 105, 176–82
time-dependent volatility 106–10
univariate implementation framework 101–2
violations 143–66, 208
value-weighted indices 2–9, 32–3
var() 107–8, 148–53
VaR see Value at Risk

variance 14–15, 16–21, 35, 57–71, 73–6, 93–110, 174–5, 199–210, 220, 224, 234, 242–3, 245–53
  see also covariance; GARCH ...
  definition 102, 199, 202
  properties 202–3
variance–covariance method (VCV) 93–110, 181–2
  see also parametric estimation methods
vector() 128–9
vectors
  Matlab concepts 7–9, 128–9, 232–3, 240
  R concepts 128–9, 218–19
violation ratios (VRs) 145–66
violations
  see also backtesting; Value at Risk
  concepts 143–66, 208
  definition 143, 145
VIX 2
volatility 1–29, 31–56, 73–4, 75–6, 90–1, 106–10, 111–20, 202, 216, 245–53
  see also conditional ...; risk measures; squared returns; standard deviations; standard error; unconditional ...
  critique as a risk measure 11, 75–6, 91, 152–3
  cycles 10–11
  definition 9–11, 75–6, 202
  high volatilities 5–6
  interest rates 111–20
  latent variables 31–56, 75
  leverage effect 51–2, 56
  predictability benefits 12
  proxies 45–6
  S&P 500 from 1791 to 2009 5–6
  S&P 500 summary return statistics from 1928 to 2009 6–9, 10–11, 12–14
  square-root-of-time scaling 90, 178–9
  subadditivity aspects 82–3
  underestimates of risk 76, 143–66
volatility clusters 1, 7–29, 31–56, 153, 155–60, 216
  see also skewness ...; stylized facts of financial returns
  definition 9, 11–14
volatility models 31–56, 57–71, 73–4, 93, 106–10, 146–7, 148–53
  see also ARCH; EWMA; GARCH ...; implied ...; moving average ...; multivariate ...; realized ...; stochastic ...; univariate ...
  alternative models 54–6
  application 34–5, 46–53, 58–71, 106–10, 146–7, 148–53
  challenges 31
  definition 31–2
  diagnosis 44–56, 65–7
  goodness-of-fit measures 45–51
  lags 31–56
  LR 44–51, 52–4
  MLE 41–4, 155–60
  out-of-sample forecast comparisons 44–6
  practical multivariate models 57–71
  simple volatility models 32–5
  types 32–56, 57–71
volatility of volatility, concepts 38
VRs see violation ratios

Wald test 251, 253
Wall Street Journal 21
Weibull distributions 169–70, 172–3, 223
while loops 227–8, 240–2
white noise 210–12, 215
  see also stationarity
who, Matlab concepts 231–3
Wiener process see Brownian motion
window sizes 97–8, 143–66
writing functions, R 225–7

yield curves 112–15, 125–9, 164
  see also duration
  shape changes 129, 164

Z test statistic 215–16
zero-coupon bonds 125–9